TONI MORRISON
FORTY YEARS IN
THE
CLEARING

THE GRIOT PROJECT
Series Editor: Carmen Gillespie
Bucknell University

This book series, associated with the Griot Project at Bucknell University, publishes monographs, collections of essays, poetry, and prose exploring the aesthetics, art, history, and culture of African America and the African diaspora.

The Griot is a central figure in many West African cultures. Historically, the Griot had many functions, including as a community historian, cultural critic, indigenous artist, and collective spokesperson. Borrowing from this rich tradition, the Griot Project book series defines the Griot as a metaphor for the academic and creative interdisciplinary exploration of the arts, literatures, and cultures of African America, Africa, and the African diaspora.

Expansive and inclusive in its appeal and significance, works in the Griot Project book series will appeal to academics, artists, and lay readers and thinkers alike.

Titles in the Series

Carmen Gillespie, ed., *Toni Morrison: Forty Years in the Clearing*

Myronn Hardy, *Catastrophic Bliss*

Angèlé Kingue, *Venus of Khalakanti,*
translated by Christine Schwartz-Hartley

TONI MORRISON
FORTY YEARS IN
THE
CLEARING

EDITED AND WITH AN INTRODUCTION BY
CARMEN R. GILLESPIE

Bucknell
UNIVERSITY

Bucknell University Press

Published by Bucknell University Press
Co-published with The Rowman & Littlefield Publishing Group, Inc.
4501 Forbes Boulevard, Suite 200, Lanham, Maryland 20706
www.rowman.com

Unit A, Whitacre Mews, 26-34 Stannery Street, London SE11 4AB

British Library Cataloguing in Publication Information Available

Library of Congress Cataloging-in-Publication Data

The hardback edition of this book was previously cataloged by the Library of Congress as follows

Toni Morrison : forty years in the clearing / edited and with an introduction Carmen Gillespie.
    pages cm.—(Griot Project book series)
  Includes bibliographic references and index.
  1. Morrison, Toni--Criticism and interpretation.
PS3563.O8749 Z9134 2012

                         2012474303

ISBN 978-1-61148-491-5 (cloth)
ISBN 978-1-61148-634-6 (pbk.)
ISBN 978-1-61148-492-2 (electronic)

To Chloe Wofford

Step by Step

Step by step the longest march can be won, can be won
Many stones can form an arch, singly none, singly none
And by union what we will can be accomplished still
Drops of water turn a mill, singly none, singly none

—TRADITIONAL

The Gathering

Acknowledgments

I offer my most sincere gratitude to each of the contributors to *Toni Morrison: Forty Years in The Clearing*. I was overwhelmed at the response we received to the initial invitation to gather in this space to reflect upon Toni Morrison's forty and more years of artful expression, and I remain awed by the generosity, grace, and gift of each contributor.

Books do not produce themselves and there were many involved in the creation of this one. James Peterson was an important agent at the beginning of this project, and I acknowledge and am grateful for his help. Particular thanks goes to Nina Forsberg for her assistance, as well as to Kate Parker whose insights, creativity, and syntheses gave the book an original and dynamic structure. Thank you to Patrick Henry for his assistance with the initial assemblage. For their reading, research, and technical support, my appreciation to Catherine Joos, Heather Hennigan, Rebecca Willoughby, and Karen Holstead.

I am appreciative of Greg Clingham, director of the Bucknell University Press, for his belief in this project. Thanks to Bucknell University for their support of the Griot Institute for Africana Studies and of the Griot Book Project Series. I express particular gratitude for the artistry of Adrienne Beaver, who designed the Griot Book Project insignia, as well as the book and the template for the Griot Project Book Series.

To Lucille Fultz, Maryemma Graham, and Susan Mayberry I am indebted for your support and for your reaching out to console and encourage. Lucie, "quiet as kept."

Harry, you are my sanctuary.

Permissions

Acknowledgment and appreciation is due to the following holders of copyright for their permissions to use and/or reprint the following:

Photograph of Toni Morrison taken by Bernard Gotfryd (back cover), conveyed through Getty Images.

Bobbie Crews for the Griot Tree photograph.

Richard Danielpour and the G. Schirmer Library for permission to reproduce the synopsis, sound clip, lyrics, and score of "Margaret's Lullaby" from *Margaret Garner.*

Timothy Greenfield-Sanders for the reproduction of his Morrison photographs.

Republished with the permission of John Leonard, "First Three Novels on Race," in *New York Times,* November 13, 1970, 35; permission conveyed through Copyright Clearance Center.

"'Letter to the Editor,' in Response to Sara Blackburn's *New York Times* review of *Sula*," Alice Walker Archives, Manuscript, Archives, and Rare Book Library, Emory University.

Mendi and Keith Obadike for reproduction of the lyrics and soundclip of "Praise Song for Toni Morrison."

CBS News Information Resources and CBS News for permission to reproduce *Presidential Questions* "Candidates Favorite Books."

"The Sisterhood," Photograph, Alice Walker Archives, Manuscript, Archives, and Rare Book Library, Emory University.

Theodore Gericault's *The Raft of The Medusa, Salon of 1819,* Oil on canvas, 4.91m x 7.16m. Paris, *Musee de Louvre.* Public domain.

Forty Years and More in the Clearing
Selected Morrison Chronology, 1970–2012

1970

Works as a senior editor at Random House in New York.

Achieves critical acclaim, but not commercial success, with the publication of her first novel, *The Bluest Eye.*

1971-72

Resumes teaching career at the State University of New York at Purchase.

Appointed as an associate professor at the university.

Continues work as an editor for Random House.

1973

Builds on literary success by publishing second novel, *Sula.*

1974

Edits and publishes *The Black Book,* a landmark collection documenting the African American experience.

1975

George B. Wofford, Toni Morrison's father, dies on September 9.

Sula nominated for a National Book Award and receives an Ohioana Award.

1976-77

Accepts a visiting lectureship at Yale University in New Haven, Connecticut.

Serves as a faculty member at the Bread Loaf Writer's Conference in Vermont.

1977

Publishes *Song of Solomon,* which achieves commercial success.

Recognized with the National Book Critics' Circle Award for *Song of Solomon.*

Song of Solomon is also awarded the American Academy Award, the Institute of Arts and Letters Award, and is selected as a Book-of-the-Month Club choice.

Appointed by President Jimmy Carter to the National Council on the Arts.

1978

Purchases a house in the Hudson River Valley, near Nyack, New York.

1981

Publishes *Tar Baby*.

Elected to the American Academy and Institute of Arts and Letters.

Appears on the March 30, 1981 cover of *Newsweek* magazine. Morrison is the first black woman to be so featured since Zora Neale Hurston.

Writes the story and lyrics for *New Orleans: The Storyville Musical* with Donald McKayle and Dorothea Freitag.

1983

Publishes "Recitatif," her only short story to date.

1984

Decides to pursue teaching and writing full-time. (See Nikki Giovanni's essay in this volume "And Everyone Will Answer.")

Accepts an endowed chair as the Albert Schweitzer Professor of the Humanities at the State University of New York at Albany, a position she holds for two years.

Workshops *New Orleans: The Storyville Musical* at the Public Theater in New York.

1986

Writes and assists in mounting a production of her play, *Dreaming Emmett*, in Albany, New York.

Accepts a position as a visiting lecturer at Bard College in Annandale-on-Hudson, New York.

1987

Publishes *Beloved*.

Beloved selected as a Book-of-the-Month Club choice and nominated for the National Book Award.

Appointed as a lecturer at Bowdoin College and at the University of California, Berkeley.

1988

Defended by almost fifty prominent African American writers in an open letter to the *New York Times Book* Review written in protest of the fact that Morrison had not yet won the National Book Award. (See in this volume, "In the Beginning: Two Rewiews")

Honored with the National Organization of Women's Elizabeth Cady Stanton Award.

Wins the Pulitzer Prize for Fiction for *Beloved*.

Accepts a position as a Tanner Lecturer at the University of Michigan.

1989

Becomes the first African American woman to hold an endowed chair at an Ivy League university when she becomes the Robert E. Goheen Professor in the Council of Humanities at Princeton University in Princeton, New Jersey.

Granted the Modern Language Association's Commonwealth Award in Literature.

1990

Delivers a series of lectures as part of the William E. Massey, Sr. Lectures in the History of American Civilization at Harvard University.

Awarded the Chianti Ruffino Antico Fattore International Literary Prize.

1992

George C. Wofford, Toni Morrison's brother, dies after a short illness.

Publishes *Jazz*, which becomes a *New York Times* bestseller.

Publishes *Playing in the Dark: Whiteness and the Literary Imagination*.

Publishes *Race-Ing Justice, En-Gendering Power: Essays on Anita Hill, Clarence Thomas, and the Construction of Social Reality*, a book of essays on the Clarence Thomas hearings.

Becomes a founding member of Elie Wiesel's Académie Universelle des Cultures.

1993

Raymond Wofford, Toni Morrison's brother, dies of colon cancer.

Wins the Nobel Prize in Literature. She is the first black woman and the first African American to win the prize.

Experiences the loss of her much-loved house on the Hudson River, some original manuscripts, and several irreplaceable family heirlooms as a consequence of a December fire.

1994

Ella Ramah Wofford, Toni Morrison's mother. dies on February 17th.

Establishes the Atelier program at Princeton University as an interdisciplinary arts program to bring artists from various disciplines together to work closely with students to produce a work of art or an artistic production. Atelier artists have included Richard Danielpour, Gabriel García Márquez, Yo Yo Ma, Maria Tucci, Peter Sellars, Lars Jann, Roger Babb, and Mendi and Keith Obadike. (See Obadike song in this volume, "Praise Song for Toni Morrison").

1995

Explores interests in theater, dance, and music with creation of the collaborative and interdisciplinary work *Degga* with composer Max Roach and dancer/choreographer Bill T. Jones.

Honored by her hometown of Lorain, Ohio with the establishment a reading room in her name in the Lorain Public Library.

Edits and publishes the writings of Huey P. Newton in a volume entitled *To Die for the People: The Writings of Huey P. Newton*.

Records *Honey and Rue,* her musical collaboration with composer Andre Previn.

1996

Awarded the National Book Foundation Medal for Distinguished Contribution to American Letters.

Gives one of her most important and well-known speeches: *The Dancing Mind: Speech upon Acceptance of the National Book Foundation Medal for Distinguished Contribution to American Letters on the Sixth of November, Nineteen Hundred and Ninety-Six,* and publishes the speech in 1996 as a short book.

Song of Solomon chosen by talk show personality Oprah Winfrey for her show's book club.

Edits and publishes the multi-genre collection of Toni Cade Bambara's writings, *Deep Sightings and Rescue Missions: Fiction, Essays and Conversations.*

Writes the libretto for *Sweet Talk: Four Songs on Text,* with composer Richard Danielpour.

Selected by *Time* magazine as one of America's 25 most influential people.

1997

Edits and publishes *Birth of a Nation'hood: Gaze, Script, and Spectacle in the 0. J. Simpson Case* with Claudia Brodsky Lacour, professor of Comparative Literature at Princeton.

1998

Publishes *Paradise.*

Oprah Winfrey produces and stars in the cinematic version of *Beloved* directed by Jonathan Demme. The film also stars Danny Glover, yet is a critical and commercial failure.

Edits and publishes the collected works of James Baldwin under the title *James Baldwin: Collected Essays: Notes of a Native Son / Nobody Knows My Name / The Fire Next Time / No Name in the Street / The Devil Finds Work / Other Essays.*

Organizes a writers' and scholars' protest against the impeachment of Bill Clinton with the assistance of Stephen Holmes, Paul Berman, and Sean Wilentz.

1999

Begins a literary collabotation with her youngest son Slade with their joint authorship and publication of *The Big Box,* the first in a series of children's books. Giselle Potter is the book's illustrator.

Recognized as Woman of the Year by the popular magazine *Ladies Home Journal.*

2000

Receives the National Humanities Medal.

Publishes the poems "I Am Not Seaworthy," "The Lacemaker," "The Perfect Ease of Grain," and "The Town Is Lit" in the literary magazine *Ploughshares*.

Receives the Library of Congress Bicentennial Living Legend Award.

2001

Celebrates her 70th birthday at a gala held at the New York Public Library.

2002

Publishes the poem "black crazies" in *Ms. Magazine*.

Publishes *The Book of Mean People* with her son, Slade Morrison.

2003

Publishes *Love*.

Publishes the children's book, *Who's Got Game: The Lion or the Mouse*, with her son, Slade Morrison.

2004

Publishes the children's book, *The Poppy or the Snake? (Who's Got Game?)*, with her son, Slade Morrison.

Publishes the book *Remember: The Journey to School Integration* for young readers.

2005

Serves as a Feature Films Jury Member at the Festival de Cannes.

Writes the libretto for the opera *Margaret Garner* with composer Richard Danielpour. The opera premieres in Detroit, Philadelphia, and Cincinnati. (see, Toni Morrison and Richard Danielpour's "Margaret's Lullaby.")

Receives an honorary Doctor of Letters degree from the University of Oxford.

2006

Retires from Princeton University after teaching at the institution for seventeen years.

Beloved named as the best work of American fiction of the past 25 years by *The New York Times Book Review*.

Reads from forthcoming novel, *A Mercy* (2008) at the opening of the Musée du Louvre's weeks-long event in Paris entitled "The Foreigner's Home Exhibit." Serves as guest curator for the exhibition. (see Nancy J. Peterson's "Toni Morrison, Théodore Géricault, and Incendiary Art.")

Essay "Black Matters" appears in the publication *Introduction to Literature: the Arts and Cultural Diversity*.

The opera *Margaret Garner* premieres in Philadelphia, Pennsylvania, and Charlotte, North Carolina.

Honored by the Lincoln Jazz Center in New York City with a musical salute.

"The Reader as Artist" appears in *O: the Oprah Magazine* in July.

2007

Publishes with son Slade Morrison a compilation of their three *Who's Got Game* book series under the title *Who's Got Game?: The Ant or the Grasshopper?, The Lion or the Mouse?, Poppy or the Snake,* with illustrations by Pascal Lemaître.

Essay "The Habit of Art" appears in *Artworks: the Progressive Collection.*

Receives honorary Doctor of Letters from the Sorbonne.

"The Bird is in Your Hands," Morrison's Nobel lecture, appears in *Nobel Lectures: From the Literature Laureates, 1986 to 2006.*

Serves as curator for the *Art is Otherwise* Humanities Programs sponsored by the French Alliance.

Awarded the Ellie Charles Artist Award from the literary magazine *African Voices* in recognition of her literary contributions to Columbia University.

Named Radcliffe Medalist by Harvard's Radcliffe Institute "For her extraordinary achievements and impact on people in America and around the world."

Debut of *Margaret Garner* at The New York City Opera.

Named one of twenty-one Women of the Year and awarded Lifetime Achievement award by *Glamour* magazine.

Writes the foreword to a new edition of August Wilson's *The Piano Lesson.*

2008

Publishes *A Mercy.*

Releases a collection of non-fiction writings entitled *What Moves at the Margin: Selected Non-Fiction.*

Honored by hometown Lorraine, Ohio with the christening of the town's new elementary school Toni Morrison Elementary School. The school is located at 1830 West 40th Street.

Essay "10 Questions for Toni Morrison" appears in *Time* magazine.

Endorses Barack Obama for President in an open letter. (see Barack Obama, "A Literary Question for Barack Obama.")

2009

Edits and publishes *Burn This Book: PEN Writers Speak out on the Power of the Word.*

Publishes with Slade Morrison *Peeny Butter Fudge,* a children's book that derives in part from Morrison's experiences with her grandchildren.

Song of Solomon removed by a Michigan high school from the syllabus of an AP English class after public outcry over the book's profanity, sexual references and violence.

2010

Publishes with Slade Morrison *The Tortoise or the Hare* and *Little Cloud and Lady Wind*. *The Tortoise or the Hare* is illustrated by Joe Cepeda, and *Little Cloud and Lady Wind* is illustrated by Sean Qualls.

Acts as keynote speaker at the American Library Association Annual Conference.

A Mercy selected by "One Book, One Chicago" as the text by which to draw the diverse denizens of Chicago together around a single book.

Inducted into the Legion of Honor in France.

Receives the Carl Sandburg Literary Award, an award recognizing an author whose body of work enhances the public's awareness of the written word, from the Chicago Public Library Foundation.

Slade Morrison dies on December 22. Morrison has reported that the cause of her son's death was pancreatic cancer.

2011

February 18th declared Toni Morrison Day in the nation's capital by Mayor of the Washington, D. C. Vincent C. Gray and the D.C. Council.

Celebrated on the occasion of her 80th birthday at a gala held in the James Madison Hall of the Library of Congress in Washington, D.C.

Desdemona, the play production, premieres at the Theatre Nanterre-Amandiers outside Paris, France, in October. The play has US productions in San Francisco and New York.

2012

Publishes *Home*.

Desdemona produced in London.

Toni Morrison receives the Presidential Medal of Freedom from US President Barack Obama at the White House on May 29th.

"In this here place, we flesh;
flesh that weeps, laughs;
flesh that dances on bare feet in grass.
Love it. Love it hard."

TONI MORRISON, *BELOVED*

Carmen R. Gillespie

Carmen R. Gillespie is Professor of English, Director of the Griot Institute for Africana Studies, and the University Arts Coordinator at Bucknell University in Lewisburg, Pennsylvania. She is a scholar of American, African American, and Caribbean literatures and cultures and a poet. In addition to journal and poem publications, she is the author of the books *A Critical Companion to Toni Morrison* (2007), *A Critical Companion to Alice Walker* (2011). Carmen also has a published a poetry chapbook, *Lining the Rails* (2008), and a poetry book, *Jonestown: A Vexation,* which was the winner of the 2011 Naomi Long Madgett Poetry Prize. In commemoration of its 40th anniversary, *Essence* magazine named Carmen one of its 40 favorite poets. She had the privilege of working with and reflecting upon Toni Morrison's 40 years of artistic "Clearing" with the scholars and artist included in this volume.

Gather at the Clearing

CARMEN R. GILLESPIE

... a wide-open place cut deep in the woods nobody knew for what
at the end of the path known only to deer and whoever cleared the
land in the first place. In the heat of every Saturday afternoon, she
sat in the clearing while the people waited among the trees.

and ...

Her authority in the pulpit, her dance in the Clearing,
her powerful Call (she didn't deliver sermons or preach — insisting
she was too ignorant for that — she *called* and the hearing heard).

and ...

... love your heart, for that is the prize.' Saying no more,
she stood up then and danced with her twisted hip the rest of what
her heart had to say while the others opened their mouths and gave
her the music. Long notes held until the four-part harmony was
perfect enough for their deeply loved flesh.

These depictions of Toni Morrison's intricately crafted space — the Clearing — from her Pulitzer-Prize winning novel, *Beloved*, are most familiar territory for her readers. They are also exceedingly useful for understanding some of the intricacies of Morrison's profound cultural influence over the last forty years. Currently, Morrison is the only living American (and the only black American) to have received the Nobel Prize for Literature. She published her first novel, *The Bluest Eye,* in 1970. In the ensuing forty plus years, her work has become synonymous with the most significant artistic and intellectual engagements of our time. The publication of her tenth novel, *Home* (2012), as well as the 2011 and 2012 productions of her play *Desdemona*, recalls the range and acuity of her verdant imagination.

Toni Morrison: Forty Years in The Clearing embraces Morrison's metaphor as its structural imperative. The Clearing is a complicated and dynamic space. Like the intricacies of Morrison's intellectual and artistic voyages, the Clearing she imagines is both luxuriant and deadly, a sanctuary and a prison. Her vision invites consideration of these complexities and confronts these most basic human conundrums with courage, resolve, and grace. *Forty Years in The Clearing* attempts to reproduce the character and spirit of this metaphorical terrain through multifaceted and multidisciplinary contributions and considerations. *Forty Years in The Clearing* is not a hagiography, nor is it a work comprised of the reflections of Morrison "fans;" rather, the collection is a serious and interactive consideration of Morrison's diffuse and divergent impact over the past four decades by professional, acclaimed, and emerging artists and scholars. Employing Morrison's theoretical model, this volume provides spaces for its readers to enter, occupy, and interrogate from their own subjective positions.

Forty Years in The Clearing attempts to mirror Morrison's own multiplicity and range of interests and explorations by gathering a variety of responses to her work from various creative artists and scholars. Through its self-reflexive engagement with its subject, the collection originates a genre of scholarly publication that includes personal reflections, literary criticism, as well as creative writing, photographs, and music in order to give Morrison's audiences/readers, critics, and students an opportunity to reconsider the breadth of her cultural and literary impacts. This collection collaboratively reflects upon the import and influence of her legacies in her multiple roles as writer, editor, publisher, reader, scholar, artist, and teacher over the last four-plus decades.

This interdisciplinary collection features contributions from scholars, artists, public figures, and others whose lives, art, and work have been affected and/ or influenced by Morrison's fiction, speeches, essays, and interviews written by Toni Morrison. Hopefully, *The Clearing* will inspire fresh reviews, examinations, and (re)discoveries of Morrison's body of work as defined by those who have already become central voices in this conversation as well as by those emergent voice who are now beginning to discover Morrison's landscapes.

" . . . a wide-open place cut deep in the woods
nobody knew for what . . ."[1]

When Morrison published her first novel in 1970, the year proved to be a landmark in African American women's history. In the wake of the civil rights and feminist movements of the 1950s and 1960s, African American women acquired — or perhaps more appropriately claimed — public voice and presence in spaces that had previously been elusive and exclusionary.

An ironic starting point for contextualizing the publication of *The Bluest Eye* can be found in popular culture. The popular hits of the year included top 100 best-selling songs from Diana Ross, Freda Payne, Aretha Franklin, and Dionne Warwick. That same year, Cheryl Adrienne Brown won the Miss Iowa pageant and went on to become the first black Miss America Beauty Pageant contestant. Jayne Kennedy, who would later become a well-known African American actress, won the Miss Ohio beauty pageant and became the first black woman to compete in the Miss USA Beauty Pageant. The significance of this accomplishment: "achieving the crown" is indirectly articulated by Morrison's interest in the consequences of the construct of beauty and the myriad ways in which she addresses its problematics throughout her canon, but most expressly in *The Bluest Eye*. As critic John Leonard noted in the first line of his *New York Times* review, "*The Bluest Eye* is an inquiry into the reasons why beauty gets wasted in this country."[2]

The 1970s began with African American men and women facing an unemployment rate nearly double that of their white counterparts. The percentage of unemployed African American men that year averaged almost thirteen percent compared with nearly six percent for white men. Rates of unemployment for black women were at eight percent compared with nearly five percent for white women.[3] Stating economic inequity as one of its primary concerns, the New York Coalition, later called the National Coalition of 100 Black Women, was formed in New York City.

Angela Davis, who would later meet and become friends with Morrison when Morrison edited Davis's autobiography in 1970,[4] was fired from her position at the University of California, Los Angeles, for her involvement in the defense of the Soledad Brothers, including George Jackson. Davis was then charged with murder after Jonathan Jackson, using guns Davis had purchased, tried to free his brother. After being placed on the FBI's most-wanted list and evading capture for two months, Davis was captured. She was eventually acquitted.

In 1970, *Essence* magazine, with the slogan "for today's black woman," began publication. For her portrayal of Peggy Fair, a character on the television show "Mannix," Actress Gail Fisher became the black first woman to receive an Emmy Award. Director Madeline Anderson's short *I Am Somebody* cataloged the struggles of a strike by black women workers and was among the first documentaries by a black woman. That same year, Shirley Chisholm began her second year of service as the first black woman elected to the United States Congress. Later, Chisholm would become the first black person to become a candidate for the United States Presidency.

In addition to this new public and political visibility and, arguably, viability, for black women, writings by African American women entered a period of astounding productivity. This proliferation, termed the Afra-American renaissance[5] by literary critic Joanne Braxton, ushered in early publications by the major figures in contemporary American and African-American literature. In addition to *The Bluest Eye*, 1970 saw the publication of a critical and groundbreaking compilation of writings by black women, Toni Cade-Bambara's *The Black Woman: An Anthology* that included poems, short stories, and essays by a wide-range of black women writers, among them Alice Walker, Audre Lorde, Nikki Giovanni, Paule Marshall, and Abbey Lincoln. Other works published by black women in that same year include, among others, are Maya Angelou's *I Know Why the Caged Bird Sings*, Mari Evans' *I Am a Black Woman*, Nikki Giovanni's *Black Feeling, Black Talk/Black Judgement*, Lorraine Hansberry's posthumous *To Be Young, Gifted and Black: An Informal Autobiography*, Sonia Sanchez's *We a Baddddd People*, and the first of Alice Walker's novels *The Third Life of Grange Copeland*. Further indication of the import of the Afra-American renaissance was the double reprinting of Paule Marshall's *Brown Girl, Brown Stones*, originally published in 1959.

Morrison was part of an impressive group of black women. The spaces she and her sister artists and activists entered, they (re)imagined and claimed with their diverse individual subjectivities, talents and divergent visions. In 1970, what may have been the common denominator for these black women was the recognition that their accomplishments were made possible by those who had come before. No matter the anonymity of the "whoever cleared the land in the first place," there is an implicit acknowledgment of the essential role of that historical clearing. In a 2012 interview with London's *Guardian* newspaper, Morrison recalls 1970 and her ambitions for *The Bluest Eye*.

> All the books that were being published by African-American guys were saying 'screw whitey', or some variation of that. Not the scholars but the pop books. And the other thing they said was, "You have to confront the oppressor." I understand that. But you don't have to look at the world through his eyes. I'm not a stereotype;

I'm not somebody else's version of who I am. And so when people said at that time black is beautiful — yeah? Of course. Who said it wasn't? So I was trying to say, in *The Bluest Eye*, wait a minute. Guys. There was a time when black wasn't beautiful. And you hurt.[6]

Two members of the literary class of 1970 who also refused to ignore the complexities of that era or any other are contributors to this collection. Nikki Giovanni was the first to respond to the invitation to write an essay for this collection. In "And Everyone Will Answer," Giovanni demonstrates the continuity between the previous generation's and her own aspirations as a young writer.

I was studying social work in the hopes of emulating my mother and one of her best friends and an incredible "aunt" to me, Theresa Elliot. All the social workers I knew were cool, and I had been awarded a scholarship. Unfortunately, I was never meant to work in any real sort of system. After a year it was decided by all, respectively (and I might add, lovingly), that social work was not for me.

The second writer to respond to the invitation to be a part of *Toni Morrison: Forty Years in The Clearing* was Sonia Sanchez, who shared a poem written for Morrison, "15 Haiku for Toni Morrison,"

in the beginning
when memory was sound. there was
bonesmell, bloodtear, whisperscream;
and we arrived
carrying flesh and disguise
expecting nothing.

Like her friends and contemporaries Morrison and Giovanni, Sanchez posits that the origin of their overlapping artistic journeys is rooted in her acknowledgment of the historical African American struggle. These writers ensure that their responses to the questions at the core of their work are contextualized and rooted in their common history. Their work evinces a methodology *Toni Morrison: Forty Years in The Clearing* readily embraces.

One of the frequently neglected aspects of investigation of Morrison's scholarship is serious consideration of her Howard University experiences. While at Howard, Morrison shared space and time with Jessye Norman, Sterling Brown, Roxy Roker, Stokely Carmichael, Leroy Jones (Amir Baraka), Claude Brown and many others who would go on to achieve national and international stature. Her good friends at Howard University, Florence Ladd and Mary Wilburn, in an interview with novelist A. J. Verdelle provide a first-hand account of those years and share the intriguing insight that, even then, Chloe Wofford/ Toni Morrison was "Staring Shakespeare in the Face."

For some of our contributors, being in company with Morrison has come through their interrelationships with her work — associations that catalyzed and supported their artistic and intellectual growth. Although she started her professional career as a literary critic, today Elizabeth Beaulieu, author of *The Toni Morrison Encyclopedia*, is a university dean. From that position, she has perhaps a broader perspective on the relationship between faculty and students and Morrison's work. Intriguingly, Beaulieu reimagines the Clearing as "interdisciplinary inquiry" and her occupation of that space as representative of her professional journey. Her essay "In Search of the Clearing" documents the struggles she encountered while introducing *The Bluest Eye* to the general education curriculum. Her essay also speaks to the challenges of teaching Morrison's work.

Novelist A. J. Verdelle (re)constructs the creative dialogue between Morrison's work and her own by crafting a series of letters, "The Making of a Novelist (Epistolary)." In the piece, Verdelle asserts that "About no other writer can this be said. My Morrison reading is as Complete as Sorrow's chosen name. And this has happened without duty, without fanfare, or trumpet. Your production has been the horizon of my literary coming of age." The various letters that constitute the piece document Verdelle's on-going relationship with Morrison as intellectual and artistic mentor.

Literary critic and artist Farah Jasmine Griffin catalogues the necessary role Morrison's work has provided for her both as a perpetual challenge and as a source of consolation, even redemption. She notes,

> In this context, Toni Morrison was not only Novelist. The implications of her fiction on thought were becoming clearer. She was engaging, informing, and shaping my understanding of history, narrative, power, domination, and language. Her prose started to shape and define my sense of the relationship between space and time. She taught me about form and content. In Morrison there was no ahistorical celebration of fragmentation; fragmentation was not only psychic. It was real, it was literal. She understood that pre-modern, modern, and postmodern forms of power operated on black bodies simultaneously.

For Griffin, Morrison's works are signposts, sites of memory, by which she can trace and (re)construct her maturation as an intellectual and, simultaneously and more centrally, as a black woman. Koritha Mitchell explores a similar interrelationship with Morrison in her "Belief and Performance, Morrison and Me." Mitchell attributes her career as an academic and her acquisition of psychological survival techniques directly to Morrison.

> Reading Toni Morrison's *The Bluest Eye* at age eighteen ultimately led me to pursue a Ph.D. in Literature, so Morrison's work literally shaped the life that I now lead as a college professor. The insights that I gleaned from that novel have proven valuable throughout my journey as a black woman living in the United States.

For those who were gifted with Morrison's company through her works, as well as for those who shared that momentous entry with her in 1970, her Clearing, indeed their Clearing, has always been occupied— a shared space peopled with those who would come forth to laugh, cry, sing, and dance.

"(she didn't deliver sermons or preach . . . she *called* and the hearing heard)" [7]

Toni Morrison: Forty Years in The Clearing broadly surveys the range of responses generated by Morrison's four decades of artistic production. Such has been her generative impact that a comprehensive assessment would be nearly impossible. As an experiment, I Googled the phrase "inspired by Toni Morrison." The 2,954 results are but one anecdotal indication of the range and depth of her influence. Among the examples were a dance piece by Urban Bush Woman choreographer Christina Jones entitled *Naked City*, inspired by Morrison's novel *Jazz*; a song by rapper Chris Brown, called "Amazing Grace," based on *Beloved*; a documentary film by Natalia Almada entitled *All Water Has a Perfect Memory*, titled after a Morrison quotation; an exhibition by artist Deanna Bowen entitled *Stories to Pass On*, from a line in *Beloved*; and literally hundreds of other creative responses. This range of Morrisonian inspirations is not well-documented, but it is an essential starting point that *Forty Years in The Clearing* provides.

This volume includes diverse perspectives and contributions; from those of the President of the United States to literary critics, creative writers, and choreographers. One motivation for this collection is the recognition that the vast body of published responses to Morrison has come from literary critics and that, while I wish to acknowledge the breadth and range of that work (the Modern Language Association lists 2101 published journal articles, books, and dissertations that engage Toni Morrison's work) I want this collection to reflect Morrison's own multiplicity, refusal to be categorized, and disregard of artificially imposed boundaries in her own artistic and intellectual project by weaving multiple genres into its contents.

That said, *Toni Morrison: Forty Years in The Clearing* adds to the flourishing literary critical conversation about Morrison's works with new offerings from some of the major voices in the field. Kathleen Marks, author of *Toni Morrison's Beloved and the Apotropaic Imagination*, revisits *The Bluest Eye* in search of its underexplored contributions to discourses about the definitions of melancholy. Marks notes that "it is one of the novel's main insights that there is a fruitful melancholic stance as well as a destructive one, or to put it in terms closer to the novel's, there are both vincible and 'invincible' melancholies. One leads to perception and insight, while the other leads ultimately to self-directed anger."

Marks's reexamination of Morrison's first novel complements Susan Mayberry's exploration of what is, perhaps, Morrison's most critically neglected novel, *Tar Baby*. Mayberry, author of *Can't I Love What I Criticize?: The Masculine and Morrison*, maps Morrison's navigations of the contemporary theoretical currents. Mayberry contends that Morrison's employment of food and its consumptions in *Tar Baby* function as signifiers that enable Morrison "to address complex modern philosophical dilemmas about conditions of knowledge, cultural hybridity, rejection of fabricated history, and uncertainty of language."

The other literary critical works in this volume employ cross-canonical examinations and complement the original and essential single-text studies by Marks and Mayberry. Missy Dehn Kubitschek, author of *Toni Morrison: A Critical Companion*, uses a trope coined by Elaine Showalter, "the wild zone," to interrogate some of Morrison's novels in light of their creation and negotiations of such spaces. In her reading of *Beloved*, Kubitschek characterizes the attempted rescue of Sethe while the women of the community gather at 124 Bluestone as a moment where the wild zone emerges.

> … it was as though the Clearing had come to her … where the voices of women searched for the right combination, the key, the code, the sound that broke the back of words." These passages certainly suggest a linguistic wild zone, transcending patriarchal language, empowered by primal female energy.

Kubitschek's evocation of the Clearing establishes it as a metaphor ungrounded in place but emanating from the expressive desire of the community in the service of one of its own. Ultimately, she argues that the wild zone, although present in Morrison's works, is elusive and transient and does not present a viable "home" for Morrison's characters.

Linden Peach, author of *Toni Morrison*, offers a fresh, cross-textual look at the issue of body image in Morrison's fiction. Peach suggests that much of the scholarship on bodies in Morrison's canon focuses on markers of gender and race. By examining other ways in which Morrison represents difference, Peach refocuses our gaze and considerations of these bodies and introduces new ways of reading somatically. Peach asks readers to reevaluate their former understandings of phenotypically and "differently-bodied" Morrison characters. A similar reframing occurs in "American Romance, the Moral Imagination and Toni Morrison: A Theory of Literary Aesthetics," by Jan Furman, author of *Toni Morrison's Fiction* and *Song of Solomon: A Casebook*. Furman reminds us that Morrison is not only a novelist but also a literary critic. Furman uses Morrison's arguments articulated in the critical volume *Playing in the Dark: Whiteness and the Literary Imagination* to flesh out Morrison's literary aesthetics and moral imperatives as they manifest in her criticism and in her novels. Furman discusses

Morrison as theoretician in the context of *Playing in the Dark*'s analysis of the major literary figures of American Romanticism:

> Against a contested background of dark stereotype in Poe, Hawthorne, Melville, and others, Morrison redraws landscape, character, and incident. Her novels set right the subject of critical commentary in *Playing*. Giving the shadow human shape and dimension in her narratives, Morrison has re-imagined American romance and its founding narratives.

Furman establishes that Morrison's literary project is grounded in a carefully outlined and considered self-fashioned literary theoretical paradigm.

Hearing the call — finding inspiration in the example of Morrison's project — is not contained within the often steep boundaries between academe and other artistic and professional enterprises. Morrison's endorsement of then Senator Barack Obama during the 2008 election was a first for Morrison. President Obama expresses his thoughts about Morrison's work in an interview with Katie Couric and in a speech from the award ceremony in which he presented Morrison the Presidential Medal of Freedom. These articulations from the President and Morrison's commentary on Obama are combined in the chapter "Morrison and Obama."

In her essay, "Trouble in Paradise: Representing Bliss in Non Orgiastic Language," theologian Katie G. Cannon reflects on the impact of Morrison's works and vision for her discipline. Cannon discusses the 1995 annual meeting of the American Academy of Religion when Morrison delivered the plenary address, "Trouble in Paradise." Cannon contends that by problematizing religious discourse, "Morrison shows a generation of intellectuals how faith in a system of belief is inextricably linked to endurance, leadership, and seasonable opportunities in the material worldliness of fiction." Cannon's reflections illustrate that genuine inspiration often generates struggle and hard work.

That struggle to transform inspiration into understanding and then to (re)imagine — to create something new from that genesis — is the outcome produced by the choreographers whose engagements with Morrison are included in this collection. Dustyn Martinchic, choreographer, dancer, and professor, details the catalytic effects of Morrison's novel *Paradise* on her imagination and the consequent steps from that inspiration to creation and staging of her original piece entitled *Co(n)ven(t)*. *Co(n)ven(t)* was performed by students in the Bucknell University Dance Company in December 2009. Martinchic understands "Morrison's narratives as offering artists of various mediums the opportunity to open vivid and imagistic details, using her rhythmic language as a beat. The stories demand to be performed." Another choreographer L. Martina Young finds similar correlations between Morrison's language and the foundations and practices of dance. Like Martinchic, Young is attracted to Morrison's fundamental understanding of the physical body as having and expressing its own languages. Young theorizes on Morrison's *Beloved* and, through her reading of the novel, develops the notion that ritual movements, both actualized on the page and enacted between the text and the reader, perform a type of self-reflexive catharsis that reverberates on multiple levels. "The purposive rhythm in *Beloved* activates a process that, according to writer Wole Soyinka, is a 'symbolic disintegration and retrieval of the protagonist ego [and thereby] reflects the destiny of being.' The ordeal is a clearing. Furthermore, Morrison's reader is part of this clearing and retrieval process."

Education professor and school psychologist Lakeisha Meyer aspires towards fully-fleshed articulation of her work merging the lessons of Morrison's project with the clinical definitions and applications of bibliotherapy. Meyer asserts that "narrative, specifically Morrison's canon, can be utilized to encourage conscious (re)membering of trauma and the exploration of trauma's impact on development and psychological well-being." Such an interaction is critical to the writing process for poet Christine Jessica Margaret Reilly. Reading Morrison's works led her to an unexpectedly generative moment in the creation of her own work — one that she describes as therapeutic. "I have always been drawn to the philosophy that reading and writing poetry can be therapeutic or a coping mechanism for both the writer and reader. I hope that my poems reflect the richness I've gained from Morrison's language." This ekphrastic impulse and its connection to healing are also found in literary critic and poet Joanne Gabbin's "Meditations on Love." Gabbin reflects on Morrison saying, "In your hand is a map of these woods. / You trace a jagged path / To a clearing, to a great heart urging me / To stroke my sullen flesh / Into imagination."

> **"the others opened their mouths and gave her the music.**
> **Long notes held until the four-part harmony was**
> **perfect enough for their deeply loved flesh."** [8]

In 2011, Morrison's new play *Desdemona* premiered in France. Subsequent short runs were staged in 2012 in San Francisco and New York. Another production was staged in London in the summer of 2012. *Desdemona* began as a disagreement between Morrison and her friend Peter Sellars about the merits of Shakespeare's *Othello*. The argument evolved into a collaboration between Sellars, singer/songwriter Rokia Traoré, and Morrison. The play emerges from Desdemona's perspective, with text by Morrison and music by Traoré. This type of collaborative creativity is primary to Morrison's understanding of the artistic process. Whether it is the interactive relationship she demands of her readers or her establishment of the Atelier at Princeton, Morrison defines her project as inclusive and participatory.

Several of the contributors to *Toni Morrison: Forty Years in The Clearing* share their experiences or the product of their collaborations with Morrison. Literary critic Nancy J. Peterson is not a direct collaborator, but in her essay "Toni Morrison, Théodore Géricault, and Incendiary Art," Peterson documents the "collaboration" between Morrison and painter Théodore Géricault, whose 1819 painting, "The Raft of the Medusa,"Morrison chose as the focal point of her guest curatorial project, "The Foreigner's Home," at the Louvre Museum in 2006. As Peterson notes, "Both Morrison and Géricault as artists understand how to make history come alive by narrowing it and deepening it." Peterson extends her discussion of the collaboration between Morrison and Géricault and Morrison's crafting of "The Foreigner's Home" exhibit to a reading of Morrison's novel *A Mercy*.

Performance, sound, and new media artists Mendi and Keith Obadike were invited to participate in Morrison's Princeton Atelier in 2005, where they created the collaborative project *Four Electric Ghosts*. The Obadikes contribute an original music composition to this collection, a song based on Morrison's Nobel Prize Acceptance Speech. The Obadikes's lyrics remind us that,

> Sometimes what's held is not just a bird.
> It could be the charged and necessary word.
> Unbound quills inscribe the sky,
> Calling us to fly.
> And the sage says:
> *Once in the hand,*
> *All dreams of flight depend*
> *On the holder's plan,*
> *Not on the blowing wind.*

One of Morrison's primary musical collaborators is Grammy-Award winning composer Richard Danielpour, who has partnered several times with Morrison, most prominently with the production of the opera *Margaret Garner*. Morrison created the lyrics for Danielpour's score.

Danielpour generously gave us permission to include the lyrics, sound clip, and score for the song "Margaret's Lullaby," excerpted from the as yet unpublished *Margaret Garner*.

There is an interesting intersection between Morrison's work with Danielpour and her creative interactions with photographer Timothy Greenfield-Sanders. According to Greenfield-Sanders, Morrison was discussing *Margaret Garner* with him when they happened upon the idea of what would become *The Black List*, a series of photos (and, ultimately, a documentary series) of prominent black Americans created by Greenfield-Sanders. "On February 24, 2005, Toni Morrison was having lunch in my East Village kitchen. The conversation turned to 'divas' as Toni described the extraordinarily talented performers she had auditioned for her opera, *Margaret Garner*. 'Timothy, we should do a portrait book on these women. Call it . . . *Black Divas*.'"[9] As a consequence of his conversation with Morrison, Greenfield-Sanders went on to collaborate with Elvis Mitchell to produce the photographs and accompanying HBO documentary. Greenfield-Sanders was as gracious as Danielpour when I asked him to contribute to *Toni Morrison: Forty Years in The Clearing*, and he readily offered us ten of his Morrison portraits for inclusion in this volume.

The Bluest Eye has been reimagined in a theatrical version written by playwright Lydia Diamond. In an interview with Diamond that appears here, she discusses the process of writing the play. Diamond observes that the creation of the play was collaborative even though she did not work directly with Morrison. Diamond notes, "If my voice is in there, it's just in the way that I made structural decisions and the prose that I wrote as much in her vernacular as possible — to the extent that there are passages that sometimes I don't know if they are mine or hers." The resulting play is an interweaving Morrison and Diamond artistry into something else, derived, but distinct from the original. Diamond details her creative process and engagements with Morrison and her work in her interview "Creatively Serving — The Process": An Interview with Playwright Lydia Diamond, Author of *The Bluest Eye*.

"Bit by bit, at 124 and in the Clearing, along with others, along with others, she had claimed herself."[10]

In a recent interview with *New York Magazine*, Morrison makes an important distinction between her public persona, Toni Morrison, and her *self*, Chloe Wofford. She states, "I still can't get to the *Toni Morrison place* yet."[11] [emphasis added] As evidenced by this volume, Morrison's intellectual and artistic project is the genesis of a Clearing, derived from, but expanding well beyond, its fictional origins — a Toni Morrison place that, since her emergence during the Afra-American renaissance of the early 1970s, has been for literary critics, scholars, artists, and many others as a generative space of inspiration, creativity, and collaboration. There is so much more to explore. For example, Morrison's work at Random House and interactions with a generation of black writers calls for multiple examinations of her influences and interactions in her role as editor. *Toni Morrison: Forty Years in The Clearing* and its examination of facets of Morrison's forty-plus years as an artist and a public figure and intellectual will engender what I hope will be many published considerations of Morrison's multiple influences, engagements, and interactions.

The Toni Morrison of 2012, writing in a very different context than in 1970, is one of the most widely-read and admired writers in the world. In recognition of her global stature and contributions to American literature and culture, in May of 2012, President Barack Obama, the first African-American to hold that office, awarded Morrison the Presidential Medal of Freedom, the highest honor an American civilian can receive. Acclaim, recognition, and post-raciality and attendant presumptions aside, the questions Morrison asks us to consider through her work are arguably as salient as they were when she published her first novel. It is my hope that this volume will expand the conversations about Morrison's project over the last four plus decades and help define those discussions as inclusive, broad, and unlimited in their imaginative boundaries as is the source that inspires them.

I also issue an invitation to Chloe Wofford to join the "exhausted and riven, all and each . . . [gathering in] the Clearing damp and gasping for breath,"[12] for I am certain that she has always been here with us — in this Toni Morrison place — in this, the Clearing.

NOTES

1. Toni Morrison, *Beloved* (New York: Random House-Knopf, 1987), 87.
2. John Leonard, "Three First Novels on Race." *New York Times*, November 13, 1970, 35.
3. Susan Carter, et al., eds. *Historical Statistics of the United States, Millennial Edition* (New York: Cambridge University Press, 2001), http://www.hks.harvard.edu/fs/phall/HSUS.pdf.
4. Angela Davis, *Angela Davis: An Autobiography* (New York: Bantam Books, 1975).
5. Joanne Braxton and Andree Nicola McLaughlin, eds. *Wild Women in the Whirlwind: Afra-American Culture and the Contemporary Literary Renaissance* (New Brunswick, NJ: Rutgers University Press, 1990).
6. Emma Brockes, "Toni Morrison: 'I Want to Feel What I Feel. Even If It's Not Happiness,'" *The Guardian*. April 13, 2012, http://guardian.co.uk.
7. Ibid, 177.
8. Ibid, 89.
9. Timothy Greenfield-Sanders, "Artist Statement," *The Black List*, National Portrait Gallery Exhibition, October 28, 2011-April 22, 2012, http://www.npg.si.edu.
10. Morrison, *Beloved*, 95.
11. Boris Kachka, "Who is the Author of Toni Morrison?" *New York Magazine*, April 29, 2012, n.p.
12. Morrison, *Beloved*, 88.

John Leonard and Alice Walker

John Leonard's *New York Times* 1970 Review
of Toni Morrison's *The Bluest Eye*

and

Alice Walker's *New York Times* "Letter to the Editor"
in Response to Sara Blackburn's 1973 Review of *Sula*

CHAPTER ONE

In The Beginning:
Two Reviews

John Leonard's Review of *The Bluest Eye*

Nancy J. Peterson noted in the introduction to the 1993 double-issue of *Modern Fiction Studies* entitled "The Canonization of Toni Morrison," that Morrison's novels have always generated commentary that quite often was more reflective of the anxieties of the reviewer/critic and of the particular cultural moment than they were illuminative of the works they purported to address. Peterson's observation seems even more accurate some twenty years later.

> "Toni Morrison" has become the name around which debates of considerable significance to American literature, culture, and ideology have amassed—these include debates about multicultural curricula; about the relation of slavery to freedom; about the degree of determinism and/or free will African Americans might experience; about the possibility of creating literature that is both aesthetically beautiful and politically engaged; about the interlocking relation of racism, sexism, and classism; about the ability to construct meaningful dialogues across entrenched differences; about the possibility of laying claim to our lives and imaginations from within a postmodern, capitalist society.[1]

As John Leonard's review of *The Bluest Eye* attests, the literary gifts and the impending import of Toni Morrison and her work were appreciated by some from the beginning. Reprinted here, in its entirety, is that 1970 review.

November 13, 1970
Books of the Times
By John Leonard[2]

Toni Morrison's *The Bluest Eye* is an inquiry into the reasons why beauty gets wasted in this country. The beauty in this case is black; the wasting is done by a cultural engine that seems to have been designed specifically to murder possibilities; the "bluest eye" refers to the blue eyes of the blond American myth, by which standard the black-skinned and brown-eyed always measure up as inadequate. Miss Morrison exposes the negative of the Dick-and-Jane-and-Mother-and-Father-and-Dog-and-Cat photograph that appears in our reading primers, and she does it with a prose so precise, so faithful to speech and so charged with pain and wonder that the novel becomes poetry.

Taking Refuge in 'HOW'
It all takes place in Lorain, Ohio, a sort of black Winesburg. We are told at the outset that Pecola Breedlove, age 11, is impregnated by her own father; Pecola will live and her child will die. "There is really nothing more to say," writes Miss Morrison, "except *why*. But since why is difficult to handle, one must take refuge in *how*." She proceeds to tell us how, and thus explains why, in a series of portraits of "ideal" domestic servants, high-yellow children, preachers, drunks, whores and those abiding back women who so torment Daniel Moynihan:

> Then they were old. Their bodies honed, their odor sour … They had given over the lives of their own children and tendered their grandchildren. With relief they wrapped their heads in rags, and their breasts in flannel; eased their feet into felt. They were through with lust and lactation, beyond tears and terror. They alone could walk the roads of Mississippi, the lanes of Georgia, the fields of Alabama unmolested. They were old enough to be irritable when and where they chose, tired enough to look forward to death, disinterested enough to accept the idea of pain while ignoring the presence of pain. They were, in fact and at last, free. And the lives of these old black women were synthesized in their eyes—a puree of tragedy and humor, wickedness and serenity, truth and fantasy.

I have said "poetry." But *The Bluest Eye* is also history, sociology, folklore, nightmare and music. It is one thing to state that we have institutionalized waste, that children suffocate under mountains of merchandised lies. It is another thing to demonstrate that waste, to re-create those children, to live and die by it. Miss Morrison's angry sadness overwhelms.

In his response to Morrison's first published novel, Leonard demonstrates what Morrison would later coin as the phenomenon of the reader as artist.[3] His review is included here as a starting point for consideration of professional public reactions to Morrison's writings.

Alice Walker's "Letter to the Editor"

When *Sula* was published in 1973, however, Sara Blackburn's *New York Times* review was more problematic and, in many ways, symptomatic of the complex currents of the time with respect to the intersections of race, gender, class, and the publishing industry. Blackburn begins her review by retracting the earlier praise the newspaper had given to *The Bluest Eye*. Blackburn attributes the acclaim the novel had received as having "reaped the benefits of a growing, middle-class women's movement that was just beginning to acknowledge the reality of its black and poor sisters."[4] Blackburn does, however, praise aspects of *Sula's* characterizations, and even compares Morrison to Gabriel García Márquez, eventually noting that "the comparison can't be extended: Morrison hasn't endowed her people with life beyond their place and function in the novel, and we can't imagine their surviving outside the tiny community where they carry on their separate lives."[5] Finally (and, perhaps, most egregiously), Blackburn advises Morrison that she must "transcend the early and unintentionally limiting classification 'black woman writer' [in order to] take her place among the most serious, important and talented American novelists now working."[6]

This last admonition was addressed by writers Clarence Major and Alice Walker in separate "Letters to the Editor." By 1974, Walker and Morrison knew each other and were supportive of each other's work. Eventually, both women would join a black women writers' support group called The Sisterhood.

The group, begun by Walker and June Jordan, also included writers Vertamae Grosvenor, Lori Sharpe, Nana Maynard, Ntozake Shange, and Audrey Edwards.[7] Responding to Sara Blackburn's review in *The New York Times*, Walker wrote the following in defense of her friend and fellow writer.

> Dear sir: I am amazed on many levels by Sarah Blackburn's review of *Sula*. Is Miss Morrison to 'transcend herself?' And why should she and for what? The time has gone forever when black people felt limited by themselves. We realize that we are as ourselves unlimited and our experiences valid. It is for the rest of the world to recognize this, if they choose.[8]

This kind of solidarity was, perhaps, essential in order for African American writers to counter the prejudice and discrimination they encountered, even in reviews.

The New York Times would again provide a platform for a similar defense of Morrison and her work when, in 1988, African American writers (including Robert Allen, Maya Angelou, Houston A. Baker Jr., Toni Cade Bambara, Amina Baraka, Amiri Baraka, Jerome Brooks, Wesley Brown, Robert Chrisman, Barbara Christian, Lucille Clifton, J. California Cooper, Jayne Cortez, Angela Davis, Thulani Davis, Alexis De Veaux. Mari Evans, Nikky Finney, Ernest J.

Gaines, Henry Louis Gates Jr., Paula Giddings, Vertamae Grosvenor, Cheryll Y. Greene, Rosa Guy, Calvin Hernton, Nathan Irvin Huggins, Gloria T. Hull, Gale Jackson, June Jordan, Paule Marshall, Nellie McKay, Louise Meriwether, Louise Patterson, Richard Perry, Arnold Rampersad, Eugene Redmond, Sonia Sanchez, Hortense Spillers, Luisah Teish, Joyce Carol Thomas, Eleanor Traylor, Quincy Troupe, Alice Walker, Mary Helen Washington, John Wideman, Margaret Wilkerson, John A. Williams, and Sherley Anne Williams) published a letter to the editor entitled "Black Writers in Praise of Toni Morrison." This group of writers and public intellectuals represent the depth and breadth of support Morrison enjoyed from her peers, as well as the lengths they were willing to go to defend her place in the canon of American letters. These writers felt that a proclamation regarding the merits and value Morrison's literary contributions expressed directly by a community of black writers was a necessary reparation in the face of what they saw as blatant disregard of her artistry when Morrison did not receive the 1988 National Book Award. The writers and critics end their collective letter, written by June Jordan and Houston A. Baker, with the following line, "we here record our pride, our respect and our appreciation for the treasury of your findings and invention."[9] Morrison eventually was awarded a Pulitzer-Prize for *Beloved*, as well as the Nobel Prize for Literature. She has not received a National Book Award.

NOTES

1. Nancy J. Peterson, "Introduction: 'The Canonization of Toni Morrison," *Toni Morrison. Modern Fiction Studies*, Special Double Issue, 39, no. 3-4 (1993-94): 465.

2. John Leonard, "Three First Novels on Race," *New York Times*, November 13, 1970, 35.

3. Toni Morrison, "The Reader as Artist," *Oprah Magazine*, Harpo Productions (July 2006), http://www.oprah.com/omagazine/Toni-Morrison-on-Reading.

4. Sara Blackburn, "Review of *Sula*, 'You Still Can't Go Home Again," *New York Times Book Review*, December 30, 1973, 3.

5. Ibid, 3.

6. Ibid, 3.

7. Rudolph P. Byrd and Alice Walker, eds., *The World Has Changed: Conversations with Alice Walker* (New York: The New Press, 2010), 24.

8. Alice Walker's response to Sara Blackburn's 1973 review, "*Sula*," Letter to the Editor, *New York Times*. January 20, 1974, 328.

9. Houston A. Baker, Jr. and June Jordan, et al. "Black Writers in Praise of Toni Morrison," *New York Times Book Review*, January 24, 1988, 36.

Elizabeth Beaulieu

Elizabeth Beaulieu is Dean of the Core Division at Champlain College in Burlington, Vermont, where she oversees the design and implementation of a new interdisciplinary general education curriculum. Beaulieu holds a Ph.D. in twentieth-century literature, with a specialty in African-American literature from the University of North Carolina at Chapel Hill, and is the author of *Black Women Writers and the American Neo-Slave Narrative: Femininity Unfettered*, and the editor of *The Toni Morrison Encyclopedia*, and *Writing African American Women: An Encyclopedia of Literature by and about Women of Color*. Beaulieu's essay for this volume collects and names a variety of ways in which readers can engage Morrison, whether sensory, political, affective, or antagonistic. Beaulieu's position as Dean offers a keen insight into Morrison's continued relevance in the undergraduate classroom, particularly in a curriculum invigorated by questions of moral and social aesthetics.

In Search of the Clearing

ELIZABETH BEAULIEU

The film *Precious* (2009), based on Sapphire's 1996 novel *Push*, triggered its share of controversy, including an inflammatory *New York Times* Op-Ed piece by Ishmael Reed, in which he alleges that black men and women feel "widespread revulsion and anger" over the Oscar-nominated film that features an obese teen protagonist and depicts abuse, incest, illiteracy, and HIV in the African American community.[1] Reed argues that such works cast "collective shame upon an entire community," and it is clear that he doesn't buy into the redemptive message of *Precious* that other critics (critics he identifies as largely white) and audience members laud. Sapphire responded to Reed's Op-Ed piece with a simple but powerful justification for her work: "Silence will not save African Americans. We've got to work hard and long, and our work begins by telling our stories out loud to whoever has the courage to listen."[2]

The most important and provocative literature of any culture is often a re-telling of that culture's most important truths, and such work is frequently contentious. Reading Reed's and others' remarks on *Precious* and Sapphire's impassioned defense of her art reminded me of Toni Morrison's *The Bluest Eye* and Morrison's own motivation for writing her first novel. Both are admittedly ugly stories — stories of violation, shame, disgust. These are stories that many believe have no value in being told, stories better left hidden. And yet both writers push beyond convention to challenge contemporary audiences to acknowledge silenced voices and honor the struggle they represent.

I was drawn to Toni Morrison for precisely that reason. Reading *Song of Solomon* and *Sula* in college introduced me to a world I knew very little about and crystallized my decision to pursue African American literature in graduate school. Studying *Beloved* in graduate school led me to write a dissertation on the neo-slave narrative. I envisioned a future teaching African American literature to undergraduate students like my undergraduate self — young white women who wanted to understand the struggle and celebrate the endurance of black women. I recognized Toni Morrison as one of the great American writers of the twentieth century, standing side-by-side in canon formation with Faulkner, Fitzgerald, and Hemingway. She belonged in the English department, a place where I also believed I belonged.

Alas, although Toni Morrison's works are regularly taught in English departments across the country and few would argue her place in the canon (whatever that means these days), I never spent a day as a faculty member in an English department, and my relationship with Toni Morrison and her works is significantly different because of this fact. This essay, then, is a window into what I learned when I moved out of the English department and into the "Clearing" that is interdisciplinary inquiry . . . and took Morrison along with me.

After several years teaching various women's studies courses and always seeking to include one or more of Morrison's works, I left my teaching position to assume a deanship at a small private college that was looking to invigorate its general education curriculum. The courses would be interdisciplinary, inquiry-focused, and would not rely on conventional textbooks. Of course, I wondered whether I'd find a place for Morrison's work in the new curriculum but was careful not to insist that others embrace my own area of expertise and interest. However, *The Bluest Eye* turned out to be an excellent choice to anchor a sophomore-level aesthetics course.

What did I learn about Morrison and her work once I viewed it through an interdisciplinary lens? I had always considered Morrison a "great" writer, but I had not closely questioned how I defined "greatness." *The Bluest Eye* invites inquiry, and that became for me one of the central tenets of greatness. How many ways can a reader enter the story? In *The Bluest Eye*, students can connect through music (especially the blues and rap), through film, through popular culture references, through sweet Mary Jane candies, and through their own preschool Dick and Jane readers. While my middle-class white Vermont young adults may not relate to the racial self-loathing of a young black girl in post-Depression Ohio, the novel provides a raw emotional experience that many readers can't — or won't — forget. An interdisciplinary approach, especially one that encourages readers to frame questions as they read and discuss rather than seek definitive answers in a text, allows for multiple points of entry and rich context for absorbing and internalizing the novel's themes. Students grapple with the beauty of Morrison's language juxtaposed with the ugliness of the story she is telling. They encounter poverty, physical deformity, incest, and madness, and they experience discomfort. They question hegemonic ideas of beauty (the very purpose of our course on aesthetics), and they question the very world that could give rise to a family like the Breedloves. In short, they question. And they learn that Morrison provides no easy answers.

We encountered some resistance from students when we included this text in the new curriculum. Quite a few had read it in high school and viewed it as a "problem" novel — a novel intended to draw attention to the plight of an underrepresented group of people. They questioned whether we chose it (placing it alongside works like Michelangelo's *Sistine Chapel* and Beethoven's *Third Symphony*) to be "politically correct," which is how many of them viewed its inclusion in the high school curriculum. Like Reed, they weren't interested in downtrodden black folks; after all, they had just seen the first black president elected.

To students, we positioned the novel in precisely the way Sapphire defended her work in response to Reed's *New York Times* piece. These stories make up the American experience; we need to listen to them with humility and humanity, and we need to recognize that it takes courage to listen. Our core curriculum challenges students to first ask and then confront "big" questions, to prepare for life in an increasingly complex and impersonal world. Pecola's world is foreign to most of them, and Morrison's interrogation of beauty, when placed alongside Michelangelo's work or the *Erotica*, is disturbing.

Recently, a senior accounting major spoke up in class; he had "done the math," and Haiti should be wiped out, because economically it's simply not a viable place. A responsibility to address thinking such as this guides the design and work of our core curriculum; we aspire to enable our students to see the world from multiple perspectives — Pecola Breedlove's, Precious's, a Haitian refugee's — and to inspire them to act to make a difference. Life is challenging, complex, and troubling. It is ugly sometimes. We seek not to provide answers but to pose questions for deep thought and careful response. Toni Morrison is our model; I see now that she resides not just in the English department (a place where she rightfully belongs) but among us everywhere — in and between and among the disciplines, in the eyes of Precious, in the grimace of a Haitian earthquake survivor. Like Sapphire, she calls us to the complex and contradictory face of humanity, and leaves us stunned by its beauty, crushed by its pain. It is my hope that by including Morrison's work in our curriculum she will come to reside in our students' hearts as well, urging them on to ask, to seek, to listen even when it is difficult, and finally to act with courage.

NOTES

1. Ishmael Reed, "Op-Ed: Fade to White," *New York Times*, February 5, 2010, A25.
2. Sapphire. "Letter — Why Stories Like 'Precious' Need to Be Told," *New York Times*, February 12, 2010, A20, http://www.nytimes.com/2010/02/12/opinion/l12sapphire.html.

Katie G. Cannon

Katie Cannon is currently the Annie Scales Roger Professor of Christian Ethics at Union Theological Seminary in Richmond, Virginia. The first African American woman to be ordained in the United Presbyterian Church, Cannon was also the first to receive a Ph.D. from Union Theological Seminary in New York, which she completed in 1983. She has lectured widely on issues of Christian ethics and Womanist theology and has written or edited six books, including *Teaching Preaching: Isaac R. Clark and Black Sacred Rhetoric, Katie's Canon: Womanism and the Soul of the Black Community* and *Black Womanist Ethics.* Her essay marks the message of Morrison's plenary lecture to the American Academy of Religion, delivered in 1995. Cannon, who recounts her own experience hearing Morrison speak, also interprets the significance of Morrison's concept of "paradise" in the context both of academic religious scholarship and of contemporary theological and spiritual discourses.

Trouble in Paradise: Representing Bliss in Non-Orgiastic Language

KATIE G. CANNON

When Toni Morrison delivered her plenary address, "Trouble in Paradise," at the annual meeting of the American Academy of Religion in November 1995, she launched an ethical critique of paradise that still reverberates throughout womanist theology. Black women religious scholars who heard this lecture (and who were also privileged to engage in a dinner conversation with Professor Morrison following her public presentation) continue to wrestle with the challenges she set before us: (1) to bring into sharper focus the re-imagining of blissful abode in a capitalist political economy thriving on marketable evil, (2) to investigate the malignant push-pull tension between *paradiso* and *inferno*, and (3) to elaborate rhetorical strategies in constructing texts in which religious belief is central to the narrative itself.

Far too many critics leave religion out of the universe of influences that shape the literary genre of creative imagination. To address this glaring omission, I will exegete my notes recorded during Morrison's lecture. For it is in this work, "Trouble in Paradise," that Morrison pulls no punches. By problematizing religious discourse, she shows a generation of intellectuals how faith in a system of belief is inextricably linked to endurance, leadership, and seasonable opportunities in the material worldliness of fiction.

Introduction

Toni Morrison's plenary lecture, "Trouble in Paradise," at the 1995 annual meeting of the American Academy of Religion, was a landmark event. As the winner of the 1993 Nobel Prize in literature and the 1988 Pulitzer Prize for her powerful and complex works of fiction, Morrison is a seminal thinker for many educators and researchers who belong to the American Academy of Religion (AAR). Her subject range is enormous and has profound moral, epistemological, and philosophical significance. For the more than 10,000 AAR members who teach in some 1,000 colleges, universities, seminaries, and schools in North America and abroad, Morrison's literary clairvoyance gives us almost unbearable descriptions of the multilayered misery and contradictions in the black American experience. Her texts acknowledge the joys and sorrows, ups and downs, gains and losses of African Americans searching for meaning in an unjust world. Even while affirming possibilities, Morrison exposes realistic details of the painful limits set against black existence in the United States.

Deservedly, Morrison is one of the novelists liberation theologians turn to most often. Her narrative powers exemplify truth claims about the bygone days of slavery and interweave the mythic into survivalist intentions of freed people. James H. Cone, the preeminent and leading exponent of Black Theology since the late 1960s, says that the following questions should come to mind whenever religious scholars read Morrison:

> How is it possible to articulate the liberating experience of faith, a faith that enables people to love their blackness, to endure terrible hardships and to withstand pain without losing their sanity in their struggle to be free? How do we construct a theology that empowers people to survive and to struggle for liberating change?[1]

Morrison's oeuvre speaks directly to womanists, black women religious scholars who affirm an intimate connection between justice making and the meaning of authentic faithful discipleship. It is correct to point out how womanists, despite our many denominational differences, continue working together to excavate suppressed memories and to investigate embedded testimonies of adherents of religious systems in the midst of struggles of resistance, so that the God consciousness of African American women in particular, and of black religious communities in general, is made intelligible to the world.

Thus, Morrison's bold articulation of re-membering as no less than reincarnation is a central motif in womanist theological ethics. If we are willing to journey to a site to see what remains have been left behind, Morrison says literary archaeology enables us to reconstruct the worlds these remains imply.[2] When womanists exegete novels, we find that these artistic compositions speak volumes about how we ought to behave and what it is that we ought to know.

Morrison asks, "Where else can we find information about how to hang onto what it is that is important and how to give up things that are not?"[3]

Anticipating an eager demand to hear Professor Morrison's lecture in such a scholarly venue, the womanist design team sketched out a three-fold action plan as soon as the program booklet arrived in our mailboxes. We organized a festival of books to celebrate black women's writing lives. For the first time in the eighty-six-year history of the AAR, we highlighted womanist publications with a splendid book signing party. Next, we orchestrated a womanist panel to explore religious themes in Morrison's writings. Our final strategic act was to camp out in the grand ballroom of the Philadelphia Marriott Hotel several hours before Toni Morrison was scheduled to speak.

After the womanist professors, seminarians, and graduate students — nearly 100 strong — filed in, the security guard locked the doors. The grand ballroom belonged to us. So we opened our carryout supper containers and broke bread together. We shared memories of ministers, liturgical language, and contestable issues in Morrison's novels. We wrestled with whether characters such as Pecola, Pauline, Cholly Breedlove, and Maureen Peele in *The Bluest Eye*; or Sula, Nel, Shadrack, Eva, Plum, Ajax, and the Deweys in *Sula*; as well as Macon "Milkman" Dead, III, Freddie, Guitar, Pilate, First Corinthians, Magdalene, and Ruth in *Song of Solomon* resonate with theologies consistent with beliefs stated in our articles of faith and practices of worship. Illuminating various aspects of ambiguities in our collective histories and personal religious lives, we discussed questions related to the plausibility, irresolutions, and counterproductive behavior in *Tar Baby*, *Beloved*, and *Jazz*. All of these texts were page-turners for us. Our Holy-Ghost-goodtime conversations charged the space with positive energy in preparation for Morrison's arrival.

It all came down to a womanist sitting in every chair in the "Amen Corner." We resembled the folk in James Baldwin's 1954 play, *Amen Corner*, wherein as fervent supporters we occupied a conspicuous part of the meeting space. In the spirit of call and response, we rehearsed assisting Professor Morrison with enthusiastic refrains of "Amen!," "Say it, Sister!," "Teach!," and "Make it plain!" Our act of talking back to the plenary speaker from our strategic location would be one of creative resistance. Such expressive responses are anomalies at learned society gatherings. Of course, we erupted into a spontaneously standing ovation, full of thunderous applause, as soon as Professor Morrison stepped to the podium.

In pure Morrison style, she framed her lecture, "Trouble in Paradise," by asking us to think about what, precisely, paradise really is and by talking about the difficulty in writing her forthcoming novel, *Paradise*, a richly detailed portrait of a black community in Oklahoma. Morrison launched her presentation with a bold stroke of self-disclosure:

> Although I have been working on *Paradise* for two years, it still is presenting
> me with apparently insurmountable problems. While each novel I have written,
> other than the first two (*The Bluest Eye* and *Sula*), perhaps most of you know,
> seemed equally un-doable. It still astonishes me how the more work one does,
> the more difficult it becomes, the more impossible the task.
>
> This instance, I am trying to recreate in those Black towns of the West a
> narrative about paradise—the earthly achievement of paradise, its possibility,
> its dimensions, its stability, or even its folly; certainly its desirability. The
> novel's time frame is 1908 to 1976, and its population, former slaves and first
> generation children of former slaves.[4]

In the context of academic religious scholarship, the direction of Morrison's
lecture was clear. One did not need to be a devotee of any religion to be interested
in paradise as an ideal connection to the divine, but it helped that this audience
was full of theologians willing to imagine why some people embrace the eternal
condition of peace and changelessness seriously. However, for the vast majority
of weekly worshippers, paradise is the final resting place on the other side of
death where there will be no suffering, a place of rest, refreshment, and reunion
with loved ones in spiritual happiness.

More specifically, how can Christian theologians resolve the statement Jesus
is reported to have said to the penitent thief hanging beside him on the cross:
"Truly, I say to you, today you will be with me in paradise?"[5] Liberationists need
to think hard about whether the promise of a fuller life beyond the grave truly
brings believers closer to God, or if it takes them further from working for heaven
right here on earth. Morrison says the bottom-line, fundamental question is:

> How can we narrate profound and motivating faith in paradise to a highly
> secularized, "scientific" world? I think that is the problem with trouble in
> paradise — the poverty of our ability to re-imagine and re-articulate it as a
> worthy idea for its own sake.[6]

After all, what use is paradise to researchers of religion, people who teach and
preach in a twenty-first century globalized world, a world that moves with
extremely rapid, break-neck speed, a world with interlocking economies,
cultures, governmental policies, military affairs, and political movements? The
cultural shifts in our internationalized reality — both within the academy and
outside it — transcend spatial barriers well beyond the boundaries of countries,
continents, and oceans. Morrison posits that the testament to this fundamental
dilemma is that paradise is no longer imaginable, or rather it is over-imagined,
which amounts to the same thing. Paradise has become familiar, common, and
even trivial.

So, in short, how do we re-imagine paradise in a world of wireless com-
munications and electronic commerce interconnected by webs of transoceanic

reciprocity? "The question that surfaces immediately," says Morrison, "is 'Why re-imagine it at all?' since the ablest geniuses have already, and long ago provided unsurpassed and unsurpassable language to describe paradise."[7] Among those who do seek some answers to inquiries about the solidity of paradise in our contemporary contexts, we must understand that paradise as an earthly project has serious intellectual and visual limitations. Morrison speaks at length about the language of religion being dependent on the Bible:

> Historically, the language of religion, although I am speaking here of Christianity, I am relatively certain that it is true of all texts-based religion, depended upon and gains its strength, beauty, and understandability from biblical or holy texts. Contemporary religious language, that is the speech and the script which seeks to translate divine speech into popular or everyday common parlance, works brilliantly in song, in sermon, in anecdote and in rhetorical art.
>
> I understand that the reason for modernizing traditional language of the Bible is an effort to connect with and proselytize a population that may be increasingly indifferent or unresponsive to the language that moved our ancestors. To compete for the attention of a constituency whose discourse has been shaped by the language of media and commerce and whose expectation of correlating images to accompany and clarify the texts is a difficult enterprise. And it appears reasonable to accommodate altering circumstances with alternate modes of discourse. While I cannot testify to the success of such efforts, I suspect that the modernization of God's language has been rewarding. Otherwise, these attempts would not be so plentiful.[8]

As we struggle to wrap our minds around the complexities embedded in a modern-day discussion of paradise, Morrison invites us to join her in wrestling with "Trouble in Paradise." "Right now, I want further to outline what my problem is," says Morrison, "and to tell you why I think I have it." She continues,

> I am having two kinds of trouble in paradise. Both kinds are writerly ones. I am hoping that they are difficulties that will interest an audience with your credentials and interests. The first problem involves the novel that I am writing, the title of which is *Paradise* and lies in the language of the narrative. The second problem concerns the idea of *paradise* and lies in the language of the text, that being how we read the text.[9]

In response to Morrison, I will discuss the following theological challenges she set before members of the AAR. First, I will examine her understanding of what it means to bring into sharper focus the re-imagining of blissful abode in a capitalist political economy thriving on marketable evil. Next, I will investigate Morrison's claims of a malignant push-pull tension between *paradiso* and *inferno*. Finally, and related to the preceding, I will elaborate Morrison's rhetorical strategies in constructing texts in which religious belief is central to the narrative itself.

Re-imagining Blissful Abode in a Capitalist Political Economy

In perhaps the most succinct inquiry about paradise in recent history, Morrison is quite direct with her questions:

> How can I invoke paradise in an age of theme parks? How can a novelist in a land of plenty render undeserved limitless love, the one that passes all understanding, without summoning the consumer pleasure of a lotto win? How can I represent bliss in non-sexual, non-orgiastic terms?[10]

Unfortunately, her inquiry is not yet unanswerable.

African American theologians in the ballroom immediately made connections between Morrison's interrogation and the urgent problem of envisioning a twenty-first century paradise that parallels the ethical ideal of acknowledging the good in each of us. But for many believers, our existential contexts encourage passive neglect when it comes to living as doers of justice. Nowadays, we hear a lot about how the laws of capitalism are imposed worldwide. Capitalist political economy consists of organizing free-market production by way of large multinational corporations and hybrid conglomerates. Each step in the chain of the high-tech, strategic planning process — from research and development to processing of raw materials, to production of parts, to the assembly of components and marketing of final products — is carried out in geographical locations that maximize the greatest profit, regardless of where corporate headquarters might be located or where the end product is sold. National borders are broken down. More than that, we end up living amalgamated existences like robotic automatons watching the same three-minute audio-visual news clips of major events, financial forecasts and ecological disasters circulating on twenty-four-hour news loops.

Liberationists continue to critique the elite powerbrokers, situated at the top of the hierarchal pyramid, who have gained control over entire sectors of the economy by seizing small companies and creating monopolies that exploit both labor and natural resources. International trading companies are growing fat at the expense of the majority. They are swallowing up self-sustaining smaller markets, smashing local economies, and forcing indigenous, homegrown industries out of existence. These conglomerates have so much power that they can tell governments what to do and bring them down if they refuse to obey.

At heart, this analysis of our existential reality interfaces with Morrison's plea for theologians to pay more attention to half-hearted flirtations and overt pressures around us, especially the restrictive demands of learned guilds that cause professors of religion to acquiesce, to dumb-down, to mortgage ourselves to conservative close-mindedness. According to Morrison,

Marketing religion requires new strategies, new appeals and a relevant sense of meaning, not contemplative. Thus, modern language, while perhaps successful in the acquisition of converts and the spiritual maintenance of the confirmed, is too often forced to kneel before the denominator that is most accessible, that is lowest. Religious language is sometimes forced to bankrupt its subtlety and its mystery in order to bankroll its effect.[11]

This means that, in the work world of the Academy of Religion, we need to embrace a vision of paradise that integrates character and behavior. An internal ethical criterion of heaven and earth being intimately in tandem, possibly touching, requires humans to participate responsibly in the world. Authentic faith can never be divorced from practical life. Since reality hinges on the moral laws of the universe, we need to be honest, just, and loving if we are serious about changing conditions that thwart life.

Historically, Morrison says that the images of paradise in poetry and prose were intended to be grand but also accessible, graspable, seductively precise, so that we could recognize and strive towards them. Paying close attention to her overall theme, Morrison notes,

> I have chosen this task, this obligation, partly because I am alarmed at the debasement of religious language in literature, its cliché riddle expressions, its apathy, its refusal to refuel itself with non-marketable vocabulary or its insistence on healing itself with marketable vocabulary. The terminology of philosophical clarity is substituted for popular psychology, for patriarchal triumphal-ism, for morally opinionated dictatorial praxis, for the unearned pleasure it takes in its performability of miracles rather than content. In short, in the language of literature, the religious language has a very low opinion of itself.[12]

Thus, Morrison purposes a sensitive, nuanced overview of five traditional characteristics of paradise that must be examined. She discusses the following watchwords: beauty, plenty, rest, exclusivity, and eternity.

Beauty matters. Beauty as a philosophical and theo-ethical concept denotes a pleasing quality associated with harmony, contemplative delight, and other unspecific properties of loveliness. This quality can be present in a person or a thing. Beauty can be the high spiritual qualities in benevolent individuals possessing blessed felicity, or it can be the intense satisfaction arising from sensory attractiveness as in colors, shapes, textures, et cetera, perceived by sight, sound, smell, touch, and taste. Morrison's apt observation is thus: "Beauty is a duplicate of what we already know, intensified. Or, beauty is what we have never known, articulated. What it cannot be, and ought not to be, is beauty beyond imagination, beyond enunciation."[13] Beauty in *Paradise Lost* (1667, 1674), a biblical epic in blank verse by the seventeenth-century English poet John Milton, is depicted as the goodliest trees loaded with fruits and blossoms of golden hue, enamel colors dripping with delicious taste. In this poem, considered the greatest poetic epic in English, Milton talks about nature booming forth profusely on hills, dales, and plains covered with curls of gold sand. Flowers without thorns are full of nectar. Morrison poignantly argues that even though we might be comfortably moved by such visual and aural incantations, such language is useless in postmodern fiction. Milton's scenario of a beautiful paradise before the temptation, fall, and expulsion of Adam and Eve from the Garden of Eden no longer commands our attention because we are living in a world owned by the wealthy, visited and viewed by guests and tourists, regularly on display for the rest of us in products and promises sold by the media.

Another key concept related to paradise is plenty. Here, too, Morrison contends that in our current world of excess and its companion, greed, resources are tilted to the haves, and the have-nots are forced to locate bounty within what has already been acquired by the haves. For Morrison, the stubborn fact is that abundance has now become an obscene feature of paradise:

> In this world of mal-distributed resources, of outrageous, shameless wealth, squatting, skulking, careening itself before the dispossessed, the very idea of plenty, of sufficiency as utopia ought to make us cringe. With what we know now and what we can do technologically, it is intolerable that plenty is regulated to a paradisiacal state rather than normal, everyday humane life.[14]

Alongside beauty and plenty, rest is the third essential characteristic when envisioning paradise. And yet, Morrison insists that the search for work as survival, wherein one labors in order to eke out the bare necessities of life, occupies millions all over the world. The frightening repercussions of multinational corporations, systemically crushing the socio-cultural foundations of local economies that sustain much of the population, cause widespread hunger, chronic disease, environmental spoliation, mass emigration, and chaotic unrest. Morrison's assessment is that the idea of freedom from activity is now contaminated and interpreted by powerbrokers as desirelessness. Due to vast changes in socioeconomic circumstances, rest as a positive value is now considered moot: "Rest from the pursuit of working or fighting for the rewards of food and luxuries has dwindling currency these days, suggesting a special kind of death without dying."[15]

Exclusivity is also an essential aspect of paradise. Morrison states emphatically that exclusivity is still an attractive — even a voluptuous — feature of paradise in these times because some of the unworthy are not there: "Our dreams are secure — watchdogs, gatekeepers, and security guards are there to verify the legitimacy of the inhabitants."[16] Morrison does not waver in her keen analysis of enclaves popping up more and more, like moated fortresses.

She says that it does not seem possible or desirable for a city to be envisioned, designed, and built wherein poor people are accommodated rather than tolerated. Exclusivity is not just an accessible dream for the well-endowed, but an increasingly popular solution for the growing middle class. Morrison is quite exacting in her discussion of the negative consequences of exclusivity:

> The concept of exclusivity extends beyond these private conclaves. It now encroaches on what used to be known as public space. Streets are understood to be populated by the unworthy and the dangerous. Young people are forced off of them for their own good. Public space is fought over as though it were private. Who gets to enjoy a park, a beach, a mall, a corner? The term "public" itself is a site of contention, a struggle for exclusivity and exclusive rights. The exclusiveness of paradise therefore continues to be a very real attraction to our society just as it was to certain elements of earlier ones.[17]

In tapping tradition and reworking it, Morrison addresses concerns about eternity in an inventive way. What is relevant here is that eternity is the fifth and final defining feature of paradise. To bolster her evaluation, Morrison straightforwardly proclaims that eternity, since it avoids the pain of dying again, probably has the greatest appeal for paradise. Eternity, as the state of everlasting bliss, is connected to the unfolding of the human life cycle. In the natural scheme of things, finite corporeal beings are born, we mature, and we die. Eternity is a concept of sacred time wherein the human spiritual existence continues after death of the physical body. Even though the nature of future existence is conceived in very different ways, for many religious practitioners, eternity is the timeless state where the never-dying soul resides:

> Many folks embrace eternal life as a key component of their religious tradition and reject secular, scientific arguments to the contrary. Moreover, it is worthwhile to note that medical and scientific resources are directed toward more and bigger life. They encourage in us the desire for an earthbound eternity rather than eternal afterlife. Still the length and fitness of life are paramount to human yearnings.[18]

Weaving eternity terminology into her observations of contemporary times, Morrison says that, of the five features of paradise, only two (exclusivity and eternity) excite us. Due to our trouble with paradise, we are especially attracted to exclusivity and eternal life, a paradise *only for us, forever.*

Essentially, paradise, in the context of religious studies, is a utopian value that cannot be limited and bound up. Each of the five elements is a postulate of morality. As we ascertain our duties in faith communities, we grasp that earthly harmony is free of licentious extravagance. In turn, paradise is a symbolic image of the divine commonwealth available to and for all. Morally and aesthetically, there is miniscule distance between the only two coordinates that matter, the nexus of being and doing. In other words, implicit in this causal link of living in paradise is a dynamic, non-static pattern of purposive behavior and intentional involvement, whereby the kind of person one is bears upon the decisions one makes. At its best, a theo-ethical vision of paradise closes the circle of meaning securely around the fact that who we are determines what we ought to do; the flesh and blood of what we do tells others who we are.

Investigating the Malignant Push-Pull Tension between *Paradiso* and *Inferno*

Though committed as ever to wrestling with paradise as a moral compass, Morrison asserts that hell does indeed provide answers to paradise's questions. Paradise has always depended on its opposite for its juice. Morrison succinctly grapples with this binary: "It is hard not to notice how much more attention has always been given to hell. Dante's *Inferno* beats out *Paradiso*. The visionary language of antithesis reaches heights of linguistic order with which the thesis language seldom can compete."[19] Based on her approach in dealing with this push-pull tension, Morrison argues directly that John Milton's brilliantly rendered pre-paradise world known as chaos is far more fully realized than his idyllic, sin-free heaven. His brilliantly rendered pre-paradise world of utter confusion, disarray, and large-scale warfare is far more fully realized than his hopeful vision of salvation. Morrison observes that there are many reasons why the images of the horrors of hell were meant to be virulently repulsive in the twelfth, fifteenth, and seventeenth centuries. The arguments for avoiding afterlife in hell needed to reveal how much worse such an eternity was than the hell of people's living life. "The need for hell, rather than paradise, as stimulus has persisted in our times and with significant addition."[20]

For instance, even now, Morrison's message says much about how essential it is for theologians to pay attention to the way bearers of inherited white supremacist privileges engage in disparaging remarks, grievous offense, and widespread assaults against people of color with impunity. Many who teach religion in colleges, universities, and seminaries participate in creating and sustaining institutionalized assaults that become living hells. Academic orthodoxy justifies such death-dealing behavior in a myriad of legitimating myths that sanction exclusive categories of reality. Power relationships in the ivory tower keep selected academicians in the traditional, hegemonic center as normative subjects while pushing the designated "other" to the despised periphery as marginalized objects.

Due to an "invisible package of unearned assets,"[21] some members of scholarly guilds consciously minimize, ignore, trivialize, or deny institutional-ized racial oppression. Others are indifferent to black misery and pain.

However, in this hellish state of de facto racism, professors of religion differ greatly regarding the degree to which their interactions with racially ethnic colleagues and students inhibit their ability to see patterns of habituation and social forces as a result of destructive intellectual handiwork. Once the ready-made theological rationale for this type of dominant adaptation of systemic exclusion based upon rigid constructions of scholarly identity of excellence is in place, it becomes a cultural practice that takes on a life of its own.

In her effort to reinvigorate our understanding of paradise, she infuses it with a critique of the pervasiveness of hell-making evil. Her success in this regard is thorough:

> There is an influx in print devoted to consternation about the absence of our sense of evil, if not evil itself, of a loss of shame about evil in contemporary life. One wonders how to account for the melancholy that accompanies these exhortations about our inattention to the muteness, the numbness toward an anti-paradisiacal experience. Evil is understood, justifiably, to be pervasive. But, evil has also lost its awe, its awfulness. It doesn't frighten us. It is merely entertainment.

What's more, Morrison provides ample reasons to substantiate that trouble in paradise is related to a radically anthropocentric need for hell:

> Why are we not so frightened by the possibility of hell that we turn toward good? Why is the language of good, moral, and spiritual so banal? Is afterlife of any sort too silly for our complex, sophisticated modern intelligence? Or, is it that unlike paradise, evil needs costumes constantly refurbished and replenished?
>
> Evil has always lent itself to glamour, headlines, a tuxedo, cunning, gruesome seductiveness. Evil needs blood and slime, roaring simply to get our attention — to tickle us, to draw from us, to outwit our imagination, our energy, our heights of performance.[22]

Morrison is concerned, above all else, with the reasons we allow hell to trump paradise. For some, paradise is simple. For others, it seems too passive:

> Paradise has an edgelessness and perhaps an unavailing lack, and an already perceived, recognizable landscape. Great trees with shade, true lawns, palaces, precious metals, jewelry and animal husbandry. Outside of fighting evil, waging war against the unworthy, there seems nothing for inhabitants of paradise to do. The unspoken tragedy is that a non-exclusionary, un-bordered, come-one-come-all paradise without dread, minus a nemesis, is no paradise at all.[23]

Morrison reminds us that our dismissal of paradise has the teleological consequence of living in a society that lacks an inclusive vision of the well-being of us all:

> My literary problem is trying to use contemporary language to reveal not only what I believe to be the intellectual complexity of paradise, but to find language

that seizes the imagination. Paradise is not about weakness. Nor is it naïve or neurotic. But rather, paradise is sane, intelligent life itself.[24]

Elaborating Rhetorical Strategies in Constructing Texts in which Religious Belief Is Central

It is important to note that, in this particular novel, Morrison wants to convey how the earthly achievement of former slaves and first generation children of freed people is incapable of being disconnected from their perception of the divine:

> The history of African Americans that narrows or dismisses religion in both the collective and individual life, in their political and aesthetic activities is more than incomplete, it may be fraudulent. Therefore, among the difficulties before me is the daunting one of showing not just their civic and economic impulses that respond to their religious principles, but how African Americans were inextricably bound with these principles.[25]

Morrison presents a clear and convincing argument for using credible and effective expressive language in the construction of postmodern fiction in which religious belief is central to the narrative itself. In writing her novel, *Paradise*, Morrison is clear that she does not want to submit to vague, poly-tarianism, nor to some form of late twentieth-century environmental spiritualism, nor to modern-day schools of goddess religion, nor to a loose undiscriminating conviction of the innate divinity of all living things, nor to biblical-political scholasticism of the French dictatorial reign, because none of these approaches seems to represent the everyday practices of nineteenth-century African Americans and their children, nor do they lend themselves to innovative narrative strategies.

Progressive writers can no longer sacrifice ambiguity, depth, and moral authority, because to do so reinforces oppression rather than liberation. Our task is not to sanitize tragedy and horror, but rather to exegete such texts so that, as embodied readers, we can witness both the abominations and the searing conflicts for freedom. Morrison is aware of the audience's possible objections to her proposed methodology, so she sensitively presents her dilemma in this way:

> Paradise is a textual problem in the broadest sense of the word. Therefore, the questions as a writer that I put to myself are these: Is it possible to write a religious inflected prose narrative that does not rest its case entirely or mainly on biblical language? Is it possible to make the experience in journeys of faith fresh, as new and as linguistically unencumbered as it was to early believers and they themselves had no collection of books to rely on?[26]

Morrison's methodological assumption, the rhetorical strategies emanating from this paradisiacal discourse, will not allow her to minimize or ignore the rich textures of African American religious concerns: "The polls of 1994 indicate that 96% of African Americans believe in God. I suspect that the 4% who do not believe are recent phenomena, unheard of among slave and ex-slave populations."[27]

In toto, Morrison's lecture is a clarion call for theologians to use our keenest critical thinking skills in the struggle to fill in holes of religious curiosity and doubt. She avers that spiritual belief as an animating force cannot be taken for granted anymore. Embedded in an ideal, such as paradise, is innate passion commanding us to tease out hidden meanings. There is no one single template for African American religiosity. Morrison's decipherable lecture is full of religious source documentation. When we piece together the situated-ness of paradise of which she speaks, we find a variety of ways to assess how the first generation of freed people strained against unutterable anguish. Morrison's foremost agenda is this:

> The integrity of my project, in a highly secularized world, demands peaks of imagination that may be beyond me, straining the credulity of any reader because the job is not to layer religiosity onto an existing canvas of African American migration and the quest for African American citizenship. Nor is it simply to tip one's hat to characters whose belief is unshakeable. The job, my job, is rather to construct a work in which religious belief is central to the narrative itself, naturally, if any, in the expressive language that renders it.[28]

Such texts end up carrying weight, possessing a type of religious gravitas that impacts theological studies. Morrison's novels usher us into a space that enables us to cultivate a potentially life-changing capacity of empathy. To bolster her stance, Morrison straightforwardly and uncompromisingly proclaims:

> If I am to do justice, bear witness to the deeply religious population of this project and render their profoundly held moral system affective in these uninspiring times, where religion among some quarters is understood to run the gamut from scorned, unintelligible fundamentalism to literate, well-meaning liberalism, to tele-evangelistic marketing, to militaristic racism, I have serious problems.[29]

Morrison read from her novel, *Paradise*, two brief scenes: one that opened with a sermon; the other speculated on another sermon that had no speech at all. Both selections represented the core essentials of the religious-driven life made real. Morrison's words brought the religiosity and social worlds of African Americans into existence, allowing us to see stunning glimpses into the souls of foremothers and forefathers who migrated from the South as homesteading exodusters to Oklahoma. Morrison's point is that, although prosperity, ownership, safety, and self-determination were thinkable and hungered-for goals for former slaves, design alone could not and did not animate the treacherous journey they took to get to unknown territories to build cities, to build towns, and to build their own communities. By simultaneously mixing historical details with purposeful fictitious characters, she gives us accessible entry to the socio-cultural religious world behind the representation.

Indeed, the focus of redeeming paradise as an aspect of "intelligent life" is the major undercurrent throughout this presentation, "Trouble in Paradise." Morrison's overarching strategic answer to the numerous methodological questions posed throughout her lecture is this:

> So, I have chosen to do something else. I have chosen strategy in order to inform old fashion passions in a post-modernist world. And that something else is not to describe paradise, but to do it. To activate its possibilities. To domesticate its realization and then to interrogate its desire.[30]

Again, at the end, when Morrison stepped away from the podium, members of the Amen Corner, who engaged in call-and-response throughout the lecture, erupted into a spontaneously standing ovation full of thunderous applause.

NOTES

1. James Cone's commentary during the Womanist Panel at the 1995 AAR Meeting.
2. See Wilfred D. Samuels and Clenora Hudson-Weems, *Toni Morrison*, Twayne's United States Authors Series, 559 (Boston: Twayne, 1990).
3. Carolyn C. Denard, ed., *Toni Morrison—Conversations*, Literary Conversations Series (Jackson: University Press of Mississippi, 2008), xiv.
4. Toni Morrison, "Trouble in Paradise." (speech, American Academy of Religion Annual Conference, Marriott Hotel, Philadelphia, Pennsylvania, November 1995).
5. Luke 23:43
6. Morrison, ibid.
7. Morrison, ibid.
8. Morrison, ibid.
9. Morrison, ibid.
10. Morrison, ibid.
11. Morrison, ibid.
12. Morrison, ibid.
13. Morrison, ibid.
14. Morrison, ibid.
15. Morrison, ibid.
16. Morrison, ibid.
17. Morrison, ibid.
18. Morrison, ibid.
19. Morrison, ibid.
20. Morrison, ibid.

21. Peggy McIntosh, "White Privilege and Male Privilege: A Personal Account of Coming to See Correspondences through Work in Women's Studies," in *Working Paper No. 189* (Wellesley, MA: Center for Research on Women, Wellesley College, 1988), 1.
22. Morrison, ibid.
23. Morrison, ibid.
24. Morrison, ibid.
25. Morrison, ibid.
26. Morrison, ibid.
27. Morrison, ibid.
28. Morrison, ibid.
29. Morrison, ibid.
30. Morrison, ibid.

Richard Danielpour

Richard Danielpour is one of the most gifted and sought-after composers of his generation. A Grammy Award-winning artist, Danielpour counts some of the world's most prominent musical artists and institutions among his commissions, including the New York Philharmonic and the National Symphony. Danielpour has been recognized with a Lifetime Achievement Award from the American Academy of Arts and Letters and has received a Guggenheim Foundation Fellowship. With Morrison, Danielpour created *Margaret Garner*, his first opera, which premiered in May 2005 and which had a second production in the fall of 2007 with the New York City Opera. The selection of Danielpour's music featured here, "Margaret's Lullaby," an excerpt from *Margaret Garner*, exemplifies the potent fusion of his deeply moving music — which he describes as "speak[ing] to the heart as well as the mind" — and Morrison's earthy and prescient words.

"Margaret's Lullaby"
(from Act I, Scene 2 of *Margaret Garner*)

RICHARD DANIELPOUR

Toni Morrison's collaborative works include creations with musicians such as Max Roach, Andre Previn, and, perhaps most prolifically, with composer Richard Danielpour. Danielpour wrote the music, and Morrison wrote the story and lyrics, for their collaborative works *Sweet Talk: Four Songs on Text* (1997), *Spirits in the Well*, (1997), and *Margaret Garner* (2005).

The opera *Margaret Garner* is loosely derived from Morrison's novel *Beloved*, which itself is based on the true events in the life of the opera's title character, a Kentucky slave in the 1850s who escaped to Ohio but, upon her recapture, killed one child and attempted to kill her other children, rather than see them returned to slavery. Morrison wrote the opera's libretto, and Richard Danielpour composed the music for *Margaret Garner*. The two-act opera has nearly 100 cast members, including two choruses: one for the slaves and one for the slave owners. Co-commissioned by the Michigan Opera Theatre, the Cincinnati Opera, and the Opera Company of Philadelphia, *Margaret Garner* debuted on May 7, 2005, in Detroit, with mezzo-soprano Denyce Graves singing the lead role.

Margaret Garner *Synopsis*
Act 1

The story opens in 1856 at a property auction in Kentucky. Edward Gaines, standing among the bidders, is from the area, but he has been away for twenty years. When his family plantation, Maplewood, is brought onto the block, he interrupts the bidding and says that the plantation cannot be sold because it belonged to his dead brother. The other people have a hard time remembering him, but they accept his claim, so he takes possession of Maplewood. While signing the ownership papers, Gaines hears the singing of one of Maplewood's slaves, Margaret Garner. He recalls his childhood and grows wistful.

As the slaves of Maplewood return from the fields, Cilla — the mother-in-law of Margaret Garner — joins her son and daughter-in-law for supper. Their eating is interrupted when Maplewood's foreman, Casey, arrives with terrible news. Robert — Margaret's husband — has been sold to another plantation. Margaret is to remain at Maplewood.

Gaines hosts a marriage reception for his daughter, Caroline. Gaines and his new son-in-law, George, argue about the nature of love. Later, Caroline asks Margaret, now a servant in the Gaines house, for her views on love. The guests are horrified that Caroline should solicit a slave's opinion, and they leave. Gaines is also horrified and scolds Caroline. Later, he watches Margaret clean the parlor, and he forces himself on her.

Act 2

Margaret goes to Cilla's cabin to meet her husband, Robert, who is to visit from the plantation where he now lives. Robert is not there, but Margaret finds her mother-in-law packing and her own children missing. Cilla explains that Robert is planning an escape to the Ohio. When he arrives, Robert confirms the news. This thrills Margaret, but she is upset that Cilla will not join them. Casey storms into the cabin, and this leads to a fight between him and Robert. It ends with Robert killing Casey. Robert and Margaret are now under even more pressure to escape. They flee and arrive at a shelter in Ohio. They are close to freedom, but Gaines catches up and captures Robert. Margaret fights back and witnesses Robert getting lynched. Unwilling to see her children returned to slavery, she murders them.

Margaret is returned to Kentucky, where she stands trial for the theft and destruction of another's property — that is, her own children. Caroline says that Margaret should not be charged with theft but with murder. She says the children are not property. They are human beings. The judges disagree. They sentence Margaret to be hanged for theft. Caroline begs her father to seek clemency for Margaret, and Gaines must choose between his daughter's respect and the morality of the times.

The next morning, Margaret ascends the scaffold. Gaines runs in with a legal document. The judges have granted Margaret clemency. She is on the gallows, with the rope around her neck; Margaret expresses her refusal to live as a slave. She gives herself her own freedom by hanging herself. The onlookers, both Black and White, pray for their own repentance and for Margaret's soul.

Margaret's Lullaby
LYRICS BY TONI MORRISON

Sad things far away.
Soft things come and play lovely baby…
Sleep in the meadow, sleep in the hay.
Baby's got a dreamin' on the way.
Bad things, far away.
Pretty things, here to stay.
Sweet baby smile at me.
Lovely Baby to sleep.
Sleep in the meadow, sleep in the hay.
Baby's gonna dream the night away.
Lovely baby, pretty baby.
Baby's gonna dream the night away.
Sleep in the meadow, sleep in the hay.
Baby's gonna dream.
Baby's gonna dream.
Baby's gonna dream.

The excerpt from *Margaret Garner* included as a contribution to this collection is entitled "Margaret's Lullaby." It occurs in Act I, scene 2 of the opera. The recording of this excerpt can be found by following this QR code or linking to: www.bucknell.edu/MargaretsLullaby.

Act I–Scene 2

Act I–Scene 2   183

184   Act I–Scene 2

186   Act I–Scene 2

Act 1–Scene 2

Act I–Scene 2

188

Act I–Scene 2

Act I–Scene 2

* mm 335-336 ossia: "mmm" (humming)
** Going gradually from closed mouth to partially open mouth.

Lydia Diamond

Lydia Diamond is a Huntington Playwriting Fellow, resident playwright at Chicago Dramatists, and an Assistant Professor of Playwriting and Theatre Arts at Boston University. She has written several celebrated plays, including *Stage Black*, *The Gift Horse*, *Stick Fly*, *Voyeurs de Venus*, *The Inside*, and *Harriet Jacobs*, which premiered at Steppenwolf. Her adaptation of Morrison's *The Bluest Eye* won the Black Arts Alliance Image Award for Best New Play. Two of Diamond's plays — *Stick Fly* and *The Gift Horse* — have been published by Boston University Press. In this interview with Carmen Gillespie, Diamond reflects on the powerful and visceral transformation she experienced while adapting *The Bluest Eye* for stage production. Her clear reverence for the work, and her thoughtful negotiation of the shared consciousness between author and playwright echo Morrison's visionary conviction in the force and strength of literary representation.

CHAPTER FIVE

"Creatively Serving — The Process"
An Interview with Playwright Lydia Diamond, Author of the Play *The Bluest Eye*

LYDIA DIAMOND WITH CARMEN GILLESPIE

Toni Morrison's first novel, *The Bluest Eye* was adapted for the stage by Lydia Diamond. The theatrical version of the novel focuses on the novel's central character, Pecola Breedlove, an eleven-year-old girl in 1940s Ohio who thinks she will be loved by her family and friends, if only she can acquire blue eyes. Directed by Hallie Gordon, the original theatrical production of *The Bluest Eye* received strong reviews upon its debut performances in 2005 at Chicago's Steppenwolf Arts Exchange. In 2006, the play premiered in Manhattan. Since that time, it has been produced nationally and internationally, creating a new audience for Morrison's narrative and acclaim for Diamond's skillful adaptation.

During the summer of 2010, Lydia Diamond and I discussed her engagement with and adaptation of *The Bluest Eye* for the stage.

CARMEN GILLESPIE (CG): Would you speak a little bit about your experiences in becoming a playwright before we speak specifically about your adaptation of *The Bluest Eye*.

LYDIA DIAMOND (LD): I realized I was a theatre artist in high school and leaned toward the performance side of things. For college I picked Northwestern because at the time it was rated the number one school for acting training and was still a liberal arts college. I majored in theater, and I got a great education. While there I was going I became more and more interested in something in the department called performance studies, which was more of a sociologically and anthropologically-based approach at performance. I also found it more inclusive because it looked at other cultures. So the canon of theatre — not black theatre — that was presented to me was so white and so dead that I felt excluded, and didn't know how to access works, and so I presumed that they didn't exist. As such, part of my becoming a playwright was my desire to put roles and images into the world that I wanted to be in, to act.

It wasn't until after graduation that I was exposed to the great canon of African American and African diaspora theatre. That's when I discovered Wole Soyinka and sadly, much later, Adrienne Kennedy. Dicsovering these black voices was fortuitous in thay I found my voice before I learned to imitate voices that already existed. Prior to hearing those voices, I thought I was inventing something. Sometimes when I watch young people going through various stages of consciously emulating various writers, I am aware that I didn't have that opportunity. So as I was honing my writing skills, I fell into my own voice very naturally, very organically.

CG: I was thinking, as you were speaking, that your motivations to write sound, in some ways, similar to what Morrison says about her reasons for wanting to write novels. She has said that she wanted to read the books that weren't available to her.

LD: Right.

CG: Did you have much exposure to Morrison, either as a young person or as a student?

LD: I did, as a matter of fact. As an undergrad, I was introduced to Toni Morrison in literature classes. I believe it was the summer of my sophomore year that I decided I was going to read every Toni Morrison novel. And I did. Reading her novels was sort of like medicine. But at the time I didn't have the skills and the depth to really understand what I was reading (laughs). So much of what I read just washed over me. But I continued to immerse myself in her work. And that was great, but I still wasn't really *being* in it. I think some of the themes brushed against my own vulnerabilities and unresolved issues. I dismissed *The Bluest*

Eye because it was painful. And I didn't come back to it until the Steppenwolf Theatre Company said that they had acquired the rights to do the play as a one-time production and they wanted me to write the adaptation.

CG: What was that moment like for you, when they invited you to do the adaptation?

LD: I had just had my son and I was in the middle of finishing my play *Stick Fly*, and a theatre company had said that they wanted to produce it. And I was scrambling to finish it, so that it could go into production. I was actually holding Baylor [her son] — he was days old! — in the bathtub when I got the call about the commission. It was wonderful, because, with all of the hormones of having just had a baby I was convinced that I would never be a playwright again. Who can be a mommy and a playwright? So it was very affirming to know that somebody still wanted me to write a play, even though I was someone's mommy.

But what was extraordinary was that it opened me up in amazing ways to being able to receive the story. I re-read the novel in an afternoon. I had the time because I was just nursing and sitting in a chair and rocking Baylor. The rereading was shattering. I began to feel what the novel meant.

The venue that I was being asked to adapt the play for was the Steppenwolf's Theatre for Young Adults program, which is run by a woman named Hallie Gordon, a wonderful, wonderful director and a wonderful administrator and director, who would also direct the play. The theatre brings kids from all over the city, so there are also privileged white kids who come and see the shows, but there is also a larger audience of people of color that see the regular productions in the evenings.

The dynamic of having kids walk into the lobby of the Steppenwolf, which at the time had only one African-American ensemble member, K. Todd Freeman, was astonishing. You walk in and there are pictures of the ensemble members all over the lobby. It is very beautiful, and then there's a big, wall-sized picture of the whole ensemble together. But it's very, very white. I felt the pressure of trying to understand what it means when kids that look like me walk into a lobby and walk past images that don't look like them. You feel the money when you walk into the lobby. And so then they're going into the theater and are presented with these stark images of one piece of American reality that doesn't define the whole African-American experience, that is sort of historically-specific, but in some ways beyond their ability to grasp. It frightened me. At the time, the inherent power dynamics of the theatre made me reconsider whether or not I wanted to adapt the novel for this venue in this way. After many conversations with my husband, a lot of soul-searching and a lot of worry and thought, in concert with being aware of how privileged I was to have this opportunity, and also taking into consideration the work that the Steppenwolf does and the people I've had a chance to work with there, I accepted the challenges of the adaptaion.

So, in spite of this really weird set of contradictions and concerns, I took it because — and it might be cocky — but I decided that the very concerns I was having, I could address in the piece, and I would feel uncomfortable having somebody else do the adaptation, someone who, perhaps, wasn't coming to the table with my list of concerns.

CG: It is fascinating to me, the ways you're talking about the venue as a potential kind of meta-narrative of the issues of the play. Is that the way you perceived it?

LD: Absolutely.

CG: And, it was also an opportunity. I would imagine that you were hoping that there would be some transcendence of the powerful structural constructs for the audience while they're in the theatre space. That's really very interesting. And so, as you were in the process of writing — did you work at all with Toni Morrison?

LD: Toni — Ms. Morrison — was so generous in allowing the adaptation of *The Bluest Eye* to happen in the first place. I was aware that she just doesn't readily permit adaptations of her work. But, to answer your question, her involvement was limited to none. Her most generous and important gesture was to give the theatre permission. She started reading the first draft, and, at a certain point, decided that she would pull back further, and let that draft live without her micromanaging it, which was amazing and gracious, and — as you can imagine — also a little scary.

CG: Right [*laughs*].

LD: And then she was pleased with the reception the play received and with what had been written about the production, and then the *coup* . . . well, not *coup* . . . but it was a *coup* — she allowed the play to move into the world. That was huge.

CG: I'm gathering that your expectation was that the initial engagement would be the only engagement.

LD: It was intended to happen only at that one time, in that one place. I wasn't adapting a play that was supposed to end up in my repertoire of plays.

CG: I see.

LD: When I wrote it, I didn't know that it would be produced all over the country.

CG: Right, and the world, I understand.

LD: I was writing a play for the children and young adults of Chicago. I was actually humbled by young adult audiences because they force me to be a better writer. I have to really understand why I'm telling the story, the story has to be engaging at every second, or they're out. And the passion that I feel for getting it right — the images, the historical context, the issues of respect, the unspoken story — anticipating a young audience raises the stakes for the writer in such a way that makes the act of writing and of assembling the work so much more purposeful.

CG: I can hear that intensity in your description of the process.

LD: And so the reality that it ended up being a play that was also appealing to adults is because it was a play that young people could enter, and stay engaged, and could have a political conversation with.

CG: So it was accessible. I like your idea about having to hold youthful attention and imagination, and that goal is fundamental to good theatre irrespective of age, right?

LD: Absolutely. Also, we sometimes underestimate young adult audiences, because we're talking about audiences between the ages of . . . oh, thirteen and eighteen, I guess? They are so bright. They are so on top of it, and they don't miss a beat. I think it also has to do with knowing that while writing for any age, even for work I've done for young children, it requires honoring the plays enough to make the work sophisticated enough that they earn the respect of the audience.

CG: That's really interesting, particularly in terms of *The Bluest Eye*, because one of the things that I've been grappling with as I've been thinking about talking with you about the play is the question of whether or not it is a coming-of-age story, or if it is a sort of anti-*Bildungsroman*. And, the question of the impact that it potentially could have on young children, or young adults, must have been daunting as well, given the level of sexuality and violence that's inherent in the story. How did you approach those challenges?

LD: I think, partially, being painfully aware that those challenges, unfortunately, are already things that our young people have to address —

CG: Right.

LD: — you know, and the level of vulnerability, and sexual navigation, or sexual — what is the word I'm looking for? — the way that a twelve-year-old who is getting her breasts is asked to navigate herself sexually in the world in which she's a young person who is still ogled by old men, and vulnerable to young men and old men alike, and learning how to have agency. I guess it *is* a coming-of-age story, in that these are really important themes, and I didn't want Pecola's rape to define her — Pecola's rape, actually, in my mind, is not the coming-of-age climax of the story, it's the contextualization of what is happening politically and socially

CG: I hear that.

LD: And so, for me, it was about being brave and remembering why. It was also really helpful to hear women who aren't African American speak with tears in their eyes about how and why *The Bluest Eye* saved them when they were in high school. And my director, who is a white woman, and I had some passionate arguments about what the book was about, and I was very clear about. I don't want to have this universalized in a way that makes it not specific to me and why it's important to me. This is a play that is about a young black girl in a black family in a racist society. And she was saying, "Yes, but it is also about learning to accept yourself, and for me, that's the way it changed my life — I was a little white girl growing up in California, around the beautiful people, and feeling never enough, and I read this and I cried, and I had some sense of perspective." And that was really challenging to me, eye-opening and challenging, and still I didn't waver in my insistence that this was a culturally-specific story that has resonance for everyone. But it complicated it in a really interesting way.

CG: I've had a sort of similar experience when I've been teaching the book and some of my white students have identified with Morrison's use of the character Jane from the *Dick and Jane* readers. As you know, Jane only appears in the epigraph at the very beginning of the book. With that introduction, Morrison sets up questions of gender and the vulnerability of young girls generally. It's a very sad story if you read the mini-narrative and learn about Jane's isolation and lack of companionship. So, it's helpful to hear your experiences with non-blacks who can identify with this play, even though the work is so importantly specific to the African American experience. What has been your response from people understanding the play as a way of working through trauma?

LD: If that literature's out there, I haven't been exposed to it.

CG: I was wondering if people were perhaps writing letters to you . . . .

LD: No, we had huge conversations and had numbers to give people, as well as counselors available if the play became a trigger for people around sexual abuse—it was really a concern for us. I haven't been a part of a dialogue about my adaptation and these dynamics. And I didn't read a lot — I purposefully didn't read the sort of "deconstructing Toni Morrison's book" essays. I was not only not interested in that, but I didn't want to be messed up by it. [*laughs*]

CG: So you did not look at literary criticism at all?

LD: No. I am a writer. I'm a working writer. [*laughs*] The closest I've gotten to it was Toni Morrison's own book, you know, *Playing in the Dark*. I love that book! That's about as far into the world of literary criticism that I can go.

CG: Let me ask you about the structural challenges of creating a play from the novel form of *The Bluest Eye*. I really admire the way that you were able to extract the essence of the play and yet change the novel in a way that makes it work for the theatre. And I was wondering if you could speak about what your objectives were and how you went about achieving them.

LD: Yes. Well, initially, my objective was not to offend and alienate myself from Toni Morrison forever —

CG: [*laughs*]

LD: — and so I was just afraid and wanted to honor the book. I realized quickly and after much pain that that wasn't serving—creatively serving—the process. So, I had to let that go, and remember that I know how to write a play. That I knew I knew how to do. And so I sort of went back to the drawing board, and took a really hard look at why I decided Toni Morrison was telling the story — she speaks very clearly in the foreword [of the novel] about that herself — and I wanted to honor that. I then needed to apply what I know about playwriting to tell the story of the person I identified as the protagonist, and to make sure that I was serving and honoring all of the themes and the reasons I had decided in the first place to take this on, even with my concerns.

CG: And it seems to me that one of the voices that emerges out of the play [that] is, in many ways, absent in the novel, of course, is Pecola. Can you speak to your construction of her?

LD: Absolutely. I needed for Pecola to have a voice. I thought that, in the novel, the place where we really saw her have a voice was in her relationship with the prostitutes. I didn't have enough time. You don't have enough time, in a play, to develop everyone. And, a general rule of playwriting is not to introduce characters that you're not going to develop fully. And, along with all the other things that I've said about my concerns about what I was putting before young people, and how they would synthesize it, there was just not time to properly contextualize and protect these beautiful characters that Pecola finds her voice with. And so they [the prostitutes] couldn't be in my adaptation. It was a painful decision.

I only had 90 minutes. [*laughs*] The play needed to be 90 minutes long, because the kids come in, they have a bus, and it taught me again, I think, that 90-minute plays are kind of fabulous. I've fallen in love with the form. That's the perfect amount of time to sit in the theater and have an event, but, if I had chosen to explore her [Pecola's] relationship with those wonderful women, it would have to develop over almost a whole act, in order for us to understand the context and get over the career, and all of that. I couldn't explain this to young people, I couldn't have contextualized that, and I wasn't going to put images in an already-troubling story of more troubling female images that couldn't be properly contextualized. So I wrote some monologues for Pecola so that we could sort of understand her internal life, and I tried very hard to construct those in a voice that sounded like Toni Morrison's. I wanted, very purposefully, for the play to be the experience of the novel on stage. I chose not to take the characters and write a straight play, I wanted the language to be another character. The language is so lush, why would I not use what we all acknowledge is one of the most important parts of Toni Morrison's work?

CG: Exactly, and it's an interesting question for me to think about your use of Morrison's language and yet finding your own voice, which, clearly, you did in this play. Was there a kind of conscious effort to navigate that near conundrum, or was that something that just happened as the work evolved?

LD: I think it was actually very spiritual, and I don't — I didn't — have any desire to find my own voice in it. I only wanted to highlight Toni Morrison's voice in a respectful way, and so if my voice is in there, it's just in the way that I made structural decisions and the prose that I wrote as much in her vernacular as possible — to the extent that there are passages that sometimes I don't know if they are mine or hers, and I remember that when people talk about the play, there were times where I would feel sort of like, "Oh, but you don't understand, I wrote that." [laughs] "No, I didn't just sort of willy-nilly highlight some things in the book and then plop them down on the page. ... "

CG: [laughs] Right, right.

LD: I got to a place with directors who were new to the project where I would say, "Okay, you're going to read the book and then you're going to read my adaptation, and then you're going to want to call me, and say, 'Can we just add this?' and, 'Can we just add that?' and I want to nix that now. Because I've had two years of intense, intense, purposeful placing-in, laying-in of this story the way I need it to be. And it may look arbitrary, but indeed it is not. [laughs] And so, you're just going to have to trust that.

CG: And they have?

LD: They have! But, there was a time when I had to develop this speech, because ...

CG: And make that point.

LD: Yeah. It's like, "No, this isn't open season on what would you like to throw into the play!"

CG: And that's an interesting issue in terms of the questions about adaptation and what that work is like for the playwright. One of the questions I have for you is about that process in terms of — recovery is not exactly the right word, but I know that you've worked with Nikki Giovanni's poems, and you're also, I understand, working with Incidents in the Life of a Slave Girl. Is that work completed?

LD: Yes, that's completed. Northwestern University Press is about to publish it. They did a good job with *Stick Fly*, so I think it will be beautiful, and it had a production at the Steppenwolf in the same venue as *The Bluest Eye*, and it's had another one since, in Boston at Underground Railway Theatre Company, and it's about to have a production at the Kansas City Repertory Theatre.

CG: Congratulations.

LD: Oh, thank you!

CG: So do you see one of your professional objectives or missions as bringing African American women's literature to another venue?

LD: No. And yes. [*laughs*] The Harriet Jacobs is actually really not an adaptation. It's a play based on the life as told in *Incidents in the Life of a Slave Girl*, which is tricky, and it does get called an adaptation, and to some degree I suppose that's fair. It's not what I did with *The Bluest Eye*, because I wasn't interested in capturing Harriet's literary voice. I was interested in pulling out the psychological complexities around her existence and her choices. So, it's a really different project.

CG: And you created a dramatic interpretation of Jacob's story?

LD: A dramatic interpretation of her story that I tried to make as historically accurate as possible, but was interested most in making a psychological exploration of Harriet Jacobs, and the perverse, weird hierarchy of slavery, how the institution works.

CG: And the evidence that we have based on her response to slavery — that people would incarcerate themselves in that way — I am always so horrified to think about what slavery must have been like and the realities of it, and to also try to stay so proximate to your children, it's just astonishing. Was that a difficult journey as well?

LD: Oh, yeah, yeah, that was painful. It remains painful. I get vertigo every time I go into a process with it, and I'm in the process of getting over my most recent bout of vertigo, and I think that's not a coincidence. It's horrific. Yeah, it's horrifying.

CG: Absolutely.

LD: But, your question was: do I feel a mission? So when I first started writing plays, what I thought my mission was, was to present, was to put on stage contemporary stories inhabited by people who looked like the people in my world. Which meant a range of socioeconomic realities, a range of genders and races, and sexual identifications . . . and, so that was my passion. Every time I saw a play with people of color in it, most of the time, it was in a historical perspective and it was a story that was about our reaction to the white people's boot on our back.

CG: One of the reasons that I asked the question is because of Alice Walker saying at one point that the reason she let *The Color Purple* become a film adaptation is because she wanted more people to have access to the story. So, that made me curious about what your thoughts were.

LD: Well, there's more. …

CG: I'm sure! [*laughs*]

LD: So that was the first part of my artistic mission, in my twenties and in my early thirties. And then, I think Toni Morrison taught me, and the experience of doing the *Bluest Eye* taught me, the importance of articulating our history honestly and with complexity, and in a way that will help people hear it, not in a way that it's sort of been packaged and made precious, exoticized, or infantilized, and that emboldened me to do Harriet Jacobs, with some conviction that my initial rejection of telling a story about enslaved people was maybe a little bit around my own shame that I hadn't acknowledged, and a lot about how the telling of those stories had been mishandled, and a lot about how there aren't the telling of enough *other* stories to balance the telling of those stories. So, I feel that I've been working really hard to do that, and so I had earned the telling of, giving of some historical perspective and accuracy, around thus.

CG: So, *The Bluest Eye*, in some ways, enabled you or gave you the confidence to do the next works? What is happening with *Stick Fly* now?

LD: We're in the process now of trying to get *Stick Fly* to Broadway. We've been working hard. [note: *Stick Fly* opened on Broadway on December 9, 2011 and is still running as of publication.]

CG: Congratulations.

LD: Well, that would be nice. We'll see if it happens.

CG: I remember you said you had finished one act of *Stick Fly* when you got the call about *The Bluest Eye*.

LD: Yes, yes. So I finished that quickly before I started *The Bluest Eye*.

CG: I see. Well, I'm even more impressed. On another note, many critics have written about the idea of the blues as one of the central motifs of *The Bluest Eye*. I know that music is an important part of the play. How did you envision the blues as either a metaphor or even just as a sound of the play, since the novel only suggests sound and relies on readers to create or imagine it?

LD: I think I heard jazz more than I heard the blues, and Toni Morrison actually speaks about it specifically in some of her narration about Cholly, about jazz.

CG: His "dangerous freedom," right.

LD: Right. I think I felt that, especially, the musicality was in her language. I thought her language *is* the blues, and *is* the jazz, and the many layers of the different instruments and the rhythms and the syncopations, so I just tried really hard to preserve that and honor that. And I'm not a sound designer. I tend, actually, to hear the musical elements — and I think this is actually problematic, creatively, for me — but I hear the musical elements layered on last. I see the play visually and I hear the rhythm and the musicality of the language, but I don't actually hear the music itself while I'm writing.

CG: So the language is the music.

LD: The language is the music.

CG: That sounds very much like Morrison's own description of the ways that language exists for her, and I think the way that audiences have experienced your play is as a kind of music. The language is so compelling that it's seamless, in some ways, with the music. May I ask you, also, if you would be at all interested of doing adaptations of Morrison's other works?

LD: Oh, that's interesting. I just had this conversation with someone. Originally, my thought was, "No, I don't want to be the 'Toni Morrison writer.' I am a playwright!" [*laughs*]

CG: [*laughs*] I don't think you have to worry about that!

LD: Well, that was my initial response because I got a lot of that right after *The Bluest Eye* came out and did so well. Secondly, I think that I really, *really* respect wherever Toni Morrison is with regard to her feelings about adaptation of her work. So, it's almost presumptuous for me to even think that I might be able to adapt something else of hers. And then my third part of that answer is, "Yeah, I really want to adapt *Sula* one day. . . ." [*laughs*] But I've never mentioned that to Toni Morrison, and I haven't even read it with that in mind, I just . . . It feels like it would live nicely on the stage, and I've seen other people in academic contexts play with that text performatively. So it's not like I'm the only one who's ever thought about it, but I have so many commissions right now — I have five commissions right now.

CG: Congratulations, Lydia. That's wonderful!

LD: Thank you. But before I can even think about what's next I have a lot of institutions who are being very patient, and also probably annoyed, that it is taking me a while to get those done, so I can't actually even think about what's next outside of the things I am committed to. But yes, I think it would be an amazing honor to maybe take that on again one day.

CG: Did you see a lot of theater when you were a young girl?

LD: I did, I did. I saw a lot of everything. In my middle school years my mom was getting her Ph.D. at UMass and she helped manage the performing arts center there, and so I remember being backstage while the Alvin Ailey dancers were running around. And I saw *Bubblin' Brown Sugar,* and I saw Yitzhak Perlman and got to meet him backstage, yeah, Pinches Zukerman, *Ain't Misbehavin'* — I saw the original cast of *Ain't Misbehavin'.* I found out that a woman who I'm hoping is helping with this endeavor to get *Stick Fly* to Broadway, produced the first straight play that I ever saw, which was *Elephant Man.* I must have been about nine when I saw *Elephant Man.*

CG: That must have been transformative.

LD: Yes. My mom always took me to the theater, and to operas, and concerts, and things like that.

CG: Lydia, I want to return to an earlier point in our conversation and your detailing the process of your creation of the play *The Bluest Eye.* You mentioned the prostitutes as an element of the novel that you admire that you weren't able to include in the play. Were there other aspects of the novel that you weren't able to include that were difficult to exclude?

LD: Oh my gosh, is his name Junior? The boy with the cat? Oh, I wrote that scene, and wanted so desperately for it to be in the play, and it just couldn't. There just was no way because, psychologically, it's such a sophisticated and specific piece of the story, so fully developed, I couldn't honor it in the time I would have had to give it, and so he would have been just another bad boy, not this complicated product of racial confusion and class dysfunction, just this bad boy who did bad things. I made the character of Father more present, because I needed to balance the images of black men who are dangerous, and so Junior — I couldn't do him justice. But it's one of my favorite parts of the book, it's so . . . when he flings that cat around . . . it's heartbreaking.

CG: Especially the construction of his home and his world.

LD: The construction of his home, that's what it is! The act of the cat thing is the culmination of the construction of his home life, and the way the home life fits into the story is so important. I couldn't get it in. It broke my heart. It just killed me. I tried valiantly, in many different ways, and it couldn't happen.

CG: Have you seen the play recently? Have you seen many of the productions?

LD: I've seen lots of productions of it, and lately I haven't had the privilege of seeing many recent productions. It is being produced at a lot right now at colleges. Jasmine Guy just directed a production of it.

CG: At Spelman [College], right?

LD: Yes. But I haven't had a chance to see that production. In the beginning, I try to stay with a script through its first three or four productions — it's still becoming what it is — and then I have to release it into the world.

CG: And I also have to ask you, speaking of releasing things into the world — which is what, obviously, Toni Morrison did when she allowed this production to take place—have you had a conversation with her about the play?

LD: No, not really. I had an opportunity to go dinner with her, and she was very generous, and I got to sit next to her and talk. We talked as much about — I didn't want to talk about *me*, because I was sitting with Toni Morrison! We got to talk about her experience writing *Margaret Garner*, the opera. It was about to open at the time that we had our dinner, and it was a dinner with lots of other people, but she was generous, and I got to engage with her for a long time. *Margaret Garner* was about to open, I think in Philadelphia first. I saw it in Detroit.

So we talked about that, and I thanked her for allowing *The Bluest Eye* to happen and we talked about that, but we didn't really do the down-and-dirty talking about my play. I just feel that there was this huge generosity of trust, that she had let it go, that she gave it to me. She's never been to a production, and I'm so cool with that. It's sometimes hard to explain to people who produce it; I often get a call: "Do you think you could get Toni Morrison to come to our production?" I say, "No, that's not going to happen." [*laughs*]

But I also find myself defending her position. "No, this isn't a lack of generosity — quite the opposite, actually. You should be grateful that she's letting it exist in this way apart from herself."

CG: I understand. Through her permission to allow the play to have a larger life, I think you've gotten an answer about how she feels about it. I would imagine, in any case.

LD: I hope so.

CG: Do you have any thoughts about any other adaptations of Morrison's work? For example, *Beloved* — it's very interesting, the contrast between the success of your play and the complex response to the film adaptation of *Beloved*. I'd be curious to know your thoughts, any general reflections on the difficulties of adapting her work.

LD: It's hard. And I don't know to what degree she had a part in *Beloved*. I don't know. I think it's just hard, and doing *The Bluest Eye* humbled me around the way I respond to other people's adaptations of anything. And I'm thinking, for film, then layer on to the screenplay so many different, other elements, and there's casting, and there's the music and the score and the visual and . . . oh, God, so many variables . . . I didn't think that the film necessarily looked like what the book looked like in my head. It would be surprising if there weren't people who felt the same about my adaptation because, when we read a book, we get to have a relationship with it that is so much more intimate than someone making those decisions for us. And so, I'm not just trying to be graceful.

CG: [*laughs*] You're doing a great job!

LD: Well, I'm not trying to be. I really, sincerely think that it's a ridiculously huge undertaking, and it works, or it doesn't work. I just can't make myself the authority on who gets it right.

CG: Right. Well, I have to tell you, the one of her books that I wanted to see as a film, really — in my head, it seems like a film — is *Song of Solomon*.

LD: I could see that being a film.

CG: I have this fantasy of Whoopi Goldberg as Pilate that I can't get out of my head.

LD: Oh, that's interesting. I could see that, too. What I knew about the play *The Bluest Eye* was that people would say, "Do you think that this could be a film?" I have no desire to see *The Bluest Eye* be a film. Ever. And, having said that, I'm sure that if Toni Morrison said, "Hey, would you adapt this, make this a film?" I would probably do it. But I don't think it wants to be a film.

CG: It seems to me that the theatre, in its intimacy, is a much more appropriate venue for *The Bluest Eye*.

LD: I think where it's hard, with the intimacy of *The Bluest Eye*, or any piece that you — as an artist of color — spend a lot of time laboring over, the politics, the nuances of it, the political ramifications of the visuals and such, is that a lot of the time, in theatre right now—particularly when it's being produced in a venue with lots of money — is that it tends to be a white venue, and I'm interested and continually sort of frustrated and aware of the dynamic of what it means when a very, very privileged white audience watches these stories in the context of a very privileged white institution. And so, I don't know.

CG: And I would imagine that's the conundrum, right? Because, what is the alternative?

LD: And so, to *that* degree I think film can reach more people.

CG: So film is more democratic, potentially?

LD: Yes, democratic in this great American country. [*laughs*]

CG: One more question, Lydia. This book, *Toni Morrison: Forty Years in The Clearing* refers to the period from 1970 until the present, and in looking at your biography, I realize that that's just about your life span.

LD: Yes . . . [*laughs*]

CG: It is interesting. You came of age in a world where Toni Morrison and other African American women were writing, being published, and taught. *The Bluest Eye* obviously takes place in a very different time frame from when you grew up. I'm wondering if you see the literature as bridging that gap? What is the difference between being born in 1969 and living when Pecola lived, and how do you think writers like Toni Morrison have changed that geography?

LD: Oh, that's such a complicated question. It's a beautiful question. I just want to honor it. First of all, I grew up all over the country, so I was a very little girl in Itta Bena, Mississippi, and I went to high school in Waco, Texas. And my mother's family, which is the family I grew up with most, from a small town in southern Illinois called Sparta, Illinois. And my mother's worldview is very much shaped by her experience growing up as a contemporary of Toni Morrison. And so, I was socialized, sort of, in that space. I remember the movie theater in Sparta, Illinois, still had the two rows of chairs that were missing, and I think then they were calling them "wheelchair accessible" or something, but those were the two rows of chairs that divided where the black people sat in the back of the theater and the white people in the front.

So there were these tangible images of segregation, and my grandparents taught at the black grammar school — my grandfather was the principal and my grandmother was a teacher there. And there was a lot of political resistance around integration, from them — they were all on board with it but wanted to do it slowly, and there was a faction in town that wanted to do it quickly and all of the political ramifications of that, so I grew up, sort of, with a healthy sense of — maybe healthy and unhealthy sense of — racial distrust, and perhaps a more palpable understanding of those injustices than if I had, say, grown up in an all-black neighborhood in Chicago. I was always, *always* in the minority, wherever I was living, but with these kind of politically-aware adult figures around me, very interesting.

CG: Sounds like it.

LD: So, I think it's great that Toni Morrison and her contemporaries were able to write about these things and articulate them in a way that liberated *me*. And also, I don't know that I felt, when I was writing it, that we had come all that far. I've been challenged in another way by working with young people, who have such different paradigms around race, and how they think so different—I find it, really, very threatening and very hopeful. And then the way the Obama thing has happened has also been, for me, promising and unsettling.

CG: You know that in an interview during the 2008 campaign, Obama stated that *Song of Solomon* is his favorite novel.

LD: Wow! Michelle Obama came to see *The Bluest Eye* when it was at the Steppenwolf!

CG: She is just phenomenal in so many ways. I hear what you're saying, though, about being nervous that the Obama presidency has prompted this generation to feel like racial struggles are resolved or past or don't involve them.

LD: It scares me and makes me feel old. I think maybe things have come further than I'm comfortable giving them credit for having come sometimes.

CG: Lydia, thank you so much for your time. It has been a pleasure. The care that you express in talking about the construction of *The Bluest Eye* and the responsibility that you felt is astonishing. I haven't heard many artists talk in that particular way about that kind of engagement with their audiences. It is moving and inspiring.

LD: I hope it is Morrisonian.

Jan Furman

Jan Furman is Professor of Early American literature and Director of the Master of Liberal Studies Program at the University of Michigan, Flint. She is authored or edited *Toni Morrison's Fiction*, *Slavery in the Clover Bottoms: John McCline's Narrative of his Life in Slavery and during the Civil War*, and *Song of Solomon: A Casebook*. She has published widely on Morrison, Civil War narratives, and slave narratives. Her essay unravels the moral imagination at the center of Morrison's aesthetics, recognizing the productive link between what one composes and what one teaches. In contextualizing Morrison within the robust intellectual tradition of the American canon, particularly through Morrison's own reading of Edgar Allan Poe, Furman revels in the claim that "[n]arrative remains the best way to learn everything."

American Romance, the Moral Imagination and Toni Morrison: A Theory of Literary Aesthetics

JAN FURMAN

Playing in the Dark: Whiteness and the Literary Imagination remains Toni Morrison's most sustained work of criticism. In it, she re-views American fiction from the twin perspectives of practiced reader and writer and proposes to outline new territory for critical study: "to draw a map, so to speak, of a critical geography and use that map to open as much space for discovery, intellectual adventure, and close exploration as did the original charting of the New World—without the mandate for conquest."[1] In tracing this critical terrain, Morrison points to the importance of examining the imaginative space that must be created by any writer who is interested in telling the truth in a racialized society. Based on her own experience, Morrison wonders about the kinds of narrative choices other writers make. What creative, intellectual, and social understandings inform their decisions about content and form? How conscious or unconscious are those choices? How and why might the work of white and black authors differ in these selections? "How compelling is the study of those writers who take responsibility for *all* of the values they bring to their art," Morrison observes in this statement, which is also the essential question for her. For how many writers of American texts, historically, have cared enough to stand sentinel against the prospect of unintended politics determining their art? Morrison contends that too many have not, and she initiates a process, which she is recommending to other scholars, of identifying those authors and examining all of the meaning in their narrative choices. As Donald Klein and Hisham Amin point out in their clever review of *Playing*, "Morrison's lofty objective is to expand the study of American literature to include a critical perspective that is at once African American, unique, and modern."[2]

Composed as it is of three Harvard talks in the William E. Massey, Sr. Lectures in the History of American Civilization, *Playing* is not (nor is it intended to be) systematic in its investigations. "Informal," Morrison calls it. But the study is instructive in its insistence upon keeping focus primarily on racial content, which is to be distinguished from racist content. A work may have racial content, but not every work with racial content is racist. The latter is limiting and even prosaic, Morrison suggests. In her words, "these deliberations are not about a particular author's attitude toward race."[3] In making a distinction between the two approaches, Morrison is claiming the value of literary criticism as an intellectual enterprise and acknowledging the awkwardness and unproductiveness of identity politics that might result in misdirecting her critical theory. An African American exploring racist content (or racial content for that matter) might be seen as having "vested interests." By contrast, racial inquiry shifts critical perspective toward consideration of the demands of narrative art and opens conversation about not only how a writer thinks about race, but also what effect that thinking has on the creative process. Morrison believes that in a "wholly racialized society," where there is no escape from "racially inflected language," it is the complex, creative obligation of the writer to "unbundle the imagination from the demands of that language."[4] That requires the kind of radical self-awareness that anticipates and cautions against "taking oneself intact into the other." For the writer, this is a consciousness-raising act of "becoming," of transcending the limitations of social identity, which may be rooted in race, in an effort to expand and facilitate creative thought.[5] This large effort shapes a moral imagination that, at its best, is generous and honest in representations of race, gender, and class. Such a liberal aspect of moral imagination would seem to be a defining requirement of Morrison's literary aesthetic, and that is the focus of this discussion — the writer's responsibility for the role of his or her work in the development of human life.

This view of the writer's responsibility to truth corresponds to a theory of moral aesthetics—the concept of literature playing a role in producing and acquiring moral knowledge and education. Children's stories and fairy tales fall into this category; these are not merely exercises in imaginative play, but are generally recognized to have pedagogical purposes. In Morrison's words, "[n]arrative remains the best way to learn anything."[6] Indeed, didacticism in poetry and story has a long tradition in American writing. As Christopher Clausen points out in his essay collection on the subject, "few . . . critics denied the instructive functions of literature before the middle of the nineteenth century."[7] Clausen understands the resistance to moral criticism on the grounds that it is potentially anti-intellectual and that applying moral judgment to art subordinates creativity to propaganda. Clausen argues, however, that commenting on and even evaluating the values being promulgated in a work is just another useful critical tool. "[I]n a successful literary work," he writes, "instruction and esthetic delight are one thing—instruction delights, or what is delightful instructs."[8]

Admittedly, this is a treacherous area for literary criticism. Questions such as "What is the moral imagination?," "What is its relation to aesthetic merit?," and "How and to what extent is art able to shape virtue?" are more comfortably the province of philosophical inquiry. A particularly helpful statement on a way of viewing philosophy in literary art is Martha Nussbaum's *Love's Knowledge*. Nussbaum, who is a philosopher, declares that conventional philosophical prose is "remarkably flat and lacking in wonder." But literature can be "more complex, more allusive, more attentive to particulars" in its "views of the world and how one should live in it — views, especially, that emphasize the world's surprising variety, its complexity and mysteriousness, its flawed and imperfect beauty."[9] Nussbaum shows with her work on Henry James that "the novel is itself a moral achievement"— both its content and its author's relationship to that content. The moral imagination, as reflected in "moral attention and moral vision, finds in novels its most appropriate articulation."[10]

Philosopher Noel Carroll's discussion in "The Wheel of Virtue: Art, Literature, and Moral Knowledge" is appropriate here, too, and offers a thoughtful rationale for the way in which aesthetics relates to literary theory. Carroll agrees that a story can teach self-knowledge and social knowledge, both of which are necessary in the construction of cognitive strategies for successfully navigating one's world. In an innovative consideration of philosophical significance in literature, Carroll likens literary narratives to philosophical thought experiments, which can and do impart moral knowledge by deepening and refining what one knows, intuitively. Carroll argues for the potential of literature "to challenge the standing ideas of a culture — moral, political, and even theoretical"— and to be "entertaining" as well.[11] Morrison makes a similar claim. Her writing is not a mere technical exercise of the imagination; it must have a message about and for communities and individuals. "The best art is political," she says, "and you ought to be able to make it unquestionably political and irrevocably beautiful at the same time"[12]

Theories of moral imagination are broadly applicable to literary and non-literary genres in providing a way of talking about the role of ethics in human activity, and this discussion draws from the common themes in those genres. Mark Johnson, for instance, in reviewing the role of imagination in moral reasoning in the context of cognitive science, defines moral imagination as "an ability to imaginatively discern various possibilities of acting in a given situation and to envision the potential help or harm that is likely to result from a given action."[13] Similarly, Patricia Werhane, looking at organizational design, recognizes moral imagination as "the ability to see new possibilities."[14] Barack Obama, in his Nobel speech and elsewhere in his public life, locates moral imagination in the "sense of possibility," a space apart from conventional chronology where solutions to what appear as intractable problems may lie.[15] All of these concepts share a progressive quality, an imagination free of dogma, which is particularly relevant to Morrison's conception of the writer's obligation to "becoming," to crossing a threshold of knowledge toward epiphanies of insight. I am referring to what Amy Mullin calls "the ability to view new things imaginatively from a variety of perspectives."[16] Moral imagination creates possibilities — not merely options, but the potential for transformation of some sort. That is my use of the term, which owes a great deal to Mullin's discussion of an imaginative treatment of morally significant literary content. Mullin allows for morally defective imagination, and her use of the term "morally problematic act of imagining" is beneficial in addressing Morrison's concern with writers who fail to take creative responsibility for the values they bring to their art. In such cases, Mullin is willing to assign moral culpability, especially if the narrative treats a morally significant situation or topic in a morally problematic way.[17]

Morrison addresses such a failing in her discussion of Edgar Allan Poe's *The Narrative of Arthur Gordon Pym*. She refers to Poe's "pretensions to the planter class" as context for his treatment of racial content in the narrative.[18] As a Southerner, Poe may or may not have been a staunch supporter of slavery.[19] Scholarship reflects that uncertainty. He certainly did, however, aspire to Southern nobility. Poe's letters to John Allan, the Virginia slaveholder who took him in as an orphaned child but who later rejected him as an heir, make clear Poe's disappointment and often his determination to restore what he felt Allan unfairly withheld.[20] A Southern sympathizer, at the least, Poe did not, as Morrison says, reject all of that. His predictable attitudes toward race are reflected in stereotypically negative characterizations of blacks in *Pym*. Maurice Lee proposes an interesting critical context for these attitudes by pointing to a conflict between Southern values and Transcendental ideals that were so popular in the middle third of the nineteenth century — between

Poe's attention to the idealism of German philosopher Friedrich Schelling and the realism of Southern values. Poe was drawn to Schelling's conjecture of a self capable of complete understanding, which was achievable through a synthesis of the subjective and objective, through the merger of feelings with experience. In Poe's case, that would require a reconciliation of imaginative power (the beautiful) with (Southern) life (the unbeautiful). Despite a yearning, Poe achieved no such reconciliation, and he brings this pathology to his texts. Lee makes his reading of Poe's psychology relevant to the stories, including "Ligeia" and "Metzengerstein," Poe's first published story. In *Pym*, the dualism is expressed in terms of white and black, master and slave, and subjective absolutism and objective, unlovely reality. The dualism remained unassimilated in fiction and experience, because the historical black/white opposition persisted in Poe's thinking. In Lee's words, "Poe cannot celebrate Transcendentalism that synthesizes black and white."[21]

Morrison takes up a version of this last point in *Playing* with her brief textual analysis of the final scene in *Pym*, whose tropes of racial difference surface often in American literature. At the end of a long and treacherous journey, Pym and Peters, the only survivors of the *Jane Guy* who escape the murderous Tsalalians, paddle off toward the South Pole. White and black images pervade the scene: white Pym; half-white Peters, black Nu-Nu, milky waters, white linen handkerchief, white ashy shower; floating white animals, white birds, a white-shrouded human figure. Nu-Nu perishes in the encounter with this total whiteness as if it were a deadly antidote to the utter blackness and inchoate evil of the Tsalalians. Morrison calls Nu-Nu "the serviceable and serving black figure."[22] For Pym and Peters, whiteness soothes and then relieves a residual dread of the islanders, "the most wicked, hypocritical, vindictive, blood thirsty, and altogether fiendish race of men upon the face of the globe."[23] Seeing the white curtain, they anticipate its approach "without . . . terror." Beyond that appears a superhuman "[o]f the perfect whiteness of snow."[24]

The end of struggle, the "dreaminess of sensation," the authority of something larger than the self: each dimension of the final movement fits Lee's interpretation of Poe's failed bid for "absolutism," that merger of black and white, subjective and objective. Nu-Nu's presence in the scene, followed by his death, undermines the momentum toward the harmonious, unified ideal. In the end, there is only the white self headed toward either annihilation or salvation. Dirk Peters, as John Carlos Rowe shows, hardly matters in this reading. He "is Poe's fantasy of the faithful and grateful servant" and, as such, threatens no infusion of appreciable color to the white narrative.[25] Indeed, in the end he is washed white by the ash. Just as Thomas Jefferson's pseudo-scientific hierarchy of color and beauty had raised Native American people, with their "fine mixtures of red and white . . . [and] flowing hair" above African slaves of "eternal monotony . . . that veil of black," so Peters has the advantage over blacks in Poe's narrative.[26] That is not the case with the "black cook" of the *Grampus*, "who in all respects was a perfect demon." Associated with "the most horrible butchery" of the mutiny, the black cook bludgeons twenty-two sailors and throws another overboard. Among the mutineers, he alone refuses to release their captives.[27] That Poe's and Pym's reductive othering is given free expression in the text returns to Morrison's concern with the writer's responsibility to a truth that admits of possibility.

Poe saw no connection between ethical and aesthetic convictions. He had but two considerations: emotional appeal and marketability. The reader's experience of beauty was paramount, and beauty for him was incident, tone, and the vivid effect they wrought. Affect trumped argument and theme; a moral or philosophy flattened art and occluded emotive response. "*He* must be blind, indeed, who does not perceive the radical and chasmal differences between the truthful and the poetical modes of inculcation," he wrote in "Philosophy of Composition."[28] His comment applies to narrative as well, as seen in a May 1842 review of Nathaniel Hawthorne. In opposition to the Concord Romantics, Poe claimed to eschew systems of ideas in his poems and stories. But in Hawthorne he saw something of himself. In reviewing *Twice Told Tales* in *Graham's Magazine* in tones complimentary of Hawthorne, Poe sets out, in its essence, his own philosophy of literature: If a writer is wise, "he has fashioned his thoughts to accommodate his incidents, but having conceived, with deliberate care, a certain unique or single *effect* to be wrought out, he then invents such incidents — he then combines such events as may best aid him in establishing this preconceived effect."[29] The exoticism of discovery in *Pym* depends for its effect upon the anticipated danger and adventure of distant voyaging in uncharted water and on disturbing perversions of human nature. Poe also aimed for what Richard Kopley refers to as "verisimilitude — a semblance of reality."[30] Tapping into the widespread interest in polar exploration, *Pym*, as Richard Wilbur demonstrates, "borrow[ed] from nautical literature [and] adapted ideas from . . . [Poe's] other reading." Of all Poe's works, "*Pym* most frequently filches or reprocesses the materials of other writers."[31] *Pym* should appear to be the story of an actual exhibition — only more exciting and wondrous. To that end, Poe invented a narrative for his *Narrative*: the true perils of one who lived to recount his near-death experience. Many reviewers and, apparently, most readers rejected the invention. In an examination of annotations in three extant copies of the narrative, Kopley found readers annoyed and unimpressed with Poe's attempt at verisimilitude. According to Kopley, "Pym's earnest presentation of his adventure, weighted with an abundance of nautical and scientific detail, did not convince or please."[32] Ironically, the effort to achieve verisimilitude carried Poe very far afield of credulity. In an attempt to explain, for example, publication of earlier installments of *Pym* in *The Southern Literary Messenger*, Pym states in "his" Preface that after meeting Poe in Virginia, the latter advised him to write his story. But fearing ridicule, Pym refused, and Poe proposed writing the account himself and presenting it as fiction. Pym wants readers to know that:

> [t]he manner in which this *ruse* was received has induced me at length to undertake a regular compilation and publication of the adventures in question; for I found that, in spite of the air of fable which had been so ingeniously thrown around that portion of my statement which appeared in the *Messenger* (without altering or distorting a single fact), the public were still not at all disposed to receive it as fable, and several letters were sent to Mr. P's address, distinctly expressing a conviction to the contrary. I thence concluded that the facts of my narrative would prove of such a nature as to carry with them sufficient evidence of their own authenticity, and that I had consequently little to fear on the score of popular incredulity.[33]

Pym and Poe were wrong about that. *Pym* was not a critical or financial success. William E. Burton's September 1838 review in *Burton's Gentleman Quarterly* was typical. Burton panned it thoroughly. "There is nothing original in the description," Burton wrote. The "rapid succession of improbabilities destroys the interest of the reader."[34] It is noteworthy that Burton finds nothing original in Poe's narrative: nautical voyages had been done better. The improbabilities he catalogues are plot related: volcanoes erupting from the ocean, showers of white ashes, Pym's survival of a bolt thrust through the neck, and "a few ambushed savages" affecting the avalanche of rocks "by merely pulling at a few strong cords of grapevine." For Burton, the ambushed savages themselves were believable creations. Burton and his contemporaries did not question (nor should we expect them to) Poe's characterizations or the narrative strategies Morrison sees: Poe's "estranging language, metaphoric condensation, fetishizing strategies, the economy of stereotype, allegorical foreclosures, strategies employed to secure his characters' (and his readers') identity" as rational and civilized.[35] These narrative shortcuts determine Poe's effect without inviting meaning. They reflect the very inattention to meaning that Poe claims while, nevertheless, delivering a significant message about color and culture that Poe and his readers took for granted. Mullin's morally problematic act of imagining applies here.

The second factor informing Poe's aesthetic was the marketplace. He wrote what he believed readers wanted — a concession to the exigency of financial need and an attempt to satisfy an audience with a taste for adventure, exploitation, the far and away. Three years before the publication of *Pym*, Poe responded to an editor's complaint that "Berenice," the tale he had submitted, was in bad taste by protesting that such stories were popular. The public liked "the ludicrous heightened into the grotesque; the fearful colored into the horrible; the witty exaggerated into the burlesque; the singular wrought out into the strange and mystical." Poe reminds the editor that "to be appreciated you must be read and these things are invariably sought after. . . . "[36] Thus, like "Berenice" and much of Poe's work, *Pym* is market-driven. Impoverished in New York, with a wife and aunt (who was also his mother-in-law) to support, Poe took an editor's advice to write a long work in an effort to meet public demand for such. He began *Pym* and finished it over several months; it was published in its entirety within a year after its inception.

In a letter to Burton nearly two years later, Poe referred to *Pym* in passing as "a very silly book," an interesting assessment even on its face. Poe almost certainly did not think *Pym* ridiculous when he wrote and published it, having, as he did, the serious purposes of literary success and financial solvency. But by 1840, in the wake of *Pym's* failure in both purposes, it may have seemed face-saving to play down his ambitions. In addition, it is significant that Poe's remark was made in the context of responding to Burton's dissatisfaction with him as the now-assistant editor of the *Gentleman Quarterly*. I am not vindictive, he was saying: "Your criticism was essentially correct and therefore, although severe, it did not occasion in me one solitary emotion either of anger or dislike."[37] Poe may have believed, however, that as a marketable enterprise, the book had missed its mark. That may have entered his estimation of the silliness.

Poe's work in the final scene of *Pym* invites a clarifying contrast to Morrison's final chapter in *Song of Solomon*. *Pym's* quest stands in nearly direct opposition to Milkman's, and in their difference is reflected a clash of moral imaginations. Each adolescent (at thirty-three, Milkman was conducting an extended adolescence) leaves home to find adventure and fortune, more or less. Neither comes by fortune, and their adventures, in time, turn to misfortune. At the end of both texts, three characters stand or lie in proximity to each other. In each novel one is dead, and the other two are moving inexorably toward an unknowable and potentially transformative destiny.

There, the similarities fall away. *Pym's* journey over the course of the narrative takes him farther and farther from home and further from his authority as a narrator, which may be measured in his increasing inability to inscribe experience. He loses eleven of the last twenty-two days, and in the final brief entries, a dispassionate review of events suggests some sort of resignation or defeat. By then, he is shrouded in mystery. Milkman's geographic journey is 360 degrees. He returns to the place where he began. He comes psychologically and spiritually far, ending up fully realized, passionate and compassionate. The final scene of *Song of Solomon,* in which flight is the dominant motif, marks Milkman's overdue coming of age. Birds fly off into the air; one carries Pilate's name in the snuffbox, prompting Milkman's realization that "without ever leaving the ground, she could fly." Earlier, he had sung his memory of Solomon's flight: "Sugargirl don't leave me here," intoning a deep and sorrowful understanding of Pilate's human accomplishment as she lay dying from Guitar's bullet. "'There must be another one like you,' he whispered to her."[38] Following Solomon's example, Milkman stands, whirls, rides the air. But unlike Solomon, Milkman's movement is not selfish; his is not leaving anyone behind. In an ultimate yielding up of materiality, Milkman flies at Guitar in an instant of extravagant love and fierce rebuke.

Therein lies Morrison's meaning. I and others have seen *Song of Solomon* as a manifesto on self-knowledge as liberating and humanizing. Milkman is an apostle of human freedom, having jettisoned the material life that no longer serves him. As Morrison says in a different context (but one that is appropriate here), "sometimes with the proximity of the end you strip away all of the weighty, vain comfortable things that we yearn for. . . . "[39] As with the peacock, Milkman cannot fly with the "jewelry" and "vanity" weighing on him. "Wanna fly, you got to give up that shit that weighs you down."[40] Guitar does not heed his own words; Milkman does. And so does the reader. The balance is struck between credulity and incredulity. Morrison's deep embrace of human flight as spiritual and cultural archetype is far different from Poe's market and society-driven stereotypes. Hers is the story "one would have been just as drawn to write without readers, without publishers."[41] A parting contrast is Solomon and Tsalemon. One we know nothing of, except that he presides over a barbarous people. The other leaves a legacy of power and abandonment in flying back to Africa and leaving a wife and twenty-one children behind. One is complex; the other is not. The difference is not merely in terms of space and time allotted in the text, but one rendered in terms of moral vision as well. Solomon is essential to Milkman's lessons on the importance of empowerment and commitment. Tsalemon serves Poe's verisimilitude: as a seemingly organized human society with a king, the Tsalalians' inhumanness, because it is associated with unrelenting blackness, is simultaneously shocking and believable.

The historical context for Morrison's commentary on Poe is American Romance and the beginning of *Belles Lettres* in the nineteenth century. Morally problematic imagining as defined here is not universal; it is, however, pervasive. Morrison points to Hemingway and Cather in the modern period and to William Styron in the postmodern period. But the case for close study is Romance, the period from about 1820 to 1865 in which an American tradition in literature came of age and helped shape the canon. As late as 1828, nearly fifty years after ratification of the Union, James Fennimore Cooper pointed to a dearth of original writers in his travel book *Notions of the Americans*. Owing to a common language and heritage, English literature was the literature in America, but this was not a concern for Cooper. After all, Americans "had . . . just as good a right to claim Milton and Shakespeare and all the old masters of the language as any Englishman."[42] (Perhaps modesty prevented Cooper from recommending himself as an original writer.) By the time *Notions* was published, the first two of six novels in his *Leather-Stocking* series had appeared, including *The Last of the Mohicans* (1826), the most well-known. It could also be that Cooper thought of himself as less an American writer than an international one. His *Leather-Stocking* stories are styled after the novels of Sir Walter Scott and Western epic, even if his subject is Indians and pioneering whites on the eastern frontier. As the critic John McWilliams observes, Cooper's "style is . . . memorably inappropriate to his subject."[43]

But others observed the absence of American writers, although they, unlike Cooper, decried the fact and called for the bold and new. In 1837, Emerson told the Phi Beta Kappa students in Cambridge—future men of letters as they were —"Our day of dependence, our long apprenticeship to the learning of other lands, draws to a close."[44] In the same speech, Emerson reminded his audience that "[t]he English dramatic poets have Shakespearized now for two hundred years." This is not the model for American artists, he was suggesting. Four years later, setting out a path for the poet or the artist with imagination, Emerson calls forth the creative genius and charges him or her with, among other duties, celebrating the American landscape, people and spirit:

> We have yet had no genius in America, with tyrannous eye, which knew the value of our incomparable materials. . . . Our logrolling, our stumps and their politics, our fisheries, our Negroes, and Indians, our boasts, and our repudiations, the wrath of rogues, and the pusillanimity of honest men, the northern trade, the southern planting, the western clearing, Oregon, and Texas, are yet unsung. Yet America is a poem in our eyes; its ample geography dazzles the imagination, and it will not wait long for metres.[45]

Emerson's is not a call to literary formalism, didacticism, or nationalism. His writer-poet will give expression to what is universal, honest, and soulful. The artist will not be bound by tradition or convention. He or she will be an interpreter of unlimited human potential and of what is good and authentic in human and physical nature. Emerson's is a liberating ideal in Morrison's view. His "plea for intellectual independence," she writes, "was like the offer of an empty place that writers could fill with nourishment from an indigenous menu. The language no doubt had to be English, but the content of that language, its subject, was to be deliberately, insistently un-English and anti-European, insofar as it rhetorically repudiated an adoration of the Old World and defined the past as corrupt and indefensible."[46] Emerson's ideological context of nineteenth-century liberalism certainly did inform the struggle, broadly speaking, between institutional and individual authority, and that encouraged social and political reform. Calls for an end to slavery, renegotiation of women's domesticity and place in society, experiments in education, and the overthrow of Locke for Kant all brought an intellectual energy to American life and letters.

It is compelling that in this promise-filled landscape of the emerging literary imagination, writers of what F. O. Matthiesson has termed the American Renaissance chose to ruminate on darkness. Morrison theorizes that to argue themselves free and innocent, American writers meditated on the not-free and the diabolical. For a people who made much of Emerson's call for "newness" in American thought and character, "it is striking," Morrison says, "how dour, how troubled, how frightened and haunted our early and founding literature truly is."[47] Morrison reasons that such echoing of the bleak and feudal immigrant past, more than two centuries later, was an unconscious attempt to inoculate the present against that troubled past. She calls this dynamic "romancing the shadow," and the symbol and shorthand for expressing that shadow was Africanist. Enslaved blacks were not only the not-free, but the not-me: "The result was a playground for the imagination. What rose up out of collective needs to allay internal fears reflected in a national psyche and to rationalize external exploitation was American Africanism, a fabricated brew of darkness, otherness, alarm and desire that is uniquely American."[48] In renaming Romanticism "Africanism," Morrison calls attention to what she sees as pervasive objectification of "repressed darkness" through a stereotyped African persona.

Politics matter here. The dark Romantics — Poe, Hawthorne, and Melville — did not oppose slavery. The case with Poe is clear. Hawthorne's circumstance is different; the influence of racial politics on his creativity is more subtle but, one could argue, just as evident. Take, for example Hester's extravagant rehabilitation at the conclusion of *The Scarlet Letter*. In effect, she recants the radical Emersonian individualism of earlier chapters and accepts the convention of Puritan repentance in the end. Sacvan Bercovitch refers to: the enormous cultural pressure brought to bear upon the conclusion.... It is as though Hawthorne had to overcompensate for the enormous radical potential inherent in his characters and symbols; had to find some moral absolute —

some equivalent in the liberal imagination for the *Thou Shalt Nots* delivered from Mount Sinai — powerful enough to recall all those unleashed energies of will, eros, and language back into the culture from which they arose and, in his view, which they belonged.[49]

Despite being married to Sophia Peabody, whose family was abolitionist and Transcendental, and living in Concord, Massachusetts, where his neighbors were Bronson Alcott, Ralph Waldo Emerson, David Thoreau, and other abolitionists and Transcendentalists, Hawthorne bore an affinity for Franklin Pierce, a like-minded college friend, a pro-slavery Democrat, and the fourteenth president. Hawthorne's sensibility did not conform to Emerson's view of the (American) writer's duty. Recalling Hawthorne after the latter's death, Emerson wrote in his journal, "I thought him a greater man than any of his works betray, that there was still a great deal of work in him, and that he might one day show a purer power,"[50] a truer moral imagination. Emerson associated Hawthorne's writing with "paltry politics." The limitations of his race thinking shuttered not creativity, but a dimension of creative possibility. Morrison's requirement here is that the writer be "mindful of the places where imagination sabotages itself, locks its own gates, pollutes its vision."[51]

Melville's racial themes are more self-conscious than those of his sometimes friend Hawthorne. Presenting morally relevant material as though it is not, Melville brooded on the individual and his confrontation with power, a theme that often took on a frightful, malevolent aspect. In "Benito Cereno," the black slaves are wicked usurpers of power; Amasa Delano, the American Captain, and Don Benito Cereno, captain of the *San Dominick*, are innocent, if not authentic. The "negroes" who overtake the ship and murder the crew are given no context, historical or otherwise, that might explain their mutiny. They are merely available to Melville in a meditation on evil. No mitigating evidence is required from him for his readers. In the tradition of Romance, this Africanist presence and dark shading involve the genre in "repeated" imaginings of a morally problematic sort. This is worrisome in Mullin's theory because the "repeated adoption in the imagination of an immoral perspective might have morally damaging effects."[52] At the least, it may have set a tone for later writers of fiction.

Morrison tells what the high Romantics did not in a manner they, perhaps, could not have. (The writer must not enter the telling intact; the telling itself is a *becoming*, a journey to the site of new understanding for the writer.) Against a contested background of dark stereotype in Poe, Hawthorne, Melville, and others, Morrison redraws landscape, character, and incident. Her novels set right the subject of critical commentary in *Playing*. Giving the shadow human shape and dimension in her narratives, Morrison has re-imagined American romance and its founding narratives. For example, *Beloved*, a thought experiment on the absolute necessity and the limits of human authority, is set in the historical and ideological context of nineteenth-century liberalism, the core ideal of which is Emerson's "infiniture of the private man." Trust in one's own thoughts is the first step in all reformation, Emerson believed. "A greater self-reliance — must work a revolution in all the offices and relations of men; in their religion; in their education; in their pursuits; their modes of loving; their association; in their property; in their speculative views."[53] Sethe's awful insistence upon defining for herself what it means to be her children's mother derives its force and complexity from this radical self-reliance.

As Morrison revises the nineteenth-century text, recasts characters, and re-contextualizes historical setting, she, interestingly and paradoxically, takes on a semblance of the Romantic ideal. Unlike Emerson's anxious contemporaries, Morrison answers a century and a half later the philosopher's call for an aesthetic of organicism and truth. Over the course of her writing career, she increasingly embodies Emerson's artist as "the world's eye" and "the world's heart"— the one who "guides men and women by showing them facts amidst appearances."[54] Emerson's focus on transcendent language—liberating, intellectually independent, absent false motives and traditions—is not different from Morrison's view of art that is "unquestionably political and irrevocably beautiful at the same time." Like the wise old woman in her Nobel Lecture, Morrison is a crafter of language and moral images who seeks to restore what Emerson calls "the light that can lead . . . back . . . to prerogatives" and what Morrison says "may be the measure of our lives."[55]

It must be noted, however, that Morrison's work is not about nineteenth-century liberalism as suggested in Emerson's privileged place in Concord, where he had time to ponder important individual and American ideals. That kind of nostalgia is "deleterious," Morrison thinks. Her work, even her historical fiction, "speculate[s] on a future where the poor are not yet, not quite, all dead; where the under-represented minorities are not quite all imprisoned." Morrison's texts are part of the strategy, "the means by which [critical] values are taught."[56]

NOTES

1. Toni Morrison, *Playing in the Dark: Whiteness and the Literary Imagination* (New York: Random House-Vintage, 1992), 3.
2. Donald Klein and Hisham M. Amin. "Racial Legacies," *African American Review* 28, no. 4 (1994): 659.
3. Morrison, *Playing in the Dark*, 90.
4. Ibid., 13.
5. Ibid., 4.
6. Thomas LeClair, "'The Language Must Not Sweat': A Conversation with Toni Morrison," in *Conversations with Toni Morrison*, ed. Danille Taylor-Guthrie, Literary Conversations Series (Jackson: University Press of Mississippi, 1994), 23.
7. Christopher Clausen, *The Moral Imagination: Essays in Literature and Ethics* (Iowa City: University of Iowa Press, 1986), 6.
8. Ibid., 6.
9. Martha Nussbaum, *Love's Knowledge* (New York: Oxford University Press, 1990), 3.
10. Ibid., 148.
11. Noël Carroll, "The Wheel of Virtue: Art, Literature, and Moral Knowledge," *Journal of Aesthetics and Art Criticism* 60, no. 1 (2002): 10.
12. Toni Morrison, "Rootedness: The Ancestor as Foundation," in *Black Women Writers (1950-1980)*, ed. Mari Evans (New York: Random House-Doubleday, 1984), 64.
13. Mark L. Johnson, *Moral Imagination: Implications of Cognitive Science for Ethics* (Chicago: University of Chicago Press, 1993), 202.
14. Patricia H. Werhane, *Moral Imagination and Management Decision Making* (New York: Oxford University Press, 1999), 5.
15. Barack Obama, "A Just and Lasting Peace," Nobel Prize Acceptance Lecture, *Los Angeles Times*, December 10, 2009, http://latimesblogs.latimes.com/washington/2009/12/barack-obama-nobel-peace-prize-speech-text.html, n.p.
16. Amy Mullin, "Moral Defects, Aesthetic Defects, and the Imagination," *Journal of Aesthetics and Art Criticism* 62, no. 3 (2004): 258.
17. Ibid., 251. Mullin also points to morally problematic failure to image in instances where a narrative fails to take a stance on morally significant material. She acknowledges that "it can be hard to draw a clear line between morally problematic failure to image and morally problematic acts of imagining since the latter may lead to the former."
18. Morrison, *Playing in the Dark*, 58.
19. Terrance Whalen, "Average Racism: Poe, Slavery, and the ways of Literary Nationalism," in *Romancing the Shadow: Poe and Race*, eds. Gerald Kennedy and Liliane Weissberg (New York: Oxford University Press, 2001), 3-40. The question of Poe's support of slavery has rested on the matter of Poe's authorship of an 1836 review in *The Southern Literary Messenger* of two pro-slavery publications (*Slavery in the United States* by James Kirke Paulding and *The South Vindicated for the Treason and Fanaticism of the Northern Abolitionists*, attributed by William Drayton). As editor of the *Messenger*, Poe was supposed to have written "to be subjected to the whims & caprice, not only of your white family, but the complete authority of the blacks. . . . "
20. After a break with Allan, Poe writes repeatedly and melodramatically of Allan's broken promises of support. Often threatening never to contact Allan again, Poe, nevertheless, continues to request financial assistance and to express disappointment over lost opportunities to assume his place as Allan's son. On one occasion, he complains that Allan has humiliated, causing him "to be subjected to the whims and caprice, not only of your white family, but the complete authority of the blacks. . . ." See Edgar Allan Poe, *The Letters of Edgar Allan Poe*, ed. John Ward Ostrom (New York: Gordian Press, 1966), 8.
21. Maurice S. Lee, "Absolute Poe: His System of Transcendental Racism," *American Literature* 75, no. 4 (2003): 776.
22. Morrison, *Playing in the Dark*, 32.
23. Edgar Allan Poe, *The Narrative of Author Gordon Pym* (Boston: David R. Godine, 1973), 150.
24. Ibid., 155.
25. John Carlos Rowe, "Antebellum Slavery and Modern Criticism," *At Emerson's Tomb: The Politics of Classic American Literature* (New York: Columbia University Press, 1997), 55.

26. Thomas Jefferson, "Query 14 'Laws' The administration of justice and description of the laws," *Notes on the State of Virginia* (London: John Stockdale, 1787), 265.

27. Poe, *The Narrative of Arthur Gordon Pym*, 150.

28. Edgar Allan Poe, "Philosophy of Composition," in *Essays and Reviews*, ed. G. R. Thompson (New York: Literary Classics of United States, 1984),13-14.

29. Edgar Allan Poe, "Nathaniel Hawthorne: *Twice-Told Tales*," in *Essays and Reviews*, ed. G. R. Thompson (New York: Literary Classics of United States, 1984), 572.

30. Richard Kopley, "Readers Write: Nineteenth-Century Annotations in Copies of the First American Edition of Poe's The Narrative of Arthur Gorgon Pym," *Nineteenth-Century Literature* 55, no. 3 (2000): 401.

31. Richard Wilber, ed., "Introduction," in *The Narrative of Arthur Gordon Pym,* by Edgar Allan Poe (Boston: David R. Godine, 1973), ix.

32. Kopley, "Readers Write," 401.

33. Poe, *The Narrative of Arthur Gordon Pym*, 4.

34. William E. Burton, "Review of Poe's The Narrative of Arthur Gordon Pym," *Burton's Gentleman's Magazine* 3 (1838): 210.

35. Morrison, *Playing in the Dark*, 58.

36. Poe, *The Letters of Edgar Allan Poe*, 57.

37. Poe, *The Letters of Edgar Allan Poe*, 129-30.

38. Toni Morrison, *Song of Solomon* (New York: Random House-Knopf, 1977), 340.

39. Toni Morrison, "Speaking of Reynolds Price," in *What Moves at the Margin: Selected Nonfiction*, ed. Carolyn C. Denard (Jackson: University Press of Mississippi, 2008), 96.

40. Morrison, *Song of Solomon*, 80.

41. Toni Morrison, "A Bench by the Road: *Beloved*," in *Toni Morrison: Conversations*, ed. Carolyn C. Denard, Literary Conversations Series (Jackson: University Press of Mississippi, 2008), 44.

42. James Fennimore Cooper, "To the Abbate Giromachi, &C. &C., Florence," in *Norton Anthology of American Literature*, vol. 1, 3rd ed., ed. Nina Baym (New York: Norton, 1989), 855.

43. John P. McWilliams, "Introduction," in *The Last of the Mohicans*, by James Fenimore Cooper (New York: Oxford University Press, 1990), xv.

44. Ralph Waldo Emerson, "The American Scholar," in *Emerson's Prose and Poetry*, ed. Saundra Morris (New York: Norton, 2001), 56.

45. Ralph Waldo Emerson, "The Poet," in *Emerson's Prose and Poetry*, eds. Saundra Morris and Joel Porte (New York: Norton, 2001), 196.

46. Morrison, *Playing in the Dark*, 48.

47. Ibid., 35.

48. Ibid., 38.

49. Sacvan Bercovitch, "Hawthorne's A-Morality of Compromise," Special Issue: American Reconstructed 1840-1940, *Representations* 24 (Autumn1988): 21. Hawthorne was certainly not an abolitionist. He thought them extremists. But neither was he, in the strict meaning of the term, pro-slavery. He has some idea that, if left alone, the institution would eventually fall. For an interesting discussion of the effect of Hawthorne's slavery politics on *The Scarlet Letter*, see Sacvan Bercovitch, "The A-Politics of Ambiguity on *The Scarlet Letter*," *New Literary History* 19, no. 3 (1988): 1-27.

50. Ralph Waldo Emerson, "The Burial of Nathaniel Hawthorne" in *The Journals of Ralph Waldo Emerson*, vol. 10 (Cambridge: The Belknap Press, 1969), 122.

51. Morrison, *Playing in the Dark*, xi.

52. Mullin, "Moral Defects," 252.

53. Ralph Waldo Emerson, "Self-Reliance," in *Emerson's Prose and Poetry*, ed. Saundra Morris, (New York: Norton, 2001), 132.

54. Emerson, "The American Scholar," 63.

55. Toni Morrison, *Lecture and Speech of Acceptance, Upon the Award of the Novel Prize for Literature, Delivered in Stockholm on the Seventh of December, Nineteen Hundred and Ninety-Three* (New York: Random House-Knopf, 1994), 22.

56. Toni Morrison, "How Can Values Be Taught in the University?" in *What Moves at the Margin: Selected Nonfiction*, ed. Carolyn C. Denard (Jackson: University Press of Mississippi, 2008), 197.

Joanne V. Gabbin

Joanne V. Gabbin is currently Professor of English at James Madison University. She is the author of *Sterling A. Brown: Building the Black Aesthetic Tradition* and the children's book *I Bet She Called Me Sugar Plum*. She has also edited four collections of poetry, including her most recent, *Shaping Memories: Reflections of African American Women Writers*. As Executive Director of the Furious Flower Poetry Center at James Madison University, she has organized two international conferences for the critical exploration of African American poetry. She is the founder and organizer of the Wintergreen Women Writers' Collective, serves on the board of the Virginia Foundation for the Humanities, and has served as a member of twenty-five professional and service organization. Gabbin's contribution to this volume traces the dense and succulent imagery delivered from the furrows culled by Morrison's hand as they mature in the forestry of her narratives. A fellow traveler, Gabbin meditates with the reader on her love for Morrison and her work.

Meditations on Love
~ *for Toni Morrison* ~

JOANNE V. GABBIN

In your hand is a map of these woods.
You trace a jagged path
To a clearing, to a great heart urging me
To stroke my sullen flesh
Into imagination.

I go panting to your territory,
A place at the bottom of heaven,
And I sing, rehearsing
The rhythms of my youth.

You turn my face toward mercy
And I crave a mother's love.
Thick as buttermilk
And dark as Alaga syrup.

I open myself to your music,
Soulful and mango sweet.
Your touch is gentle
Like dandelion puffs
That disperse and blow in the wind.

I go to your keeping room.
Memories like brightly colored jars
Line up.
Love is heavy
And put away.

Yours is a path toward forgiveness
That hugs the ground
Like bent waves
On a ruby road.

With you I travel along rivers
And learn that love is water,
Gurgling up, running swiftly

With force enough
To etch *beloved* in stone.

Nikki Giovanni

Nikki Giovanni is the Gloria D. Smith Professor of Black Studies at Virginia Tech University. The author of thirty books and one of the most distinguished African American poets of the past fifty years, she has received six NAACP Image Awards, The Langston Hughes Medal for Poetry, and is the first recipient of the Rosa L. Parks Woman of Courage Award. Giovanni holds more than twenty-five honorary degrees, and she published her first book of poetry, *Black Feeling Black Talk*, in 1968. Her contribution to this volume, "And Everyone Will Answer," is an account of her intersections and conversations with Toni Morrison in the 1970s. Giovanni captures the extraordinary vulnerability of both authors at a time in their careers when real success was only glimpsed, not guaranteed. This is a stunning portrait of an earlier Morrison — and an earlier Giovanni.

And Everyone Will Answer

NIKKI GIOVANNI

I had driven to Buffalo. As a Midwesterner with southern roots, driving a car has always been fun and comforting. I had had a 1960 Volkswagen that I had purchased for about six hundred dollars. I was in grad school at the University of Pennsylvania. I was studying social work in the hopes of emulating my mother and one of her best friends and an incredible "aunt" to me, Theresa Elliot. All the social workers I knew were cool, and I had been awarded a scholarship. Unfortunately, I was never meant to work in any real sort of system. After a year it was decided by all, respectively (and I might add, lovingly), that social work was not for me. Through the good offices of a great social worker, Louise Shoemaker, I was accepted into the MFA program at Columbia. I had a car, a scholarship, and New York City. Could there be anything better?

Now I was in Langston Hughes territory. I lived in a wonderful apartment building at 84th and Amsterdam. I had exciting neighbors in film, dance, Broadway, and jazz. I was also a bit of a rebel, so I knew the young people who were changing the world. I don't care what anybody says: we were the Great Generation. But I lent my car to a friend who took a job in another city, and it was towed. I purchased another. But I gave that to my nephew who had other issues, and it was totaled. So I purchased a Peugeot Diesel, which I gave to my sister when she got her third divorce, but that would be a few years off.

It was my thought that the MFA program was there to help me/let me/ encourage me to write a book. I did. By the end of my first year. I was ready to receive my degree and go on. Columbia didn't look at it that way, so I, degreeless, just went on. We in the Black Arts Movement (which wasn't really a movement but a group of people who had similar objectives) took a page from the Beats, who had taken lessons from Langston Hughes. Read your work to the People. I wasn't afraid of a job, but my thought was if I could pay the rent, have some food on the table, with gas at twenty-five cents a gallon, and have something left over for those things that make life fun like Barbados and clothes, then I would be okay. After my son was born, I understood I needed a bit more structure than that, but still a job seemed so foreign. Get a lecture bureau, I said to myself. So I began to read poetry and lecture.

I had driven to Buffalo because driving is so relaxing. No one can get to you. You can think or daydream or sing old songs to yourself that nobody else knows or cares about. I know it wasn't winter because only an idiot would drive to Buffalo in winter, but it wasn't summer either. It seems it was after Christmas, so I'm thinking spring. But early spring, since I had a remembrance of a heavy jacket. I hadn't had a coat since college, but I remember it was important to stay warm.

I arrived at the university, greeted folks, laughed, talked, signed books, those sorts of things, when someone came to me with "An Urgent Message: Call your office." I didn't know what the "urgent message" could be: Thomas, my son, hurt himself; Debbie, who was babysitting him, hurt herself; Wendy, the dog, ran away; or something might have been wrong with one of my parents. I really couldn't see anything else. But I knew for certain if I called and found out, I wouldn't be able to go on stage that evening. So I tucked the note in my pocket and did what I had been invited to do. When I got to the hotel, I called. My father had had a stroke and was in the hospital. I called Mommy to tell her I was in Buffalo and that I'd be home as soon as I could. Being a great believer in peppermint and coffee, I checked out of the hotel, got in the car, bought a cup of joe, and hit the road. I made it to Painesville, Ohio, where I pulled over for a couple of hours, then repeated step one and went on to Cincinnati.

It's funny how you can live in a house and never notice things falling apart. Walking through the back door, which is always how we entered the house, I noticed the floor was not right; the upstairs bathroom had a damp floor; the walls were not dirty (Mommy was a great housekeeper), but need attention. There was no question of what needed to happen. They needed help. I don't know. It's funny, though not humorous, to see that your parents have grown old. I called Debbie to ask if she would bring Thomas down.

My thought was a couple of months and all would be set right. But it wasn't just the stroke; there was intestinal cancer. And there was no health insurance. Next step: sell the apartment in New York. I know people think that cancer doesn't hurt and that people think your insurance co-pay is reasonable, but neither is true. 20% of cancers will put you into bankruptcy. My first thought was Mommy should divorce him; then he would eligible for one of the programs. This is over thirty years ago, but Mommy would have none of it, so we needed a lawyer to get things straightened out. We had known Gloria Haffer for a very long time. She and Mommy were friends. And her Dad, Ben, had hired me when I was in high school to work the cash register at his store. Now, Gloria was a lawyer considering starting her own firm. We caught the gold ring.

Nothing makes me as nervous as filling out forms and things. All I had to do now, which is a strength of mind, is get the physicalities right. Mommy had taught third grade before she went into social work. One of her students, Bobby Hunter, now did construction. When he heard what was happening, he came and retiled the bathroom. Rather than paint the walls, I convinced Mommy to put wallpaper on them. We both hated the kitchen floor, so we put a wood floor in. Things were shaping up. 1168 Congress was a three-bedroom house. Mommy had her room; Gus, my father, would have his when he came home from the hospital; and Thomas had the third. That left the entire basement to me. It was a good space. Friends and I built cabinets, bookshelves, and stuff for a den. The bathroom was papered and made special with photos. The other big room was where I showered and dressed. I should explain: the bathroom was really une toilette and a basin. I found, as I am a lover of antiquities, an old claw footed tub for $25 in Newport, Kentucky. It cost about the same to have it delivered to the basement; a plumber hooked it up, and I had a "magambo"-type shower. The washing machine emptied into it. I put a refrigerator down there, and I was set. *Essence Magazine* came down to do an article on me and photographed the whole house. We looked good. The bedroom was small with no clock and no phone. There was only one rule: If I am asleep . . . Do Not Wake Me Up. To this day, I can and do wake up when I should. If I do not, I am either sick or too tired to go on. In either case: Do Not Wake Me Up.

My father was a nervous man. If nothing else, he would tap his foot or wring his hands. He was always in motion. In the spring and summer his yard and garden got his attention. He'd always be outside planting or pulling or doing something. He had a beautiful yard. But in the winter the basement got the brunt of this attention. He would wax and wax the floor. After fifteen or twenty years, the build up was incredible. I kept looking at the floor, and it was making me crazy. I guess to some extent I am kin to Gus, too, though I am neither mean nor impatient. As the house was pulling into being a lovely, comfortable place again, my part still needed work. One night, in what I recognize to be a Gus move, I took a straight razor and began getting the wax up. At first it was only a tile or two, maybe four or six. Then looking at the entire three rooms, I knew I'd have to do more. So every night when everyone else was in bed, I worked on removing the wax. It wore me out, but the wax was yielding.

I am an admirer of many writers and their poems, plays, essays, and novels. I love nonfiction, too. But being in the business, I had enough sense to know writers are not the work they produce. You may love a writer's book, but meeting the writer can break your heart. Yet, I could not resist wanting to meet Toni Morrison after reading *The Bluest Eye*. Maybe reading it two or three times. I was still in New York, and I knew she worked at Random House. One day I got up my nerve. "This is Nikki Giovanni, I write poetry, and I wonder if it is possible to speak to Toni Morrison." I was incredibly nervous, but then she came on the phone, and I had no idea what I wanted to say. She was kind enough to invite me for a drink after work, and I must say I was thrilled that she actually read my work. At that time I didn't drink, so a "drink" to me was Campari or coffee. I walked down to Random House, and we went somewhere. It seems there were other people there, but I don't remember. Toni is a great storyteller, and she was telling the table about meeting Mohammed Ali. It was fun.

Of course, when *Sula* was published, she was on track to do what she did: become one of the greatest novelists of her generation. Whenever I could, I would go to her readings, and she always said nice things about me. I am not much with phones, though we talked a few times. Then my father had a stroke, and I moved to Cincinnati and began working to restore my mother's home. Details take a lot out of you. I was up in the morning to make breakfast, some mornings took Mommy to work. Worked on the house. Worked on my poems. Things. Things one does to keep things running smoothly. By habit, which I still have, dinner was started or laid out while breakfast dishes were being washed.

One day, Mommy had not gone to work. I don't know why she didn't. She wasn't sick or anything, and it wasn't snowy or icy. It threw my routine off, though. Since I was spending a great part of my night with a straight razor getting wax up, I was tired during the day. I was a napper. I still am. I said to Mommy, "I think I'll take a nap." Thomas came home about four, so it must have been early enough that I could get an hour in before school was out. Mommy knew the rule. I had just drifted when I heard the phone ring. I knew if it was for me Mommy would take a message. But I heard her footsteps on the stairs. I am not a particularly angry person, but I could feel myself working up a lather. "Baby," she almost whispered, "it's for you."

"I'm asleep."

"But Baby," she timidly insisted, "it's Toni Morrison. You have to get up."

And I did. And this was Toni's question: "I'm thinking about quitting my job and writing full time. I've been working since I was fourteen years old. What's it like not to have a job? You're the only person I know who doesn't work."

I poured a cup of coffee. "You're Toni Morrison. You don't need a job. You're great. Run an ad: WANTED: SOMEONE TO TAKE CARE OF A GREAT NOVELIST. Everyone will answer."

"Do you really think so?" she asked.

"Guaranteed," I replied. "I'm a poet. We know these things."

And they lived happily ever after.

CHAPTER NINE

Timothy Greenfield-Sanders

Timothy Greenfield-Sanders is the most prolific and respected portrait photographer working today. He is a contributing photographer at *Vanity Fair* magazine and has portraits in the collections of the Museum of Modern Art, the Metropolitan Museum of Art, the Whitney Museum, and the National Portrait Gallery, among others. In 2004, seven hundred of his art-world portraits were accepted into the permanent collections of the Museum of Modern Art and the Museum of Fine Arts, Houston. Greenfield-Sanders has also produced and directed five films, including the acclaimed *The Black List Project*. The portraits of Toni Morrison featured here combine her characteristic earthy warmth with a philosophical and intellectual intensity. Greenfield-Sanders captures the writer in poses that, like her books, recall powerful archetypes of feminine power and knowledge.

Morrison as Subject:
The Photographs

TIMOTHY GREENFIELD-SANDERS

In 2008, Toni Morrison was one of the African American luminaries featured in Timothy Greenfield-Sanders and Elvis Mitchell's HBO documentary, *The Black List*.[1] In the documentary, Morrison reflects upon her experience of winning the Nobel Prize and the racist responses of some individuals who suggested that she had been awarded the prize because of her race not on the merits of her writing. In the interview she details the messages her family imparted about race while she was growing in Lorain, Ohio. She explains how that foundational information has allowed her to discount those assessments that are mired solely in racism.

In *The Black List* and in his many photographs of Morrison, Greenfield-Sanders captures on film the essence of her self-articulations. Collected here are twelve Morrison portraits by Greenfield-Sanders. They are their own narrative.

To see full color versions of the portraits, please follow the QR code or link to: www.bucknell.edu/MorrisonPortraits.

NOTES

1. Timothy Greenfield-Sanders, *The Black List Documentary*, directed by Timothy Greenfield-Sanders and Elvis Mitchell (HBO Documentary Films, 2008.)

Farah Jasmine Griffin

Farah Jasmine Griffin is William B. Ransford Professor of English and Comparative Literature and African American Studies at Columbia University. She is the author of *Who Set you Flowin – The African-American Migration Narrative* (New York: Oxford University Press, 1995), *If You Can't Be Free, Be a Mystery: In Search of Billie Holiday* (New York: The Free Press, 2001), and *Clawing at the Limits of Cool: Miles Davis, John Coltrane and The Greatest Jazz Collaboration Ever* (Thomas Dunne Press, 2008). Her most recent book, *Harlem Nocturne: Black Women Artists and Politics in Mid-Century New York*, will be published by Basic Books in 2013. She has edited collections of African American travel writing and editions of W.E.B. Dubois and Harriet Jacobs. Griffin's essay for this volume explores her intellectual coming-of-age through the evolving role Morrison's work has come to mean to her — both as a black woman, and also in her development as a scholar in African-American studies. She advocates reading Morrison "consistently, closely, attentively," in a way that allows her work to truly inform "our way of seeing and knowing in the world."

Wrestling Till Dawn:
On Becoming an Intellectual
In the Age of Morrison

FARAH JASMINE GRIFFIN

Now I discover that in your company it is myself I know.
That is the astonishing gift of your art . . .
You gave us ourselves to think about, to cherish.

TONI MORRISON
James Baldwin: His Voice Remembered; Life in His Language (1987)

I.

Summer brought Bomb Pops, endless games of Double Dutch, *Wildflower* by New Birth, and *Sula*. In those days, everything was measured "before Daddy died" and "after Daddy died." That summer was certainly after Daddy died, but not too long after, because I was still a girl, not yet a teen, still jumping rope, still missing my daddy. And into that big, empty space came books and music and daydreams of endless summers. There was never any shortage of books, music, and daydreams. And yet, somehow, there was never enough.

The boys in South Philly wore their hair cut close, Black Muslim style, and girls not much older than me were starting to get pregnant. My Pierce Street friends and I passed around paperback books after dog-earing the sex parts. There was *Howard Street, Daddy Was a Number Runner, Black Boy*, and there was *Sula*. Some of these books had the stamp from the Point Breeze Branch of the Philadelphia Public Library, others belonged to the Philadelphia School System, and still others had been previously owned by some unknown somebody. No one really understood *Sula*, but some of the older girls did say that she "slept with" her best friend's husband: "How could she!!!" (I don't think I knew what "slept with" meant.) Mostly, I remember the sound of the words and that some of the people seemed familiar. I *knew* people who used drugs like Plum did. I *knew* Plum — so sweet, so high. I knew mad men like Shadrack who had gone to Vietnam or "the white people's college" or on a bad drug trip only to return home "not right in the head." And Sula herself reminded me of my Aunt Eunice, who always said had she been a boy she would have runaway forever, but she was a woman so she always ended up back home. Like Aunt Eunice, but more like Sula, I wanted nothing more than to leave and come back after a long mysterious trip somewhere out there. And I had a friend like Sula's best friend Nel, only her name was Sandra and I loved her.

The cover of the book had a thin brown woman kneeling down, face surrounded by a halo of an Afro. And, there was a yellow rose, like the ones my Aunt Eartha grew. This was a time when Black women graced the cover of books: Angela Davis on her autobiography and the beautiful model on Toni Cade's *The Black Woman*. But this one was different; it was a painting, not a photograph. (At the time I did not know Morrison edited both women's books.)

Sula contained a world not unlike my own: a world where magic occurred, except we didn't think of it as magic. I wanted to live in those pages where ordinary life took on a deeper dimension because of the sound and order of the words used to describe it. I wanted to hear those words, to be as beautiful as they were, to stay forever enveloped in their embrace. The very fact of this book, with the soft brown woman on the cover, said I could and should read and dared to suggest that maybe, just maybe, one day I could write as well. In *Sula*, I found music in words.

II.

At the Baldwin School for Girls in Bryn Mawr, Pennsylvania, we didn't read *any* books by Black authors. There was an essay by James Baldwin in eleventh grade English; he and Richard Wright joined Truman Capote and pages of others on the Summer Reading List. As a scholarship student at this elite school, I had been given detailed instructions by my mother: You are not there to make friends; you are there to get A's. Your identity as a black girl is not to be found there. It probably won't even be affirmed. That is why you come home. That is why you "remember where you come from." I did make friends there. And, I learned to read critically and to write. We read Chaucer in Middle English, the Metaphysical poets, *Hamlet, Wuthering Heights, Crime and Punishment, Portrait of the Artist as a Young Man, The Love Song of J. Alfred Prufrock, Long Day's Journey Into Night*. The Baldwin School nurtured what had been a longstanding passion for literature. In learning *how* to read, this I knew for sure: Toni Morrison could hold her own in this company. Her prose could withstand the most rigorous of readings. And, just as she seemed to know the world from which I came, she also seemed to know this one. I could connect her to these writers. She seemed to speak this tradition at the same time that she spoke to me. At this time, she led the pack of my growing collection of black women writers: Gwendolyn Brooks, Toni Cade Bambara, Maya Angelou, and Ntozake Shange. I read them on my own: outside of school but away from my friends on Pierce Street.

Along with these new authors, I'd acquired another group of friends, girls from my old magnet middle school, especially Vanessa Garrett, and a small group of girls who also attended Baldwin, many of whom shared my secret passion for the emerging group of black women writers. These writers were my spirit guides and my word warriors. These women were a bridge between the world of South Philly and the world of the Baldwin School and beyond. I met Pecola Breedlove and wept. To have limned the depths of that tragedy made Morrison a witness. She *saw* Pecola's reality and told her story to a world that had refused to listen to a black girl's cry. To bear witness: *this is what white folk do to us and this, in turn, is what we do to each other*. I was a dark-skinned girl who had been called BLACK with the venom that only ghetto children can hurl the word. And yet, I came from a fiercely protective family, so my experience was more that of Claudia and Frieda than Pecola. At times, within my family, I was as precious and adored as Maureen Peal! They tried fiercely to protect me from the color prejudice of my own people and the tactics of older men who often preyed upon girls that, like Toomer's Karintha, ripened too soon. (There was a copy of *Cane* in Baldwin's library.) Karintha, whose "skin is like dusk on the Eastern Horizon . . . when the sun goes down."[1] But it was to *Sula* I returned again and again, because even in death she was less defeated than either Karintha or Pecola. At this stage, I turned to Morrison not only to find a reflection and affirmation of a world that was familiar to me. Without knowing it, this was the beginning of my development as a literary critic. I didn't know that then; I wanted to be a creative writer. I began to read her not only for the stories she told but for the way she told them.

When allowed to pick my own texts for one of my final papers, I chose *Sula* and *For Colored Girls Who Have Considered Suicide*. I focused on the tree imagery with which both books end. One describing a transcendent death: "'Sula?' she whispered, gazing at the tops of trees. 'Sula?' Leaves stirred; mud shifted; there was the smell of overripe green things. A soft ball of fur broke and scattered like dandelion spores in the breeze."[2] The other describes a recommitment to a transcendent life:

> I fell into a numbness
> Til the only tree I cd see
> Took me up in her branches
> Held me in the breeze
> Made me dawn dew
> That chill at daybreak[3]

In both instances, the trees are associated with, embody, and nurture the spirits of these complicated, tortured women. In both instances, the trees contain a life force that insures a kind of immortality and that acknowledges the sacred in the individual.

During the spring of 1981, Diane Jarvis Hunter, one of the best English teachers the world has produced, gave me the *Newsweek* with "Toni Morrison: Novelist" on the cover. Fellow members of our black student union, which I led, gave me a hardback copy of *Song of Solomon* as a going away gift. I read *Tar Baby* that summer.

Toni Morrison: Novelist. What did she have to know to write like this? What did she read? Did she write at dawn? At midnight? Where and how far did her imagination roam?

III.

At Harvard, I lost — then found — my way. I still loved to write, but I realized I wasn't a very good poet. (That was obvious once I read my classmate Fred Moten's work.) I wrote for *The Crimson*, but soon learned I didn't want to be a journalist. I fell for a dark chocolate boy whom I loved almost as much as I loved books. During one of our multiple dramatic, tumultuous break-ups, he gave me a gift: two books he'd seen in one of Harvard Square's multiple bookstores, Gloria Naylor's *The Women of Brewster Place* and Mary Helen Washington's *Midnight Birds*. He knew my mind and my heart's true longing. As a student, I met Maya Angelou, Paule Marshall, Toni Morrison, and Alice Walker, all of whom came to read and give talks. My professors, Nathan Huggins and Werner Sollors, made sure I got to meet each of them. Marshall and Morrison were the kindest. Once again, outside of class, I began to read those pamphlets published by the Kitchen Table Press; I discovered the Combahee River Collective, the essays and poetry of Audre Lorde. I discovered Adrienne Kennedy and Frances Harper and Zora Neale Hurston. (I also started to read Edith Wharton—who blew, blew, *blew* my mind.) Harper would be the subject of my senior thesis, but it was Alice Walker who dominated my literary psyche. Mostly, because she published *In Search of Our Mother's Gardens* and helped me to really, really appreciate the essay as a literary form. Yes, *The Color Purple* came out then, and I admired it almost as much as *Meridian*. But it was those essays, those critical, literary, personal, and political essays that set the stage for the future I saw unfolding before me. The essays on Hurston were influential, yes, but she also wrote about Flannery O'Conner *and* Frances Ellen Watkins Harper. Because of Walker, I began to settle into, became comfortable with, a form that would claim me: the nonfiction essay. And, I learned that criticism could indeed be poetic.

As for my relationship with Ms. Morrison — I began to distrust her seduction of me. And I grew angry because of all the damaged and dead women in her corpus. I wanted answers, and she left me with too many questions. Truth be told, I was not yet ready for her, not for what she still had to offer me. There were others who gave voice to my pain and my longings, others who affirmed the space from which I had come, others who wrote bold and beautiful language, others who said this is what it might mean to be a black woman in a white man's world. Morrison seemed to say that and something more, something deeper. And, she questioned that framing: that we were living in a white man's world. In fact, she seemed to think it was her world, to be made and remade according to her liking. She seemed to be saying something big and expansive, and I did not yet have the intellectual tools to wrap my brain around it. This was the moment — a moment, one of many — when I became aware of my own intellectual and imaginative limitations. I understood the story but I needed to know more. She eluded even as she continued to beckon.

IV.

And then came *Beloved*. I started it three times. During the spring semester of my first year in graduate school, I came home to Pierce Street. I sat on my mother's couch after she had gone to bed, and I opened the book again. As I had done with Cornel West's *Prophesy and Deliverance* only months before in that same spot, I opened the book and did not close it until well after dawn. I read it all night long. I read parts of it aloud. I scribbled notes and expletives in the margins. I cried at its pain and at its beauty. I thought "Aw, Toni . . . ," and "Damn, Toni!" I heard the poetry and I saw the colors. By daybreak I was spent. She had whipped my ass and blessed me at the same time. I sat in a state of awe at the accomplishment and at the witness. I had come face to face with her genius. My head buzzed like a madwoman. Could she have? Did she really? I read *Beloved* in the midst of other reading. I was also encountering Luckacs, Adorno and Benjamin, Foucault and Gramsci, Fanon, Spivak and Said, the Western Marxists and the French Feminists. Cornel West, John Blassingame, Robert Stepto, Hazel Carby, Michael Denning, Jean Agnew, and Margaret Homans were among my teachers. Saidiya Hartman, Errol Louis, Tera Hunter, and Lisa Sullivan were my classmates, teachers, and intellectual compatriots. At every encounter my intellectual equilibrium was shattered and rebuilt.

In this context, Toni Morrison was not only Novelist. The implications of her fiction on thought were becoming clearer. She was engaging, informing, and shaping my understanding of history, narrative, power, domination, and language. Her prose started to shape and define my sense of the relationship between space and time. She taught me about form and content. In Morrison there was no ahistorical celebration of fragmentation; fragmentation was not only psychic — it was real, it was literal. She understood that pre-modern, modern, and postmodern forms of power operated on black bodies simultaneously. She knew that black diasporic peoples were the first modern, indeed the first postmodern, subjects. Herein lie the answers. And, she did all of this in absolutely breathtaking prose. No ugly language here. Her words opened doors, welcomed you in, insisted you become involved with them. After reading *Beloved*, I knew I could write about my people and call them my people and do so with a sense of awe, wonder and a critical sensibility. I also knew that "my people" contained multitudes.

Cornel West invited Saidiya and me to come to Princeton because Ms. Morrison would be giving an inaugural lecture. "I will introduce you to her." It was February. It was freezing cold. We left New Haven at daybreak, took Metro-North to Grand Central, the subway to Penn Station, New Jersey Transit to Princeton Junction, the dinky to Princeton, and then we walked up. It was a pilgrimage. In those days, we traveled near and far to see and hear Toni

Morrison and Hortense Spillers. Morrison gave a talk that shared much with her essay "Unspeakable Things Unspoken," and she read from what would become the final pages of *Jazz*. That talk and reading changed the course of my intellectual life. Until that moment, I had been wavering between a dissertation on black women writers and the legacy of slavery and one focusing on black artists and the African American migration experience. I was leaning heavily toward the latter, but the former seemed hipper, trendier. It would allow me to demonstrate my ability to engage some of the theorists I'd been reading who made connections between the body and writing, especially Luce Irigary, Hélène Cixous, and Jacques Lacan. However, I left Princeton knowing that I would write about migration and that to do so would broaden my intellectual contribution to a body of knowledge about Black peoples. I also left Princeton committed to writing about literature and the arts with clarity and the conviction of my own voice.

Later, while constructing a framework informed by Antonio Gramsci, Michel Foucault, Georg Simmel, and Richard Wright, I realized that my most important theorist would be Toni Morrison. Through her criticism and her fiction, she gave me critical categories like the ancestor, and she suggested a literal and narrative space that I would theorize as "safe space" or "the South in the City"; she helped to identify the literary history I sought to document and was situated at the center of the shift in dominant portrayals of migration that would take place after the Civil Rights Movement. Prior to that movement, Richard Wright's representation of the South and the migrants' experience of urbanization dominated (in spite of Hurston's presence). In this view, the South was the site of the crime: our enslavement, brutalization and exploitation. The city enacted a more sophisticated form of power, one that constructed us as urban subjects. It kept us confined and contained in ghettos and limited our social mobility even as it created our desire for a life denied us. With *Song of Solomon* Morrison reconsidered the South. Yes, it was the site of the crime against our humanity, the site of our suffering. But it also housed the bodies and spirits of our ancestors, whose blood nourished the soil and established our birthright. Furthermore, unlike Albert Murray's *South to a Very Old Place*, Morrison's South was very African.

That talk at Princeton and a re-reading of her oeuvre also affirmed what my reading and experience taught me: that mobility and migration were the dominant tropes of Black life in the modern world: "Move. Walk. Run."[4] While *Jazz* did not appear in the dissertation, it would become the subject of the final chapter of the book.

V.

Toni Morrison's criticism was important, yes. "Unspeakable Things Unspoken," "The Ancestor As Foundation," and eventually *Playing in the Dark*. But the fiction, especially *Song of Solomon* and *Beloved*, also had tremendous theoretical and philosophical implications. In her corpus she put forth an intellectual agenda just as powerful as that of Eliot or Joyce or Wright or Ellison. She had their intellectual ambition, yet she wasn't as beholden to the Western Literary Tradition. She certainly wasn't dismissive of it; in fact, she was as grounded in it as were they. But it did not seem to mystify or mesmerize her. Nor did she find the nationalist implications of the black struggle stifling. She seemed genuinely fond of black people, certainly more so than did Wright and even Ellison; she was not afraid of painting them in a critical light. Yet, unlike James Baldwin, she did not seek the role of spokesperson. In the pages of *Paradise*, she gives us dark-skinned town founders, so imprisoned by memories of their own victimization by lighter-skinned blacks that they become the victimizers. (I finished *Paradise* on a plane from Illinois and upon landing went directly to a phone booth and called my friend, the poet, Harryette Mullen: "What does this ending mean?")

I also read *The Iliad*, *The Odyssey*, and *The Medea* because of Morrison. I came to Faulkner through her, and not vice versa. (An aside: I came to a deeper understanding of him through Thadious Davis, whose brilliant work on the Mississippian anticipates Morrison's insights in *Playing in the Dark*. But that is for another essay.)

I find that Morrison informs the large as well as the small, the sweeping epic and the specific gesture. Her words enter your imagination and provide a way of knowing and seeing the world we inhabit. For example, let us return, yet again, to *Sula*:

> In that place, where they tore the nightshade and blackberry patches from their root to make room for the Medallion City Golf Course, there was once a neighborhood.[5]

In this opening sentence we have the disruption, the displacement, the dispossession: this could be the rupture of the slave trade, black farmers land loss at the hands of racial terrorists, the towns bombed and burned, urban renewal, or gentrification. The organic landscape destroyed to make way for a site of elite leisure, the pesticide ridden, manicured greens of a golf course. While the blackberry patches and nightshade are a metaphor for the neighborhood's black inhabitants, later Morrison gets more specific, naming a that space so that it becomes place:

> They are going to raze the Time and a Half Pool Hall, where feet in long tan shoes once pointed down from chair rungs. A steel ball will knock to dust Irene's Palace of Cosmetology, where women used to lean their heads back on sink trays and

doze while Irene lathered Nu Nile into their hair. Men in khaki work clothes will pry loose the slats of Reba's Grill, where the owner cooked in her hat because she couldn't remember the ingredients without it.[6]

A community is violently torn from its roots, resulting in what Mindy Fullilove brilliantly calls "root shock." For Fullilove, "root shock" describes the consequences of such dispossession, particularly the loss of income, social organization, and ability to adequately organize a political response as well as the resulting psychological trauma of communities that experience urban renewal.

Through the use of metaphor and metonymy, Morrison's prose provides vivid, concrete imagery to explain complex social and historical phenomena. In other instances she provides explanation for something familiar, naming a feeling or an action that we have long experienced or witnessed, but for which we have no name or working definition. Consider this moment, when the fair-skinned Helene encounters the devaluing gaze of the white conductor on the Jim Crow car. She is struck by "[a]n eagerness to please and an apology for living."[7] From the moment you reads this, whenever encountered with that sensibility in yourself or another, you will be taken back to this explanation: it describes a price paid by some oppressed people in a context that offers them nothing but disdain. As with Richard Wright's Bigger Thomas, who never feels blacker than when he is under the insistent and defining white gaze, Helene, a woman separated from him by class and skin tone, possesses a different impulse but a similar sense of self-hatred.

In most of Morrison's novels, she will step away from a central character, away from the plot's action, to give us a meditation on the group. In so doing, she identifies a sensibility, a worldview, a history. In an oft-quoted passage from *The Bluest Eye*, she introduces us to a group of Black migrant middle class women:

They come from Mobile. Aiken. From Newport News. From Marietta. From Meridian. And the sound of these places in their mouths make you think of love . . . You don't know what these towns are like, but you love what happens to the air when they open their lips and let the names out. . . . These girls soak up the juice of their home towns, and it never leaves them. They are thin brown girls who have looked long at hollyhocks in the backyards of Meridian, Mobile, Aiken, and Baton Rouge. . . . Their roots are deep, their stalks are firm, and only the top blossom nods in the wind. They have the eyes of people who can tell what time it is by the color of the sky. Such girls live in quiet black neighborhoods where everybody is gainfully employed . . . They go to land-grant colleges, normal schools, and learn how to do the white man's work with refinement . . . Here they learn the rest of the lesson begun in those soft houses with porch swings . . . : how to behave. The careful development of thrift, patience, high morals, and good manners. In short, how to get rid of the funkiness. The dreadful funkiness of passion, the funkiness of nature, the funkiness of the wide range of human emotions.[8]

For pages Morrison gives us a detailed, poetic portrait of this particular group of migrant women. In so doing, she distinguishes them from other migrants. She tells us what they've kept and what they've given up in their steady climb toward respectability, toward representativeness. She at once creates a category and uses it to show that black people are not homogenous. In these moments, Morrison steps back, takes in the entire history and psychology of a people or a group or a nation—and provides a portrait grounded in the complex humanity of those she describes, whether it be the free men and women of *Beloved* or the Black Southern men of *Song of Solomon*. She gives us what the historians cannot give us, what the anthropologists reach for: "a knowing so deep." In so doing, she articulates a particular philosophy of history. One that turns to the scrap in the archive, to those who live on the edges of town, the ones who sit just outside of history's conventional narrative. She calls our attention to that which moves at the margin.

Until *Beloved*, those marginal ones, ignored by historians, invisible to urban planners and mapmakers, were living individuals and their communities. With the publication of *Beloved*, Morrison includes those who were even more marginal: "the sixty million and more," those with the unmarked graves. As early as *Sula*, she had suggested that the dead dwell among us. Recall Nel's encounter with Sula's spirit in the windblown tree. Morrison's notion of history is not straightforward, linear, or necessarily progressive. History is always there, right next to the present. Left unattended, it haunts, makes a mess of things. With attention, it may give of itself, may inform, and, sometimes, it may provide a map. And, yet, one must not become its prisoner. With *Beloved* she seemed to give me a sense of direction for my own work. What she says of Sixo and the Thirty Mile Woman describes not only a beautiful romance but also the task of those of us who would write about the forgotten ones: "She is a friend of my mind. She gather me, man. The pieces I am, she gather them and give them back to me in all the right order. It's good, you know, when you got a woman who is a friend of your mind."[9] Who doesn't want a lover like that? But here we also have a metaphor for the task of the engaged intellectual, those of us who would be scholars or artists: to gather the pieces, the scraps, to give them shape, form, narrative, meaning, to put them together in the right order and to give them back, an offering, a gift. Also, to the young feminist that I was then, Paul D's desire to put "his story next to" Sethe's had a particular resonance. It challenged me to write not the story of men as if it were the story of all black people; nor to write only the story of black women. Instead, I should write a narrative where the stories of men and women were next to each other, side by side.

VI.

In that 1981 *Newsweek* article, Morrison describes herself as "a middle-aged colored lady." I now occupy that stage in life, except after a lifetime of reading Morrison, I am not sure I can lay claim to colored lady-hood. I am still reading, wrestling with, and learning from her, the towering intellectual figure of our time. (Unfortunately for me, her publication record still defines the number of books that constitute a "body of work." It's a horribly abusive game that I play with myself. To have a body of work, I must publish the number of books she has published. It was simply aspirational in 1987; now it feels impossible!)

For those of us who read her consistently, closely, attentively, Morrison continues to inform our way of seeing and knowing the world around her. (Her phrases are as close to my tongue as Biblical verses are to those raised in the church.) As she said about James Baldwin, we can say of her that she has given us a "language to dwell in" (1987). Many of us have become comfortable with what we think we know about Morrison. We come to her work seeking what we are already sure we will find there. We look for the clever new way she may tell us something she has told us many times before. But she refuses. She is too busy thinking, imagining, standing at the edge of the unknown and daring to go there.

With *A Mercy*, Morrison goes back before the beginning. She reminds us that there is always a "before" that makes our "beginnings" possible. She looks at this place in North America before it becomes the United States of America: a place with limitless obstacles and limitless possibility. She is *the* premier U.S. writer, and this is her meta-statement. In *A Mercy* she presents a world, as yet untamed, with pliable boundaries. A world filled with birds, bugs, natural beauty, disease, passion, pestilence, and utter chaos. As in the past, with Hagar, Reba, and Pilate or Sula, Hannah, and Eva, she gives us a household of three "unmastered" women, but this time they are the white Rebekka, the Native American Lina, and Sorrow, who is of mixed heritage. And there is Florens, the young slave girl "with the hands of a slave and the feet of a Portuguese lady."[10] After the death of Jacob, Rebekka's husband, the women become a family of orphans, left to fend for themselves. This is a new American narrative. The moment of what might have been . . . the moment when those who would possess power turned away from one set of possibilities: a family of orphans, needing and clinging to each other in spite of emerging hatreds.

At this time, race is moored in myth and mystery, but does not yet define one's status as slave or free. White supremacy is not yet the dominant governing ideology, and thus white characters are not flattened by it. Instead they are as interesting and complicated as the Africans and Native Americas, and all are shaped by the others.

Significantly, the landscape may be the novel's most animated character. The topos Morrison describes is so distant from our own that it appears magical and magnificent without needing to be described in surrealistic terms. Morrison reveals the magical in the ordinary: "Sudden[ly] a sheet of sparrows fall from the sky and settle on the trees. So many the trees seem to sprout birds, not leaves at all."[11]

Here we get a land more ancient than Eden. The land (not Founding Fathers, sacred documents, religious exiles, or settler colonists) sits at the beginning of this history. And to that land came the dangerous, superstitious theologies of the Baptists, Anabaptists, and the Catholics. The so-called Pagan beliefs of the Native American Lina honor the sacredness of the landscape far better than the newcomer Christians.

A Mercy is an exploration of the meaning of freedom at a time when it could have been much more expansive, a time when our national identity was beginning, to be but not yet entirely, constructed at the expense of its black and indigenous peoples. It is not insignificant that the book was published just a week after the United States elected its first non-white president. A perfect time to reconsider our beginnings to explore our origins and to question our received myths and meanings.

In our own time Morrison, our spellbinding storyteller, continues to teach, to instruct, to question. She brings heartbreaking pain, breathtaking beauty, and awe-inspiring mystery to the stories we tell about ourselves. To wrestle with her on the page is still a struggle and a blessing — one that awakens a yearning for more from her and most importantly, more (and better) from ourselves.

NOTES

1. Jean Toomer, *Cane.* (New York: Harper & Row, 1923 and 1969; repr., New York: Norton, 2011), 3.

2. Toni Morrison, *Sula* (New York: Random House-Knopf, 1973), 174.

3. Ntozake Shange, *For Colored Girls Who Have Considered Suicide When the Rainbow is Enough* (New York: Charles Scribner, 1977), 63.

4. Toni Morrison, *Beloved* (New York: Random House-Knopf, 1987), 80.

5. Morrison, *Sula*, 3.

6. Ibid., 3.

7. Ibid., 22.

8. Toni Morrison, *The Bluest Eye* (New York: Random House-Knopf, 1970 and 1994; repr. New York: Holt, Rinehart and Winston, 1993), 82.

9. Morrison, *Beloved*, 321.

10. Toni Morrison, *A Mercy* (New York: Vintage International, 2009), 4.

11. Ibid, 83.

Missy Dehn Kubitschek

Missy Dehn Kubitschek is Professor of English, Africana Studies, and Women's Studies at Indiana University-Purdue University Indianapolis. She has written extensively on African American literature, including her books *Toni Morrison: A Companion Volume, Claiming the Heritage: African American Women Novelists and History,* she has numerous articles in *African American Review, MELUS, CLA Journal* and *Frontiers.* Kubitschek's essay considers Morrison's writing in relation to the paradigm of a "wild zone" that must allow for the performative and relational character specific to African American women's texts. She probes the ways in which Morrison writes, reads, and forges relationships with her reader both within and without her texts, ultimately concluding that it is the sensual aspects of love and yearning, rather than the abstract yet persistent hope for transcendence, that Morrison "passes on" through her texts.

Playing in the Wild:
Toni Morrison's Canon and the Wild Zone

MISSY DEHN KUBITSCHEK

I. In the Zone: Evolving Ideas of a Women's Wild Zone

Over a forty-year creative career, Toni Morrison has participated in (and in some ways set the agenda for) redefinitions of African American culture, of African American women's and men's lives, and finally of American history. She has shown black women's beauty, their significance in the world, their love for and with black men, the complexities of black communities—and the history of racist and sexist attacks on all of them. Morrison has participated in what Michel Foucault called "the insurrection of subjugated knowledges" by voicing and revoicing African American experiences.[1] As part of the feminist critical exploration contemporary with Foucault's work, Elaine Showalter discussed Edwin Ardener's concept of dominant and subjugated (or muted) groups in relation to patriarchies and women. Here, she describes feminist attempts to theorize and realize the experiences of women, a subjugated group, and the possible existence of a "wild zone" beyond patriarchal control:

> We can think of the "wild zone" of women's culture spatially, experientially, or metaphysically. Spatially it stands for an area which is literally no-man's-land, a place forbidden to men. . . . Experientially it stands for the aspects of the female life-style which are outside of and unlike those of men; again, there is a

corresponding zone of male experience alien to women. But if we think of the wild zone metaphysically, or in terms of consciousness, it has no corresponding male space since all of male consciousness is within the circle of the dominant structure and thus accessible to or structured by language. In this sense, the "wild" is always imaginary . . . French feminist critics would like to make the wild zone the theoretical base of women's difference. In their texts, the wild zone becomes the place for the revolutionary women's language, the language of everything that is repressed, and for the revolutionary women's writing in "white ink." It is the Dark Continent in which Cixous's laughing Medusa and Wittig's guérillères reside. . . . The concept of a women's text in the wild zone is a playful abstraction.[2]

Given that her title is "Feminist Criticism in the Wilderness" and her subtitle "Pluralism and the Feminist Critique," it's no surprise that Showalter uses "the Dark Continent" ironically. Women-centered practices, Showalter implies, are not "subjugated knowledge" but are, true to Foucault's formulation, "subjugated knowledge*s*," the focal points of Toni Morrison's novels. Showalter contrasts the imaginary of the wild zone, the "playful abstraction," with the inescapable social factors that affect and effect literary productions, whether fiction or criticism.

Like many later feminists, Showalter highlights difference, for "when feminist critics see our task as the study of women's writing, we realize that the land promised to us is not the serenely undifferentiated universality of texts but the tumultuous and intriguing wilderness of difference itself."[3] A specific African American difference must inflect any discussion of Morrison's texts. A wild zone for African American women necessarily differs from the terrain of the imaginary for other women. African American identities and spiritualities, for example, are performative and relational. Any linguistic expression, space, or experience that is liberatory for African American women must exist not for a single, individual woman, but for a plurality, women-in-relationship.

In the decades since the emergence of the Ardener paradigm, other writers and critics have attempted to conceptualize forms of a wild zone that would destabilize patriarchy and transform the conditions of real life. Critic Cordelia Chávez Candelaria examines wild zones in Chicana texts, concluding that the writers configure "thematic *zones* that interconnect experience and imagination. Sometimes that configuration centers on the geography of birthplace and homeland; sometimes its center is the home and personal surroundings."[4] Candeleria thus restores geographic space and cultural ethnicity necessarily absent from the wild-zone-as-imaginary. John Kanthak builds on Candeleria's work by adding time as a crucial descriptor of wild zones. Kanthak concentrates on the psychological mechanisms of women who call evanescent wild zones into being and maintain them; these zones last only as long as the participants agree to the risk. That risk comes into being at the moment when the zone empowers women in the actual world, as soon as their behavior threatens the patriarch — or as soon as the patriarchy perceives them as a threat. Ardener's model postulated safety in wild zones because the dominant power is blind to their existence — self-blinded because the zone's existence lies outside the power's epistemological premises. In recent formulations, the wild zone is no longer an abstraction: clothed in the social, geographic, and temporal, it becomes a visible target.

In a loosely analogous way, Morrison's early work plays with the abstract concept of the wild zone, interrogating its possibilities by imagining different relationships between elements of a wild zone in each work from *Sula* through *Jazz*. The "wild zone" as metaphor or myth holds enormous emotional attraction for the subjugated, who look to transcend or to recover Utopian pasts, or to build Utopian futures. Morrison's early readers may well have hoped for at least a vision of, if not a working model of, experience in a wild zone. After *The Bluest Eye,* each of the early novels contains characters and plot structures that permit such a reading. Each novel works with a different element of the wild zone, and each suggests some initial hope via its depiction of African American spirituality as offering the needed spatial, linguistic, or experiential freedom.

Sula ponders subject matter that had been excluded from the dominant discourse, the friendship of black women, and gestures toward spiritual transcendence in its final scene. *Song of Solomon* portrays a wild woman in Pilate. *Tar Baby* shows mythic energies and spirits available to the social world. In *Beloved*, Baby Suggs attempts to found an independent, empowering spirituality, and though she fails, community women rally to rescue Sethe. *Jazz* proffers the possibility of familial transcendence, suggested in Wild and Golden Gray and re-embodied in Violet, Joe, and Felicity.

Even in these early novels, Morrison depicts the social world's hostility toward and ultimate victory over the abstract wild zone. Each novel discovers a problem that is finally not resolvable in or by the spiritual sphere. Pilate liberates only Milkman; she is destroyed by forces personified in Guitar. *Tar Baby* shows how deeply mythos is infused with the social and, therefore, the patriarchal. *Beloved* comes close to mocking belief in spiritual efficacy. In many ways the most optimistic, *Jazz*, alone of Morrison's novels, ends with an unambiguously positive ending: two happy couples and a now-parented child in the social world. The novel focuses on a willed reinterpretation of personal and social history, albeit one negotiated not only between characters, but between narrator and reader. What can be willed can also be unwilled; the victory might be both partial and temporary.

Morrison's later novels — *Paradise, Love,* and *A Mercy* — deal with attempts to establish a wild zone that is no longer abstract, not the pure imaginary but the time/place/action of the social world. *Paradise* emphatically disavows the ambiguity of *Jazz*: the women of the convent establish a concrete expression of the abstraction of women's wild zone spiritualities and powers to heal; Ruby's men destroy it the following morning. *Love* and *A Mercy* foreclose the possibility of a wild zone by clearly re-forming the crucial tropes of the earlier novels into tragedies as bleak as those of *The Bluest Eye*. Characters may still long for the wild zone — perhaps even think that they have access to it — but the structures of the novels repudiate those beliefs.

II. Finding the Wild Zone: Sula through Paradise

Sula shows the gate to the promised land of the wild zone but doesn't provide an image or analysis of the entry or of the lived experience there. It's difficult to remember now, in the wake of its cultural influence, the originality of *Sula*'s subject: two African American women's friendship. *Sula* asserts the primacy of the bond that Sula and Nel establish as girls. After Nel's marriage, after Sula's sexual encounter with Nel's husband Jude — and even after Sula's death — the bond endures. In the novel's final scene, Nel realizes that she is grieving not for the long-gone husband, but for Sula. Critic Margaret Homans dubs Nel's stricken cry "her very own howl," a suggestion of the linguistic expression possible in a wild zone.[5] In the decade following the publication of *Sula*, the centrality of women's emotional bonds with other women suggested to critic Barbara Smith a larger and more enduring wild zone: lesbianism. Smith offered a textually based lesbian reading of a novel with no explicit sex between women. She identified an imagery of female erotic energies and the primary commitment of Sula and Nel to one another, thus broadening the definition of "lesbian" (then and now a contested term).

For Nel to establish a wild-zone friendship with Sula, she must see an alternative to her mother, Helen, who always on guard lest Nel inherit the "wild blood" of her grandmother Rochelle.[6] In their only brief meeting, Nel responds intensely to Rochelle's sensuality, and though they literally don't speak the same language, they exchange first names. Rochelle is the return of the historically and psychologically repressed in Helen's powerful, obsessive propriety. Meeting Rochelle gives Nel the knowledge necessary for an insurrectionary friendship, hence her final cry *de profundis*. *Sula* thus ends with a glimpse of the wild zone but no sense of how an adult might live within its transcendence.

Song of Solomon carries this suggestion of the wild zone much further into an experiential realm. It shows, however, one — and only one — woman capable of living in a wild zone: Pilate. Critics have always identified Pilate as one of Morrison's most vital, original contributions to world literature. Pilate does not choose life in the wild zone; she is thrust out of the social world by the physical peculiarity of lacking a navel. She does choose not to accept a definition of herself that is destructive. Instead, "[s]he threw away every assumption she had learned . . . When am I happy and when am I sad and what is the difference? What do I need to know to stay alive? What is true in the world?"[7] Pilate establishes her home as a center of fiercely protective femaleness, reaching out from it to protect the pregnant Ruth from Macon, to threaten a man menacing Reba with a knife, and to rescue Milkman and Guitar from the police. Looking into the window of Pilate's home, Macon shows the quintessential male ambivalence toward a female wild zone — fascination and fear.

Song of Solomon hedges on why Pilate's wild zone cannot protect Hagar as it protects Ruth and Milkman *in utero*. Temperament appears to play a role, for Pilate and Reba can see Hagar's difference from themselves very early. Equally important, Hagar places her self-worth in the hands of the patriarchy. With Hagar's death, the borders of Pilate's wild zone have been breached as definitively as those of Baby Suggs when the four horsemen arrive, or those of Consolata when the convent is stormed. The wild zone can coexist with the social for unpredictable lengths of time, but its literal, spatial dimension remains vulnerable to physical and psychic attack. When a bird—perhaps Pilate's mother, Sing Bird — reclaims the earring with Pilate's name from the ground that will be her body's grave, *Song of Solomon* shifts the wild zone from a marginalized part of the social world to a spiritually charged nature.

Far more pessimistic than *Sula* or *Song of Solomon*, *Tar Baby* implies through the swamp women and the night women a zone of ancestral female energies that are at best passive toward — and at worst destructive of — living women. Even the spirit world of *Tar Baby* remains dualistic, one set of energies for men (the horsemen) and another for women (the swamp women). The reader never sees or overhears the male horsemen, but one should note that the narration gives the swamp women consciousness (if not individuality) and large claims:

> The women looked down from the rafters of the trees and stopped murmuring. They were delighted when first they saw her, thinking a runaway child had been restored to them. But upon looking closer they saw differently. This girl was fighting to get away from them. The women hanging from the trees were quiet now, but arrogant — mindful as they were of their value, their exceptional femaleness; knowing as they did that the first world of the world had been built with their sacred properties; that they alone could hold together the stones of

pyramids and the rushes of Moses's crib; knowing their steady consistency, their pace of glaciers, their permanent embrace, they wondered at the girl's desperate struggle down below to be free, to be something other than they were.[8]

This female, spiritually animated nature bears no resemblance to any archetypal earth mother. Disappointed that Jadine is struggling against them — against drowning in the swamp, that is — they dismiss her as not their problem.

The novel appears to dismiss the swamp women in the same way. The horsemen figure in Son and Valerian's confrontations and in Son's final decision. The swamp women, however, are heard from in only one scene. Jadine does not call on them or even refer to them in making her decision. The spirit world seems static, even stagnant, particularly the part associated with women. Further, the spirits are local, available only on a single Caribbean island, not in the mainland U.S. settings of New York or Eloe. Ultimately, if the swamp women constitute a wild zone, Jadine would have to die — literally, physically die, not be reborn somehow into a different self — to partake. It is not simply Son and Jadine who cannot meld the spiritual with the social; unless Morrison wanted to depict a world that offers no hope for a beautiful, educated black woman with family, the novel has lost control of its allegory. Morrison never again depicted the social and spiritual worlds as simply parallel rather than interactive.

Beloved deepens the pessimism of the early novels. While Morrison acknowledges that female dyads can construct partially successful wild zones, she depicts only ineffectual or doomed communal zones. The novel depicts two dyads: Sethe/Amy and Denver/Beloved. This first operative wild zone, Sethe and Amy Denver's temporary alliance, both returns to the dyadic implications of *Sula* and anticipates *A Mercy*'s emphasis on the impermanence and limitation of any experiential wild zone.

Only two scenes offer glimpses of a wild zone *in potentia*: Sethe's birthing Denver and the assembly of women who try to free Sethe from Beloved.[9] Birthing children is a uniquely female experience, but with rape a profitable part of slavery, birthing in *Beloved* certainly is not free of male control. However, Amy and Sethe are alone together when Denver is born. Their language is perforce that of racist and sexist authority—it's the only language that they know—but it also includes a faint echo of the wild zone in Amy's mother's lullaby. Further, "[t]here was nothing to disturb them at their work. So they did it appropriately and well."[10] In an interstitial wild zone, they have helped another female into the world. Morrison accents the brevity of such companionate labor by musing on bluefern spores:

> Often they are mistook for insects — but they are seeds in which the whole
> generation sleeps confident of a future. And for a moment it is easy to believe

each one has one — will become all of what is contained in the spore: will live out its days as planned. This moment of certainty lasts no longer than that; longer, perhaps, than the spore itself.[11]

Sethe preserves the memory of that moment when she names her child "Denver." This story of Denver's birth involves a second wild zone, in which Denver and Beloved collaboratively create a story from the "scraps her mother and grandmother had told" Denver.[12] Alone together, as Amy and Sethe were, Denver and Beloved expand the one-word text of Denver's name to a detailed narrative of fugitive women's temporary alliance. Together, they create a narrative of wild zone experience.

Two attempts to create a larger, more communal wild zone fail. Despite the gatherings in the Clearing, the four horsemen violate Baby Suggs's yard, Beloved dies, and the family is destroyed. Baby Suggs dies too, of communal psychic homicide. Ultimately, no space is shielded from white control: Sethe trades her body for the gravestone carved "Beloved."

The empowered wild zone of Pilate's Michigan household does not exist in either of Sethe's ensuing all-female households, because of or despite their succoring Beloved in different forms. Baby Suggs does appear for a cameo when Denver needs a supportive push. But by that time, conditions are beyond desperate, and it is not clear whether Denver could have requested aid earlier or whether Baby Suggs could offer help again. The ancestral spirits' own space is the ghastly nightmare of perpetual Middle Passage from which Beloved emerges to claim Sethe.

Baby Suggs, Holy creates a communal wild zone, but it cannot withstand a single community party. Eighteen years later, the community women achieve at least a temporary wild zone — and Morrison shows its complete power-lessness in the social world. When the women gather at Sethe's gate to try to free her from Beloved, they see themselves "[y]ounger, stronger, even as little girls . . . Baby Suggs laughed and skipped among them, urging more. Mothers, dead now, moved their shoulders to mouth harps."[13] Finding prayer insufficient, Ella hollers, and the group "took a step back to the beginning. In the beginning there were no words. In the beginning was the sound, and they all knew what that sound sounded like."[14] Their voices carry that vision to Sethe: "it was as though the Clearing had come to her . . . where the voices of women searched for the right combination, the key, the code, the sound that broke the back of words."[15] These passages certainly suggest a linguistic wild zone, transcending patriarchal language, empowered by primal female energy. Like Nel's own howl, this cry is genuine yet communal, rather than individual, perhaps a primordial birth cry.

Beloved thus sets up an expectation that the women use wild zone energies to protect Sethe as they did not protect her and Baby Suggs earlier. And then it mocks that expectation. The women do prevent Sethe from killing Mr. Bodwin; Beloved leaves, so Sethe is freed, but not by wild zone energies. Ella stops Sethe with a hard right to the jaw, a real comedown from any transcendent wild zone. Perhaps more importantly, the women do not drive off Beloved. Beloved leaves because she thinks that Sethe has abandoned her again. Readers know this because the narrator gives us access to Beloved's thoughts and feelings; the women must make their stories, individually and communally, without this knowledge. Can a wild zone be founded on a misunderstanding? *Beloved* says that we'd better hope so.

More optimistic, *Jazz* shows a wild zone intersecting frequently with the social world. It can be entered by conscious decision, and while it cannot offer safety, it offers the self-knowledge on which a tenable social identity must rest. *Jazz* includes a female character named Wild, who cannot be connected to a linguistic wild zone because she utters no sound. Experiential? Scots verdict, not proven. She's a fleeting presence, and we have no access to her experience. An important part of the plot, she provides focus and occupation as Golden Gray and Hunters Hunter, father and son, negotiate during their first meeting. Hunters Hunter names her Wild when she bites him after he and Golden Gray have helped her birth her child. In another iteration of the mother/child relationship disrupted in almost every Morrison novel, Wild refuses to nurse or even notice this child.

The persistence of two ancestral women, Wild and Violet's mother Rose Dear, may return to *Song of Solomon*'s sense of a sacred nature. Wild and Rose Dear are connected by spatial symbols of female physicality: Wild, with the underground cave-as-womb, and Rose Dear, with the vagina-like well in which she drowns her sorrows. Like Pilate's mother Sing Bird, Wild flashes unexpectedly into presence in the novel's penultimate scene. Wild has always been associated with red-winged blackbirds, and now, as Joe and Violet happily snuggle in bed, "he sees through the glass darkness taking the shape of a shoulder with a thin line of blood. Slowly, slowly it forms itself into a bird with a blade of red on the wing."[16] The quasi-biblical language of Joe's vision suggests that it is true ("but now we see as through a glass, darkly," Corinthians 1:13). Violet, too, is metaphorically involved in renegotiating the maternal: "Meanwhile Violet rests her hand on his chest as though it were the sunlit rim of a well and down there somebody is gathering gifts . . . to distribute them all."[17] If these visions are tenable, both Joe and Violet have recovered the maternal, which exists in a wild zone that borders on the social.

Jazz highlights the radically contingent nature of human knowledge, history, story, and personal identity. Distant kin to Pilate, Violet seems first to stumble into a wild zone and then to collaborate on making one with Alice Manfred. Pilate, however, always participates in and continually creates a wild zone in a deeply spiritual context of interchange with the ancestors. Violet's context is more like Sethe's, with no traditional spiritual rituals to rely on. Thus, when Violet simply sits down in the street, unable or unwilling to carry on the social roles available, she's something like Pilate inventing her own options. After many miscarriages, the aging Violet feels that she has no access to the role that helps to energize Pilate: motherhood. By the end of the novel, Violet has redefined motherhood to include surrogacy, as she mothers Felice. Violet's ability to make a way out of no way depends on entering and experiencing, then on constructing and re-experiencing, the wild zone.

In *Jazz*, the wild zone is as close as the nearest street, if one is willing to sit down in it. This deliberately inglorious passage to the wild zone and Violet's subsequent actions highlight a buried assumption in most feminist constructions of the wild zone: we know that it will not be "nice"; we know that we might not be able to perceive its order, trained as we are to identify only patriarchal orders; but we assume that it is a thing of beauty and a joy forever to free women. That it might be violent or ugly comes as a shock. Morrison's construction here resembles what *Sula* identifies as the reason that the Bottom does not oust Sula: in addition to the Christian trinity, there's a fourth side of god; evil cannot be so easily expunged. The wild zone will be liberating, but what forces exist in women to be liberated?

In *Jazz*, Violet enters the wild zone and becomes Violent, who interrupts a wake to stab the corpse of her husband's adolescent lover Dorcas. After this action, she unconsciously recruits another woman, Dorcas's aunt Alice, to make and experience a wild zone. Socially, these women have nothing in common. Experientially, they are both dealing with loss and great grief. As they become friends, they restructure a private space, Alice's apartment — not the public space of a street — and together learn to communicate in ways that lead them to substantially different, much more emotionally energized relationships. This wild zone does not exist for long, but the women do not need it to. Besides, the wild zone has multiple points of entry, and *Jazz* offers jazz as a form to contain and express what linguistically and experientially pertains to the wild zone.

Morrison's next novel, *Paradise*, offers the most complete description of a wild zone, its ability to free women, and the violence that inevitably attacks it in the social world. *Paradise* is at once the high-water mark of the wild zone's efficacy and a transition to the deep pessimism of *Love* and *A Mercy*. *Paradise* juxtaposes two orders: the stagnant, essentialist, and patriarchal all-black town called Ruby versus the progressively wilder "convent" just outside Ruby. Because the novel opens with the male power brokers of Ruby storming the convent and killing its women, the reader knows immediately that this incarnation of the wild zone has been destroyed. Nevertheless, the place marking the wild zone endures longer in *Paradise* than in any other Morrison novel, and it involves a community of women rather than a single woman or a dyad of friends. The convent's wild-zone work includes one resurrection, one death, one birth, and much healing.

Under its leader Connie/Consolata, the convent becomes a haven for abused women who eventually create a wild zone. All have experienced catastrophic disruptions of their mother/daughter relationships or have been so damaged that they fail to mother their children. All are damaged by patriarchal violence, generally sexual violence. No one is healed for some time. As Connie has to believe herself to be Consolata Sosa, a powerful healer, the others have to want to heal, and the process takes years. Consolata initiates the women into "loud dreaming":

> That is how the loud dreaming began. How the stories rose in that place. . . . And it was never important to know who said the dream or whether it had meaning. In spite of or because their bodies ache, they step easily into the dreamer's tale. . . . In loud dreaming, monologue is no different from a shriek; accusations directed to the dead and long gone are undone by murmurs of love. So, exhausted and enraged . . .[18]

As anger replaces shame, the women gain strength to paint visions of their authentic selves. At the same time, Consolata tells them of Piedade, a divine female force, who sings a miraculous song without words. The women exchange their stories through words. In return, Consolata gives them a vision and an experience beyond words — the linguistic, experiential, and metaphysical aspects of the wild zone ouat of which they have created an incarnation of.

The spatial aspect of this wild zone lays the convent women open to male fascination and subsequent visceral, deadly rejection. The Ruby men simply walk to the convent and shoot all the women as threats to the purity of their town. The healed women all die. Here, though, *Paradise* ventures into new territory. The dead women's bodies disappear from the convent and its grounds. Later, they are seen in places important to each individual's experience. One forgives, one simply greets, one refuses to forgive, one heals her mother. Spirits survive the body's death frequently in Morrison's novels: Sula wants to tell Nel how death felt; Pilate's father says, "Sing," and her mother flies off with Pilate's earring; Beloved wants her mama; the red-winged blackbird perches outside Joe and Violet's bedroom. These represent, however, those with particularly strong life forces. Most are tied to a particular locale important during their physical lives. The spirit women of *Paradise*, however, return from the convent grounds to the crucial settings of their earlier experience. The reader has no idea of how long their disembodied lives will persist, or even if that is important.[19]

The ending of *Paradise* posits the continuing existence of an active female force constitutive of the wild zone, Piedade: "a woman black as firewood . . . singing," on a beach, holding another woman's head on her lap.[20] Singing of solace, Piedade looks "looks to see what has come. Another ship, perhaps, but different, heading to port, crew and passengers, lost and saved, atremble, for they have been disconsolate for some time. Now they will rest before shouldering the endless work they were created to do down here in paradise."[21] Four of the convent women's spirits reappear, but not Consolata's. Consolata Sosa, then, is likely an avatar of Piedade. The imagery of ships is fraught in African American history and literature, but like the traumatized convent women, these crews and passengers can rest. And then work.

While Morrison's conclusions frequently challenge by insisting that readers interpret and synthesize to make a coherent reading, *Paradise* ends in a stasis in which the reader has no such work assignment. Contrast the finale of *Paradise* with that of *Jazz*: *Jazz* concludes with "[i]f I were able I'd say it. Say make me, remake me. You are free to do it and I am free to let you because look, look. Look where your hands are. Now."[22] We are directed to labor; we are to make and remake our interpretations. In the same way, *Song of Solomon* tells us that it does not matter which man gives up his life to his killing brother, and the reader must discover what could make that true. The final picture of Piadade, however, is static. She awaits. The wild zone is perhaps more powerful, more enduring, even more accessible in *Paradise* than in any of Morrison's earlier books, but it has a *Brigadoon* feel. It's out there somewhere in a transcendent realm, not here in our embodied forms or in our cities.

III. Love, A Mercy, and the Triumph of the Social World

Paradise is the zenith of a transcendent, available wild zone, albeit one that cannot survive patriarchal rage. Morrison's next two novels, *Love* and *A Mercy*, systematically destroy the earlier intimations of a wild zone by recursively examining the themes of earlier novels. *Love* takes on *Sula*'s subject, the love of girlhood friends become women, and *A Mercy* reworks the mother love of *Beloved*. Denying the very existence of wild zones, these late works brand believers as naïve and self-deluded. In this way, they return to the tragedy of Morrison's first novel, *The Bluest Eye*. *The Bluest Eye* does not gesture toward a wild zone, whether linguistic, experiential, or metaphysical. Its business is to document the racist patriarchy's complete destruction of a black girl child. The novel offers no active spiritual world. Pecola's tragedy resonates so powerfully in part because she cannot imagine even a temporary respite from her pain, much less a wild zone in which she could heal. She attempts to provide for herself what her society has denied her—affirmation—by creating an invisible friend. The reader, made privy to those conversations between parts of a fractured self, is forced to see that no part of Pecola's being has escaped deadly damage. Though often romanticized in 1970s feminist criticism and feminist works, madness here is no breakthrough for wild-zone consciousness. It offers Pecola no spatial, experiential, or metaphysical freedoms. The implosion of the Dick-Jane-Sally primer's conventions of spacing between words bespeaks not a new linguistic expression, but an even more concentrated racist pedagogy. Metaphysically, the only people who even seem to try to help Pecola, the MacTeer girls, cannot re-energize the myth of Demeter and Persephone.

This bleak worldview of death-dealing oppression with no wild zone as a site of resistance constitutes *Love* and *A Mercy*. Referring to several of the earlier novels, *Love* resembles *Sula* most because it reprises the girlhood friendship ruptured by patriarchal values. Christine and Heed are *Love's* analogs to Nel and Sula respectively, but the novels have markedly different tones and outcomes. *Sula* never feels like a tragedy, perhaps because of Sula's insouciance (even after her death) and Nel's epiphanic validation of their friendship. *Love* is unrelieved tragedy, with all earlier wild zone possibilities absent, with their energies depleted. While *Love* draws heavily on *Sula*, it fuses that novel's portrait of women's primary links to one another with the grim outcome of *The Bluest Eye*. In *Love*, the hotel owner Cosey and his fishing buddies, who include a white sheriff, provide the context of oppressive, racist male power that creates the need for a wild zone. And in *Love*, it's not there. Not just inaccessible: not there.

Christine and Heed's friendship re-examines the wild zone possibilities of Nel and Sula's bond, but it is presented as both weaker and as more virulently attacked by patriarchy. Like Nel and Sula, the girls come from different backgrounds. Christine has middle class status as the grandchild of Bill Cosey, while Heed comes to the Cosey hotel from poverty. Patriarchy interferes with the friendship so early that Christine and Heed lose years of experience that would have strengthened their relationship. Heed is eleven when Cosey fondles her nipples. Released, she runs. Cosey then retires to Christine's bedroom to masturbate, and Christine sees him through the window. Neither girl feels able to tell the other what she has experienced. The marriage of twelve-year-old Heed and Cosey solidifies the girls' alienation. The character Love may have loved Cosey, but she assigns him responsibility for the rupture and the wasted lives that followed it: "*See, he chose a girl already spoken for. Not promised to anyone by her parents. That trash gave her up like they would a puppy. No. The way I see it, she belonged to Christine and Christine belonged to her.*"[23] Christine blames Heed for a marriage that she sees as a betrayal:

> [s]he would never forget how she had fought for her, defied her mother to protect her, to give her clothes . . . They shared stomachache laughter, a secret language, and knew as they slept together that one's dreaming was the same as the other one's.[24]

Conscious or unconscious, Christine and Heed are one until Heed's wedding. Describing the ménage forced upon them years later by Christine's poverty and Heed's disabled hands, The narrative says: "So the one who had been sold by a man battled the one who had been bought by one."[25] The references are ambiguous; in crucial ways, and in their relationship to patriarchy, they are still indistinguishable — and still only victims.

The girls' secret language, a gesture to a linguistic wild zone, is merely a form of "pig-Latin," with the first consonant moved to the last position of the spoken word, with "hidegay" added. Its structure remains patriarchal, its sound too much like standard language to hide or express meanings beyond the patriarchal. Not surprisingly, then, after the wedding, Christine uses it to call Heed a slave. Heed remembers that scene in the kitchen, which might be but is not a female-defined space:

> The one time she [Heed] tried to make peace with Christine, offering to let her wear her wedding ring, the kitchen exploded. The four of them — May, L [Love], Christine, and Heed—were preparing vegetables when Heed slipped off the ring, held it out to Christine, and said, "You can wear it, if you want."
> "You little fool!" May shouted.
> Even L turned on her. "Watch yourself," she said. "The streets don't go there."[26]

The adult women may have been thinking of incest, for Christine is Cosey's granddaughter, and May soon ships her to a boarding school to protect her from Cosey. However, the intensity of the response suggests that the kitchens' denizens reject a marriage between Heed and Christine as formalizing the primary emotional bond that cannot survive patriarchy and its required heterosexuality. "The streets don't go there"— a primary relationship between women has no social existence, institutional support, or place to be.

Heed and Christine's reconciliation decades later reiterates both the yearning for the wild zone and the patriarchy's ability to crush it. The scene takes place in Christine's old bedroom after Heed has had a bad fall:

> On her knees again, she turns, then gathers Heed in her arms. In light sifting from above each searches the face of the other. The holy feeling is still alive, as is its

purity, but it is altered now, overwhelmed by desire. Old, decrepit, yet sharp. . . .
There in a little girl's bedroom an obstinate skeleton stirs, clacks, refreshes itself.[27]

The women's positions recall the Piedade image from *Paradise*, but instead of being on a shore of the eternal ocean, they are in Cosey's long-abandoned hotel, the bedroom adorned with tacky forget-me-not wallpaper. The obstinate skeleton is not merely the apparition of death, which need not stir or refresh itself. No, the women lose as the girls did, to male desire and power.

Overwhelming patriarchal power and the death it brings to girls and women echo the dominant themes of *The Bluest Eye*. In this context, then, the echo of the earlier phrase "where the streets don't go" shows a yearning for the wild zone but no chance that it exists:

[Christine] I was in a fancy apartment banging my head over some rat. . . .
Traded?
Bought. Like a fifth of whiskey. And, well, you know, at some point you have to buy more. I lasted three years. Miss Cutty Sark.
You were nobody's liquor.
Neither were you.
What then?
A little girl. Trying to find a place when the streets don't go there. . . .
We could have been living our lives hand in hand instead of looking for Big Daddy everywhere.
He *was* everywhere. And nowhere.
We make him up?
He made himself up.
We must have helped.
Uh-uh. Only a devil could think him up.
One did.
Hey, Celestial.[28]

Unlike the kitchen scene, this passage is written without identification of speakers and without quotation marks because it is not speech. Heed has just died. It may represent a kind of telepathic communication that signals a return to girlhood closeness. However, Christine and Heed affirm one another only as victims, for the patriarch Cosey is described in god-like terms, as self-creating and omnipresent. More importantly, the passage parallels the end of *The Bluest Eye*, in which Pecola speaks with an imaginary friend who answers. Pecola's conversation manifests the total ruin of her very being because, having internalized racial hatred and served as the black community's doormat, she can imagine only critical, racist company for herself. Pecola never had a friend and thus never had a model for creating supportive dialogue. Christine did. Thus, though the non-dialogue dialogue might be a transcript from a female wild zone, it might also signify the supremely self-serving nature of Christine's imagination.

The exchange ends with "Hey, Celestial," another girlhood code whose meaning is present only to Heed and Christine. "Celestial" is the name of a local woman on whom Christine and Heed project their need for power and escape, their fantasy of a woman from the wild zone. Nor are they alone: Celestial frightens Christine's mother, May, who counsels the girls to avoid her "[b]ecause there is nothing a sporting woman won't do."[29] To Christine and Heed, she becomes a mythic figure, free to act as she chooses, her name a celebration of women's capabilities. To the reader, she seems a little less grand. Her face is scarred. She accompanies Cosey and the white sheriff, Buddy Silk, on Cosey's fishing boat and there services them sexually. Heed later uses photos from these outings to blackmail Buddy. It's one of several occasions in which harm to Celestial does not enter into the women's calculations.

Love, too, constructs Celestial as powerful and independent, a wild woman. Like all of the novel's women, Love is dissatisfied with the development of sexual mores and much else in the late twentieth century. Needing a means of making not just her own life but her society meaningful, Love meditates in the prologue on "*Police-heads — dirty things with big hats who shoot up out of the ocean to harm loose women and eat disobedient children.*"[30] Police-heads are the mythic creation of Up Beach, an area where factory workers and hotel workers live, disdained by the Cosey hoteliers. Love cannot sustain her belief in Police-heads: "*I know it's trash: just another story made up to scare wicked females and correct unruly children. But it's all I have. I know I need something else. Something better. Like a story that shows how brazen women can take a good man down. I can hum to that.*"[31] That's Celestial's story that Love wants, or at least it's the story that she makes up about Celestial.

Watching after Celestial and Cosey have had sex on the beach, Love makes Celestial into a force of nature:

> . . . *she got up naked as truth, and went into the waves. . . . Police-heads were on the move then. . . . I could tell she wasn't afraid of them — or anything — because she stretched, raised her arms, and dove. I remember that arc better than I remember yesterday. . . . Her hair, flat when she went in, rose up slowly and took on the shape of the clouds dragging the moon. Then she — well, made a sound. I don't know to this day whether it was a word, a tune, or a scream. All I know is that it was a sound I wanted to answer.*[32]

The ambiguity of the utterance — word, tune, or scream — connects Celestial to the wild zone, as does the moon. This fantasy of Celestial-as-wild-woman marginalizes her yet again in the social world — Love disinherits her, confident that Celestial will survive.

Other women unconsciously postulate an indestructible, wild Celestial the better to advance their own weaker selves in a world controlled by men. Love may admire and even fear Celestial, but her loyalties are to May, Christine, and Heed, and that's where she spends her strength. In the novel's last pages, we learn that Bill Cosey intended to leave his entire estate to Celestial, with nothing for his daughter-in-law, his grandchild, or his second wife. Love thwarts him, feeling justified by his dementia or moral perfidy. First, she stops his heart with digitalis in his tea. Then she constructs a purposefully ambiguous false will in which he leaves his estate to "my sweet Cosey child," so that Christine and Heed wind up sharing the money.[33] With such a strong sense of justice and empowerment that she can murder a man and forge his will, Love still makes another woman her projection of the wild zone. Or perhaps, not the woman alone, but the woman as another:

> Her scar has disappeared. I sit near her once in a while out at the cemetery. . . .
> I like it when she sings to him. One of those down-home raunchy songs that used
> to corrupt everybody on the dance floor. . . . Either she doesn't know about me or
> has forgiven me my solution [the will] because she doesn't mind at all if I sit a little
> ways off, listening. But once in a while her voice is so full of longing for him, I can't
> help it. I want something back. Something just for me. So I join in. And hum.[34]

Does Love want Cosey or Celestial, or both? If Celestial, then there aren't words for it yet, either in her world or in Morrison's canon.

The discussion thus far has focused on *Love*'s parallels to *Sula* and *The Bluest Eye*. Even at her most recursive, however, Morrison repeats with a difference, in effect signifying on her own earlier work. In *Love*, that difference resides in a younger generation comprised of Romen, an adolescent boy being temporarily reared by his grandparents, and Junior, an adolescent girl on her own, who survives an abusive family and an abusive legal system. Their lives show Police-heads not only coming, but arrived at the funeral rites for any female wild zone.

Patriarchy is even more powerful in the novel's present (the 1990s) than in Cosey's era. The ferociously misogynist society surrounding Romen's decent, loving grandparents overwhelms their efforts to help him become a decent man. Romen unexpectedly finds himself unable to take his turn raping a girl who is tied to a bed at a party. He feels shame that he cut her loose, and his male peers harshly marginalize him. Enter Junior. Constant sex with Junior restores Romen's self-esteem. Baffled, his male foes retreat before his "older man" airs. In the end, however, Morrison undercuts Romen's decency by showing that it is defined in a way that makes literal Junior's imprisonment by patriarchy.

In the world of *Paradise*, Junior might have drifted into the Convent's wild zone and been healed, or become Consolata. Instead, she has the same sort of freedom as Cholly, and she's reminiscent of both Wild and Dorcas in *Jazz*. She's eleven when she first runs away from abusive brothers — the same age as Heed when Cosey buys her, a similarity that Junior notes — and the men of her family ruin her foot by running a car over it. Detained in a corrupt juvenile legal system, she moves on to prison and is finally released alone, with no support system, certainly without Romen's advantage of a caring family. Hired by Heed ostensibly to help write a memoir, but really to forge a will in Heed's favor, Junior knows that she's being used and returns the favor. She has neither respect nor pity for Christine and Heed, now old women, and abandons them in the wreck of the Cosey Hotel after Heed falls through its attic floor. Instead, she favors Cosey, spiritually present to her through his portrait, and Romen.

Junior's outsider, outlaw position might point to strength like Pilate's, a walking wild zone, but instead exposes her to the same marginalization as Celestial. Love even identifies the likeness. When Junior verbally slams a young man ogling her while he spoils the plate of food that she's buying, Love thinks, *"This Junior girl — something about her puts me in mind of a local woman I know. Name of Celestial."*[35] Junior's active sexuality at first delights Romen, but then, advised by his grandfather and responding to his own anxiety over Junior's masochism, he develops classic patriarchal power and ambivalences:

> Now with the tender mixed with the rough, the trite language of desire
> smithereened by obscenities, he was the one in charge. He could beat her up
> if he wanted to and she would still go down. Funny. She was like a gorgeous
> pet. Feed it or whip it — it lapped you anyway.[36]

Thus Romen chillingly disposes of Junior's humanity, but it shouldn't surprise the reader: Romen worries about damage to his idea of himself if he's sadistic, not damage to Junior or what might have developed that masochism. His "gorgeous pet" thought comes after he first sees Junior's deformed foot, which seems to him "a hoof."[37] When Romen makes love to Junior by licking her foot, Junior feels a promise, an acceptance of her as she is. Romen promptly reneges.

Romen has a budding patriarch's decency. He is not immediately appalled to hear that Junior has left Heed and Christine alone in the ruin of the Cosey Hotel and intends to attend to them after sex, if at all. Then, however, he leaves Junior

> chased by the whisper of an old man. "You not helpless, Romen. Don't ever think
> that." Stupid! Clown! He was trying to warn him, make him listen, tell him that
> the old Romen, the sniveling one who couldn't help untying shoelaces from an
> unwilling girl's wrist, was hipper than the one who couldn't help flinging a willing
> girl around an attic.[38]

Romen cannot "decipher" Junior's speech.[39] Cosey is not counseling decency —

how could he, having raped a twelve year-old bride? — he is telling Romen that Romen's in danger of being pussywhipped, that Junior's sexuality can enslave him. It is true that weeks before Romen did not rape the girl tied down and that he releases her, but he goes no further — does not report the rape, does not see that the girl gets help, does not mention her again. Refusing to rape was good because, in the patriarchal view, it would have made Junior's masochism even more attractive, and Romen could lose himself — and his control — in it.

Junior lies, steals, and abandons two old women when one of them is fatally injured; she's not a nice girl. On the other hand, she is absolutely alone, and being nice is not a quintessential virtue in Morrison's world. As a matter of fact, Heed and Christine aren't nice either, and their malice is not expended only on each other. They agree on Junior's character and fate with Romen's subtlety and dispatch:

> What do we do with her?
> A bullet sounds about right.
>
> . . .
>
> Should we let her go, little rudderless, homeless thing?
> We could let her stay, under certain circumstances.
> What difference would it make?
> To me? None. Do *you* want her around?
> What for? I got you.
> She knows how to make trouble.
> So do we.
> Hey, Celestial.[40]

Junior and her sexuality helped Romen pull himself out of a position so marginal that it was dangerous. Now, at Christine's behest, he locks Junior into a room in the Cosey house. No one has any use for her — not Christine, not Heed, not Romen. This girl with the "Amazon hair,"[41] the vibrant sexuality, the one who understands patriarchy's structures best — in short, the best candidate to inhabit or create a wild zone — is instead locked in her fourth prison. Hey, Celestial.

Did we create the world of *Love*, or did we just inherit it? How could our attempts at paradise come to this? How, because "*since why is difficult to handle, one must take refuge in how.*"[42] *A Mercy* shows how by focusing on an America not yet colonized but colonizing, around 1690. As *Love* re-examines the themes of *Sula*, *A Mercy* dwells with *Beloved* — in the hold of a ship, where the mother/daughter bond is broken, where even limited freedom is only apparent, where an isolated female household is doomed. Even at a moment of historical transition, when one might expect great potential for creating new, freer spaces, *A Mercy* shows no female wild zone at all and only one temporarily successful resistance to patriarchal, capitalist, and religious hegemony.

Morrison resolutely demystifies spaces that might suggest female control and a wild zone. Of the "exiled, thrown-away" women in the dark hold of the *Angelus*, a perverse patriarchal womb, only Rebekka is there by choice.[43] We hear that "[w]retched as was the space they crouched in, it was nevertheless blank where a past did not haunt them. Women of and for men, in those few moments they were neither. . . . For them, unable to see the sky, time became simply the running sea, unmarked, eternal and of no matter."[44] The description sounds transcendent, if not triumphant, but it comes to us from the viewpoint of a sixteen-year-old, Rebekka. Throughout, Morrison underlines the importance of viewpoint in *A Mercy*, for instance, when this unadorned sentence constitutes the first paragraph of a chapter: "Jacob Vaark climbed out of his grave to visit his beautiful house."[45] The following dialogue clarifies that, through Willard's and Scully's consciousnesses, we are seeing an interpretation that the reader will likely reject based on additional information about Florens's nighttime activities in the abandoned house — and then perhaps re-evaluate in light of Lina's opinion that Vaark will haunt the house in a more symbolic way. Rebekka's youth and inexperience — her unconsciousness of her white privilege at this point, for example — render her an unreliable narrator. At any rate, when the *Angelus* arrives in port, the women know that they will never see one another and waste no time in sentimental gestures as they look to see what male on the pier will control their lives.

Initially, the Vaark farm looks like a promising wild-zone. Rebekka and Lina soon put aside their animosity over control of the household because it is "utterly useless in the wild."[46] They become "friends."[47] By the end of the novel, Rebekka attends long church services while she leaves her "friend" Lina outside to wait regardless of the weather. Lina is not surprised. She knows that "[a]s long as Sir [Jacob] was alive it was easy to veil the truth: that they were not a family — not even a like-minded group. They were orphans, each and all."[48] But all orphans are not created equal. An orphan himself, Jacob buys the indigenous Lina, who has lost her tribe and her culture to disease. He accepts Florens as payment for a debt. The white male orphan can and does aspire to be master of a grand house. Nor does the death of this local patriarch free the women. When Lina prays that Rebekka will survive the pox, she prays not so much for her friend as for a tenable female identity:

> Don't die, Miss. Don't. Herself, Sorrow, a newborn and maybe Florens — three unmastered women and an infant out here, alone, belonging to no one, became wild game for anyone. None of them could inherit; none was attached to a church or recorded in its books. Female and illegal, they

would be interlopers, squatters, if they stayed on after Mistress died, subject to purchase, hire, assault, abduction, exile.[49]

Conditions on the Vaark farm, like those on the Garner plantation, depend upon the commitment and longevity of a single white male. Unmastered women are not free; they are in the ghastly womb of the *Angelus*. But if the white one of their number dies, they will be born into the hell for those lacking socially recognized identities.

A Mercy thus shows female friendship to be contingent, situationally based, and corrupted by power differentials inherent in racist patriarchies. What this novel, like *Beloved*, shows as enduring is the mother-daughter bond. Florens' separation from her mother happens in the first chapter, and the novel closes with "Oh Florens. My love. Hear a tua mãe,"[50] a plea for Florens to hear her mother. Sorrow, Florens, and Lina all lose their mothers early. Shipwrecked, Sorrow creates a double, something like Pecola's invisible friend, called "Twin." Like Pecola, Sorrow loses a baby. Unlike Pecola, Sorrow seems to receive some comfort from Twin, but Twin cannot provide a relational identity. At the end of *A Mercy*, Sorrow has seized on such a relation; she is now self-named "Complete," with daughter. That definition has no social power; unmastered mothers are even less tenable than other unmastered women, as Sorrow, like every other woman in *A Mercy*, must discover.

With geographic space for a wild zone unattainable, Lina tries desperately to make a psychic wild zone for her surrogate daughter Florens through storytelling. Like Beloved, Florens believes that her mother willfully abandoned her. Lina attempts to give her an empowering narrative with a stricken but caring maternal, and strong daughters. Lina tells of an Edenic space and a female eagle with a nest of eggs. Then a male traveler asserts dominion by repeating "Mine." His claim reverberates ever louder, and when the eagle attacks him, he wounds it. The eagle falls forever, leaving the hatchlings alone:

"Do they live?" Florens' whispering is urgent.
"We have," says Lina.[51]

In the end, however, the oral tale cannot compete with Rebekka's letter, intended to give Florens safe passage, telling any and all that Florens is her slave. Only the written word prevails in the social world, and it is no respecter of women's bonds.

Ironically, this letter facilitates Florens's only contact with wild-zone resistance. On the road to bring her lover, the smith, back to the farm to help the deathly ill Rebekka, Florens shelters with the white Widow Ealing and her daughter Jane. Jane is under suspicion of witchcraft, and her mother has wounded her legs to show a committee that she bleeds, as a demon would not. An investigating village worthy (print literate), his entourage of two white women (not print literate), and a small white girl arrive and are horrified by Florens's dark skin. With the Widow gone to the village to defend herself, Jane, and possibly Florens, Jane explains the route that Florens must take to the smithy. When Florens sardonically asks if she's a demon, daughter Jane enthusiastically affirms it. The scene acquires more gravitas because the setting of *A Mercy* is two years before the Salem witch trials in which an enslaved African woman, Tituba, was identified as a catalyst. So while Florens escapes this time, we do not know the outlook for Jane or her mother. It may be that we see here wildness in Jane the moment before it's made criminal. At any rate, women may be able to help one another but only briefly, only intermittently and in small places — a house with the master away, the hold of the *Angelus*, a closet in the Ealing cottage.

The end of the novel complicates the idea of any possible psychic wild zone, what actions might signify it or gesture toward it, and whether it can mount any substantial counterattack. Florens returns to the Vaark farm a literate, self-affirming woman but, like a newborn, covered in blood. Florens has injured an orphan boy, a toddler, whose care the smith assumed that she would undertake during his trip to aid Rebekka. Florens's motive is complicated. She has hurt the child because he would not stop screaming, because she sees in him the brother that she mistakenly thinks her mother preferred to her, because the smith has left her—but perhaps also because she does not wish to mother a son. In this time and place, fertile women will have children. They will. Furious that the orphaned child has been harmed, the smith refuses to listen to Florens, justifying his refusal by calling her a slave in a quarrel that she presents verbatim:

> What is your meaning? I am a slave because Sir trades for me.
> No. You have become one.
> How?
> Your head is empty and your body is wild.
> I am adoring you.
> And a slave to that too.
> You alone own me.
> Own yourself, woman, and leave us be. You could have killed this child.
> No. Wait. You put me in misery.
> You are nothing but wilderness. No constraint. No mind.
> You shout the word — mind, mind, mind — over and over and then you
> laugh, saying as I live and breathe, a slave by choice.[52]

It is the old tale of the male traveler and his "mine, mine, mine" again, and the much older patriarchal tale of women's irrationality, their lack of discipline, and their disgusting sexuality. Proving the smith wrong about her enslavement, Florens goes after the would-be master, literally hammer and tongs.

Like Daughter Jane, Florens proudly owns her inner demon: "You say I am wilderness. I am."[53] Florens explicitly connects herself to wildness: "Still, there is another thing. A lion who thinks his mane is all. A she-lion who does not. I learn this from Daughter Jane. Her bloody legs do not stop her. She risks. Risks all to save the slave you [the smith] throw out."[54]

Florens has bloodied the smith, but, despite her bravado, she is not free of him:

> I am remembering what you tell me from long ago . . . That it is the withering
> inside that enslaves and opens the door for what is wild. I know my withering
> is born in the Widow's closet. I know the claws of the feathered thing did
> break out on you because I cannot stop them wanting to tear you open the way
> you tear me.[55]

Florens acknowledges herself wounded by racism and slavery, but she does not accept the smith's patriarchal conflation of "wild" and "wicked." At the same time, she has no wild zone in which to make a stand and no wild zone linguistics to aid her.

What she has, in the end, is the master's house and the master's tools. Determined that the smith will acknowledge her story, Florens scratches words into the walls of Jacob's abandoned house with a nail, only to remember that the smith cannot read. Deprived of her audience, she decides to burn the house and, Jane-like, defies him: "See? You are correct. A minha mãe too. I am become wilderness but I am also Florens."[56] With a nail and a flame Florens contests patriarchal definition of wildness as the obliteration of personhood. Patriarchy does not appear to notice.

The reader already knows that *A Mercy* will be fundamentally tragic because we have seen the results of this time later in the horrific suffering of *Beloved*, in communal and individual madness in *The Bluest Eye*, in the demonization and isolation of female energies in *Love*. Although no novel can restore communication between mothers and daughters separated by slavery, the ending chapters of *A Mercy* testify to the thoughts that they continually prepare for one another, to their eternal yearning for one another. And that, rather than Utopian hopes for transcendence to a Wild Zone, is the story that Toni Morrison passes on.

NOTES

1. Michel Foucault, *Power/Knowledge: Selected Interviews and Other Writings, 1972–1977*, ed. Colin Gordon (New York: Pantheon Books, 1980), 81.

2. Elaine Showalter, "Feminist Criticism in the Wilderness: Pluralism and the Feminist Critique," *Writing and Sexual Difference. Critical Inquiry* 8, no. 2 (1981): 200-201.

3. Ibid., 205. Ardener's paradigm of the relationship between dominant groups and subjugated groups—and hence the wild zone--is applicable to many different power differentials besides those of patriarchy and women: to heterosexuals and gays or lesbians, for example; to whites and any racial and ethnic minority; to social and economic classes; to industrialized nations and what we euphemistically call "developing" nations. Toni Morrison's works offer ample materials to discuss any of these. *Tar Baby* (New York: Random House-Knopf, 1981), for instance shows that different events engage different parts of consciousness, so that gender will sometimes be the determinative element in a response, while at other times race, class, or nationality dominates. Various critics have contributed analyses of one or more of these differentials. In some ways, an analysis of only one element of necessity distorts by oversimplifying overdetermined responses. My view is simply that if we readers develop interpretations on several differentials, we will eventually have a better chance of formulating readings that acknowledge and explicate the simultaneity of diverse structures of domination and subjugation.

4. Cordelia Chávez Candelaria, "The 'Wild Zone' Thesis as a Gloss in Chicana Literary Study," in *Feminisms: an Anthology of Literary Theory and Criticism*, 2nd ed, eds. Robyn R. Warhol and Diane Price Herndl (New Brunswick, NJ: Rutgers University Press, 1997), 252.

5. Margaret Homans, "'Her Very Own Howl': the Ambiguities of Representation in Recent Women's Fiction," *Signs* 9, no. 2 (1983): 192.

6. Toni Morrison, *Sula* (New York: Random House-Knopf, 1973), 15.

7. Toni Morrison, *Song of Solomon* (New York: Random House-Knopf, 1977), 149.

8. Morrison, *Tar Baby*, 183.

9. John Kanthak explores the construction and continual re-negotiation of terms in this wild zone. See John F. Kanthak, "Feminisms in Motion: Pushing the 'Wild Zone' Into the Fourth Dimension," *Literature Interpretation Theory* 14 (2003): 157-61.

10. Toni Morrison, *Beloved* (New York: Random House-Knopf, 1987), 85.

11. Ibid., 84.

12. Ibid., 79.

13. Ibid., 258.

14. Ibid., 259.

15. Ibid., 261.

16. Toni Morrison, *Jazz* (New York: Random House-Knopf, 1992), 225.

17. Ibid.

18. Toni Morrison, *Paradise* (New York: Random House-Knopf, 1998; repr., New York: Penguin-Plume, 1999), 264.

19. For an intriguing argument that some of the convent women may already be dead and that their spirits might be connected to Ruby women, see Sarah Appleton Aguiar, "'Passing On' Death: Stealing Life in Toni Morrison's *Paradise*," *African American Review* 38, no. 2 (2004): 513–19.

20. Morrison, *Paradise*, 318.

21. Ibid.

22. Morrison, *Jazz*, 229.

23. Toni Morrison, *Love* (New York: Random House-Knopf, 2003), 105.

24. Ibid., 132.

25. Ibid., 86.

26. Ibid., 129.

27. Ibid., 177.

28. Ibid., 189-190.

29. Ibid., 188.

30. Ibid., 5.

31. Ibid., 10.

32. Ibid., 106.

33. Ibid., 88.

34. Ibid., 202.
35. Ibid., 67.
36. Ibid., 155.
37. Ibid., 154.
38. Ibid., 195
39. Ibid.
40. Ibid., 198.
41. Ibid., 23.
42. Toni Morrison, *The Bluest Eye* (New York: Random House-Knopf, 1970 and 1994; repr. New York: Holt, Rinehart and Winston, 1993), 4.
43. Toni Morrison, *A Mercy* (New York: Random House-Knopf, 2008), 82.
44. Ibid., 85.
45. Ibid., 143.
46. Ibid., 53.
47. Ibid.
48. Ibid., 59.
49. Ibid., 58.
50. Ibid., 169.
51. Ibid., 63.
52. Ibid., 141.
53. Ibid., 157.
54. Ibid., 160.
55. Ibid.
56. Ibid., 161.

Florence Ladd and Mary Wilburn

INTERVIEWED BY A. J. VERDELLE

Florence Ladd and Mary Wilburn were classmates of Toni Morrison's at Howard University. Ladd is an author, social critic, psychologist, scholar, and a fiction writer. She has held numerous academic posts and fellowships, and has published several works of nonfiction, prose, and poetry, including her award-winning novel *Sarah's Psalm*.

Mary Wilburn also attended Howard with Morrison. A highlight of Wilburn's college years was performing in Scandinavia and Germany with the Howard University Players. News of this groundbreaking international trip is part of what attracted Morrison to Howard University. Wilburn earned an M.A. in German and two decades later, also earned a J.D. In this interview with A.J. Verdelle, Ladd and Wilburn discuss the significance of the experience at Howard University for Chloe Wofford's transformation into Toni Morrison and for her emergence as a world-renowned intellectual and artist. The interview details the heady and rich environment of Howard in the 1950s and 1960s as well as the originality and perspicacity that, apparently, was always a part of Morrison's character. The interview also elucidates a possible and original reason for Morrison's name change, one that will — perhaps — end much of the speculation on this controversial topic in Morrison scholarship.

"Looking Shakespeare in the Face:"

An Interview with Toni Morrison's Howard University Friends, Florence Ladd and Mary Wilburn

A. J. VERDELLE

In December of 2010, Toni Morrison's classmates from Howard University, Florence Ladd and Mary Wilburn, conversed with novelist and scholar A. J. Verdelle about the significance of that experience as a foundation in the transition of Chloe Wofford to Toni Morrison and her emergence as a world-renowned intellectual and artist during the past four decades.[1] This interview is annotated with details about contextual and biographical information that might not be familiar to the reader.

A. J. VERDELLE (AJV): Well, I heard you all talking about C-U-L-L-U-D.

MARY WILBURN (MW): Yes. It's in a letter I received from Toni back in 1967 just as she was moving to New York with Random House.

AJV: So, she wrote you a letter in 1967 when she was going to Random House?

MW: She was just on her way to Random House, yes. They were moving to New York. She had been working for Random House, but I think she was living in Syracuse, where she edited textbooks for them. And then Random House moved their whole operation into Manhattan. It was in March 16th, 1967, she said, and they were to be at work on the 1st of June. So that's when she wrote.

AJV: And she spelled colored in a way that expressed the vernacular?

MW: She wrote the letter, and they were moving on May 26, and, yes, she did write it spelled that way in this letter.
I'm sharing it with Florence, who hadn't heard it before. We both laughed about it.

AJV: Did both of you have correspondence with her? Or do you think you were writing because the times were different? Do you still correspond?

FLORENCE LADD (FL): Well, I don't correspond with Toni now, but we had a brief correspondence, which I don't think I kept. I came across a brief note on her Random House stationery about a year ago, and I expect I put it in the box that's going to the Schomburg Center.[2]

MW: The last letter I ever had from her was in 1998. It was about a teacher whom we wanted to honor, a teacher at Howard. She hadn't taught either of us. She was the head of the drama department, but Toni had worked for her and had been in plays. I had traveled with her and had been in plays for her, so we were interested in having the Howard University honor her in some way. We corresponded about that. But, no, we're not pen pals anymore.

AJV: Did you ultimately get to honor the teacher?

MW: We did create an annual production in her honor, the Anne Cooke Memorial Production.[3] It is the second play performed by the Howard Players every year.[4] She deserved much more, and so we're still working on that.

AJV: Why do you say, Mary, that she deserves much more?

MW: She was an extraordinary woman who headed the drama department and, in fact, established it. The Howard Players were at the university for many decades, but there was no department of drama. She came to Howard from Atlanta University, as a member of the English department staff.[5] While in Atlanta, she started a summer theater, which still goes on. She was a person much like Mary McLeod Bethune. She created institutions and then they continued, because she nourished them.[6] She also began the internationalization of the Howard Players in 1949 when, for the first time in its history, the Department of State funded an international cultural program for students. They do it all the time now, but Miss Cooke was the one who was able to get them to do it that first time.[7] It was something that the State Department didn't fund entirely. Branch Rickey,[8] the man who brought Jackie Robinson[9] into the major leagues, was one of the major donors, and the Department of State, the governments of Norway, Sweden, Denmark, and the Department of Defense were all involved. Miss Cooke also made it possible for the University to have the Channing Pollock Theatrical Collection.[10] She was able to negotiate that acquisition. She designed with Warner Lawson,[11] the School of Fine Arts, which is still at Howard, the Ira Aldridge Theater, which she named, and the Crampton Auditorium complex was something that Miss Cooke worked on while Toni was working with her as a work study student in the drama department.

Toni and my sister, Beth Osbrooks, shared a job as Miss Cooke's secretary. So they knew a lot about Miss Cooke whose father was an architect. And she knew a great deal about architecture. I'm telling you more than you want to know about Miss Cooke, I'm afraid, [laughs] but that is why she deserves more and greater honor than she has received.

FL: But you have given us a segue to Toni [laughs].

AJV: Yes, absolutely, because she shared a job with your sister in Miss Cooke's office, you're saying.

MW: That's correct. She did.

AJV: Was your sister in her class? Is your sister younger than you?

MW: Oh, my sister does not allow me to tell our comparative ages, but she and I were in the same class, and we were both juniors when Toni was a freshman.

FL: Toni and I were in the same class. She was in the English department. None of us participated in the drama department as students or majors, but we were all involved in the Howard Players. At that time, they were almost one and the same thing in a certain sense, because there were three staff members, three professors, and those drama department professors were also the directors of the Howard Players' performances.

MW: Toni was in English. I was in German. Florence was in psychology.

AJV: Oh, I see, but you were all in the Howard Players.

FL: I wasn't in the Howard Players.

MW: We were all.

FL: I was an usher.

MW: Florence was as much in the Players as any of us.

FL: I was an usher, a groupie, and a critic. [*laughs*]

MW: Well, I would have seen you as a member, frankly. An important member.

FL: Thank you.

AJV: So somebody tell me — step back a little bit and explain to me about the Howard Players. Florence, you feel like you were sort of a satellite. Mary thought that, and Mary thinks that you were as much a part of the group as anybody. Was this a big group? A popular group? What was it like?

MW: It was a haven for our group. Wouldn't you agree, Florence?

FL: Yes.

MW: It was a place to hang out and to be together and to share common interests.

FL: Oh, I think we've considered ourselves, somewhat different, you know. We were special.

MW: We were elitist, on that campus, at that time. [*laughs*]

FL: Thank you. [*laughs*] Right word. And there weren't more than about 10 to 12 players at the most.

MW: You know, and we were in Spalding Hall, which was a decrepit building on the campus. Now it's been destroyed. The ROTC was upstairs, and we had the theater downstairs.

FL: And on weekends, we were often at 1036 Quebec Place.

MW: That's correct.

AJV: Florence, that's where you lived with your mom, on the weekends you were there?

FL: Right.

MW: Mrs. Coffin [Florence's mother] was careful to see that her daughter was at home, so she let all the rest of us in there. [*laughs*]

FL: We were, yeah — we were there with our Ouija board [*laughs*].

MW: And theatrical parts and 78 records. [*laughs*] I met Toni in December of '49. The Howard University Players travelling group that went to Norway, Sweden, Denmark, and Germany returned on the day after Thanksgiving in 1949. We had travelled in August. Toni was a freshman that year. It was my junior year. She was in a play that the Howard Players put on, the ones who were in the states, to celebrate the return of the Howard Players from this European tour.

Funny, I was just telling Florence: I was looking for old Toni stuff, and I found an issue of *The Hilltop*, which is the Howard University newspaper. It shows her [Toni] playing the role of Hetti in a play called *Overtones* in this celebratory production in December of 1949.[12] And, that's when we met.

AJV: I see. So Florence, do you remember that overseas trip at all?

FL: Yes, I was a freshman that year. I was very much aware of when they returned from abroad. It was a major event. It was during a time when, politically, Washington was charged with the pre-McCarthy atmosphere. It was unusual to have had a group of black players go abroad, and for them to have been well-received made their return an extraordinary event. We were all aware of that trip.

MW: Toni told me that she was influenced to attend Howard because of the information that she read about the Howard University Players travelling internationally. She had heard about a previous trip to Norway.

I found a picture of Toni and me in a play from which we did a scene on the television, WMAL-TV. It was *Richard the Third*.[13] Owen Dodson,[14] the poet who was our director, had seen a picture of the three queens mourning the death of George VI — his mother, his wife, and his daughter, Queen Elizabeth, who holds her daughter. The photo shows the three women draped in veils. Dobson was so struck by the photo that he wanted to do a play where he could have three queens mourning, [*laughs*] and so he chose *Richard the Third*. [*laughs*] Toni played one of the three queens, and Alice Davenport and I were the other two on stage. But at the television station, it was Juanita Tolson who played the third queen. I have a picture of it. It's amazing. I had no idea I had such a thing from that time.

Then later, Toni toured with the Washington Repertory Players Miss Cooke organized.[15] She and I both did. I went, I think in '53 and '54, and Toni in '54 and '55. So, we were on the road, and we did a show together there too. We performed *Glass Menagerie* by Tennessee Williams.[16] I played Amanda Wingfield, and Toni played, the daughter, Laura. So the last time I saw Toni perform — on stage, I'll say [*laughs*] — was in the summer of '55 in Houston. She had gotten me a job at Texas Southern for the summer, when their German teacher had to leave suddenly because he was a standby for Fulbright and it came in after the course began, so she called me to see if I could come, and they hired me for the summer. She came down with the Washington Repertory Players, and I think they did something by Shaw that summer. I can't remember what it was.

I'm not sure where she worked then. I do remember how she got the job at Random House. It was amazing. She got an ad from the *New York Review of Books*. I never knew anybody who actually got a meaningful job out of an advertisement in a newspaper before, but she found it there. She had edited a textbook while at Howard, along with Lady Austin[17] and Eleanor Traylor.[18] Toni did a lot of editing. She also edited a doctoral dissertation for Bennetta Washington,[19] who was the wife of the mayor at the time [Walter Washington[20]] and another book for John Lavelle, a professor of English, so she had that experience, but that would have been later because she came back to teach at Howard, and I worked with her then.

AJV: While she was teaching there, and so, Mary, you also taught there?

MW: Yes. For two years, from '62 to '64. I taught in the German department. It was a stellar campus.

FL: John Hope Franklin was there.[21] Ralph Bunche[22] was there. E. Franklin Frazier[23] was there.

MW: Sterling Brown.[24]

FL: Sterling Brown. God bless him.

MW: Toni wrote a poem about Sterling Brown when we were students. We took a course, Toni and I, with Sterling Brown, a writing course.

FL: And he encouraged you to write, as I recall.

MW: There were three of us in the class.

AJV: Who was the other person?

MW: I don't remember his name. It was our senior year, and it was run like a graduate seminar. Sterling Brown was much better known in the larger world — and much more appreciated in the larger world — than he was at Howard at the time. He was just a fixture there; whereas, in New England, he was a celebrated folklorist.

Howard had not yet learned to appreciate him completely. Some students and people flocked to Franklin Frasier's classes, of course. He had written *The Black Bourgeoisie*.[25] Students also were drawn to Ralph Bunch's and Franklin Frasier's classes, but not so much to Sterling Brown's. He was less well appreciated partly because he didn't have a doctorate degree. He never took the terminal degree, and that was considered really important at Howard at the time.

AJV: So even the students were judging professors by what degrees they had?

FL: Certainly, there were some celebrity faculty. Frank Snowden is somebody else whose work is invoked frequently now, more frequently than it was at the time.[26] I felt he was under-appreciated.

MW: You know, it sounds pretty good, doesn't it?

AJV: It sounds amazing.

MW: And, and we have, we had segregation to thank for that.

AJV: We did indeed.

MW: They would have been elsewhere had it not been for segregation. It wasn't only the faculty. The black community surrounding Howard was enriching. Toni used to attend a salon, a salon that Professor Kelly Miller's[27] daughter, May Miller Sullivan,[28] who was a writer and a poet, used to hold in her Victorian house on S Street, where she would receive young writers she wanted to encourage. Toni was one of them, and, in fact, I was there. She took me with her once, and I was there when she read the first draft of *The Bluest Eye*. It was a short story, or developing into a short story at the time. That was in the sixties, between '62 and '64 because I know I was teaching at the time. Then, of course later, it became her first novel.

I also remember her reading a story that is now called "Recitatif," as in opera. Florence is much more schooled about opera than I, but recitative—isn't that a spoken part of an opera or an oratorio? Well, that's how they published that, that first early story.

AJV: You know, Zora Neale Hurston talked a lot about the segregation issue that created Howard and its surrounding neighborhoods. She predicted the other side of what you all are saying, which is that integration was going to ruin these kinds of heady experiences that you're describing.

MW: Yes, indeed. We had great students on our campus, too. Andy Young[29] was there, and David Dinkins[30] was another one, and the singer, she came a little after us though, didn't she, Florence? You know, Jessye Norman.[31]

FL: Also, Flack. Roberta Flack.[32]

MW: Yes, Roberta Flack was there. Yes, it was. It was quite a campus.

FL: LeRoi Jones[33]. [*laughs*]

AJV: He was there with you all?

FL: No, he was a little later.

MW: Along with Stokely? Stokely Carmichael[34] was there when I was teaching. I don't remember them very well, though. Just that there was, a buzz about them.

AJV: Uh-huh. One of you mentioned — Eleanor Traylor. Isn't she still at Howard?

MW: She just retired as head of the department, but she's still in the department.

I knew her when I taught there. She and Toni joined the English department together. They left together after seven years. Neither had earned a doctorate at that point, and Howard had this rule that you had seven years to get the doctorate or out, and so they left. Eleanor went on to Montgomery College in Maryland, later earned a doctorate, and then returned to Howard as the head of the department years later, and Toni went on into the stratosphere.

AJV: You mentioned May Miller Sullivan's salon. Do you know about the salon program that Toni set up in her last years at Princeton? Has either of you heard about that, called the Atelier?[35]

MW: Is that the program where young people who are creative are invited in to present whatever they were working on, the work in progress?

AJV: It is sort of like that. It was definitely established for Princeton students, but participants have to be invited, and the courses are non-traditional. It sounds to me like a variant of the Sullivan salon. It's interesting to have that touchstone.

MW: There were other things happening on campus. And I think you can't talk about Howard at that time without talking about fraternities and sororities. Through our indoctrination into the AKA's [Alpha Kappa Alpha sorority[36]], I really saw Toni close up. She was a darling of one of the, one of the fraternities. She was a fraternity queen, as I recall, and she used to entertain us in the sorority room with stories.

FL: She was one of the best storytellers. I don't know whether she made them up, or if she just had an encyclopedic memory and could recall all those stories. She would act them out.

MW: [laughs] She was both amusing and witty. But very quick, you know? She, she had the line, [laughs] and we were, we were spellbound. She really could hold us in her thrall.

FL: It was very interesting. She was also physically very attractive.

MW: I remember a camel hair suit that she wore with a very snug skirt. And the walk that she could take across campus. The kind of walk from Founder's Library all the way across to the dormitory. [laughs] She twisted and turned and [laughs] turned that walk into a 15-minute performance. Well, when you say she was physically attractive. It's the understatement of the year. She just had a phenomenal figure. Once, when we were doing *Richard*, as I recall, one of my very best friends, Roland Noel, said to me about a scene he had watched, "Well Mary, the scene's great. But if you and Alice think that anybody's gonna be looking at you with Toni Wofford up there [laughs], you are very much mistaken."

She had two friends she was close to, Norma Lewis, as I recall, and Joan Carter. When they all first arrived at Howard, Jean was what they call now a "resident assistant," you know, the person who oversees the dorm. I don't think they had names then, but Jean was taking three new girls around to introduce them to people in the dormitory. She said she would stop, and she'd say "Why don't you meet so and so?" "This is Norma, and this is Joan. What did you say your name was?" Toni said, "Chloe," in her small voice; you know she has different levels. Jean misheard her and said, "Oh yes, and this is Toni."

FL: That's when it happened.

AJV: Well, what, what does that mean though? Why would the woman introduce her as Toni?

MW: Well, I think people hear what they know, and Chloe was not a name that you heard on the campus. I don't know whether Joan, or Jean, had ever heard it before. Jean heard Toni when she said her name was Chloe Wofford. You've heard Toni talk, you know that she can give you just almost a whisper, but it's a stage whisper. You can hear it all over the room. Or she can give you something that's really blatant. And she could shout it out like Ma Rainey. But apparently, she must have said it in her small voice, and what Jean heard was Toni, and so she said, "And this is Toni." And Toni was so quick. She realized that it would be a useful name for her, and so she kept it. She took it. People accepted it. She said she was Toni, and that's who she was.

FL: And then she adopted Anthony.

MW: Her name was Chloe Ardelia, and subsequently added Anthony.

FL: For St. Anthony. She was brought up Catholic, I think.

AJV: Right.

MW: For Saint Anthony, and it explains Toni, if you needed to explain it.

AJV: And do you know, when you say so matter-of-factly it was for St. Anthony? Or are you deciding that because she was brought up Catholic?

MW: I think I know it, but I don't know how. She would have told me. I mean that would be the only reason I would, but I can't remember her specifically telling me.

AJV: And Florence, do you remember the Chloe Ardelia part?

FL: Oh, I remember Chloe certainly. Chloe turned up from time to time. We were on the same line, A.J., for AKA, along with 31 others.

MW: That's right. We're the Mighty 34. [laughs] Yeah.

AJV: And have you kept in touch with any of the other Mighty 34?

FL: No, no.

MW: The girl who pinned me, who was not on my line, you know, the one I went to third grade with. I don't see anybody else on that line. I inquire from time to time about people, but don't hear much about them. Roxie Roker[37] was on our line, too.

FL: Yes, Roxie was on the line. Mighty, mighty.

AJV: I know her because she was on the television show *The Jeffersons*, [38] but also because she's Lenny Kravitz's[39] mom.

MW: You know Lenny?

AJV: I do. His father actually came to one of my early readings and told me that I explained exactly how black women are about their sons. In my novel, [*The Good Negress*[40]] the mother is just very, very tenacious about her boys. And Sy Kravitz[41] came and told me that Roxie divorced him over Lenny, because of things she felt like he shouldn't give Lenny. Like when Lenny wanted a car, he spent $300 and bought him a car, and she was outraged.

MW: I suppose so, because Lenny moved into the car rather than go to the school they wanted him to attend. These things happen, but, you know, it's interesting you should say that, because in this letter that Toni wrote me in 1967, her focus is on her boys [Ford[42] and Slade[43]]. She says, "I have to pay fantastic amounts of money to keep my family intact, but it is certainly what I'm working for. I could not bear the idea of their living with my mother while I do not. It's just endurable for me, for them to visit there in the summer, and that's only because they love it so and are so much enjoyed." It was really about the kids for her.

Even in school, she was an intellectual all the time, when she wasn't amusing us. We were walking towards my house one day, and she says, "You know, Mary, I'm ready to look Shakespeare in the face now." And I thought, what on earth is she talking about?

"I'm ready to look Shakespeare in the face now," she said. She was thinking about it, you know. See, because she taught humanities — of course. She taught the Bible and Shakespeare and the whole range — but what she was saying to me was, "I no longer have to go through other peoples' interpretations. I know what they think. Now I'm ready to address it and think what I think." And it was just kind of amazing to me. I didn't catch it immediately. But then I realized, that's what she was saying: that she could think independently, even about something that had been as worked over as Shakespeare by so many people over centuries. She was ready to confront that on her own and to meet him where he was and where she was. It helped me to understand how smart she is. [*laughs*]

FL: That's quintessential Morrison.

MW: Her ability to appropriate challenge. Reinterpret. Reinvent. Not just herself, but other works and periods of our history. One time, she was telling me a story that she was writing. I don't remember what it was, and I said, "Toni, what, do you carry that stuff around your head all the time?" She said, "Yes, I just work through it in my head, until I have it the way I want it, and then I write it down." I don't know if she continued to do that through all these books, but this was in about 1960. I think it was '63. She was teaching. Claude Brown[44] was one of her students. He wrote *Manchild in the Promised Land*.[45] He brought her his manuscript and insisted that he wanted her to read that just before he published *Manchild*.

She was teaching and mentoring students. She was taking care of her children. The woman who helped her take care of them was a woman who was one of Sally Hemings's descendants, Sally Hemings's and Thomas Jefferson's. Even then, walking along in the street, she was writing. She was writing in her head. Writing a story, changing the words, polishing and so forth. This is really quite a marvelous, and, on top of it all, she was a fine actress.

She visited us in Putney, Vermont. She was at Bread Loaf one summer, and she and Slade came and spent a day or two, and Toni was standing out there at the edge of the garden watching it, and she began to tell a story. I believe it was *Tar Baby*. She told the story right there. I probably said, "What are you working on?" And she just unfolded it all, with the texture, the language, and the drama of it. Right there all in her head.

Lewis Fenderson[46] [Dr. Lewis H. Fenderson, Jr.] told me once — he was a professor at Howard who taught Toni English when she was a freshman — He told me in the '60s that the freshman essay she wrote, he had kept, and he read it every year to his class, his freshman English class. Every year. She's had the gift since she was very young.

FL: And she knew she had a gift.

MW: She also has two personalities, two parts to her personality. It's this just great intellectual ability and also all the artistic ability. It's the combination that makes her unique, but she also had that ability to have a good time and to share it.

AJV: I want to ask if either of you had met her sister.

MW: Oh, Lois [Lois Brooks[47]]. Yes. [*laughs*] Lois came to visit us once, as a matter of fact, when Toni was still living in Washington. Lois didn't stay with us, but she came over. Toni had brothers, too. I think I met Raymond and Lois. I didn't meet her other brother. She also had a lovely father.

AJV: Can each of you talk just a little bit about what it's been like to see your friend become Toni Morrison and to have this unique perspective on her? What has that been like for you both?

FL: There's something about having known someone rather intimately, which doesn't give them the kind of aura or distance that one might have if you only know or have known the person through the media or through some other indirect way. She has remained Toni in a lot of ways. Certainly, when I've gone to her public events and have managed to get a seat near the front in Cambridge, or New York, or Paris, she's leaned over and said, "Hi, Florence." She hasn't forgotten. Rachel Kadish,[48] who was one of her students at Princeton, was another link to her later on. Through Rachel, she let me know that she wanted to visit us in Flavigny, France.[49] The summer she said she was coming, I went about the village looking for books by Toni Morrison and telling people she was coming. Nobody knew her name.

I didn't have any of her books there, and I wanted to have someone generate some interest around her visit. She was not known among either the French villagers or among people, who are fairly sophisticated people, who were coming for the summer from other places like Paris and London and Zurich and so forth, and that put things in a certain perspective for me.

She didn't come. She had a secretary call, and the message was "Petals fall." I remember, Mary, I called you and asked you what Toni meant by that. Do you remember what you said?

MW: What did I say?

FL: Shit happens.

MW: [*laughs*] Exactly.

FL: And, then later, I came across that term, "petals fall," in a Langston Hughes[50] poem ["Not What Was"[51]].

MW: Oh, did you really?

FL: It's very much Toni's way of saying something. [*laughs*]

MW: [*laughs*] Oh, she wouldn't mind quoting Langston. Once, she was doing a book signing. I think it was for *Paradise*, and I went with some friends. I had not told them that I knew Toni very well. But when I got to her, she stood up and embraced me [*laughs*]. Well, I didn't know she was going to do that, that warmth is still there. Of course she's gone on into another world. I miss her, to tell you the truth. When I see her, I feel, "Oh it's wonderful to see Toni." But then I feel I'm in that crowd outside. I'm not sitting nearby hearing her tell it like it is in a way that no one else can. . . . That's just really unique. I do miss her, miss the friendship that we had, that was close. The last time I saw her in my house was . . . she had won—It was not for the Nobel Prize, of course, it was long before that — a major award. She came to Washington to sign, and she came to the house. We had a party for her with friends, and she was just the Toni that we knew, and we were so delighted. It was really nice to have her here. But of course, that's over. I don't think I'll ever have her in my house again. When was the last time we saw her together, Florence? Do you recall? Not in Paris, but in Cambridge where she spoke, and she took us for a ride in her limousine [*laughs*]. That was a lot of fun [*laughs*]. It was good.

I remember once when we were with the Washington Repertory Players in Baton Rouge, she said "Mary, why don't you get yourself some summer clothes of different colors?" I tended to wear dark colors and stuff. I said, "Well, I don't even know how to start." She said, "Oh, come on. I'll go with you." So she took me to the store. When she saw what I picked out, she said, "Oh no, don't get that. Always buy your dresses at least one size smaller than you think you need." [*laughs*] And so I did, and I loved those clothes. I wore them all summer long, and I just had the most marvelous time. [*laughs*] She was fun. That's the thing about Toni.

She was just fun, absolutely. No question about it. One time going down Connecticut Avenue, she looked out and saw people going into the Mayflower Hotel, which was segregated at the time, and she [*laughs*] leaped out of the car, and she said, "Live, white folks, live." [*laughs*]. We couldn't go in there, you know [*laughs*].

AJV: Were you ever surprised by what she was writing?

MW: I've always been not just surprised, but astonished, by what she has produced, where the work has taken not just me personally, but has taken our generation. That she had signed on for certain causes.

AJV: Certainly, she was associated with the Obama election.

MW: Nothing that she's written, that I've read, has surprised me. There are some things I haven't read. There's some non-fiction things that are out there that I'm not aware of. But her description of the suffering that has to do with race, and of the vindications that people seek out of their own resources. That doesn't surprise me, and I think it is because she is so completely original.

I remember, Florence, when she did the "Jabberwocky" thing. She had the right skirt, pink satin. It had never been seen before. Annually, the Delta Sigma Theta sorority had an event that was kind of a talent show, the different sororities and fraternities participated and competed and there was always an award. There'd be skits, there might be music or something. But Toni did a solo thing. Now, it was a long time ago, and I don't remember precisely what it was. I remember her. It was just so distinctive. There's nothing else out there like what she did. And of course she looked fabulous. And, she wore a white fur skirt. You ever see anybody in one? [*laughs*] And it had a pink fat bow. [*laughs*] The pink fat bow. [*laughs*] She made up stuff. She made up stuff all the time. [*laughs*] She just has the gift of originality and creativity, and the ability to share it in a way that you can enjoy it completely. Even though, if you thought about it, you really could be envious. But you don't know anybody who can do that better. She just came up with stuff off the top of her head that spoke to whatever the situation was in an original, creative, and distinctive way. So nothing that she does really quite surprises me. Except that it's surprising. I'm not surprised. But I know that will be surprising when she presents it.

INTERVIEW ANNOTATIONS

1. *Howard University*: A private, historically Black university in Washington, D.C. It was founded in 1867 by an act of Congress and was named after General Oliver O. Howard, a Civil War hero.
2. *Schomburg Center*: The Schomburg Center for Research in Black Culture. A division of the New York Public Library, it archives items that pertain to or document the lives of blacks and makes these items available to the public. Its collection includes manuscripts from writers of the Harlem Renaissance, monographs from the sixteenth, seventeenth and eighteenth centuries, traditional African art and artifacts, recordings of oral histories, among others.
3. *Anne Cooke Memorial Production*: An annual production in honor of Dr. Anne Cooke Reid, who was the chair of the Drama department at Howard University.
4. *Howard Players*: Formerly the College Dramatic Club, it was renamed the *Howard Players* in 1919 by T. Montegomery Gregory, the chair of the Department of Speech. This group specializes in putting on plays that depict black life.
5. *Atlanta University*: Historically black college in Atlanta, Georgia that originally only offered graduate degrees. The University was founded in 1865 by the American Missionary Association, and received some aid from the Freedman's Bureau. Eventually, Atlanta University combined with Clark College to form Clark Atlanta University.
6. *Mary McLeod Bethune* (1875-1955) African American woman who in 1904 founded the Daytona Normal and Industrial Institute for Negro Girls, which is now known as Bethune-Cookman College.
7. *Miss Cooke*: Anne Cooke Reid, chair of the Drama department at Howard University.
8. *Branch Rickey* (1881-1965): General Manager of the Brooklyn Dodgers. In 1945, Rickey negotiated the contract with Jackie Robinson, a player for the Negro League's Kansas City Monarchs, which brought Robinson into the major leagues. When Rickey joined the Dodgers in 1942, he began to lay plans to desegregate the Dodgers. He needed someone who possessed not only a talent for baseball, but also strength of character, someone who would not be provoked into a confrontation when faced with insults, racial slurs and hostility. After signing Robinson, Rickey signed other black players.
9. *Jackie Robinson* (1919-1972): Crossed the color line in 1947 when he started his major league baseball career with the Brooklyn Dodgers. Signed a contract with Branch Rickey in 1945, but continued to play with the Kansas City Monarchs through 1946. As a Dodger, Robinson had an

outstanding ten-year career; he played in six World Series and won that National League's Most Valuable Player award in 1949. Robinson continued to be a voice against discrimination.

10. *Channing Pollock Theatrical Collection*: Collection of the playwright's papers — manuscripts, personal correspondence, published works and criticism. Donated to Howard University by Pollock's daughter, Helen Channing Pollock, in 1950. Channing Pollock (1880-1946) was a playwright who was famous in his day. He is most noted for his four major works: *The Fool* (New York: Brentano's, 1922); *The Enemy* (New York: Brentano's, 1926); *Mr. Moneypenny* (New York: Brentano's, 1928); and *The House Beautiful* (New York: S. French, 1931).

11. *Dean Warner Lawson*: Founder of Howard University's School of Fine Arts and served as its dean from 1942-1975.

12. *Overtones* (New York: D. McKay, 1914) is a play written by Alice Gerstenberg, first produced November 8, 1915. It is one of the first plays that attempted to dramatize the mechanizations of the unconscious. Two actresses played the character Harriet. One, "Harriet," played the cultured Ego, while the other, "Hetti," was the wild Id.

13. *Richard the Third* (*Richard III*), written by William Shakespeare, was the final play in the series of four plays that began with *Henry IV* .

14. *Owen Dodson* (1914-1983): An African-American poet, novelist, playwright and an important figure in black theatre. Dodson received his MFA from Yale University in 1939. Taught at Howard University between 1947 through 1979.

15. Washington Repertory Players: A theater troupe co-founded by James Butcher, who was also the Director of the Howard Players.

16. *Glass Menagerie*: A semi-autobiographical play written by Tennessee Williams. First performed in 1944.

17. Lettie Austin (1924-2008): Professor of English at Howard University, where she began teaching in 1947. Austin published *College Reading Skills* in 1966 in conjunction with Morrison, who was third author, and Traylor. She received her Ph.D. from Stanford University.

18. Eleanor Traylor: Professor of English at Howard University whose works include: *Broad Sympathy: The Howard University Oral Traditions Reader (1996), The Humanities and Afro-American Literary Tradition* (1988). Traylor received her Ph.D. from Catholic University.

19. *Benetta Washington* (1885-1991): Wife of Walter Washington, mayor of Washington, D.C. She was the daughter of the influential Rev. George O. Bullock of the Third Baptist Church.

20. *Walter Washington* (1915-2003): Became the first black chief executive of a major American city when President Johnson appointed him to the position of mayor of Washington, D.C. in 1967. He was reappointed twice by President Nixon, and finally became the first elected mayor in Washington in over a century in 1975.

21. *John Hope Franklin* (1915 - 2009): Historian whose landmark book, *From Slavery to Freedom: A History of African-Americans,* was first published in 1947. Lawyers for the plaintiff in *Brown vs. the Board of Education* consulted him when building their case against segregation. He taught at a seven universities, including Howard University, University of Chicago and Duke University. He received his Ph.D. from Harvard University.

22. *Ralph Bunche* (1904-1971): Professor and the first chair of the Political Science department at Howard University, where he taught between 1928 and 1941. Bunche won the Nobel Peace Prize in 1950 for his work as a mediator for the United Nations during the Arab-Israeli Conflict in the 1940s. After almost a year of negotiating, both sides finally signed an armistice agreement. Bunche received his Ph.D. from Harvard University.

23. *E. Franklin Frazier* (1894-1962): Director of the Sociology Department at Howard University from 1934 through 1959. Frazier published nine books and over a hundred articles and essays. His work and the work of others influenced institutions to adopt more equitable economic, political and social practices towards African Americans. He received his Ph.D. from the University of Chicago.

24. *Sterling Brown* (1901-1989): Poet, essayist, critic and scholar. He taught in the English department at Howard University for over forty years and was the first to offer courses in Black literature. Like Zora Neale Hurston, Brown drew upon his first-hand ethnographic research in rural African American folk traditions and culture in his writing. His book *The Negro in American Fiction*, published in 1937, draws correlations between how a marginalized group is depicted in the text and its actual condition outside of the text. Brown's work, both as a critic and a writer, raised the profile of African American literature and folklore. He received his M.A. from Harvard University.

25. *The Black Bourgeoisie* (1957): Book by E. Franklin Frazier. In it, Frazier criticizes the emerging black middle class for conforming to, rather than challenging, the status quo. As an example, Frazier

cites Howard University's decision to distance itself from W. E. B. Du Bois because Du Bois was blacklisted by the House Un-American Activities Committee.

26. *Frank Snowden* (1911-2007): Professor, scholar, and diplomat. Taught in the Classics department at Howard University between 1940 through 1990. His area of specialty was blacks during ancient times. His published work includes *Blacks in Antiquity: Ethiopians in the Greco-Roman Experience* (1970), *Before Color Prejudice: The Ancient View of Blacks* (1983) and *The Image of the Black in Western Art, Volume I: From the Pharaohs to the Fall of the Roman Empire* (1976, as co-author). He received his Ph.D. from Harvard University.

27. *Kelly Miller* (1863-1939): Professor at Howard University. The son of a slave woman and a free man. He received his Bachelor's degree from Howard University in 1884 and in 1887 was the first African American to enroll at John Hopkins University, where he studied mathematics as a graduate student. Two years later Miller was forced to leave John Hopkins due to a steep increase in tuition. He returned to Howard to continue his studies, receiving his Ph.D. from his alma mater and securing a teaching position there. He taught both mathematics and sociology and rose to become the dean of arts and sciences. He wrote extensively on African American issues, especially on the importance of making education available to African Americans.

28. *May Miller Sullivan* (1899-1995): Poet, playwright, actress and director. Daughter of Kelly Miller and a graduate of Howard University. She used her writing as a medium to talk about the discrimination African Americans experienced. Her work includes *Negro History in Thirteen Plays* (1935), *The Bog Guide* (1925), *Scratches* (1929), *The Clearing and Beyond* (1974), *Ransomed Wait* (1983) and the *Collected Poetry* (1989).

29. *Andy Young* [Andrew Jackson Young, Jr.] (1932 -): Civil rights leader, minister, and politician. He was the first African American to serve as an ambassador to the United Nations and graduated Howard University in 1951. Young worked closely with Dr. Martin Luther King, Jr. between 1957 through 1968, when King was assassinated. Young, the first black congressman elected from Georgia in over a hundred years, served in the United States House of Representatives (1973-1977). He won re-election in 1974 and 1976. He resigned from Congress when President Carter appointed him to the United Nations in 1977.

30. *David Dinkins* (1927-): Politician and lawyer. Dinkins was elected Mayor of New York City in 1989, the first African American to win the post. He graduated from Howard University in 1950.

31. *Jessye Norman* (1945 -) Grammy award-winning opera singer. Achieved world renown in the 1980s. She has received the Kennedy Center Honor, four Grammy Awards as well as the Grammy Lifetime Achievement Award. In 2003 she opened the Jessye Norman School of the Arts in Augusta, Georgia to help disadvantaged youth with an interest in art and the performing arts. Norman graduated from Howard University in 1967. Albums include: *With A Song in My Heart* (1984), *Spirituals* (1990), *Diva: Jessye Norman* (1995), *Honor! A Celebration of African American Cultural Legacy* (2009), and *Roots: My Life, My Song* (2010).

32. *Roberta Flack* (1939 -): Grammy award-winning singer and musician. Flack was honored with a star on the Hollywood Walk of Fame in 1999. She matriculated at Howard University when she was only fifteen years old. Her albums include: *First Take* (1969), *Killing Me Softly With His Song* (1973), *Blue Lights in the Basement* (1977), *Set the Night to Music* (1991), and *Oasis* (1989).

33. LeRoi Jones [Everett LeRoi Jones AKA Imamu Amiri Baraka] (1934 -): Poet, playwright, and activist. Jones changed his name to Imamu Amiri Baraka after the assassination of Malcolm X in 1965. He founded Totem Press (1958), the Black Arts Repertory Theatre in Harlem (1965), the Spirit House Movers and Players (a cultural group, 1967) and the United Brothers (a political group associated with Black Power, 1967). He has won a number of literary awards, including the Guggenheim Fellowship, the PEN/Faulkner Award, and the Langston Hughes Award. He has taught at Columbia University, Yale University, the University of Buffalo, George Washington University, the New School for Social Research in New York and San Francisco State University. He is now a professor emeritus at State University of New York in Stony Brook. Much of his writing expresses his frustration and anger at white society. He graduated from Howard University in 1953. Works include: *Dutchman* (1964), *Black Art* (1966), *Black Magic* (1969), *Arm Yrself or Harm Yrself* (1967), *Confirmation: An Anthology of African American Women* (1983), and the *Autobiography of LeRoi Jones/Amiri Baraka* (1984).

34. *Stokely Carmichael* [AKA Kwame Ture after 1968] (1941-1998): Activist and advocate of Pan-Africanism. Ture, frustrated with Dr. Martin Luther King, Jr's nonviolent policies, began to advocate black separatism and "black power" in 1966 shortly after he was named chairman of the Student

Nonviolent Coordinating Committee (SNCC). Prior to this move towards militancy, Ture was involved in the nonviolent struggle for "freedom"—black voter registration Alabama, the Freedom Rides of the Congress of Racial Equality, and was frequently arrested for civil disobedience. The SNCC repudiated him and his views in 1967, the same year he wrote the book *Black Power*, with Charles Hamilton. Ture organized the Lowndes County Freedom Organization, an all-black organization, and chose the black panther as its logo, which was later adopted by the Black Panther Party. Ture served briefly as their honorary prime minister before parting ways over the party's solicitation of support from white radicals. Ture moved to Guinea in 1969 and encouraged other African Americans to return to Africa. He became a strong advocate of Pan-Africanism and spoke on behalf of the All African Peoples Revolutionary Party.

35. *Princeton Atelier*: Conceived by Morrison in 1991 while working together with André Previn (composer) and Kathleen Battle (singer) on the lyrics for *Honey and Rue*. Morrison wanted to create a place where artists could experiment and push boundaries. It differed from a typical workshop in that participants — both students and professional artists — were put into a position where they had to work together and rely on each other's strengths in order to accomplish the project. The inaugural workshop brought together Jacques d'Amboise, the director of the National Dance Institute, A. S. Byatt, a novelist, and students in order to create a dance inspired by one of Byatt's novels.

36. Alpha Kappa Alpha: A national sorority first founded in 1908 at Howard University. It is the oldest Greek organization founded by African American women.

37. Roxie Roker (1929-1995): Actress and children's advocate. She performed in several off-Broadway plays, one for which she was nominated for a Tony award, but is most remembered for her portrayal of Helen Willis on *The Jeffersons*, a television show. Roker was the mother of singer Lenny Kravitz. She was a member of the Howard Players and the Alpha Kappa Alpha sorority and she graduated from Howard University in 1952.

38. *The Jeffersons* (1975-1985): A comedy that ran on CBS; a spinoff of *All in the Family*. It was one of the first primetime television programs to feature African Americans in leading roles, as well as television's first interracial couple — Tom and Helen Willis.

39. Lenny Kravitz (1964 -): Grammy Award-winning musician. Kravitz is the son of Sy Kravitz and Roxie Roker. He was married for several years to Lisa Bonet, the actress who played Denise Huxtable on *The Cosby Show*. His albums include: *Let Love Rule* (1989), *Mama Said* (1991), *Are You Going My Way* (1993), *Five* (1998), *Lenny* (2001) and *Baptism* (2004).

40. *The Good Negress* (1995): Novel by A. J. Verdelle (b. 1960). The novel was a finalist for both the Los Angeles Times Book Award and the PEN/Faulkner Award. The novel, set in 1963, depicts the plight of a young African American woman, who, raised by her grandparents, is reunited with her pregnant mother, brothers and stepfathers and is expected to cook, clean and care for the new infant. She becomes conflicted when her teacher encourages her to "reach beyond her station" through improving her education, a goal which puts her at odds with her responsibilities to her home and family.

41. *Seymour "Sy" Kravitz* (1927-2005): Sy Kravitz was a producer for NBC. He was married to and divorced from actress Roxie Roker. Kravitz was the father of Lenny Kravitz.

42. Harold Ford Morrison (1961-): Son of Harold and Toni Morrison.

43. Slade Kevin Morrison (1964-2010): Son of Harold and Toni Morrison. Morrison worked with Slade to produce children's books, including: *The Big Box* (1999), *The Book of Mean People* (2002), and the *Who Got Game?* series.

44. Claude Brown (1937 - 2002): Writer. Born in Harlem, his parents had moved from South Carolina during the Great Migration, which was the movement of African Americans from the South to other regions of the United States. New York, however, was anything but the "promised land." After a troubled childhood, including a stint in reform school, Brown put himself through high school and went on to attend Howard University, from which he graduated in 1965, and law school at Stanford and Rutgers. He wrote a second book, *The Children of Ham* (1976), as well as numerous articles.

45. *Manchild in the Promised Land* (1965): Autobiographical novel by Claude Brown. In the novel, Brown traced his rise from an impoverished childhood in violent Harlem. The text, was a departure from the works of James Baldwin and some of his other contemporaries. The novel was frequently challenged and often banned from schools and libraries between 1965 and 1975.

46. *Lewis Fenderson* [Dr. Lewis H. Fenderson, Jr.] (-1983): Poet, playwright, writer and scholar. Fenderson was a professor of English at Howard University who helped to found the journalism

department at Howard University. He was married to Lettie Austin. Fenderson received his Ph.D. from the University of Pittsburgh. His works include: *Thurgood Marshall: Fighter for Justice* (1969), *Many Shades of Black* (1969) and *Black Man in the U.S. and the Promise of America* (1970).

47. *Lois* [Lois Brooks] (1929-): Brooks is Morrison's older sister by a year and a half and her only surviving sibling. Morrison included Brooks in her novel *Tar Baby's* dedication.

48. Rachel Kadish (1969 -): Writer and teacher. Kadish instructs at the MFA program at Lesley University. She has received many awards and grants for her writing, including fellowships from the National Endowment for the Arts and Harvard/Radcliffe's Bunting Institute, as well as the John Gardner Fiction Award, a Pushcart Prize and a Koret award. Her work includes: *From a Sealed Room (1998), Tolstoy Lied: A Love Story (2006). She received her M.A. from New York University.*

49. *Flavigny, France*: Small, medieval village located in the Burgundy region of France.

50. *Langston Hughes* (1902-1967): Poet, novelist, playwright and short story writer. Hughes was a writer during the Harlem Renaissance and for decades after. Hughes won a number of awards for his work, including the Harmon Gold Medal, the Anisfield-Wolf Award, and the Guggenheim Fellowship. His works include *The Weary Blues* (1926), *Not Without Laughter* (1930), *Mule Bone* (1930), *The Ways of White Folks* (1934), *Shakespeare in Harlem* (1942), *Simple Speaks His Mind* (1950) and *Something in Common and Other Stories* (1963). His work has been translated into numerous languages. Hughes received an honorary degree from Howard University in 1960.

51. *Langston Hughes* poem. "Not What Was": "And the wild rose of the world/blooms to last so short a time/before its petals fall." The poem deals with life, death and art. First published in the *Massachusetts Review* in 1965.

Kathleen Kelly Marks

Kathleen Kelly Marks is Associate Professor of English in the College of Professional Studies at St. John's University in Queens, New York. She teaches courses on writing, world literature, and New York City, leads seminars on Toni Morrison, law and literature, and children's literature. She has published widely on Morrison's *Beloved*, including her book *Toni Morrison's Beloved and the Apotropaic Imagination*, and she is currently editing a collection of essays on the apotropaic, the set of rituals and gestures that avert evil. In her contribution to this volume, Marks uncovers the thread of melancholy in Morrison's first novel, *The Bluest Eye*, and shows how this "melancholy cast," as Morrison acknowledges, throws a "dark shadow" over the rest of Morrison's work. Through close readings that align *The Bluest Eye* with more traditionally melancholic genres — the pastoral elegy and the ode, for example — Marks meditates on the meaning of Morrison's darkness, the pockets of sadness and of introspection that infuse and inspire her work.

CHAPTER THIRTEEN

Melancholy and the Unyielding Earth
in *The Bluest Eye*

KATHLEEN KELLY MARKS

They tell me it is my melancholy;
did I infuse, did I drink in melancholy into my self?
It is my thoughtfulness; was I not made to think?

JOHN DONNE
Devotions upon Emergent Occasions

A little examination and much less melancholy
would have proved to us that our seeds were not the only ones
that did not sprout; nobody's did.

The Bluest Eye

I. *The Context of Melancholy*

Melancholy and Examination

The Bluest Eye is an under-appreciated container of a melancholy that casts its dark shadow over all of Toni Morrison's work.[1] Morrison tells us that her books have a "melancholy cast, because it's more important to make a reader long for something to work and to watch it fall apart, so that he will know what, why and how and what the dangers are, more important than to show him how they all solved their problems."[2] Melancholy has, of course, its own broad literary and psychological history. And, as Morrison mentions in one of her book reviews, it also has a social history in the African American experience.[3] However, it takes a central place in this, her first novel. It is timely and fitting then, after four decades of the artist's labor, as we glance backwards in assessment, that we look at her first work.

Just as we might tap into melancholy's power by reading Morrison's corpus retrospectively, Morrison evidently framed the issues of her first novel by looking into her own biography. Indeed, throughout the *Conversations*, Morrison talks about melancholy often, usually associating it with a retrospective perception after a loss — for example, her father's death, her own divorce. She describes this melancholic or depressed state as something of a release, a disengagement[4]: "I've said that I wrote *The Bluest Eye* after a period of depression, but the words 'lonely,' 'depressed,' 'melancholy' don't really mean the obvious. They simply represent a different state. It's an unbusy state. . . . I am very passive, like a vessel. When I'm in this state, I can hear things."[5] What she is describing is a type of leisure that attends mourning; it recalls Emily Dickinson's line, "After great pain, a formal feeling comes." Morrison observes, "It was that I was unengaged, and in that situation of disengagement with the day-to-day rush, something positive happened."[6] Like Dickinson, Morrison here connects melancholy with her formal craft as a writer.

Overlooked by critics and seen as flawed even by Morrison, *The Bluest Eye*'s very failure is part and parcel of the melancholy it explores.[7] For it is one of the novel's main insights that there is a fruitful melancholic stance as well as a destructive one, or to put it in terms closer to the novel's, there are both vincible and "invincible" melancholies. One leads to perception and insight, while the other leads ultimately to self-directed anger. The distinction between the two orders of melancholy is the degree of examination, inspection, and attendance to past events. From its two prefatory fragments before the "Autumn" section, to its unpaginated 1993 "Afterword," the novel enacts the re-casting and re-framing of which productive melancholy is capable.

The Grounding of Melancholy

Just as William Faulkner, a writer with whom Morrison is compared, "discovered that [his] own little postage stamp of native soil was worth writing about," Morrison draws on her home soil.[8] *The Bluest Eye* is set in Lorain, Ohio, Morrison's hometown: "for now it's the matrix for me."[9] The novel follows the horrors that befall Pecola Breedlove — her denigration and abuse at her family's hands, her rape by her father, the death of her premature baby, her eventual mental breakdown. The unremittingly dark plot is told through the eyes of Claudia and an omniscient narrator.[10] Central to the novel is a strange bargain that Claudia and her sister Frieda make on behalf of the pregnant Pecola: they plant marigold seeds (which they collect and sell), and if the seeds bloom, then Pecola's baby will live. The marigolds fail to grow, however, and the baby is born premature and dies. As Claudia sees much later, "[w]e had dropped our seeds in our own little plot of black dirt just as Pecola's father had dropped his seeds in his own plot of black dirt. Our innocence and faith were no more productive than his lust or despair."[11] Herein lies the conflict of finding something "productive" in such a bleak realm.

The Bluest Eye's plot therefore beholds black dirt, a postage stamp of soil; it is a story about black people who are considered dirty and nasty by whites, and more importantly, it is about the dirt within, about how Geraldine, a black girl from Mobile, can put Pecola out in the cold with the words, "You nasty little black bitch."[12] Claudia "gives us the dirt" on Pecola's violations, which almost systematically move ever inward until it is her own father who does the violating. If this story is a plot of black dirt, then it is not just private guilt that is being made public, but a widespread sickness — one that infects the very soil of this novel — that is being divulged. As Morrison writes,

> What, then, is the Big Secret about to be shared? The thing we (reader and I) are "in" on? A botanical aberration. Pollution, perhaps. A skip, perhaps, in the natural order of things: a September, an autumn, a fall without marigolds. When? in 1941, and since that is a momentous year (the beginning of World War II for the United States), the "fall" of 1941, has a "closet" innuendo. In the temperate zone where there is a season known as "fall" during which one expects marigolds to be at their peak . . . something grim is about to be divulged.[13]

In *The Bluest Eye*, war is the external pressure that affects an internal distress of soul. Yet the rape, the emphasis on soil and flowers, and the division of the novel into seasons might remind us of the rape and ritualistic sacrifice of the goddess Persephone,[14] the one who establishes seasons.

Claudia is the main narrator, a child whose memory gives shape to the story; she is the one who lends a Persephonic retrospection and unity to the novel. And yet, she also fails; she is hobbled (her name literally derived from Latin *claudus* —"lame" or "crippled")[15] and limited by a past that cannot be given to her whole, a past through which she has to break. Breakthroughs she has, but she doubts herself and participates in the very societal scapegoating and superficiality she seeks to go beneath. She therefore succeeds as a melancholic, as one who enacts limitation itself. The young Claudia, like Morrison, provides "a little examination and much less melancholy." Indeed, it is Claudia who tells us of the need for less of the melancholy and who also lets us know that we can, like her mother who survived "The Great Depression," recover our ground. It is Claudia's melancholic vision that allows for the Persephonic-underworld outlook that accounts for the novel's transfiguration from a World War II-like catalog of barbarity into a coherent tale of fruition. If in the years following the events of 1941 leading to Pecola's madness "what remains is Pecola and the unyielding earth,"[16] then Claudia is not a scene-stealer but a giver and protector of truths that perdure. Claudia plants the seeds of truth, and by the novel's end, it is still Pecola's enigmatic madness and the unyielding earth that remain.

II. Views of Melancholy

Much has been written about melancholy: Aristotle placed it in his theory of virtues, the ancient medic Galen named it one of the four humors, and most famously, Robert Burton anatomized it; others have commented on it—Kierkegaard, Nietzsche, Freud, Kristeva, just to name a few. It seems to have arisen in all eras, perhaps most fully with the hesitant disposition of Hamlet's soul, but it too can be raced or gendered. This *melan melas*, "black bile," has been seen as a mood, a temperament of artists, a fault like the deadly sin of sloth, and then a disease or a mental disorder. More recently, the sociologist Wolf Lepenies has tied it to societal boredom, and the critic Paul Gilroy has assigned it a political role—it is the expression of Britain's post-imperial confusedness of vocation. A common denominator seems to be that melancholy is a response to a perception of loss. Moreover, not only does melancholy occur when the world has become overwhelmingly sad or complicated, it is itself complicated; that is, there seems to be a duality to it, a positive melancholy and a negative one, what Freud would call *mourning* (positive, because one passes through to the other side of a terrible experience) and *melancholia* (negative, as it is a mental disorder that circumvents the process of working through a terrible experience).

Certainly the novel's setting, themes, time of writing, and publication history all demand sociological and political readings. However, I would like to read the novel's melancholy in dialogue with twentieth-century theologian

Roman Guardini's analysis of its meaning: "we are treating not a psychological or psychiatric situation, but a spiritual problem."[17] This problem is a spiritual response to the imperfection of the world, and in the context of *The Bluest Eye*, we might think of the duality of melancholy, how to break through from the stasis of violence to the transformative effects of melancholy. The "depression" that Toni Morrison tells us marked her life just prior to the writing of *The Bluest Eye* finds its artful fruition in the "melancholy" that pervades her first novel as minds, wombs, and even the earth suffer through their failure to yield and are affected by a pervasive sadness.

II. Melancholy Mentions in The Bluest Eye

A Thoughtful Melancholy

Claudia's is the first of the novel's four mentions of melancholy, and as we have seen, she connects it to the sickness that affects her entire community. In the third sentence of the italicized prologue, after revealing her awareness of the fact that no marigolds bloomed in Lorain, Ohio, in 1941, Claudia informs the reader that "*[a] little examination and much less melancholy would have proved to us that our seeds were not the only ones that did not sprout; nobody's did.*"[18] Situated between the Dick and Jane primer that signals the inaccessibility of perfection to this community, and the division of the novel into four parts entitled "Autumn," "Winter," "Summer," and "Spring," the italicized prologue establishes a kind of link of recollection between the piecemeal primer and the divided text. "Significantly," as Stephanie Li sees, the "first sentence does not directly mention the tragedy at the center of the novel, namely, Pecola's rape; rather the absence of the marigolds is the crucial secret, a natural aberration that the narrator then links to the story of Pecola."[19] What Claudia remembers is that the withholding that seemed at first so particular to her — the earth's refusal to allow the seeds she planted to sprout — was indeed the condition of all. Withholding is, in fact, one of the primary themes of *The Bluest Eye*. The prologue establishes an atmosphere of confession, even as it wants to withhold. Through the conspiratorial "Quiet as it's kept," Claudia breaks the silence about a story that has been kept quiet; she is giving up the secret and sharing it, but at the same time the "why" that wants to be answered can never be so fully resolved.[20] Thus, a tension between giving and withholding sustains the entire novel, since the story is not just about Pecola Breedlove, but is about the fact that "*there were no marigolds in the fall of 1941. . . . Not even the gardens fronting the lake showed marigolds that year,*"[21] and much can be gleaned from this.

In the context of the novel, surely, the earth is unyielding because it is sick; it has been plagued by the ideals of the primer, which are without nourishment, which of themselves are empty even for white people, and which for black people are isolating and deadly. The primer's main weakness is that it is a sterile double of a myth, the fruitlessness of which infects the entire community. Reminding us of tragedy in which even the ground is plagued, there is here a root sickness that has not been able to be warded off because the marigolds that keep back root parasites cannot grow. Likewise — and despite the efforts of Claudia and her sister to save the unborn child — the rape of a neighbor girl, Pecola, by her own father, Cholly, has deadening effects. Not unexpectedly, although Cholly's rape of his daughter conceives a child, it dies. Claudia's sacrifice to save the unborn baby that the community wished dead is key to unraveling the ways in which Morrison sees that melancholy can be fruitful, and certainly Claudia's last name suggests that she is not excluded from the pervasive sadness of the novel. But the soil fails, and the world of this novel, a world that Trudier Harris says is akin to that of T.S. Eliot's "The Waste Land,"[22] is marked by a kind of barrenness and infertility: "*the seeds shriveled and died*," along with Pecola's baby, Cholly, and "*our innocence too*."[23] What remains still requires examination.

For years, the girls lived with a wounding guilt, but because Claudia is able to come through the melancholy enough to examine a little more, she can see in retrospect, from the perspective of an adult, that there was something larger going on in the community. Thus, we can see that her efforts have in fact borne some fruit: a confessional, revelatory satisfaction that comes with knowing the truth. Indeed, Claudia's ability to break through things and analyze for examination is present even as a nine-year-old, sometime narrator of the novel: "I destroyed white baby dolls."[24] But the destruction was not the point. Claudia wished to find out what made them (and by extension white girls) so desirable; she dissects them. She says of herself that she had a kind of "disinterested violence," which as she grew she learned was repulsive and from which the "best hiding place was love."[25] Not a true love, but a "fraudulent love," and one that leads her to "worship" Shirley Temple and "delight in cleanliness" as the primer demands.[26]

Misconceived or misdirected love is a major theme of Morrison's whole corpus, and it begins here with a little black girl who is not invisible to herself and cannot understand how she is to others. Anne Anlin Cheng comments on this scene in terms of racial melancholy, in terms of the theme of black invisibility that is so prevalent in black literature:

> Morrison shows us that shame does not come from the child's own blackness per se (the debased value placed on her blackness made the child angry, as it should, revealing in fact quite a sense of self-possession) but rather from the

social message that there is no place for such anger and grief, which must go into hiding.[27]

Insofar as Claudia reflects Morrison herself, who says that through this novel, "I fell in love with myself, I reclaimed myself and the world,"[28] Claudia is also reclaiming herself and what she once knew — that even as she learned to love fraudulently, "the change was adjustment without improvement."[29]

Guardini writes that the melancholic is driven to "concealment and solitude" and that the "constant flight into concealment finds expression in the entire structure of his existence. It is an existence full of facades and masks."[30] For the typical melancholic, it becomes difficult to know and say what one really is or wants, and what is experienced is "unheard of, strange, fearful, perhaps ugly and they certainly have no place in the workaday world."[31] But in the upside-down world of Morrison, where things are doubled and inverted, the thing Claudia in her complicated melancholy conceals is love; she hides her real love behind a fraudulent one, masking the one with the other — the fact that Claudia loves a lost girl and her invisible baby, and that she loves what no one else finds lovable but *should*, is what is strange.

At the time, Claudia is also full of herself and her righteous anger, and she dares to love properly. Julia Kristeva says melancholy is a kind of corollary of the amatory state or the "somber lining of amatory passion."[32] Taking her cue from Freud, Kristeva describes a kind of "melancholy cannibalism" whereby one empathizes with a lost object and actually embeds it in the self.[33] Where this might lead one to the verge of schizoid fragmentation (and certainly we see the result of that kind of doubling of the self that occurs with the insane Pecola by the novel's end), it can also nourish the self and preserve the lost thing even if only in "fragmented, torn, cut up, swallowed, digested" form.[34] One internalizes and identifies with the lost object, but not without cost. The lost object is set up inside the ego, and a kind of compensation is effected. But there always remain feelings of ambivalence; love and hate (hate because the object has been taken away) are incorporated, hence expressions of self-depreciation or impoverishment of the ego often accompany melancholy. The result of *melancholia* is aggression of the self against the self, and an unacknowledged denigration of the lost object. Therefore, when Claudia is guilty, or when she gives in to the pressure to love fraudulently, or when she doubts her own actions, she is in danger of succumbing to a melancholy that she cannot work through. But Claudia has the strength to do something that might look like what everyone else is doing; though she loves and helps Pecola, her devoted sacrifice is to the unborn baby. That is, Claudia embeds into herself not the already lost Pecola but the still alive baby. So doing, I suggest, protects

Claudia from the most fatal aspects of melancholy and allows her to mourn, to "swallow" and "digest" food for continued thought and examination.

Though Claudia admits to having had more melancholy than was necessary, enough to keep her from examining thoroughly, the reader sees that she has been fortunate enough not to be overcome by the melancholy. Though poor and hard, Claudia's life was yet marked by love and memory, two things that ward off the sickness of melancholy taking hold in her. Once, when Claudia lies in bed with a rheumy cold, her mother rubs a vapor salve onto her chest to protect her against the sickness taking a real "holt."[35] Not just her mother's love, but also her stories, are protective. In the final division of the novel, entitled "Summer," love and memory in the form of her mother's stories dominate. Claudia describes the uncertainty of memory, the way her memory of summer becomes mixed with that of one of her mother's summer in 1929 — the year of the Great Depression. She says:

> I have only to break into the tightness of a strawberry, and I see summer —
> its dust and lowering skies. It remains for me a season of storms. The parched
> days and sticky nights are undistinguished in my mind, but the storms, the
> violent sudden storms both frightened and quenched me. But my memory is
> uncertain; I recall a summer storm in the town where we lived and imagine
> a summer my mother knew in 1929. . . . I see her. . . . One hand is on her hip;
> the other lolls about her thigh—waiting. . . . The anticipation and promise in
> her lolling hand are not altered by the holocaust. In the summer tornado of
> 1929, my mother's hand is unextinguished. She is strong, smiling, and relaxed
> while the world falls down about her.[36]

What Claudia takes and remembers of her past is the strength to weather storms and to confuse memories, even as she distinguishes between them. Her ability to connect the melancholy of her community to past depressions gives her a sense that "this too shall pass," as well as the power to shape this story — a power as important as the sacrifice she thinks fails. That particular summer of her mother's is not just a private experience; it is a matter of public record, not solely because Claudia reveals it, but because it was the summer of the Depression. She says, "So much for memory. Public fact becomes private reality, and the seasons of a Midwestern town become the *Moirae* of our small lives."[37] In other words, most either do not know or have forgotten about the summer of 1929. It is for them no matrix, no plot of dirt from which to divine meaning; it has been held at bay, perhaps too painful to be remembered for those who do not have mothers who weathered the storm and can pass on even fragments of the story. Claudia recognizes that the public fact has been reduced to a private reality that she alone is in the position to remember. The eternal springtime, which is forever disrupted by the rape of Pecola or its echo in Persephone or the national loss of innocence, and which constitutes differing seasons and thus the possibility of storms, is realized here in the year of the Depression, that time after the First World War when panic, sorrow, and dispiritedness began to settle into the American imagination. With this memory of her mother as able to weather storms, Claudia is herself able to resist the threat of an all-consuming melancholy.

An Angry Melancholy

A second mention of melancholy in *The Bluest Eye* plunges us into a fierce and discordant dwelling. It occurs in the first "Autumn" division of the novel and refers to the "abandoned store" that houses Pecola Breedlove and her family. It is an eyesore that does not "harmonize with the gray frame houses" that surround it.[38] "Rather, it foists itself on the eye of the passerby in a manner that is both irritating and melancholy."[39] The Breedloves are isolated by the "unique" ugliness of their home and, they believe, of themselves.[40] In fact, the novel's structure, from the very beginning, places Pecola on the edge of existence. The Dick and Jane primer describes what Pecola's family is precisely not. The rape of Pecola by her own father shares a weakness, however, with the white ideal of beauty as expressed in the primer; neither the ideal nor the rape succeeds in remembering the town of Lorain, Ohio, whose people move about on the "hem of life."[41] Whereas the rape has a context—at least something of a how and a why — Dick and Jane do not. Their story is without history; it is merely prescribed and flat. Consider the beginning of the primer that prefaces the description of the abandoned store: "Here is the house."[42] It is as if to say "Eureka, I have found it." Yet, there is no antecedent to this demonstrative sentence. No one in Lorain, Ohio, has misplaced the green-and-white house with a "red door," as the primer continues.[43] "Here is the house" strikes no familiar note of beholding what belongs to the poor black families of this novel.

The sentence wants to function mnemonically, as a kind of "objective correlative" to what already exists in the mind, but it cannot because there is no past for Dick and Jane and because there is no such reality for the people of Lorain. The failure of "Here is the house" to signify is echoed in the description of the Breedlove home. The description immediately and ironically throws the mind back to the primer as being itself without memory and substance. Only the memory of having had the real or imagined possibility of a green-and-white house could connect "Here is the house" with when and how it was lost and is now found. Only memory, notes Claudia, can connect a "penny" or "brooch" lost under the cushions of a sofa with the "place and time of the loss or the finding."[44] But, in the house of the Breedloves, "[t]here were no memories among those pieces. Certainly no memories to be cherished."[45] No one could say, "But I *had* it just a minute ago" or "Here it is."[46] By contrasting the idyllic green-and-white house to the very real "box of peeling gray,"[47] Morrison succeeds in exposing that the two houses are linked by a shared absence of memory. This melancholic lack countermands the encroaching effects of the white ideal of beauty that, again, is false in itself and inapplicable to the Lorain community. It keeps the already too-damaged Pecola Breedlove on the edge of the town, giving her a place while withholding from her the novel's center.

The righteous anger Claudia feels toward everything the primer proffers has already taken hold as a deep-seated anger in the head of this household without memory. Cholly Breedlove, in his very name, implies the inbreeding of a love that is angry. Cholly focuses the meaning of melancholy as the ill humor of early physiology that was one considered a secretion of the spleen and now of the liver. In fact, according to Galen, the belief in antiquity was that people with a darker complexion were most affected by the choleric disposition of melancholy.[48] The anger and aggression of the black man that finds its major expression in the rape of his daughter comes from a past of being abandoned and mistreated. Particularly, when Cholly and a young girl have a first love encounter and are come upon by white men who force them to continue in front of them, they begin to "simulate what had gone on before."[49] But Cholly "could do no more than make-believe."[50] While Cholly is protective of the girl and feels terrible, his feelings are mixed with hate, hatred of the white men and of his own lack of power to love or protect.

By the time Cholly is beating Pauline in the storefront house, a kind of impotence or joylessness has already taken root. The family orders a sofa, but it is delivered already damaged. In Cholly, it "provoked a physical reaction: an increase of acid irritation in the upper intestinal tract."[51] The sofa was new, and yet when it arrived the "fabric had split straight across the back."[52] The store refused to take responsibility, so the sofa had to be lived with and hated, hated because Cholly still had to pay $4.80 a month on a sofa he "couldn't take any joy in owning."[53] So, "the joylessness stank, pervading everything" and ultimately it "withheld the refreshment in a sleep slept on it."[54] We discover at the end of the novel, when Pecola imagines another self with whom to converse, that the couch was the site of a second rape, one in which she may have more willingly participated. Regardless, the splits in sofas and psyches had long been in the making. The sofa becomes a site of torn fabric, violation, economic exploitation, and joylessness.

That in Cholly that could make him pretend, make-believe, is part of the transference of his love for his wife into the rape of his daughter. If this novel is about black dirt or if, as Harris notes of *The Bluest Eye*, "[t]he tale is one in which the culture has been threatened from without as well as from within; it therefore takes on the form of myth,"[55] then certainly the rape calls to mind not only Persephone, who is stolen by a relative, but also the goddess mother Demeter, who in her grief withhold the earth's harvesting powers. As Robert Sardello observes, "Like Demeter grieving at the loss of Persephone, one is taken into depression."[56] Cholly is looking at Pecola, thinking about how she could ever love him, when she suddenly shifts her weight and raises her foot in the way Pauline had done so many years before, when he was young and "godlike" and brought her so much delight.[57] The pathos of the scene is that it shows a breaking, fracturing act that is the only thing that links each family member to the other. Like Hades's touch, Cholly Breedlove's "touch was fatal,"[58] but Pecola does not have a mother who can help her weather and negotiate the "gifts" of gods. And, indeed, as Morrison tells us of Cholly, "[b]y that time his embrace, the rape, is all the gift he has left."[59] Hence, "[t]he narrator explains that Cholly's final emotion toward Pecola is love. . . . The rape is thus a grossly misguided demonstration of love and an act of frustrated impotence."[60] Cholly might be said to have what was called by Sir Thomas Elyot in 1534 an "unnatural" melancholy, one that "proceedeth of the adustion of cholerike mixture, and is hoter and lighter, hauling in it violence to kill."[61] So, Cholly's angry melancholy—while providing a focus for Claudia, the other one in the novel who likes to break ("destroy") things but with a more fruitful result— engenders only the potential for life that never really had a chance and that "shriveled and died."[62] Both break into Pecola's womb: Cholly to engender the baby, Claudia to examine this hated black product of incest. But neither one's actions were the cause of Pecola's undoing. It is not merely because Cholly is the father of the baby that it dies, nor even because the entire community wishes it so; why it happens, the reader is not explicitly told. But this fruitless labor, the premature baby, like the sofa that still has to be paid off and like the eyesore of a house, is at a deeper level both irritating (from the Latin *ira*, "arousing anger") and melancholy.

An Extreme Melancholy

The third mention of melancholy is to be found in the section of the "Spring" division that is devoted to Pauline Breedlove's story and shows the fantastic sickness of melancholy. Pauline is a woman who stands in contrast to Claudia's mother and her ability to weather storms. In fact, "[c]hanges in weather began to affect her, as did certain sights and sounds. These feelings translated themselves to her in extreme melancholy."[63] Unlike Claudia's mother, Pauline has no hand on her hip. She does not smile with anticipation over and against a consciousness of the world's tendency toward de-creation and disintegration. Claudia depicts a Pauline who was always set apart and who believed her unworthiness to be a result of her "crooked, archless foot."[64] Lame (as echoed in *claudus*), Pauline was never fully grounded. Unlike Claudia's mother, who can reach out a "hand" of love to her, Pauline thinks that "the complete indifference with which a rusty nail was met when it punched clear through her foot saved [her] from total anonymity."[65] Though Cholly notices and loves her foot, their love begins to sour, and Pauline begins to fantasize and wait for someone "before whose glance her foot straightened and her eyes dropped."[66] Working for a white family, she thinks she can escape the dirtiness of her own. She begins to see movies, another escape from reality where she would get her superficial and fraudulent ideas about beauty and romantic love. Li notes that Pauline "jealously guards the joy of being part of this idyllic world, leaving her children to wallow in ugliness and the fear of a hopeless, despairing future."[67] It is when she is in such a fantastic state that the changes in weather begin to bother her. In "extreme melancholy" she "thought of the death of newborn things, lonely roads, and strangers who appear out of nowhere simply to hold one's hand, woods in which the sun was always setting."[68] Melancholy manifests itself in Pauline as a passive dejection and one that she seems to foist on to Pecola: "In none of her fantasies was she ever aggressive,"[69] but in reality she was mean and would pass her beatings onto Pecola as well. Reality for Pauline was tragic: once, while eating candy at the movies, a tooth came right out of her mouth. Like the sofa for Cholly, the loss of this tooth made her give up. She says, "*Everything went then. Look like I just didn't care no more after that.*"[70] In tragedies, it seems that the decay has already set in, so that when Pecola's baby dies, or the sofa splits, or the tooth falls out, they are merely symptoms of the more pervasive problem.

Unlike Claudia, whose memories can connect her to her mother (and therefore, the present with the past) and most importantly lead her to re-imagine and shape reality, each member of the Breedlove family lives in his or her own cell of consciousness. Melancholy, then, can spur the imagination or the unreality of fantasy. Julia Kristeva writes, "if loss, bereavement, and absence trigger the work of the imagination and nourish it permanently as much as they threaten and spoil it, it is also noteworthy that the work of art as fetish emerges when the activating sorrow has been repudiated."[71] If Claudia displayed more than a melancholic doubting of her work, and instead began to renounce it, she might fall prey to fetish. But Pauline can no longer recall the beginnings of her disconnection, and her idealized world has become the sole object of her devotion.

An Invincible Melancholy

It is perhaps because melancholy has become particularly advanced in the most damaged of the novel's women characters that neither Morrison nor Claudia can focus on Pecola, on her void of "unbeing and expose it."[72] An extreme, unrepresentative, and imagined victim of racially determined beauty, Morrison writes of her choice of Pecola as subject: "I focused . . . on how something as grotesque as the demonization of an entire race could take root inside the most delicate member of society: a child; the most vulnerable member; a female."[73] If a bit too much melancholy can prevent the proper examination needed and yet somehow through its sacrificial impulse can nourish the imagination as it does in Claudia; if melancholy, as it is for Cholly, can be a kind of anger that makes one's sacrifice be in itself wrong, but makes visible to the Claudias of the world what needs to be loved and examined; if melancholy in the extreme leads to the dwelling in a world not even of one's own making so much as a fraudulent world of someone else's making as it does for Pauline and even Pecola; then finally, for *The Bluest Eye*, melancholy is to be seen as something which can also be corrupting or "invincible."[74]

Already, the word "invincible" raises the specter of religion. One thinks of vincible and invincible ignorance, and that for which we as moral beings are culpable. The fourth and last mention of melancholy refers to the community's light-skinned West Indian "Reader, Advisor, and Interpreter of Dreams," called Soaphead Church.[75] When his Dantean "Beatrice," as he thinks of his wife, leaves him, he pursues the ministry but never really follows through. Velma "left him after only two months. She had a strong . . . affection and zest for life," and she "found his fastidious and complete lack of humor touching, and longed to introduce him to the idea of delight."[76] Soaphead, who loved cleanliness and himself above all, "resisted the introduction, but she married him anyway, only to discover that he was suffering from and enjoying an invincible melancholy."[77] The other kinds of melancholy we have discussed would seem, in Morrison's world, to be vincible, conquerable, or perhaps the sufferers are less culpable due to extenuating circumstances. But Soaphead's cannot be overcome or transfigured.

What Velma learns two months into the marriage is not that Soaphead is a melancholic, but just how important his melancholy is to him; when she recognizes that he was "very interested in altering her joy to a more academic gloom, that he equated lovemaking with communion and the Holy grail, she simply left."[78] So more than the kind of extreme or unnatural melancholy, Soaphead cultivates a kind of melancholy that is connected to authority and power not of the gods, but of God. He seems to suffer from an invited *accedia*, a kind of sadness that is almost sinful as it welcomes the "noon day devil" that sometimes comes unawares in the broad sunlight of delight. As a writer, Morrison has learned to bring melancholy "about without going through the actual event" of loss,[79] but it is something she then works her way out of though the writing. Soaphead does not wish to work his way out. He enjoys the devilish melancholy more than Velma; he has a chance to be saved, and though he never got over Velma's "desertion," he never sees that he is the deserter.[80] He rightly sees that she "was to have been the answer to his unstated, unarticulated question—where was the life to bar the encroaching non-life?"[81] But he does nothing to hold onto it. Because of his ability to see and examine, he is by degrees possessed of the most invincible melancholy in the novel. Where Claudia's response to the harshness of life is to give more of herself than she thought possible, to dig into the dirt, to get her hands dirty, to partake of life and even death as countermand to the encroaching non-life, Soaphead's response to his own harsh life is to withdraw from — and yet even lord over — creation and destruction. He rents a room from an old woman who has a dog whose runny eyes bother him. The primer preface to this "Spring" section that describes Soaphead is "SEETHEDOGBOWBOW."[82] Of course, it is Soaphead who is the dog not onlyfor bringing about the death of the sickly dog, but for contributing to the "unbeing" of Pecola's psyche.

Pecola has bought the white narrative of beauty, especially the fantasies as they have come to her though her mother, and she comes to Soaphead to request blue eyes so that she might be visible and even admired by herself and others. While he feels sorry for her (though only because he thinks she is right to wish for blue eyes), he can neither love nor hate, but can only use, and he tells her that if she feeds the dog some meat (which he has poisoned) and the dog reacts, her wish will have been granted. The dying dog then becomes the sign for the fraudulent dreams of a lost girl. Through the narration it becomes clear that Soaphead is a pedophile who holds himself back from molesting Pecola. He thinks of this as a virtue, when really it is his own attempt to be God-like. Within this novel, Soaphead's withholding is meaner than Cholly's rape; it's the kind of "thin love" that "ain't love at all" of *Beloved*.[83] Unlike Cholly's, Soaphead's is a desire to put himself first, and in his self-righteousness, he withholds himself for himself. Moreover, while Cholly's spirit is limited and damaged, he attempts to love, and "[w]ith all its might, melancholy goes after *eros* — the desire for love and for beauty."[84]

What we have always known of melancholy, from John Keats's "Ode" and beyond, is that the melancholic feels the transitoriness of life, the pressure of existence as bittersweet, as a wound, because of its lack of permanence. Melancholics feel the limits of reality. While this, as Guardini observes, "is a sign that the absolute exists,"[85] there is a "good" and an "evil" melancholy. Guardini notes that the good melancholy, as we see in Claudia — and even in Cholly's impulse that crosses the lines of love and allows Claudia to see where the examination should focus itself —"is made to bear fruit and to produce. From it proceed work and activity, as a result of which everything is transformed."[86] The evil melancholy can take over when the melancholic "does not possess the generosity of sacrifice, the daring of abandonment, the power of making a breakthrough."[87] But of course, the melancholic is always aware of not having achieved what he was after, of the lack of completion and perfection. If this takes hold, then the evil of despair and hopelessness and "failure takes definitive form."[88] Soaphead not only hides behind a fraudulent love, but he believes in it, uses it. He is like one of the self-centered souls in the hell of the Dante he professes to so admire. His melancholy is "invincible" because it is his; he cultivates it and "enjoys" it; he worships it as though it were a God in which he has embedded himself.

III. Melancholy Afterwords

The Fruits of Melancholy

In the infernal terrain that is *The Bluest Eye*, the desire for blue is the melancholic, erotic desire for love and beauty. The blues, or the sadness that pervades, provide the rich soil for Claudia to hide and protect the real love that can be then preserved for examination. That is, as one plagued by melancholy, Claudia's tale takes, as Karen Carmean says, the form of pastoral elegy. The novel is itself, then, a melancholic, funeral song that mourns the dead. On this level, it might appear to be a problematic novel, one that seems a mere inventory of brutishness.

Yet like John Donne, quoted above, Claudia *thinks through* her melancholy; she uses her eyes to examine, and she points out her own vulnerabilities, her own guilt. Something has been worked through, and melancholy is as much about the process of transformation and self-reclamation as it is about trying to answer "why." Claudia is an agent of poetic redress, and the conspiracy she lets us in on is "both held and withheld, exposed and sustained."[89] She alone confronts the novel's darkness, manifested finally in Pecola's madness and hallucination, which is both the result of her victimhood as well as a state of unbeing that continues beyond the scope of the novel; her conversation with her projected self has the sense of being outside the book. Linked to an unyielding quality of the earth, Pecola's madness is an unraveling that exposes yet hides her void of unbeing. Pecola seems to represent the extremity of a de-creative process, what the earth refuses to yield in the face of devastating loss. If Pecola's void is truly one of unbeing, of de-creation, then Claudia does well not to look at it directly, to withhold as much as she gives, to maintain a tension between being and unbeing. Yet, it has something to do with us. We can participate in de-creation, watch it, and define ourselves against it when we see it. As Claudia says, "All of our waste which we dumped on her and which she absorbed":[90] Claudia is willing to raise the ugly, even her own ugliness, in order to dissect and expose the emotional nexus of the void that is Pecola's unbeing and yet defend her state of unbeing as a significant phenomenon in itself, despite its causes.

Claudia participates in the structure of the novel when by her own presence, her own being, she de-centers Pecola's unbeing, rightly making it marginal or on the hem of her narrative. Claudia is the representative of life in this novel, and she bars the "encroaching non-life" of Soaphead Church. Moreover, she carries us as far as seeing that Pecola has now found, recalling the Oedipal warning, a permanent place on the edge: "She stepped over into madness, a madness which protected her from us."[91] But neither is Pecola fully satisfied and fully free from the world of degrees that would insist on comparisons and superlatives. It's not enough for her to have blue eyes; of course, it cannot be since it is a false desire born from a "racial self-loathing,"[92] but she wants to have the "bluest" eyes.

The singular *Eye* of the novel's title refers not so much to Pecola, but to the melancholic examination Morrison and Claudia undertake together that "pecks away at the gaze that condemned her."[93] If the melancholic Claudia ingested Pecola, she can never be fully swallowed: Smith says, "[T]he melancholic subject ingests the devalued object that can never be quite swallowed—never fully worked through."[94] If we remember that Morrison says her novels have a melancholy quality "because it's more important to make a reader long for something to work and to watch it fall apart, so that he will know what, why and how and what the dangers are, more important than to show him how they all solved their problems,"[95] we see that the examination is one for its own sake; it is the thoughtfulness and the turn of mind that provides continual fruitful insight into the ever-present problems of the human condition, and it is the countermand to the kind of self-indulgent sadness that does not reverberate with meaning. Morrison is drawn to the loss that is her subject matter, her plot of soil, her matrix, and the internalizing and analyzing of it leads to representation of absence, of loss that is difficult to examine, to hold the attention. Like Claudia, who thinks she fails Pecola by having planted the seeds "too deeply" to sprout,[96] Morrison is melancholy about how successful deep digging has been. In the "Afterword" written nearly twenty-five years after the publication of *The Bluest Eye*, Morrison notes that a new edition redresses the early dismissal of Pecola. Now, some forty years out, we recognize *The Bluest Eye* for insisting on honoring a "dismissed, trivialized, misread" girl as well as underlining the importance of the easily overlooked but essential thoughtfulness that is melancholy.

NOTES

1. I argue elsewhere that that *Beloved* (New York: Random House-Knopf, 1987), articulates most fully all of Toni Morrison's themes; melancholy is no exception, and is given some treatment in that context by Victoria L. Smith.
2. Danielle, Taylor-Gutherie. *Conversations with Toni Morrison.* (Jackson: University Press of Mississippi, 1994), 74.
3. Toni Morrison, *What Moves at the Margin: Selected Nonfiction*, ed. Carolyn C. Denard. IJackson: University Press of Mississippi, 2008), 50.
4. Even Toni Morrison's *Song of Solomon* (New York: Random House-Knopf, 1977), is marked by melancholy, and Morrison says "It's exactly what Guitar said: when you release all the shit, you can fly." See Taylor-Gutherie, *Conversations with Toni Morrison*, 168.
5. Taylor-Gutherie, *Conversations with Toni Morrison*, 167.
6. Ibid., 168.
7. "With few exceptions, the initial publication of *The Bluest Eye* was like Pecola's life: dismissed, trivialized, misread." See Toni Morrison, "Afterword," in *The Bluest Eye* (New York: Random House-Knopf, 1970 and 1994; repr. New York: Holt, Rinehart and Winston, 1993), 216.
8. William Faulkner, "The Art of Fiction No. 12," interview by Jean Stein, *The Paris Review* 12 (Spring 1956):.n.p., http://www.theparisreview.org/interviews/4954/the-art-of-fiction-no-12-william-faulkner.
9. Taylor-Gutherie, *Conversations with Toni Morrison*, 158.
10. In response to the question, "Why are your books so melancholy?" Morrison answers, "I write what I suppose could be called the tragic mode, in which there is some catharsis and revelation." See Taylor-Gutherie, *Conversations with Toni Morrison*, 125.
11. Morrison, *The Bluest Eye*, 3.
12. Ibid., 72.
13. Morrison, "Afterword," *The Bluest Eye*.
14. Elizabeth T. Hayes points out that *The Bluest Eye* is the clearest example of the African American image of Persephone.
15. One is reminded of course of the tragic figure Oedipus, as well as of Pauline's crooked foot.
16. Morrison, *The Bluest Eye*, 3.
17. Romano Guardini, "The Meaning of Melancholy," in *The Focus of Freedom*, trans. by Gregory Roettger Helicon. (Baltimore: Helicon, 1966), 55.
18. Morrison, *The Bluest Eye*, 3. The ways in which these seeds do not sprout, but do germinate in Claudia's mind as invisible potentialities calls to mind the *rationes seminales* of Augustine. The novel's first edition prints what I'm calling a "prologue" (not italicized, however) on its book jacket. Subsequent editions have graphic titles.
19. Stephanie Li, *Toni Morrison: A Biography* (Santa Barbara: Greenwood Biographies, 2010), 35.

20. Morrison, *The Bluest Eye*, 3.
21. Ibid.
22. Trudier Harris, *Fiction and Folklore: The Novels of Toni Morrison* (Knoxville: University of Tennessee Press, 1991), 28.
23. Morrison, *The Bluest Eye*, 3.
24. Ibid., 15.
25. Ibid., 16.
26. Ibid.
27. Anne Anlin Cheng, *The Melancholy of Race: Psychoanalysis, Assimilation, and Hidden Grief* (New York: Oxford University Press, 2001), 18.
28. Taylor-Gutherie, *Conversations with Toni Morrison*, 198.
29. Morrison, *The Bluest Eye*, 16.
30. Guardini, "The Meaning of Melancholy," 74, 77
31. Ibid., 78.
32. Julia Kristeva, *Black Sun* (New York: Columbia University Press, 1989), 5.
33. Ibid., 11.
34. Ibid., 12.
35. Morrison, *The Bluest Eye*, 7.
36. Ibid., 147.
37. Ibid.
38. Ibid., 24.
39. Ibid.
40. Ibid., 28.
41. Ibid., 11.
42. Ibid., 24.
43. Ibid.
44. Ibid., 25.
45. Ibid., 26
46. Ibid., 25-26
47. Ibid., 25.
48. Carol Falvo Heffernan, *The Melancholy Muse* (Pittsburgh: Duquesne University Press, 1995), 12.
49. Morrison, *The Bluest Eye*, 126.
50. Ibid., 116.
51. Ibid., 26.
52. Ibid.
53. Ibid.
54. Ibid., 27.
55. Harris, *Fiction and Folklore*, 16.
56. Robert Sardello, "The Landscape of Virginity," in *Images of the Untouched: Virginity in Psyche, Myth and Community*, eds. Joanne Trout and Gail Thomas (Dallas, TX: Spring Publications, 1982), 45.
57. Morrison, *The Bluest Eye*, 126.
58. Ibid., 163.
59. Taylor-Gutherie, *Conversations with Toni Morrison*, 164.
60. Li, *Toni Morrison*, 40.
61. Elyot qtd. in C. F. Heffernan, *The Melancholy Muse*, 22.
62. Morrison, *The Bluest Eye*, 3.
63. Ibid., 88.
64. Ibid., 86.
65. Ibid.
66. Ibid., 88.
67. Li, *Toni Morrison*, 39-40.
68. Morrison, *The Bluest Eye*, 88.
69. Ibid.
70. Ibid., 96.
71. Kristeva, *Black Sun*, 9.
72. Morrison, "Afterword," *The Bluest Eye*.

73. Ibid.
74. Morrison, *The Bluest Eye*, 134.
75. Ibid., 130-1
76. Ibid., 134.
77. Ibid.
78. Ibid., 135.
79. Taylor-Gutherie, *Conversations with Toni Morrison*, 168.
80. Morrison, *The Bluest Eye*, 135.
81. Ibid.
82. Ibid., 130.
83. Morrison, *Beloved*, 191.
84. Guardini, "The Meaning of Melancholy," 81.
85. Ibid., 84.
86. Ibid., 86.
87. Ibid.
88. Ibid.
89. Morrison, "Afterword," *The Bluest Eye*.
90. Morrison, *The Bluest Eye*, 163.
91. Ibid.
92. Morrison, "Afterword," *The Bluest Eye*.
93. Ibid.
94. Barbara Smith, "Toward a Black Feminist Criticism," in *But Some of Us Are Brave*, eds. Gloria T. Hull, Patricia Bell Scott and Barbara Smith (Old Westbury, NY: Feminist Press, 1982), 107.
95. Taylor-Gutherie, *Conversations with Toni Morrison*, 74.
96. Morrison, *The Bluest Eye*, 162.

Dustyn Martincich

Dustyn Martincich is Assistant Professor in the Department of Theatre and Dance at Bucknell University, where she specializes in jazz dance and performance. She has choreographed for the theatre, concert dance, and musical theatre stage, with an artistic base in Chicago. Martincich largely credits the study of Morrison for helping her to realize the connection between her love of narrative and movement, as well as Morrison's passionate dance with language. Her essay for this volume offers a study of Morrison's *Paradise* as speaking not simply through words, but through "movement, posture, and gesture." In considering the physical and sensual images invoked by Morrison's words alongside their own tangible and affective qualities, Martincich develops a reading of Morrison as a whole-body, sensory experience.

Co(n)ven(t): A Performance Study of Toni Morrison's *Paradise*

DUSTYN MARTINCICH

in this single moment of aching sadness . . .
we confirm, defer or lose our faith. Here in the tick tock
of this moment, in this place all our questions, all our fear,
our outrage, confusion, desolation seem to merge,
snatch away the earth and we feel as though we are falling.

TONI MORRISON[1]

As a long time reader of Toni Morrison's work, I have always thought of her words as dancing off the page. The felt qualities leap into action, inspiring dance artists like Bill T. Jones and Donald McKayle. Throughout her work, the interior complexities of the characters, how they experience pain, celebration, history, secrets, resolution, and community (especially privately) speaks to me through movement, posture, and gesture. The first time I read *Sula*, I was taken immediately by Sula's posture and the way she walks down the street; her commanding presence floats from the page as if she is entering a dance. In *Song of Solomon*, I see Milkman's journey of discovery contrasting in physical qualities of lightness and weightedness with the more he learns. I can hear a drumbeat pushing him forward. And in *Paradise*, when the Convent women come into town for the wedding or Connie gives new life to a dead boy, the characters transcend the page, writhing and swaying to their own, haunting music. The rich, purposeful symbolism contained in the settings these characters occupy gives purpose to their journeys — every turbulent road, hidden safehouse, tree-covered pathway. Morrison's narratives offer artists of various mediums the opportunity to open vivid and imagistic details, using her rhythmic language as a beat. The stories demand to be performed.

What follows is an account of Morrison's *Paradise* generated by the creation of *Co(n)ven(t)*, my recent choreographed work, performed by students in the Bucknell Dance Company on Bucknell University's Harvey Powers Theatre stage in December 2009. By applying interdisciplinary approaches to exploring *Paradise*, I could delve more deeply into Morrison's images and themes. I found myself focusing particularly on images of female archetypes in society in relation to personal identity and self-discovery and themes of community versus "outsideness."

Paradise, Morrison's third novel in the trilogy that includes *Beloved* and *Jazz*, focuses on the search for "paradise," the American dream, quintessential love, and freedom. In 1976, the all African American town of Ruby, Oklahoma, faces inevitable change, and the patriarchal leaders who clench onto tradition desperately resist it. Five women from separate lives meet at the Convent outside Ruby, a former embezzler's palace, turned missionary school for Arapaho girls, turned vacant haven for women. Connie, or Consolata, was an orphan taken from her homeland. A long-time resident of the Convent, she assimilates over time with the sisters, loses her cultural identity and her sight, and eventually sinks into depression when the Mother Superior dies. Mavis, abused physically and mentally by her husband, carries with her the haunting death of her infant twins, whom she accidentally murdered. Mavis's unintentional infanticide occurs in the context of her own abuse. Gigi, or Grace, is a rebellious, overtly sexual activist who thrives on inciting others to action, unable to find her own true happiness. Seneca, abandoned by her mother, is the child-like, hallowed soul who cuts herself in self-destruction. Pallas came from wealth, but after her mother and lover's betrayal, runs away and is raped by a gang of men. Her pregnancy is part of her denial of her loss.

These women, who have escaped various forms of abuse, pose a threat to the patriarchal powers of Ruby. Their outsideness connects them, and they journey to self-discovery and freedom from their past, toward self-acceptance and love. Their freedom from any authority or tradition symbolizes the chaos and uprising Ruby's leaders see happening in their "safe" town. To preserve tradition and bloodlines, to maintain order and control, and to assert their spiritual entitlement and righteousness, a gang of Ruby men hunts the Convent women like prey.

I. Co(n)ven(t): Pre-Production

In *Paradise*, as in so many of Morrison's novels, the characters' introductions to the reader occur through movement and gesture, and their journeys and pathways are part of that movement. When I could imagine the language as a dance, I found I understood the story, the characters, and Morrison's intention with greater depth. I was able to gain entry to a place beyond the words and actualize my imagination. Inspired and freed by these kinesthetic impulses, I focused my creative process on three aspects of the novel: first, the individual journey of each woman to the Convent (their process of remembering and coming into their definition of love and acceptance, and their convergence into their own, free community); second, the way the Convent women are perceived by the people of Ruby (both the aggressive males and sympathetic females); and third, the hunt scene that bookends the novel's plot.

The Convent women nomadically travel from outside paths. Each has experienced an ordeal that isolates her from the rest of society (rather, the rest of female society as viewed and constructed by men). The archetypes of mother, wife, virgin — the women of the Convent have failed in some way to achieve them. Arguably, the women of Ruby share this fear of failure as well, and that is what connects some of them to the Convent women. Despite physical and mental abuse, Convent women are free to move with their whole bodies (hearts, heads, and loins) into and out of the town and the Convent. They fight (Mavis and Gigi) and embrace (Seneca and Pallas) and dance seductively at weddings, "throwing their arms over their heads they do this and that and then the other . . . Just their own rocking bodies."[2] This movement and behavior defies the traditions and expectations of the women in Ruby. The intentions, secrets, pasts, and feelings of the Convent women are made clear through such freedom of movement.

Morrison titles each chapter for a woman from the Convent or town. In each chapter, she details each woman's background and journey while using other characters' points of view to isolate the Convent women and to amplify their outsideness. Most of the men, protective of their families' histories and afraid of losing control, use the Convent women's arrival and defiant presence as a scapegoat for the failures and flaws of Ruby and its people. Bolstering themselves with false but sure justifications, they define the women, riling themselves up for the hunt: "Bitches. More like witches... These here sluts out there by themselves never step foot in church . . . They don't need men and they don't need God."[3] They are "a travesty of what a woman should be,"[4] and their mere presence is assumed responsible for the abortions, miscarriages, infidelities, and disorder in Ruby. Because they are outsiders, do not abide by Ruby's historic code, and do not need men, god, or others, the Convent women become the enemies of Ruby's men, giving solid form to the ongoing disruption of the Ruby way of life.

With Morrison's attention to the women outside the Convent, the representation of these outside female voices became crucial in my conception of the dance piece. Lone and Patricia's chapters offer the reader information about Ruby's history and treatment of outsiders, especially women. Though residents of the town, Patricia and Lone's lack of pure 8-Rock blood have cast them out of the male leaders' graces, Patricia's light-skinned mother and tumultuous relationship with her daughter and Lone's orphaned upbringing and magical midwifery connection to birth and death exclude both from "acceptable" Ruby society.

Other townswomen have had connections with the Convent and the Convent women, travelling and walking there in their time of need. "Back and forth, back and forth: crying women, staring women, scowling, lip-biting women or women just plain lost."[5] For example, there is Soane's connection with Connie. Initially, Soane visits the Convent to confront Connie about her affair with Deacon, Soane's husband. Then, after Lone guides Connie to her gift of "insight," Connie resurrects Soane's son, Scout, after he is killed in a car accident. Arnette, KD's wife-to-be, arrives at the Convent, despite KD's affair with Gigi, to await her baby's birth after her attempted abortion. Billie Delia finds refuge at the Convent after the fight with her mother, Patricia. Trying to make sense of the Convent women, Soane says, "[T]hese are women . . . Just women." Her sister, Dovey, opposes her, saying they are "whores, though, and strange too."[6] The sisters' relationship epitomizes the dilemma of the townswomen; they desire to be part of and yet are restricted within the patriarchal society of Ruby.

My creation of this dance work was conceived as a result of my longtime fascination with the novel's hunt scene. Morrison offers the reader the climax of her narrative right at the opening of the novel without identifying the women by name or race. Instead, she establishes the distinct contrast between the men and women of Ruby and the threat the Convent women pose in the eyes of the dominant patriarchal tradition. During the hunt, the men stalk slowly into the Convent, armed. They take in each detail of the structure, deeming everything they see as proof of the women's evil. This forced entry, this stalking, inspires *Co(n)ven(t)*'s main source of movement energy: the outsider/female energy in the physical space, contrasted by the insider/male energies, which are heavy, destructive, but not openly explicit and visible to an audience.

In addition to drawing thematic ideas from the text and various critical resources, I focused on certain compositional tools in dance that link the text to the movement: gestural and repetitive movement vocabulary, specific attention to Morrison's rhythmic language and imagery to inform the dynamic flow and creation of movement, and distinct crossing pathways in space. Repetition proved a useful tool in choreographing movement phrases reflecting the multiple versions of the same narrative each woman in the Convent experienced: abuse, journey, and acceptance. The repetition of gestural poses developed from feminine archetypical images (mother, goddess, warrior), and images of nature from Morrison's text (does, mares, birds, etc.) unified the women in the space as well, even if the phrases were not performed in unison. The break in repetition of movement vocabulary came in each woman's acceptance of herself; structurally, I knew that the movement must change from the initial movement themes. This break would signify that break in the women's cyclical lifestyles. As the piece progresses, underlying hints of previous movement exist, especially for the townswomen, who are still tied to Ruby's past. Shared or repeated phrases between Convent women and townswomen connect the characters subliminally in a shared experience.

I defined as a primary task the work of translating the rhythm of Morrison's language directly into the movement. As a jazz dance specialist, the relationship between rhythm and movement is, for me, pinnacle, so the rhythm of the language — the accents and cadence — lends to the transition to movement. The soft, sumptuous sounding "bodacious black Eves" becomes a torso undulating and beating forward with each "b" and smoothing out into a long "e."[7] The repetition followed by the verbs of action in the quotations that begins this essay —"all our questions, all our fear, our outrage, confusion, desolation seem to merge, snatch away"— these rhythms are distinct and lead the body, often in repetition. For the dance piece, I allowed both the rhythms of the music and the cadence of the text to inspire the movement vocabulary.

As the piece developed, the textual rhythms guided the dancers as breathing would when the drumbeats and rhythms faded away.

Spatially, the idea of "coming to a crossroad" serves to define the histories of the Convent women and the town of Ruby. All characters have known nomadic wandering, either directly or indirectly through their ancestors, and have found refuge at the crossroads of Ruby. The choice in direction — for Mavis to escape her family, for Seneca to carve lines on her body, for the townswomen to act in pursuit of the male hunters — pushes the narrative forward. The Convent women's meeting, their convergence at the crossroads of Ruby, in Oklahoma, at the Convent, from all across the United States, provided a strong image that informed the initial structure of the dance work. In the dance piece, the women enter the space individually, and their indirect paths cross. They may stop abruptly, leave and return again, but their paths meet in the space. It is the convergence, the center of the crossroads, that leads them on their journey of self-discovery.

One of the foci in my academic work is researching movement and performance — bringing movement to actors, and acting to dancers — so I wanted to incorporate character study into the movement vocabulary of *Co(n)ven(t)*. To prepare for this piece, I dove into various critical readings of *Paradise* but mostly concentrated on Morrison's text itself. I highlighted excerpts and images from *Paradise* that would not only prove useful for the creation of the piece compositionally, but for the dancers to employ in developing an understanding of the women they were to portray. Seven dancers were cast from a limited pool in the Bucknell Dance Company, and each played the role of a Convent woman and two symbolic townswomen (who at times took on the role of Lone and Patricia, as well as the characters Soane and Dovey). I shared excerpts of the novel and my focus themes with the dancers, all of whom came from a variety of interests and backgrounds, none of whom were initially familiar with Morrison's work.

A dancer's process typically consists of learning movement from a choreographer and then performing it. In my process, I requested extra time and consideration from the dancers regarding *how* to perform the piece, to which they eventually adapted with gusto. The narrative of *Paradise* provided the dancers with a solid foundation, and with useful acting exercises (such as identifying objectives in terms of verbs, solidifying intentions, and uncovering given circumstances of each character), the dancers had the opportunity to *perform* these Morrison women, as well as to enact her language. In reading about and studying the Convent women and townswomen, the dancers and I chose active verbs that connected them to the motivations of their characters on their journey. Through this exercise, the dancers began to understand that, though the women of *Paradise* share in the journey, each was unique from one another. Mavis would use words like escape and (un)settle. Gigi instigates and tempts. Seneca mediates and consoles. Connie retreats and saves. Pallas denies and delivers. All of the women wander, withstand, and rebel. And eventually, they reveal, discover, and accept. The townswomen characters, though separate from the Convent women, conveyed feelings of outsideness and the verbs of searching and withstanding.

II. Co(n)ven(t): Movement Narrative

Co(n)ven(t) is structured in a rising climactic arc. This design provides a sense of order to the chronology of events. The first half of the piece deals with the personal journey of each woman to the Convent. The architecture of the Convent — with its illicit and religious connections inside — extends beyond fraudulent revelry or Biblical salvation. Women journey to the Convent in search of *something*. The women enter the space one at a time — Connie, Mavis, Gigi, Seneca, then Pallas. They approach the Convent alone; they wander in looking lost, focusing anywhere but straight ahead. Hands push to the side, arms reach, torsos writhe, sway, and contract away from an invisible, but oppressive, source. Each woman performs her own gesture and movement quality. Connie moves her hands up her newly discovered body, reaches out to a lost love, and looks up for spiritual guidance. Mavis runs into Connie's arms, as if she has just escaped. She quickly turns from one side to another, as if she hears the cries of Merle and Pearl. Gigi struts into the scene, sensuous and powerful. She bucks, but she melts when she is touched by Connie. Seneca wanders indirectly into the light, and retreats back, recessed from the action. Pallas's gesture appears to brush off any person or truth.

The non-unison movement emphasizes each Convent woman's unique personal struggles. Collectively, the women may retreat, and they may fall into and push against each other, but any resistance is without a solid connection. They move independently through a seemingly confined space. As the music grows, a sadly plucking violin reaches into a more melancholic and daunting, repetitive heaving. The women continue their journey, picking up aspects and gestures of each other's movement symbolizing that they are all composed of every female archetype — a gesture for motherhood: the hands graze the belly; a gesture for the goddess: long neck arched back and to the side; a gesture for a child: stretching out, and contracting back into a tight, fetal-like position. Each in her own world, but the Convent itself becomes more defined: an outline of a closed window appears behind them.

The townswomen, with two dancers representing Lone and Patricia as well as the sisters Soane and Dovey, keep their distance. Their movement is inspired by more traditional feminine images and gestures. They are rigid, but gentle. They enter in strength and unison, almost as one figure, remaining on the outskirts of action. They enter directly and glide with slight resistance, as if they are being forced down into the ground. They break through in beautiful, feminine poses, showing their long, strong legs, pushing their arms slowly, without anger, but with a hint of sadness. They break their unison movement into a canon, echoing one another's form.

Connie begins to move apart from the women, dealing with her own crisis of lost love, faith, and identity. In the piece, she diminishes in the background as the women take refuge. It is only her insight, her ascension and ultimatum that brings them structure and order and sets them on the direct path to revelation. Connie is the only one with the power to touch each of them. She leads the collective in new movement as it repeats in canon. Only then is the weight of actual human contact felt. The unveiling of blind eyes and the shedding of the former, bound self in movement and costume leads to acceptance and freedom. The women look out, pushing against, breaking through and retreating from invisible forces. Each of the women, with Connie's help, delves into the process of remembering, of uncovering her identity. The movement becomes stronger, somewhat lighter, and grows into unison. They fall in line, in formation, like a flock.

Morrison's language changes in the passages describing the women drawing on the floor, cooking, and dancing in the rain. The rhythm and pace are fluid and calm. The women lose their names—they "were no longer haunted."[8] Drawing on Morrison's new rhythm, the women usher their competing narratives into one, creating unison movement and signifying the moment of their peace and revelation. At this point in the piece, there is a circling in the music, a cyclical ease, followed by the sounds of a storm. The movement has completely broken from the earlier phrases and breaks from the initial repetition. Though the accompanying music is circling, the women nest together, following Connie directly, cleansed or baptized by the storm, celebrating in dance together with nature. Though they have found their peace, the music indicates a foreboding presence, an imposing sign of danger to come.

The second half of the piece begins abruptly with the call of drums. The burst, the interruption of the solace by outside forces, breaks open the group of women. A townswoman, Lone, rushes onto the scene. She is making the warning call to the remaining townspeople; she gracefully controls her momentum, but her quick and divergent pathways signal panic. As she continues in the space, she loses control, especially in her torso, as her heart goes out to the Convent women. Seneca reenters the space, the first to greet the danger. Her movement glides at first, and then violently darts vertically in the space before crashing to the ground. She is small and looks as though she has been picked up and thrown through the space. This section continues to clip quickly from the town to the Convent, with abrupt overlapping entrances and exits. Dancers run at full speed into and out of the space relaying anxiety and fear of the hunt.

The Convent women, "scattering like fowl,"[9] are blown apart in the space; Pallas, Mavis, and Gigi form a trio in the game room and tumble out into the field. They are strong, their movements like those of hawks, wings spread, claws bared. Connie dashes on her own, a sadness harkening from the first section. She finds Seneca collapsed in the space. Their movement slows for just a moment into a duet about connection, help, and female protection. The women take turns throwing themselves on each other. The townswomen arrive. Their movement pathways completely oppose one another, until they circle, gather strength, and push through the space urgently. The women meet for just a moment again, unified. Visually, they bond through the enactment of the female warrior archetype as they gather strength to fight, until the last shot is fired.

With a final drum hit, the Convent women fall into darkness. Upstage, the townswomen have arrived in time to see Connie's shooting. As the wind whips in the musical score, the sisters are slowly being separated, walking away from each other. The lack of beat, the lack of clear rhythm symbolizes an irreparable tear between the sisters, Soane and Dovey, and the town as a whole. The women are meant to go in different directions, and their pathways cease to cross. As the outline of an *open* window appears, a gravelly female voice is heard in the distance, singing "I got a new world in my view," sounding as if she is freeing herself from a basement of shackles. The sisters fade upstage as the silhouettes of moving forms on the ground appear. A new solid beat ushers the women to life again, standing, pushing, facing, shrugging off, opening up to . . . something. The Convent women inch forward and upward, climbing to their feet. Their movement is pedestrian, careful and direct. Their focus, for the first time, is forward — they peer into the audience and off into the distance. As the light fades to close, the Convent women continue moving forward, with insight.

III. Co(n)ven(t): Artistic Collaboration

When the Co(n)ven(t): left rehearsal and went into production, Morrison's language really came to life. Adding the artistic contributions of Paula Davis and Bre Eckley in costuming and Heath Hansum in lighting and sound, the characters, the Convent, and the emotional intention of each movement section coalesced. Without these additions, the piece would not have been able to signify Morrison's novel. In production meetings, I shared my research with my artistic collaborators, and we discussed what the piece needed visually to bring this adaptation of Morrison's narrative to life on stage.

The women's costumes were unified in pattern and period but had individual necklines, all within the 1970s fashion. The women were also distinguished by costume color: Convent women appeared in red and Ruby women wore blue. Lace applications, borrowed from antique nightgowns, added a general symbol of femininity (implied through the symbolic associations of lace), but not in ways that would be oppressive or overly dainty. The Convent women's dresses were designed uniquely for each character — Connie wore an apron; Mavis, a smart jacket; Gigi, a shorter skirt and belt; Seneca, a young girl's jumper; and Pallas, a belted maternity dress. The women removed these initial identifying restrictions on their costumes once Connie led them to self-discovery. The dresses then began to flow, offering no specific feminine shape to any woman. This generic quality allowed for the Convent women to become visually connected without actually shaving their heads, as they had in the novel. The Ruby women, in contrast, did not change in appearance. Their lace reached high on their necks and the cuts of their dresses were traditional and conservative, fitted through the bodice and flowing down to the knee.

Music, from artists Nick Cave,[10] Rusted Root,[11] and King Britt,[12] provided emotional ambience. However, it was Heath Hansum's sound design that completed the entry into aspects of Morrison's world; it connected the narrative to the choreography and the emotional qualities of the story to the set. Hansum and I envisioned the initial journey of a women as akin to a storm brewing, in anticipation of the hunt. He arranged the perfect sound of rumbling and refreshing rain that connected easily with the fading circularity of the Cave soundtrack. Within the momentary peacefulness and calming thunder, danger still lingered, and then BOOM! Drums! Hansum's design seamlessly drew the scenes together. The drums ended as abruptly as they began, and the sound of wind swept the stage, evoking the fields of Oklahoma. The wind pulled the townswomen apart. The gravely sounding spiritual seemed to sing through the wind, while the wild Western twang carried the Convent women to their feet, to the end, a ghostly echo fading in their new futures.

Like the score, Hansum's expert lighting created the haunting, oppressive environment that extended beyond the walls of the Convent. Silhouettes and shadows isolated the dancers from themselves and each other and created the outside forces that could be sensed, though undisclosed to the women. The lighting helped direct the audience's sensory attention to emotional transitions: from loss and sadness to acceptance and love, fear, anxiety, and finally insight. Cool colors isolated the women and gave the feeling of wandering lost, being confined to an indoor darkness. Hansum added blues and purples with more intensity directly on the Convent women as they transitioned, and found themselves in the basement tracing their bodies.

As the hunt begins, the stage is swept in amber and reds, starkly contrasting any sense of magic. The stage feels open and vulnerable, like a body full of life and blood. When the music ends, the lights change abruptly as the sisters move in on a pathway upstage. The Convent women, though still in the space, are in complete darkness on the floor. Hansum's lights turn to a surreal shade again as the Convent women arise, suggesting an out-of-body yet magically realistic experience and transformation. The lights, music, and wind fade; the women push to the end of the stage. They look as if they are floating, releasing themselves out of their world.

In *Paradise*, the aftermath of the hunt and what appears to be the murder of the Convent women lead the townspeople to debate what they have seen and understood in and outside the Convent. Hansum added a window gobo (a lighting instrument that creates a pattern in the space) to help create the ambiguity of that element of the setting. This image of a window with crossbars hinted also at religious symbolism without becoming a blatant crucifix. It also helped to reinforce and echo the various crossroads of *Paradise*. The window gave the projected confinement when it was closed in the earlier sections of the piece, making the women appear to stand inside or outside of a physical structure. With the return of the window — this time partially open — the repetition of the image helped inform the audience of the roots of the original location and the characters' emotional states.

But clearly, something has changed. There is a sense of freedom, but uncertainty. There is a link created between an outside and an inside world, between which life passes. The final image suggests the women's resurrection, or perhaps the transition of their spirits into another realm.

IV. Co(n)ven(t): Post-production

Creating a kinesthetic critical response to *Paradise* gave me a new understanding of Morrison's novel. It brought me to new questions and revelations, especially about the novel's ambiguous ending. At the beginning of the Save-Marie chapter, I found a possible thesis of the novel — and of this piece. Through the rehearsal process, the dancers and I shared feelings about giving into the earth, being chased and moving so fast that we stopped thinking about movement and gave into the momentum, trusting that the earth will catch us. In those moments, we agreed that there is a feeling of surrender — to our instincts and to the narrative's rhythmic direction. In those moments where we feel like we are falling, there is an opening to a more instinctual way of being, and we have no choice but to trust in our innate identities. The acceptance of change and love involves time, faith, action, and oftentimes a giving up of control — the freedom of falling. The Convent women experience this in the ending of the novel. The women move out of someone else's construction of paradise — something that is controlled, isolated, and defined by few — and freefall, disappearing into their own paradise. This revelation helped me find the ending of the piece and transformed how I interpreted the culmination of the novel.

The dancers and I strived to engage in an open process of widening the creative possibilities of dance, performance, and literature. Like so many dancers, their initial focus was on the aesthetic form of the movement and structure of the choreography. I checked in with the dancers as we progressed in rehearsals and often held one-on-one rehearsals with each dancer to help her delve into her character. I learned so much about each of the characters by working with them. Katelyn Tsukada, an environmental studies major and a dancer with acting training, is a great example. She took on the role of Connie. We worked on connecting her with Connie's narrative by imagining the various phases of Connie's journey in the novel — from her arrival at the Convent as a young girl, to the loss of Mother Superior, to the affair with Deacon, to the retreat to the basement, to the insight that she used to save herself and the women. I shared with her how and why I created specific movements and gestures for Connie, and she shared with me instances when the movement felt authentically connected with Connie's intentions and when it felt like movement for movement's sake.

Through this process of identification, Katelyn was able to enter Connie's experience and spoke about how she desperately wanted to help the other women, to touch them. This conversation was a revelation in the reading of Connie's character for me. I previously read Connie as moving from hopeless to empowered, but scared and slightly frustrated by the responsibility that came with her gift of insight. After speaking with Katelyn, my reading of her changed, and Connie moved from being a reluctant savior archetype to the archetypes of a teacher and a goddess. As someone with her own intuitions, dreams, and pathways, she guides the women to join her, not to rule or save them. I would not have taken this reading if it had not been for the work on Co(n)ven(t) and with Katelyn.

With the opportunity to work with students at a liberal arts institution, I embrace the possibilities of interdisciplinary pedagogies to not only inform the creation of the dance work, but to extend connections to other areas of study in my students' lives and in their own self-reflection. Working with a novel like *Paradise* gave me the opportunity to open discussions about race, gender, tradition, and identity with the dancers. These are difficult, sometimes sensitive, ideas to explore with students. Most of the dancers came from similar backgrounds (eighteen- to twenty-one-year-old female, white, New Englanders), so it proved useful to take some time to connect to the reality of the rich history Morrison offers. We started in on questions like: What was happening in the U.S. in 1976? Why did the band of "8-rock" families find themselves in the middle of Oklahoma? With only a few weeks of rehearsals, the dancers found themselves overwhelmed with the amount of new information given to them (acting techniques, movement vocabulary, spatial relationships, and excerpts from the text). I found the piece had to focus on a particular theme that we could explore in depth together—this theme became feminine outsideness. And I allowed that connection to inform the piece as we progressed in the process, concentrating the movement vocabulary to reflect the female bond. By focusing on one theme, we could not explore as in depth other significant ideas of race, tradition, religion, and the danger when one is not open to change. Retrospectively, I would have asked the students what they had learned about themselves and the way they viewed the world after this process.

As an artist, but most importantly as an educator, I believe in the power and functionality of interdisciplinary education in a liberal arts environment. While I applaud the efforts of the arts and curriculum strategies at the elementary and high school levels, the benefits of integrating multiple teaching perspectives and disciplines at the university level is necessary in order to help students achieve a more holistic and deeper understanding of various art forms. Ray Bradbury's work can inspire Elton John's "Rocket Man"; Billy Joel's repertoire can inspire Twyla Tharp's "Movin' Out"; scripture can inspire countless religious paintings: art so often thrives on other art. And in the educational system, we can look to deepen our appreciation and understanding of art through other artistic mediums. I found the process of interdisciplinary "translation" valuable, particularly in regard to the implications such cross-pollination could have in a classroom, in performing a narrative, in exploring the deeper textual concepts kinesthetically. For me, the translation itself is an art all its own.

Morrison's writing lends perfectly to interdisciplinary study because it is so rich and complex. The histories are real. The issues never feel removed from the reader, and for me, the characters have not quite left me after the narrative ends on the page. Morrison offers a way to discuss the many aspects of tradition, gender, and identity, with and without race through her narratives in *Paradise*. To have the opportunity to introduce movement into a discussion of these themes and ideas is a way to open the work to myself as a choreographer, to the dancers, and to the audience. And the characters, the Convent women, live on.

NOTES

1. Toni Morrison, *Paradise* (New York: Random House-Knopf, 1998; repr., New York: Penguin-Plume, 1999), 295.
2. Ibid, 157.
3. Ibid., 276.
4. Ibid., 280.
5. Ibid., 270.
6. Ibid., 288.
7. Ibid., 18.
8. Ibid., 266.
9. Ibid., 286.
10. Nick Cave and Warren Ellis. "Moving On," *The Assassination of Jesse James by the Coward Robert Ford*, soundtrack, Mute Records Limited, 2007.
11. Rusted Root, "Drum Trip," *When I Woke*, compact disk, UMG Recordings 1994.
12. King Britt, "New World in My View," *King Britt Presents: Sister Gertrude Morgan*, compact disc, Ropeadope LLC, 2005.

Susan Mayberry

Susan Neal Mayberry is Gertz Professor of English at Alfred University, where she teaches and writes on early modern literature, literature of the American South, African American literature, Women's Studies, and Toni Morrison. She has published numerous articles on Toni Morrison's novels, and her book on the masculine and Morrison, *Can't I Love What I Criticize?* was nominated for the 2008 South Atlantic Modern Language Association Studies Award and received the 2009 Outstanding Book Award from Denmark's Organization for the Study of Communication, Language, and Gender. She is presently at work on a multidisciplinary project, *Thoroughly Modern, Theatrically Classical Dames*. In her essay in this volume, she explores the relationship between food, racial identity, and an emerging modernism in Morrison's texts. Theoretically provocative and insightfully composed, Mayberry's essay finds in *Tar Baby* the tenuous, and indeed vexed, relationship between what we consume and what consumes us.

Guess Who's Coming to Dinner?:[1]
Food, Race, and [En]countering the Modern in Toni Morrison's *Tar Baby*

SUSAN MAYBERRY

If literary modernism implies a dense and unordered actuality as opposed to the systematic, an historical discontinuity, and an ensuing sense of loss and despair, it can also celebrate an experimental imagination that insists on containing its general frame of reference within itself to counter alienation. It offers the possibility of creating a new world in the act of perceiving it. Tracking the evolution of self, what Toni Morrison poses as "absolutely . . . the first of the modern questions," Morrison's milieu substantiates these suppositions: "The fact is, Black people were the first modernists," she claims. "As far back as the 18th century they were dealing with problems of work, family, separation long before anyone else."[1] Putting her money where her mouth is, Morrison employs in *Tar Baby* (1981) the simple trope of food to address complex modern philosophical dilemmas about conditions of knowledge, cultural hybridity, rejection of fabricated history, and uncertainty of language.[2] Its isolated, colonized Caribbean setting invites heated discussion about the intricacies of Empire that interweave with modernity, elevating the individual and the inward over the social and the outward. Ways in which Morrison's characters approach appetite, food, and eating redefine race, class, and gender constructions against and within the context of a modernism that questions traditional values and assumptions and the rhetoric by which they were sanctioned and communicated.

Tar Baby's narrative structure reflects a modernist unordered actuality and forecasts the postmodern disorder prevalent in *Beloved* and subsequent novels. Morrison specifically points up the willful innocence of controlling Valerian Street in his refusal to read encoded modern fiction like *Tar Baby*, opting instead for the literal language of seed catalogs: "He read only mail these days having given up books because the language in them had changed so much — stained with rivulets of disorder and meaninglessness."[3] Close readers clearly track the narrative thrust of the novel, however, which leads to the white patriarch's painful self-knowledge, by examining its allusions to the fruits of those seeds.

In essence, a story of [en]countering colonization subverts myths about American racial constructions through its references to food. As it depicts the first dinner at which all the inhabitants of L'Arbe de la Croix are present even in their absence, the opening scene of Chapter 3 codifies some of *Tar Baby*'s significant connections among food, identity, and a reconstituted Modern.[4] Inspired by the oppressiveness of the maiden aunt fog reflecting the novel's concerns with colonialism, civilization versus wilderness, and eco-terrorism, each eating posture reveals attitudes towards race, class, and gender. Indulgent Valerian jollies along a frowning Margaret by critiquing her dining habits; Jadine depends on a delicate soufflé to moderate tension between her patron and the wife he worships; Sydney needs no eye contact to anticipate every appetite; Ondine stays in the kitchen to cook one meal for the Streets and another for the Childs; and Gideon and Thérèse stay out of the kitchen to occupy the yard and washhouse. Everything at L'Arbe de la Croix waits for and weighs upon the arrival of Son, savior/"nigger in the woodpile" whose disruptive presence at a recent last supper will upset everybody's fruit basket.[5]

The picture of an ultra-civilized, urban[e] dinner-for-three on a hot, remote, third-world island, coolly presided over by a wealthy scion of hard-working immigrants named by his hearty German uncles for a forgotten Roman emperor, skillfully prepared by an absent Black woman "doing something difficult but useful in peace," served beautifully by a "Phil-a-delphia Negro mentioned in the book of the very same name," and totally overwhelmed by unnamed but nonetheless stifling maiden aunt fog virtually encapsulates the tragicomic contradictions of Morrison's Modernism.[6] When juxtaposed against Margaret Street's human counterpart Buffalo great-aunts, whose saffron tresses have also turned wispy garlic white, the maiden aunt fog "literally, literally" implies a dense actuality combined with historical discontinuity. But their swirling hair goes "unnoticed until masses of it gathered around the house and threw back one's own reflection from the windows."[7]

Like an inversion of his equally controlling, more upscale alter ego who dislikes island mist, Italian immigrant Joseph Lordi relies on a foggy recollection of his maiden aunts Celestina and Alicia to reassure himself of his wife's irreproachable obeisance and his own solid patriarchy. The two ordinary, Maine interloper Lordis cope in culturally specific ways with their "shock and amazement" over producing beautiful redheaded light-skinned Margarette Lenore: Leonora shrugs, covers her dark head with lace older than Maine itself, and goes to mass to beg for sanity. Bothered even more than she by hair, skin, and "little girl's blue-if-it's-a-boy blue eyes" that caught his eye and ruined his dinner, Joe strokes his thumb until he smashes his temple.[8] Then he roars his reminder to his disbelieving brothers about their neglected Buffalo aunts, faces doubt in the eyes of his friends, and shows his sudden affection for the twins in the form of bus fare for a visit. When he sees the flaming hair faded now to a disappointing gray, he can still regale them in the presence of company about such hair and such skin legitimately landing four generations later on the tiny and as yet scale-less head and shoulders of Margarette Lenore. Afterwards, both parents can finally be content to leave the extraordinary Lordi completely alone, turning their energies toward Lordi Brothers construction and "the problems of surviving in a county that did not want them there."[9]

Morrison becomes quite definite about these difficulties in *Playing in the Dark: Whiteness and the Literary Imagination* (1992). As she upholds the modern position that "cultural identities are formed and informed by a nation's literature" and theorizes "how the image of reined-in, bound, suppressed, and repressed darkness became objectified in American literature as an Africanist persona," she outlines what has long been on the "mind" of the literature of the United States: the "self-conscious but highly problematic construction of the American as a new white man," called for by Emerson in "The American Scholar." A background of rawness allows a group of new American arrivals to establish solidarity yet difference. A "complex awareness and employment of a constituted Africanism," deployed as darkness and savagery, not only shape and make possible desires for autonomy, authority, and absolute power; these become major themes in American literature. Even more accessible than the nonwhite indigenous population, a rebellious but serviceable black slave population handily enables otherwise disconnected white men to measure privileging and privileged differences. In other words, his need for New World manhood and the color of his skin transform Italian immigrant Joseph Lordi into a New Englander. Whatever his social status in Rome, or London, the new white American male becomes more of a gentle/man in the New World. Shared aversion to rawness as he struggles to survive in a hostile environment, in other words "collective needs to allay internal fears and to rationalize external exploitation," persuades him that dark savagery is "out there."[10] Enough to take anybody's breath away — or make him hold it — while trying to put food on the table.

Although the appearance of the maiden aunt fog in "that fuzzy caul" of Isle des Chevaliers makes patience and breathing hard to come by for everyone present at the time, it was when the great-aunts went home that, for Margarette, "the word 'island' had meaning."[11] If the little island of family can foster isolation, it can also offer sanctuary, though Jadine notes this about finding too much peace: "Such tranquility in sleep made for wildness in the waking hours."[12] Morrison knows very well, with the Br'er Rabbit she calls "Son," that the way we try to balance "those personal things in life," such as sleeping, eating, and sex, tells us who we are and how we will store ourselves in the modern Konigsgaarten.[13] Lordi knows this is especially the case with family dinners, which when magnified "under the tender light of a seventy-year-old chandelier" can cause otherwise civilized participants to lift their lips and bare their teeth.[14]

Anglo-American modernists from Eliot's Prufrock to the Beatles' Eleanor Rigby have sidestepped threat by splitting selves and wearing faces they "keep in a jar by the door / Who is it for?"[15] Morrison, however, argues that African traditions precede these literary modernist survival tactics, explaining that the *Tar Baby* folktale she chose to reinterpret seemed to her to be about masks coming to life, about the tensions between masks and the representational life they displace.[16] *Tar Baby's* masks also provide Morrison's initial riff on (post-)structuralist Roland Barthes's "work of the break," elaborated even more specifically in *Jazz* when Golden Gray "takes the break."[17] Terry Eagleton credits the literary movement of modernism with bringing structuralist and poststructuralist criticism to birth and asserts that Barthes's "astonishing study" of Balzac's realist novella *Sarrasine*, *S/Z* (1974), calls into question the bourgeois ideology of the sign as "representational."[18] Morrison again claims this modern shift in semantics as African American, using it to relocate the accuracy in all of her novels.

Calling something out of its name, a classic African American insult, maintains with modernism that a creative mind can free itself by mapping out its own reality. Seeing and saying can become being, as Baby Suggs admonishes her *Beloved* (1987) people in the Clearing, and as the Not Doctor Street joke reminds Southside residents in *Song of Solomon* (1977). Morrison's revision of a popular black archetype, Flip Wilson's Geraldine, highlights the particular necessity for African Americans barraged by stimuli destructive to their selves to practice visual and verbal re-creation. Because stereotypical portraits construe the virtues of black people as vices, the male comic's portrayal of a single set of traits within his campy female character provokes, according to Morrison, both hatred and affection:

> Geraldine is defensive, cunning, sexy, egocentric and transvestite. But that's not all she is. A shift in semantics and we find the accuracy: for defensive read survivalist; for cunning read clever; for sexy read a natural unembarrassed acceptance of her sexuality; for egocentric read keen awareness of individuality; for transvestite (man in woman's dress) read a masculine strength beneath the accouterments of glamour.[19]

Tar Baby's poststructuralist semantics for ingenious possibility and for deconstructed and reconstructed accuracy can be read as appetite. Perceived most clearly in the ongoing repartee between L'Arbe de la Croix's white master and black servants, Morrison reveals Sydney and Ondine's checks on Valerian's infantilism by their terms for his food habits. While blind seer Thérèse thrives on the apples of knowledge that land Milton's Eve into so much hot water, Valerian's stupid diet stunts his growth.[20] The subject of calories and healthful eating supplies constant table talk, with Margaret compulsively limiting her intake and Valerian eating freely of things that are bad for him. Ondine must sneak Postum into her boss's coffee; Sydney edges the box of saccharine tablets closer to — and the salt out of — Valerian's reach, but he inevitably demands uncontaminated coffee, plops in sugar cubes, and asks Margaret to pass the salt. Eschewing light croissant because the flakes are messy, he happily downs heavy, but artfully presented, ham and eggs or mashed potatoes and gravy with liberal quantities of fine wine and "medicinal" cognac, then instructs Yardman to pick up a bottle of Maalox to assuage the ulcer he insists is an occasional irregularity. Ondine comments tartly that if he would "leave that liquor alone" and eat foods which would naturally "[o]pen him right up," Valerian could "eat like regular people."[21] Perceiving himself to be normal, decent, balanced, simple, modest, fair, generous, and — above all — not abusive, her self-described Boy Scout employer, however, actually finds it vain and inelegant to stay in shape and remains content to impose his constipated life onto others. A mere shift in semantics finds the accuracy.

Here, Morrison nods to Barthes's poststructuralist notion that a literary work cannot be treated as a stable object or delimited structure, which also denies the possibility of an ultimate critical meta-language. The ambiguous language of the critic has "disowned all pretensions to scientific objectivity, making literature a free space in which it can sport." Even the full name of Tar Baby's conjure woman, Marie Thérèse Foucault, suggests that Morrison designed the structure of her novel not only to encourage the critic/reader to carve it up, to "transpose [it] into different discourses, produce his or her semi-arbitrary play of meaning athwart the work itself," but as commentary on such plurality and intertextuality in which the reader shifts from consumer to producer.[22] She maintains that the texture of her reinterpreted folktale required a worn, exaggerated leanness so that, like the stark symmetry of a mask sculpture or the deep eaves and light-filtering curtains that counter the heat-heavy sky over L'Arbe de la Croix, no distractions exist to prevent occupants from concentrating "on whichever of their personal problems they wished."[23] Thérèse rows Son back to Isle des Chevaliers/Horsemen's Island at the uncertain conclusion of the novel so that he might decide how to live his life according to the myth he desires to inhabit; we address our appetites and reveal our natures by writing the end of the story together with Son.

As Thérèse describes it, the place "[w]here you can take a choice" lies between living "in the garden of some other white people house" and freeing yourself to join the angels who wait for you in the hills.[24] Morrison intersperses blind, wet, and naked black horsemen galloping wildly about and among the plethora of female island spirits. Pictured as half-spirit/half-human like Caliban, these mythic beings are the three-hundred-year-old descendents of African slaves who go mysteriously blind the moment they see the domination awaiting them on Dominique. Morrison deliberately juxtaposes the plain-spoken *horsemen* against their more elegantly coined counterpart *chevaliers* to defend her free black male, determinedly unbound by Western cultural or class restrictions and bred simply to breed and play. Although she applauds all of Shakespeare's insightful fools, Morrison elevates his earthy Calibans above his airy Ariels. She also echoes his praise of plainness but converts his faith in sight into the value of hearing.

Interpretations of the horsemen/*chevaliers* myth vary with listener and teller. As relayed by easy-going local fishermen, a race of blind people descends from the blacks suddenly struck blind on board a French-owned slave ship, which foundered and sank with its cargo of Frenchmen, horses, and slaves. Forced by their blindness to float instinctively with the tides, the slaves wash up on Isle des Chevaliers along with the horses. Those only half-blinded are "rescued" by the French and returned to Dominique and servitude. Morrison makes some fun here, turning "struck dumb" into "struck blind." She also experiments with various paradoxical connotations of "blind": sightless, unable to see, refusing to see, instinctual, insightful. While the term usually suggests a disability, blindness becomes an asset in *Tar Baby*'s topsy-turvy world. Sightless slaves cannot be used for slave labor; blind seers stay un-enslaved. Among the stranded but still standing, blind horsemen yet ride.

Appropriating the story she hears from the first family to whom her husband sells property, Margaret Street insists that his island's rightful name is Isle de *le* Chevalier. To this distressed damsel, there can be only one masculine model, a gallant solitary knight — preferably on a white horse. Septuagenarian Valerian prefers the version of his Franco-Algerian friend, the exiled Dr. Michelin, which maintains that one hundred French chevaliers remain in the saddle, all as old and tired as he. Only the [dis]gracefully aging natives Gideon and Thérèse (and the young black visitors Son and Jadine) perceive the riders to be forever strong, naked, black, and many. In Gideon's words, they race each other blindly but freely through the hills, avoiding the possessive clutches of "trees and things,"[25] and sleep for sport with the self-possessed swamp women in Sein de Vieilles. These horsemen see only with the mind's eye and "can't stand for sighted people to look at them without their permission."[26] Weaving the stories adroitly together, Morrison unravels Western rationalism and its linear notion of history, illustrating that the position of the listener (or what she calls the "gaze" of the reader) determines the outcome of the story.

As the culturally encoded names for its setting indicate, *Tar Baby* acknowledges the modern shift from art as "a closed entity, equipped with definite meaning, which is the critic's task to decipher," to art as "irreducibly plural, an endless play of signifiers which can never be finally nailed down to a single centre, essence or meaning," focusing its "seething multiplicity" on the reader.[27] Unlike some modern white Anglo-American theorists, however, Morrison steadfastly refuses to propose language itself as an alternative to the social problems that plague us. Instead, she experiments with words to create a self-contained frame of reference that resists conventional boundaries, undermines attack, and counters despair by offering enticing possibilities. Scholars such as Paul de Man, J. Hillis Miller, and Geoffrey Hartman may advocate, albeit less plainly than do Morrison's black characters, that literature not only naturally opens itself right up but is, moreover, "about" this very operation. Nonetheless, Marxist Terry Eagleton accuses their work of largely ignoring the practical sphere of struggle as they reduce themselves to "a power-game, a mirror-image of orthodox academic competition."[28] Once again, a Morrisonian shift in semantics, and we find the accuracy. Such erudite literary skeptics loftily refer to themselves as the "Yale School of Deconstruction." Faithful members of the Toni Morrison Society dub the critical profession that calls for and embodies radical social change simply "word work."[29]

Hit on by the moist heat of a L'Arbe de la Croix manifestation of extensively white, excessively obscure, stuffy theoretical fog but fired up by the expectations of gratifying appetite, *Tar Baby*'s diners begin the process of recognizing and scaling back on roles prescribed to them by history and culture, adopting modernist disorder, and, in so doing, dealing with the alienation that accompanies discontinuity. The masks they appropriate to do so are emphasized by their modes of eating. Instead of heavy-handedly keeping his thumb on things like rejected blue-collar Joe, dejected lost boy Valerian signals his anxious assurance of command and his adopted courtier's *sprezzatura* by the merest pressure of "his thumb to the edge of the soup plate, pushing it an inch or so away."[30] He tells Margaret she's "dawdling," that there is a rhythm to a meal that has nothing to do with speed. With the alcoholic's firm conviction that everybody else drinks too much, he stays convinced his wife is "stewed." With the connoisseur's requirement for codependency, however, and the gentleman's for gentility, he "would squint at her, but say nothing"— except to correct her pronunciation and switch the subject when she and an uncomfortable Jadine giggle over "the hair in [Eurydi-chee's] armpits": "I would like to stay well through dessert, ladies, if you please. Could we find another topic?" A vacuum-packed Valerian creatively [circum]vents his need to bust loose as he drains multiple wineglasses, glares at a bewildered Margaret when she leaves the salad utensils on the table, and manages from her perspective to "make everything [she does] sound stupid."[31] Especially the extraordinary idea of son Michael actually coming to Christmas dinner on the island.

Charles Fishman reports that Morrison names Valerian after Emperor Valerianus, who came to Roman power "during an epoch of near national bankruptcy and, after his defeat, at the hands of the Goths . . . was taken prisoner, and disappeared from history."[32] Valerian is also a plant with sedative or antispasmodic properties. Used to calm horses or produce a soothing tea, it acts as a kind of herbal valium appropriate to Morrison's character. It also sounds like valor[ian]. While he remains in some significant ways blissfully numb towards the basic needs of his household, Valerian also tries valiantly to ignore the scars of a stolen childhood filled with what his creator calls "anaconda love." Since her admittedly unfair treatment of Maureen Peal, the "high yellow dream child" in *The Bluest Eye* (1970), Morrison has "Always!" loved all of her characters, demonstrating her respect for them by showing multiple sides of their natures.[33] If Valerian Street is an aristocratic, precocious, snobbish, aloof, petty little prince, he is also a generous, bright, gracious, lonely, sensitive Petit Prince; a semantic shift again locates the accuracy.

Born the sole male heir in a patriarchal family predominated by girls, Valerian receives the kind of complicated love and attention from men and women alike that Baby Suggs says is just "too much."[34] He inherits his wealth and an executive position, for which he has been overeducated and remains poorly suited, from the Street Brothers Candy Company, its chocolate mainstay "Teddy Boys" having been created in workaholic Grandmother Stadt's German kitchen as a treat for her youngest son Theodore. Manned by his fun-loving, big-sister mother and aunts, turned "*serioso mammas*" after the death of Valerian's father but controlled by the hearty uncles, the factory boasts six "good items" by the time Valerian takes over and "all the women were dead but not the uncles."[35] Morrison uses the disjointed family history at the center of a Street Brothers' failed confectionary to elucidate how a sweet boy comes to confuse exploitation with a respect for industry.

The death of his father finds Valerian treading "the black water in the bucket that had no bottom," imprinting the modernist's dense actuality, historical discontinuity, and ensuing feelings of despair and loss on a seven-year-old child.[36] Valerian discovers human vulnerability to limitlessness at far too young an age; even worse, with nobody to talk to him about it, he is left alone. This causes him to long for the relief and purpose he finally receives from a thin, toothless, birdlike washerwoman, who is dismissed from doing the family laundry for perceiving his distress. Valerian claims that a "respect for the [Street Brothers] industry and its legendary place in the neighborhood and the hearts of those who lived there"[37] fires his determination to retire at sixty-five —"before he got foolish"— and let his son take over. His confused sentimentality actually results from the guilt overlaying his compulsions for safety and order, represented by a black woman rejected for doing something hard but helpful.

When his son is not charmed by chocolate Teddy Boys or the island retreat Valerian has carefully prepared, "Valerian's disappointment was real." He sells the company to "one of the candy giants who could and did triple the volume in two years" and turns his attention to "measuring French colonial taxes against American residential ones, killing off rats, snakes and other destructive animal life, adjusting the terrain for comfortable living." His ultimate ode to order, when he is certain his son will always be a constant stranger to him, is to build a contained private garden as a "place of controlled ever-flowering life to greet death in," "sleep the deep brandy sleep he deserved," and eat what he desires.[38] Valerian has certainly relied upon an experimental imagination to counter alienation and recollect "having once done something difficult and important while the world was zooming away from him." The problem becomes that he blindly exploits somebody else's sugar and cocoa in order to "grow old in regal comfort."[39]

Morrison encapsulates Valerian's tragically complicated fate in the comically simple trope expressed by a failed Street Brothers sweet. To show their nephew how much they love him and anticipate the takeover of their business they call "self-understood," his uncles name a candy after him: "*Valerians*. Red and white gumdrops in a red and white box (mint-flavored, the white ones; strawberry-flavored, the red). *Valerians* turned out to be a slow but real flop, although not a painful one financially, for it was made from the syrup sludge left over from their main confection — Teddy Boys."[40] The dismal narrative of *Valerians* reflects that of its conflicted namesake: a gradual collapse resulting from the pressures of a competitive white American male system reinforced by "the way black people ignite critical moments of discovery or change or emphasis in [stories] not written by them."[41]

While they attempt to treasure the "fruity" sweetness they have minted and then chewed up, tough-nut American businessmen really perceive refined, first-generation college-educated Valerian as ephemeral and lightweight: too delicate, too pretty, too gooey, too feminine — in sum, for sissies. When the hearty uncles ask the hardball sales reps:

> What's the matter with [*Valerians*/Valerian]?
> Faggoty, said the sales reps.
> Faggoty?
> Yeah. Like Valentines. Can you see a kid sitting on a curb tossing those fairy candies in his mouth? Seasonal is all we can do. Valentine's Day. Give us something with nuts, why don't you?[42]

Shunned by white Easterners and Midwesterners, *Valerians* are picked up solely by Southern "jigs." "Nobody can make a dollar selling faggot candy to jigs," say the reps, especially when said "jigs" are leaving the South in droves and "don't want to be reminded." Nonetheless, the uncles fight gallantly to promote the box with "not even a picture of the candy or a happy face eating it," only a saying, "Ooooh. Valerian!!" They ostensibly and ostentatiously try to avoid closing out Valerian[s], who "appreciated their efforts but recognized them as sentimental and not professional." In reality, the Street Brothers scrap mightily to maintain their problematic trophy to themselves as new American gentle/ men, a self-conscious effort which forces the sweet thing to sit uselessly on display until he is "hard as marbles and stuck together [with others similar to himself] like grapes."[43]

Morrison's savagely ironic food chain forges some subtle links. First of all, the comically inverted description of frustrated white businessmen trying to foist packages with no pictures onto illiterate consumers illustrates how print cultures can lose out to oral ones if the former fails to recognize the impotence of its labels. Morrison's trope also reinforces the conflicted feelings some white Americans repress toward Americans of color, finding chocolate stimulating, desirable, but heavy to digest. Even more telling, just as Valerian treads (on/ above) the black substance in the bucket with no bottom, or the child relies on the black scapegoat to steady him, or white colonialists all over the world have generated empires on the backs of slaves, red-and-white *Valerians* are constructed from chocolate waste. Finally, Valerian's groveling gratitude toward his uncles and ultimate denial of *Valerians*, based on a noble desire to be professional, represents Morrison's connection between social climbing and racial self-hatred. Increasingly self-destructive Valerian Street learns to bite the hand that feeds him—the one Margarette Lenore Lordi Street takes in marriage for the safety of its "nice square fingernails"— his own.[44]

Making light of his obsessively dieting wife for speaking constantly in food measurements, explaining patiently — or patronizingly—that the depression is over and "There really is more,"[45] Valerian becomes the unfortunate byproduct of "too much," which Morrison laments in her acceptance of the National Book Foundation Medal for Distinguished Contribution to American Letters. *The Dancing Mind* (2003) embraces a kind of peace that is not the absence of war nor at the mercy of history nor a passive surrender to the status quo but rather "the dance of an open mind when it engages another equally open one," a give-and-take that occurs most naturally in reading and writing. Her speech defending freedom describes a man imprisoned by his privilege: "a comfortable, young American, a 'successfully' educated male, alien in his own company, stunned and hampered by the inadequacy of his fine education," who must resort to "autodidactic strategies to move outside the surfeit and bounty and excess and (I think) the terror of growing up vacuum-pressured in this country" in order to learn the "very old-fashioned skill" of surrendering to the "company of [his] own mind while it touches another's."[46] Whether or not *Tar Baby*'s sweet, courteous yet cavalier Little Prince masters the skill of solitary self-conscious service remains questionable; if he does so, however, he acquires it not by autodidactic means but seated at the family dinner table.

The bored, hardening Principal Beauty of Maine, on the other hand, is the product of too little, and, as Morrison does with the husband, she lets the wife's sleeping mask slip over supper. Always one step below or above others, judged via a different scale than they, lacking the confidence even to touch her food, Margaret finally dips her spoon into the by-now limp bisque and begins to eat just as Valerian pushes back his bowl. Their battlefield the family, their weapons "public identification of human frailty," Sleeping Beauty's lack of education and sophistication makes her vulnerable to the Prince's attack.[47] Because she cannot engage in clever repartee, she defends clumsily her social faux pas. Snapping that her pace is simply different from his, she is "never sure when the confusion would return: when she would scrape her fork tines along the china trying to pick up the painted blossoms at its center, or forget to unwrap the Amaretti cookie at the side of her plate and pop the whole thing into her mouth."[48] Blaming the black woman in the kitchen for preventing her access to the mango by propping it up in ice and leaving on the skin, delighted when she can identify as oysterettes the little white pebbles the black man serves, she prays she will recognize the soufflé. The woman whose marshmallow center Son counts on to counter tough external (chin, nose, finger) tips, sharpened from years of dinners with Valerian and his class-conscious friends, likes it as she would prefer to see herself —"hot, plain and fluffy."[49]

Like an inversion of her husband's experience and despite their opposite upbringings, Margaret wears down to dinner a face dislocated from a modern lifetime of being left alone. Not only do her parents turn their energies to surviving in a place that does not want them there, "being *that* pretty with *that* coloring" leaves its mark on her:

> Maybe her beauty scared them a little; maybe they just felt, well, at least she has that. She won't have to worry. And they stepped back and let her be. They gave her care, but they withdrew attention. Their strength they gave to the others who were not beautiful; the knowledge, what information they had they did not give to this single beautiful one. They saved it, distributed it instead to those whose characters had to be built.[50]

Here, Morrison lets the reader locate the reasons, though the results are pretty clear: Margaret's astonishing appearance cuts both ways. When she finally gives in to South Suzanne's evaluation of her looks, this hometown assessment provides an antidote to her tacky trailer-park beginnings. On the other hand, it turns poisonous because "it meant she had to be extra nice to other girls to keep them from getting mad at her. It meant having teachers go fuzzy in her presence (the men with glee, the women with distrust), fighting off cousins in cars, dentists in chairs and feeling apologetic to every woman over thirty. Privately she neither valued it nor enjoyed it. . . . " Until she meets an older man who bows to her beauty and stands for a safety that comforts her and makes her feel of consequence. In other words, Valerian's visor of knighthood enables Margaret's need to be worshipped since "her Margaret-hood lay in the same cup it had always lain in—faceless, silent and trying like hell to please."[51]

Valerian marries Margaret because he needs to know and love himself. When he spots Miss Maine standing on a winter float sporting a stuffed polar bear at a convention of industrial food appliance sales, her beautiful red-and-whiteness reminds him of the candy that had his name and "had made something kneel down in him the first time he saw her."[52] That something turns out to be a thinly concealed autoeroticism combined with a determination to adore a high school beauty queen in order to prove he is capable of love to the spirit of his dead, unloved first wife. Valerian's very identity, his lost innocence and "youth lay in [Margaret's] red whiteness, a snowy Valentine Valerian."[53]

Morrison relies on the dinner scene in chapter three to suggest that taking too much can be as problematic as having too little. It also introduces the modern education, religious, and class clashes that separate men and women. Jadine bears uncomfortable witness to Valerian's pained mockery of Margaret's awkward attempts to entice their son home to dinner. Saying with a shy smile, "Michael is coming. For Christmas," Margaret unveils the present she has promised him — a visit from his favorite teacher/poet. She includes in her letter to Michael a line, supposedly from one of B. J. Bridges's poems: "And he glittered when he walked." Valerian responds to this "hint" with a snort of laughter and a suggestion that Margaret have her breakdown now because Michael won't come: "You've misled him entirely."[54] Illiterate Margaret obviously knows little about modern poetry, including the source of the line as Edwin Arlington Robinson's frequently anthologized "Richard Cory" (1897). But Morrison depends on her readers to know. Our knowledge not only reveals Margaret's insignificant and Valerian's sophisticated literary background, but it underscores the despair produced by modern alienation. Morrison also re-envisions that despair. While wealthy, worshipped Richard Cory goes home and puts a bullet through his head, Morrison's *Sula* (1973) claims that the traditional black community scorns people who take themselves seriously enough to consider suicide — like poor, ill-bred, milky-skinned Tar Baby. Or can't laugh at themselves — like Margaret and Valerian.

A lovely dinner for three created by two black servants ends in total discord when the already humiliated white hostess resents not being invited to the wedding of the host's niece, an extended family dinner fiasco just waiting to happen. German Protestantism condescends to Italian Catholicism when Margaret complains that Valerian's sister "never liked [her]," telling her to take off her communion cross because "only whores wore crosses." Teasing Margaret for letting his sister get under Margaret's skin, claiming she really wanted to "crash some fatheaded wedding because Michael was there," Valerian scoffs: "You are too stupid to live." Masks and gloves now completely off, he calls her an idiot, she retorts that she married an old fool, he agrees that only "an old fool would marry a high school dropout off the back of a truck," and she storms out of the dining room in tears.[55]

Analysis of their publicly intimate dinner conversation suggests that Valerian and Margaret appear to have nothing in common with respect to age, class, ethnicity, education, religion, or interests. If, however, abuse of the black Son caused by aspiration to new American manhood allows white men to measure privileged and privileging difference, then abuse by that same system gives a white American couple plenty with which to distract themselves from their responsibility as they abuse their own son. Even pillow talk is disturbed by the aristocratic image of pearl-gray S's everywhere, coiling at Margaret and causing her to stiffen "like Joan Fontaine in *Rebecca* until she learned from her husband that his ex-wife had nothing to do with it. His grandmother had had some of the monograms done and his mother the rest." Margaret's description of alienation's "afterboom" applies to Valerian as well: her "relief was solid but it did nothing to keep her from feeling drowned when he was not there in the spaciousness of that house with only a colored couple with unfriendly faces to save her. Alone in the house, peeping into a room, it looked all right, but the minute she turned her back she heard the afterboom, and who could she tell that to?" Morrison's fierce irony here is unmistakable: Certainly "Not the coloreds."[56]

Margaret and Jadine attempt to disregard skin color at Emperor Valerian's dinner over deceptively fluffy discussions of soufflés and hair. While the repressive maiden aunts cause the Principal Beauty of Maine to envision her soufflé as hot and visualize her hair as stringy, the haute couture model referred to as the "Copper Venus" says the fog is souffléing her hair into an uncontrollable shaggy-dog style that has to be worked on constantly because it is not cool. Margaret's intended complimentary comparison of Jade's hair to that of Eurydice in *Black Orpheus* backfires because Jadine secretly resents and resists — or misinterprets — what she views as "the way Margaret stirred her into blackening up or universaling out, always alluding to or ferreting out what [Margaret] believed were racial characteristics."[57] Not only does the viperous maiden aunt vapor in *Tar Baby* get black men and women all mixed up, but black women and white women become confused, too.

Jadine's uncomfortably tenuous place at the modern table calls upon her to stay constantly alert "about things she did not wish to be alert about" and be able to change the subject in half a heartbeat. She must leash the small dark dogs of her basic self, subduing their silver feet in order to subvert the "seasoned and regulated arguments" of her sparring hosts, or put another way: "watch tomato seeds slide into the salad dressing" as she sets about "applying the principles of a survey course in psychology." Reimbursing Valerian's patronage by enticing his wife to stay on at Isle des Chevalier, Jadine receives a supposed "vacation with light but salaried work," just what she needs to cope with her racial conflicts over raucous white French lover Ryk and the big-breasted, large-hipped African woman in yellow so that Jade can pull herself together.[58]

This ultra-modern black woman has to eat out of one side of her mouth while, out of the other, carrying on a conversation with herself about what to do with herself. Sorbonne-educated art history major Jadine is torn between a Western high life with Ryk and the authentic high life of West Africa, epitomized by a tar black "mother / sister / she" in canary yellow carrying eggs and a black

Son whose most effective mask involves not wearing one.[59] Jadine reassures art collector Valerian that, "'Picasso *is* better than an Itumba mask. The fact that he was intrigued by them is proof of *his* genius not the mask-makers'. I wish it weren't so, but. . . . '"[60] Nonetheless, her relationship with Son remains haunted by the vision of a tall, powerful woman's woman in Paris whom she believes spits at her. An inversion of the thin, white maiden aunt expectorate, this solid black woman's force arises from her originality. She is what Morrison's Modernism offers Jadine: "someone who has no peer, who does not have to become anybody. Someone who already 'is,'" i.e. the split self unsplit.[61] In essence, Jadine's alienation enhances her desire to make herself new, an appetite whetted at a grocery store and vetted at the dinner table.

Sydney and Ondine Childs show their New World niece that the Old World black community has already adopted modern ways of coping with loss and despair. Referring to the married couples of her childhood as "comrades," Morrison creates in these servants a balance between sturdy individual and fluid cor[co-o]poration.[62] Both partners clearly separate public and private life; both devote those lives to service yet wait on others in ways distinguished by their respective culinary responsibilities. Sydney relies on what Sarah Orne Jewett calls "the gift of sympathy" to referee all the eaters. "Unbidden but right on time," he circles the table "with steps as felt as blackboard erasers." Avoiding eye contact with everybody, including his niece, he uses his "practiced sidelong glance" to anticipate their desires and "float[s]" unobtrusively to their elbows.[63] If he is the epitome of the "good old Uncle Tom," Sydney also takes pride in work well done and refuses to tolerate bad behavior. Morrison praises him as "not befuddled and confused about who he is. And when all the world seems as though it is horrible, he takes over. He does not want to do so but if Valerian is not going to run things, he will."[64]

Using hesitation, subtlety, and indirection to find out direction, this silent butler moves easily through the door connecting racially separate eating spaces. He makes a strikingly effective contrast to his outspoken cook of a wife whose expert kitchen service keeps her out of the dining room but gives her the distance to talk trash about the diners she loves. Because hot-tempered Machete-Hair is reliable enough to pull herself together when cool Bow-Tie looks to be falling apart, the two comrades counterbalance each other. Trusting the other implicitly, touching the other tenderly, needing only to feed each other partial sentences for total understanding, these hard-working black servants share in the kitchen three very full and very different meals from those they supply for the dining room. As Morrison notes in *Playing in the Dark* about the disrupting Africanness in American literature and culture, black people are indisputably present despite their seeming absence: with the black woman providing backup in the kitchen, the black man is perfect at "those dinners when his niece sat down with his employers. . . . One hardly knew if he left the room or stood in some shadowy corner of it."[65]

Even Sydney, however, is "shook" when the not-masked "nigger in the woodpile" unexpectedly provokes the Street family skeleton (mother Margaret's abuse of her beloved baby Michael) to come out of the bedroom closet, and the sacrifice of two isolated sons forces everybody to acknowledge the culturally dis-eased white elephant standing in the middle of the dining room floor. Morrison's darkly comic modern reminder of the racially refreshing *Guess Who's Coming to Dinner?* continues when a fed-up Ondine finally rushes out of the kitchen to shout, "Speak, woman!" and to bark instructions at everybody as Jadine fails to calm a screaming Margaret with a glass of wine; Sydney uses the business end of a pistol to march a filthy black man sporting dreadlock hair into the light of the sixty-four-bulb chandelier; and an openmouthed Valerian — Jade, at this point, daring to say nothing — closes his mouth "before saying, in voice made stentorian by port, 'Good evening, sir. Would you care for a drink?'"[66]

While it may upset the house, the modern mischief Br'er Rabbit does to the farmer's garden makes "something grow that was dying."[67] Like the island itself and the *Tar Baby* masks, it exaggerates everything. From the time the Son who swims towards blue water "smells" a furious Jade and she runs to find the black man "laughing to beat the band" with the white man in the greenhouse because William Green stops the red soldier ants cold with mirrors and flicks Valerian Street's closed-budded cyclamen stems, paradise prepares for after the fall.[68] The nigger in the woodpile turns out to be the kind of natural man that knows potted plants: "They like women, you have to jack them up every once in a while. Make em act nice, like they're supposed to."[69] Sure enough, his black magic makes the buds bloom along with the "goddamn hydrangea," and the entire island begins to "[vomit] up color like a drunk."[70] After taking on the "implicit dare" hidden behind the vision of his son's reconciling smile from a bowl of overripe peaches and throwing the household into disarray by inviting the intruder to have a drink, an impotent septuagenarian kneels to sexually service his fiftyish wife.[71] Margaret volunteers to cook, agreeing to follow Valerian's old family recipe for a Dutch treat of Olieballen (all uh ya ballin'). Sydney rubs Ondine's swollen feet as she fusses about not having to fix Christmas dinner, blind Thérèse envisions a romantic tale of L'Arbe de la Croix, jabbing Gideon's shoulder in her excitement as she lets "the story shimmer through the clear cascade of the French of Dominque," and Son puts his forefinger on Jadine's naked sole/soul and "held it and held it and held it there."[72]

Morrison continues to employ her characters' appetites to showcase the possibilities emerging out of shaking things up. Like her creator, Jadine has become quite astute at experimenting with the suggestive social and sexual power of food. Wondering why the picture of "[l]arge beautiful women's hats" keeps her awake at night, she recalls one of the happiest days of her life grocery shopping in Paris. Having just been chosen for the cover of *Elle*, pursued by three raucous lovers "in Yugoslavian touring cars with Bordeaux Blanc and sandwiches and a little *C*," and receiving a satisfactory score on her oral exercises from a charming old man, Jadine wants to celebrate with her fashionable clique. As such, she goes to a Supra Market sure to have "Major Grey's chutney, real brown rice, fresh pimiento, tamarind rinds, coconut and the split breasts of two young lambs . . . Chinese mushrooms and arugula; palm hearts and Bertolli's Tuscany olive oil," all the ingredients she needs for "a rich and tacky menu of dishes Easterners thought up for Westerners in order to indispose them, but which were printed in *Vogue*" in a manner calculated to satisfy a twenty-five-year-old who can look much younger when she chooses.[73]

This twenty-something can also select off-putting foods. After the initial discovery of the starving black man, Jadine still takes her meals with Margaret and Valerian in the dining room while Son eats so much of Ondine's food in her kitchen that "she soften[s] considerably toward him"; Sydney finally calls him "Son" since he cannot "doubt the man's hunger."[74] A picnic lunch prepared by the woman who never "let[s] the hunger show" to contain the man "with savannas in his face" clarifies the cultural barriers to their relationship.[75] All "temptation and dare" in Easter white cotton, a glowing Jade signals her unwilling attraction to impressively made-over Son's invitation by throwing together a deliberately unappetizing lunch of "olives, French bread, uncuttable cheese, ham slices, jar of black mushy cherries and wine" in a beautiful Haitian basket.[76]

Leaving them both yearning for more, the lunch that begins as ordinary, modern, sexually acrobatic seduction becomes extraordinary because Son remains so natural and so vulnerable. As the mediocre artist fails to sketch his disarmingly "laughing, heaven-raised face," all planes and open spaces, she receives a genuine response to the "What do you want out of life?" question she recognizes as tiresome. He longs to resurrect a past that treasures his "original, original dime," given him by scrappy old San Francisco for cleaning sheephead fish and with which he buys five (Lord) Chesterfield cigarettes and a Dr Pepper. Mocking him with "Ah got plenty of nuffin and nuffin's plenty for meeeeeee," she never thinks she'd actually hear a black man admit to laziness. He is indignant that a black woman would name *lazy* the privileging of something "nice and simple and personal" and not being able to get excited about money. She retorts, "*Get* able. *Get* excited . . . for yourself, for your future."[77] Their increasingly serious exchange moves on to Thoreau, the prison of poverty, and home. The city girl understands transcendentalism; the country boy calls it a journey instead of a job. She starts to bolt when she learns that the man who makes buds open also drives through people, and he quits trying to make an impression on her. She sits quietly under his hand when she realizes he really wants to kiss her foot.

Morrison affirms that Jadine and Son "had no problems as far as men and women are concerned. They knew exactly what to do. But they had a problem about what work to do, when and where to do it, and where to live. Those things hinged on what they felt about who they were, and what their responsibilities were in being black." Arguing that the "serious question about black male and black female relationships" should not turn on gender, Morrison maintains that "the conflict of genders is a cultural illness": "Many of the problems modern couples have are caused not so much by conflicting gender roles as by the other 'differences' the culture offers." Unlike the "perfect conversations" that take place between Sydney and Ondine, the "hooks" Son and Jadine hang on, fixed by the culturally stimulated appetites each brings to the table, prevent their wordless communication.[78] Fleeing Eloe because he drove his car through the bedroom where his wife has sex with a teenager, scared for his hands in Vietnam, frightened at sea by "punching dying fish in anger . . . pricked to fury by the outrageous claim of a snapper on its own life, stunned by its refusal to cooperate with his hook, to want, goddamn it, to surrender itself for his pleasure," the former pianist jumps the ship of violently competitive American culture to find fraternity and relocate his home in Eloe with the fat pie ladies in snowy dresses who cook for him.[79] The art historian turned high-fashion model — who desires gold, cloisonné, and raw honey-colored silk, a shiny black seal-skin coat, and dry vermouth — opts to go for industry in Paris and cooks for herself.

The arrival of the "nigger in the woodpile" allows us to discover how the local great unwashed eat uninvited. Feeling unwelcome even in the downstairs kitchen, Gideon and Therese work in Valerian's yard or washhouse and live together on Place du Vent in a pink cement house whose roof must be replaced four times a year, a situation that does not daunt Dominique natives, who do not bother to "hide the contempt they felt in their hearts for everybody but themselves."[80] Since imported produce arrives wilted because French colonial law allows only French-grown fruits and vegetables, a hardship to the rich who will not work a kitchen garden, the poor eat "splendidly from their gardens, from the sea and from the avocado trees that grew by the side of the road."[81] During his unhappy exile to that "lonely Stateside" wasteland, Yardman fails to accumulate money or obtain degrees but even so manages to supply the Witch's Tit with the tart apples of information she "had tasted once when she was seven and again when she was thirty-five and had a craving for them akin to hysteria."[82]

Returning gratefully to Dominique with twelve tucked into his electric blue leisure suit, he remains out of a grudging respect for the perpetually producing magic breasts of his mother's baby sister, her ability to out-trick the trickster and make him laugh, and because "her gratitude was so complete."[83]

Unlike Valerian, their mixture of pride and humility makes this "laughing, lying crone" and her older sister's boy share willingly the best they have even without others' asking. If he usually drinks warm beer and she picks stones out of the rice, they offer Son a feast: "With country people's pride in a come-from-far guest, they paraded the American Negro through the streets of town like a king." Thérèse sends Alma Estée to the market for brown sugar and canned milk, reaching into the bag that hangs underneath her dress to give her niece money for goat's meat and two onions. She brews thick coffee while she waits her turn to talk. Morrison makes clear the gendered role differences. Although Gideon will tell Thérèse stories on Isle des Chevaliers, he does not socialize with her in Queen of France, spending his free time with old cronies and treating the powder-pink house of the out-of-work wet nurse as his castle. Having given over the single bedroom to the nephew two years her junior, Thérèse joins the men at the table only after they have eaten, and Son, drinking rum-laced, sugar-sweetened coffee, stretches his legs and permits himself "a hearthside feeling." If Gideon's sole regret at leaving "the country too terrible for dying" is the loss of his unemployment insurance, Thérèse, too, foregoes certain benefits to enjoy Gideon's presence. The blind seer, however, "had her own views of understanding that had nothing to do with the world's views."[84] If, in Valerian's case, "pride goeth before a fall," these local blacks have already fallen and so are able to offer compassion and good company. Another manifestation of Br'er Rabbit in the briar patch, they make something grow that is dying.

Dinnertime permanently disrupted by the savior in the woodpile, the white skeleton of Western patriarchy imminently out of the closet, *Tar Baby*'s conclusion finds everybody changing up but the Petit Prince, who sits and smiles and waves his hands.[85] The Principal Beauty folds; the Copper Venus flies; Br'er Rabbit runs; The Witch's Tit rows; Yardman still puts the roof back on; still comrades, Bow-Tie and Machete-Hair make themselves comfy while they still stand and wait. Isle des Chevaliers is returning to its pre-colonized wilderness. The novel ends in ambiguity because Morrison could not envision a harmonious juncture then or now for authentic African American men and women or for black and white Americans. She does assert, however, that Americans of either gender or any color cannot dwell altogether in the past or look only toward the future. *Tar Baby* confirms that the tragic imperative of enslaved Africans in the United States to make themselves new within the context of community in order to survive predates, and even counters, the more sour impulses of modernism of the late nineteenth and early twentieth centuries. Morrison's tragicomic Modernism says, "Close, but no after-dinner cigar," signifying a satisfying first supper among disciples and friends. Nevertheless, by way of contradiction and experimentation, the afterboom of sweet modernist possibility continues to sound.

NOTES

1. Laura B. Randolph, "The Magic of Toni Morrison," *Ebony* 43, no. 9 (1988): 106. Among the various studies that support Morrison's assessment and reflect today's more inclusive understanding of modernist thought is Bonnie Kime Scott's ed., *Gender in Modernism: New Geographies, Complex Intersections* (Urbana: University of Illinois Press, 2007), sequel to her 1990 edition, Scott and Mary Lynn Broe, eds. *The Gender of Modernism: A Critical Anthology* (Bloomington: Indiana University Press, 1990). Marc Conner is currently completing a study of African American manifestations of modernism titled "Modernity and the Homeless: Ethics, Aesthetics, and Religion in the African-American Novel."

2. Writers and scholars have become increasingly aware that food represents way more than what we put in our mouths. Michael Pollan, for example, has published several best-selling books on the connections between appetite and culture, including most recently *The Botany of Desire* (New York: Random House, 2001); and *The Omnivore's Dilemma: A Natural History of Four Meals* (New York: Penguin, 2006). The latter examines aspects of the industrial, pastoral, and personal food chains to consider food within the contexts of competition, communication, power, and ecology; Pollan's answers to the age-old question "What should we have for dinner?" hold political, economic, psychological, and moral implications. Carole Counihan and Penny Van Esterik's, eds., reader *Food and Culture: A Reader.* 2nd ed. (New York: Routledge, 2008), recognizes the "productive cross-fertilization between food studies and gender studies," notably Doris Witt's *Black Hunger: Food and the Politics of U.S. Identity* (New York: Oxford University Press, 1999); *Black Hunger: Soul Food and America* (Minneapolis: University of Minnesota Press, 2004); and Psyche Williams-Forson's *Building Houses out of Chicken Legs: Black Women, Food, and Power* (Chapel Hill: University of North Carolina Press, 2006) books on African American food and gender (4). Morrison's *Tar Baby* (New York: Random House-Knopf, 1981), predicts and expands these food facts with her modern perspective on "Guess who's coming to dinner?" addressing food as emblematic of race, class, gender, and aesthetics.

3. Morrison, *Tar Baby*, 14.

4. Morrison's trademark irony appears in her phonetic spelling of *L'Arbe*. Sounding like a cross between the French word for tree (l'arbre) and the English abbreviation for a financier who

engages in arbitrage (arb), the misspelling of the symbol of his island takeover indicates that Valerian's impeccable bearing is vulnerable. He designs his paradise to bear any number of crosses, some anticipated, but the heaviest arrives unexpected. Although Morrison's French, as spoken through Valerian, is usually flawless, she deliberately misspeaks enough words, through Margaret's bumbling efforts, to suggest playful digs at nouveau-riche Americans who establish their pedigrees by imitating things Parisian, including its French. Valerian mocks Margaret's halting French as a way to remind her of her working class origins. As his protégé, Jadine studies at French schools, takes French lovers, and becomes a Parisian haute couture model. It takes Son to remind her "whatever you learned in those colleges that didn't include me ain't shit" (*Tar Baby* 264). Trying to think in English stops the flow of island conjure woman Therese's imagination until she spits it out of her mouth altogether and lets "the story shimmer through the clear cascade of the French of Dominique" (*Tar Baby* 108). Like Morrison's *Song of Solomon* (New York: Random House-Knopf, 1977), *Tar Baby* acknowledges the power that print cultures assume by controlling the names of things and people. It also recognizes that oral cultures must locate ways to defuse this power and ignite their own.

5. Morrison unloads her "nigger in the woodpile" off the king's storage boat to stir up the ironic contrast between spontaneous island funk and the calculated artifice of L'Arbe de la Croix. The figure itself implies an association with and disruption between natural and manmade. Like the medieval Vice character or the family skeleton stuffed for years in a back closet, this provocateur finally escapes to wreak gleeful havoc among household members. The woodpile or garden exists as nature carefully accumulated, cultivated, measured, and groomed, arranged neatly for future warmth, promising order, possession, control. The human hidden in its midst is grotesquely misplaced, and the trickster figure of the nigger introduces comic disharmony, with its usual sexual overtones. Certainly the woodpile indicates white male ownership, potency, and mastery of a tight ship; to him the nigger represents the frightening possibility of emasculation, mutiny, or miscegenation. Margaret Street appropriates the term when, exhausted by anticipation of her son's Christmas visit and the wilderness creeping into the seasoned and regulated arguments between her and her husband, she takes to her bedroom and opens her closet door wide to find Son Green inside. The morning after leaves her drained of panic and sleep, acknowledging: "Things were not getting better. She was not getting better. She could feel it and right smack in the middle of it, with Michael on his way, *this* had to happen: literally, literally a nigger in the woodpile" (83).

6. Morrison, *Tar Baby*, 142, 163.

7. Ibid., 83, 62. A number of reviewers object to what they consider the overdone anthropomorphism of the novel. Other scholars accept the ubiquitous presence of the island's plant and animal life by associating it with the magical realism of contemporary South American writers. Gurleen Grewal compares the airs and sprites of Isle des Chevaliers to those on Prospero's island. Morrison prefers to define these figures as expressions of black people's imaginative fusion of shrewd practicality and supernatural visitations. See Thadious Davis, *Faulkner's Negro: Art and the Southern Context* (Baton Rouge: Louisiana State University Press, 1983), 414. The kissing maiden aunt fog and shriveled fogbound swamp act as chorus or bear witness to human actions and epiphanies.

8. Morrison, *Tar Baby*, 56.

9. Ibid., 55-57.

10. Toni Morrison, *Playing in the Dark: Whiteness and the Literary Imagination* (New York: Random House-Vintage, 1992), 38-51.

11. Morrison, *Tar Baby*, 62.

12. Ibid., 68.

13. Ibid., 210. See Aurelia Espinosa, "Notes on the Origin and History of the Tar-Baby Story," *Journal of American Folklore* 43, no. 168 (1930): 129-209; and Laura Jarmon, *Wishbone: Reference and Interpretation in Black Folk Narrative* (Knoxville: University of Tennessee Press, 2003), for details about the story of Br'er Rabbit and the Tar Baby.

My reading of Morrison's decision to call Son's ship H.M.S. *Stor Konigsgaarten* resembles the process by which illiterate Macon Dead Senior names his beloved daughter not for the "Christ-killing Pilate," but for the sheltering way the large, majestic figure in the group of letters bends protectively over the smaller ones (*Song of Solomon* 19). Deconstructing print because I could not read the words, I relied directly on my senses to locate the accuracy. I spotted "H.M.S.," "store," "nigs," and "garden" to make my own meaning before I acquiesced to a more "knowledgeable," i.e. powerful, reader who translated the ship's title as "Big Garden of the King." Since Morrison knows that most of her English readers will not be able to decode other languages, I am convinced that she does this deliberately here and elsewhere in *Tar Baby* to illustrate her modernist's faith in the uncertainty of language.

14. Morrison, *Tar Baby*, 68.

15. Maintaining with Dante Alighieri's Guido da Montefeltro that he would never speak about his situation if he thought he would escape from the modern inferno that tears him apart, J. Alfred Prufrock remains resigned that "There will be time, there will be time / To prepare a face to meet the faces that you meet." See T. S. Eliot, "The Love Song of J. Alfred Prufrock," in *T. S. Eliot: The Complete Poems and Plays (1909-1950)* (New York: Harcourt, Brace, 1971), 4. Prufrock also forecasts Morrison's *Tar Baby* by erotically anthropomorphizing fog.

16. Toni Morrison, "Unspeakable Things Unspoken: The Afro-American Presence in American Literature," *Michigan Quarterly Review* 28, no. 1 (1989): 30.

17. Caroline Brown observes in "Golden Gray and the Talking Book: Identity as a Site of Artful Construction in Toni Morrison's *Jazz.*" *African American Review* 36, no. 4 (2002): 629-42, that the Golden Gray segment would appear to rest outside the boundaries of the jazz ethos. It actually represents, however, the "voice of the non-hermeneutic, the textual negotiation of freedom." The non-hermeneutic in Toni Morrison's *Jazz* (New York: Random House-Knopf, 1992) "is deployed to destabilize the text, rejecting strict aesthetic order, interpretive certainty, or linear progression" (630, 639). The story of Golden Gray attempts through narrative what Jelly Roll Morton calls a musical surprise or "the break." Arguably the first jazz composer ever published, this Creole pianist, who got his start at age fourteen in a New Orleans "sporting house," affirms the importance of breaks and the beautiful ideas they inspire. See Ted Gioia, *The Imperfect Art: Reflections on Jazz and Modern Culture* (New York: Oxford University Press, 1988), 75. An appropriate alternative to the *Jazz* trope depicting Golden Gray taking a break, *Tar Baby's* diners must learn to break (the) fast and feed the self. Derrida uses the term *breach* to indicate possibilities for disruption and discovery. The deepest breach or "the unnameable bottomless well" is "the abyss" as well as the center. In *Tar Baby* Valerian's bottomless bucket of time becomes one example of both "the absence of play and difference, another name for death" and a wide-open opportunity for self-development. See Jacques Derrida, *Writing and Difference*, trans. Alan Bass (Chicago: University of Chicago Press, 1978), 296-98.

18. Terry Eagleton, *Literary Theory: An Introduction* (Minneapolis: University of Minnesota Press, 1983), 137-9.

19. Toni Morrison, "What the Black Woman Thinks About Women's Lib," *New York Times Magazine*, August 22, 1971, 63.

20. Lauren Lepow, "Paradise Lost and Found: Dualism and Edenic Myth in Toni Morrison's *Tar Baby*," *Contemporary Literature* 28, no. 3 (1987): 363-77, recognizes that *Tar Baby* represents its creator's attempt to recast Milton's misogynist version of the Genesis myth in a feminist mode.

21. Morrison, *Tar Baby*, 37.

22. Eagleton, *Literary Theory*, 137-38. The name alludes to French post-structuralist philosopher Michel Foucault. With books to his credit like *Madness and Civilization: A History of Insanity in the Age of Reason*, trans. Richard Howard (London: Travistock Publications, 1967); *The Order of Things: An Archaeology of the Human Sciences* (New York: Random House, 1970); *The Archaeology of Knowledge*, trans. A. M. Sheridan Smith (New York: Pantheon Books, 1972); *Discipline and Punish: The Birth of the Prison*, trans. Alan Sheridan (New York: Random House, 1977); and *The History of Sexuality: Vol. I, An Introduction.* trans. Robert Hurley (New YorK; Pantheon Books, 1979). Michel Foucault numbers among the foremost French post-structuralists.

23. Morrison, *Tar Baby*, 81.

24. Ibid., 305.

25. Ibid., 153.

26. Ibid., 152-3.

27. Eagleton, *Literary Theory*, 138.

28. Ibid., 145.

29. See *The Nobel Lecture* in Literature New York: Alfred A. Knopf, 1994), 22.

30. Valerian's house mockingly models the publicly casual but privately tightly rehearsed recklessness that Renaissance courtiers aspired to and called *sprezzatura*. See Susan Neal Mayberry, *Can't I Love What I Criticize? The Masculine and Morrison* (Athens: University of Georgia Press, 2007), 122-6. In this casually designed place where "Graceful landscaping kept the house just under a surfeit

of beauty," the master must maintain his aplomb, and the servant must keep his cool – Sydney because his excellent service demands a "Phil-a-delphia Negro mentioned in [Du Bois's] book of the very same name," Valerian because "When he knew for certain that Michael would always be a stranger to him, he built the greenhouse as a place of controlled ever-flowering life to greet death in." See Morrison, *Tar Baby*, 163, 53.

31. Morrison, *Tar Baby*, 62-66.

32. Charles Fishman, "Naming Names: Three Recent Novels by Women Writers," *Names: Journal of the American Name Society* 32 (March 1984): 40.

33. Morrison, *Tar Baby*, 62; Nellie McKay, "An Interview with Toni Morrison," in *Toni Morrison: Critical Perspectives Past and Present*, eds. Henry Louis Gates Jr. and K. A. Appiah (New York: Amistad, 1993), 405. During a conversation with Gloria Naylor, Morrison confesses to showing unfairly only a "façade" of the Maureen Peal that "everybody has . . . in his or her life": "I never got in her because I didn't want to go there. I didn't like her. I never have done that since. I've always regretted the speed with which I executed that girl. She worked well structurally for [Claudia and Frieda] and this and that, but if I were doing that book now, I would write her section or talk about her that way plus from inside." See Gloria Naylor and Toni Morrison, "A Conversation," *Southern Review* 21, no. 3 (1985): 581.

34. Morrison, *Beloved* (New York: Random House-Knopf, 1987), 137.

35. Morrison, *Tar Baby*, 52-54.

36. Ibid., 142.

37. Ibid., 52-53.

38. Ibid., 53-55.

39. Ibid., 203.

40. Ibid., 50.

41. Morrison, *Playing in the Dark*, viii.

42. Morrison, *Tar Baby*, 50.

43. Ibid., 50-51.

44. Ibid., 83.

45. Ibid., 67.

46. Toni Morrison, *The Dancing Mind* (New York: Random House-Knopf, 2003), 7-13.

47. Morrison, *Tar Baby*, 68.

48. Ibid., 63.

49. Ibid., 64.

50. Ibid., 56-57.

51. Ibid., 83.

52. Ibid., 242.

53. Ibid., 54.

54. Ibid., 66.

55. Ibid., 70.

56. Ibid., 58.

57. Ibid., 64

58. Ibid., 67-68.

59. Ibid., 45-46.

60. Ibid., 74.

61. McKay, "An Interview," 404.

62. Ibid., 398.

63. Morrison, *Tar Baby*, 62-63.

64. McKay, "An Interview," 405.

65. Morrison, *Tar Baby*, 74.

66. Ibid., 79-80.

67. Ibid., 192.

68. Ibid., 121,149.

69. Ibid., 148.

70. Ibid., 187. Grewal views the island setting as Morrison's re-writing of Shakespeare's *The Tempest*, one which effects a "disidentification with Prospero's ordering of the world," and *Tar Baby* as post-colonial fiction (94). As apt, however, would be a comparison to Shakespeare's *Othello*, with its scenic shift from city to island, its exploration of sex and race, and its presentation of the Moor as

the figural enactment of the fall, repository of truth, sink of uncertainty and error. If it be such, however, Morrison's fall occurs upside down. The paradoxes of falling to fly, dying to live already inherent in its myth become further complicated so that blackness, darkness, dirt, chaos are signed as ascendant and the hegemony of whiteness renders descent. The writer records with her fourth book "unphotographable beauty." See Morrison, *Tar Baby*, 46). Instead of *Othello's* dramatization of wilderness and wildness threatening civilization, *Tar Baby's* white civilization bears the guilt of attacking black wildness. The dark, blind, and naked horsemen on Isle des Chevaliers roam in league with the swamp women and the champion daisy trees to defend its natural lushness against the encroaching swords and stiff, ornate epaulets of glittering Napoleonic chevaliers.

Morrison adds color to her basic black and white to indicate the spectrum of human states. Red represents excitement and danger; blue is freedom and chaos; green represents order and possession; yellow is vitality and self-absorbency.

71. Morrison, *Tar Baby*, 144. Prufrock's despairing "do I dare to eat a peach" certainly comes to mind here, in Eliot's, "The Love Song of J. Alfred Prufrock."

72. Morrison, *Tar Baby*, 108, 179.

73. Ibid., 44-45.

74. Ibid., 164.

75. Ibid., 124, 205.

76. Ibid., 168-9.

77. Ibid., 169-71.

78. McKay, "An Interview," 404-6

79. Morrison, *Tar Baby*, 167.

80. Ibid., 110.

81. Ibid., 109.

82. A colonized human counterpart of island life reaction to the white saws' eco-terrorism, Therese of the magic milk embodies the "Poor insulted, brokenhearted" river's response to the rain forest rains no longer being equal: "Now it sat in one place like a grandmother and became a swamp the Haitians called Sein de Vieilles. And witch's tit it was: a shriveled fogbound oval seeping with a thick black substance that even mosquitoes could not live near" (10).

83. Morrison, *Tar Baby*, 108-10.

84. Ibid., 149-151, 218.

85. Possessed of all the indicators, Valerian simply will not interpret clear signs of dysfunctional family behavior. He does not see that Margaret projects the rage she cannot contain towards an emotionally abusive husband, who dumps his overflow into her, onto what Ondine later calls *his* baby. Morrison treats "the first full-fledged portrait of a child abuser in all of literature" with understanding and sympathy, focusing on the cultural conditions that swamp her into another Sein de Vieilles. See Karla F. C. Holloway and Stephanie Demetrakopoulos, *New Dimensions of Spirituality: A Biracial and Bicultural Reading of the Novels of Toni Morrison* (New York: Greenwood Press, 1987), 138. Because she does not have the words to describe what she has "come to know, remember," Margaret spoon feeds her husband, "a sip here a drop there" her story of being held hostage by mind-numbing monotony, compelled to pierce an infant's "prodigious appetite for security" along with his "sweet creamy flesh." See Morrison, *Tar Baby*, 236.

Lakeisha Meyer

Lakeisha Meyer is an Assistant Professor of Education at Bucknell University where she currently teaches courses in educational psychology, assessment, and counseling. She has worked in K-12 schools as a school psychologist and behavior consultant. She credits the reading of Toni Morrison's work as the reason she began to connect narrative and therapy in an effort to think through and to innovate bibliotheraputic methodologies. Meyer here details her attempts to synthesize psychological theory and therapy into practice by analyzing the narratives of Toni Morrison's works.

Testimony and Transformation: An Exploration of the Intersection of the Arts of Toni Morrison and the Potential Therapeutic Uses of Narrative

LAKEISHA MEYER

The old tales, the old myths often times carry within themselves more truth than recorded history.[1]

As a school psychologist, I often view the world through both narrative and therapeutic lenses. Though I am not a literary critic, I am interested in the ways that psychological theories inform literary criticism. It seems to me important to move beyond Freudian and Lacanian psychoanalytic interpretations of Toni Morrison's works, as these interpretations limit the therapeutic use of narrative, and instead I recommend consideration of more experientially grounded processes that directly engage theories of feminist and multicultural counseling and therapy. One promising hybridization exists in the melding of feminist and multicultural theoretical approaches of counseling with bibliotherapy, wherein psychology and counseling theoretical models are used to interpret literary works with the goal of generating therapeutic change. I briefly sketch here the nascent outline of a form of bibliotherapy, grounded in my understandings of the relationship between Morrison's readers and her works. This theraputic methodology I hope to develop more fully over the course of my career.

My desire to explore connections between the works of Toni Morrison and possibilities for therapeutic change arose from my personal experiences reading Morrison's novels and my professional experiences as a counseling psychologist. As an African American woman, narrative plays an important cultural role in my life as *testimony*. To testify means to do more than just "narrate but to commit oneself, and to commit the narrative, to others."[2] Morrison's works resonate with the tales and myths of the African and Voodoo deity Papa Legba, the storyteller. Legba is described as the essence of communication and, takes precedence over all of the other Loa of Voodun.[3] For me, Legba represents the connection between narrative and therapy, between testimony and therapeutic change or transformation. As African American poet and Morrison colleague Audre Lorde noted, "I have come to believe over and over again that what is most important to me must be spoken, made verbal and shared, even at the risk of having it bruised or misunderstood."[4] Through her storytelling, Morrison's works testify to the broad range of human experience. Her canon and the relationships that it assumes and achieves with her readers is a potent model for an ideal therapeutic relationship.

I. Literature, Therapy, and Culture

The relationship between the arts and therapy is well established. Bibliotherapy refers to the use of literature as a tool for achieving resolution of a client's presenting conflicts and, in this context, reading is considered to be a therapeutic experience that can promote psychological and/or emotional healing.[5] The process of bibliotherapy consists of three phases: the reader identifies with a character, then begins to relate to the character and to share some of the character's feelings and thoughts and, finally, the reader learns successfully to address his or her personal problems through identification with some aspect of the character's struggle.[6] While these steps have been formally documented, there exists a limited amount of research on bibliotherapy, most of which is focused on the use of bibliotherapy as a methodological tool for working with children.[7] In spite of these limitations, it is my contention that literature can and should be an essential tool in many forms of counseling. A critical employ of literature as a therapeutic tool can help move the practice of bibliotherapy beyond the most basic level of direct identification with characters (as described above) to a more complex relationship between the narrative and the therapeutic process. Morrison's novels with their distinctive power, immediacy, and relevance, generate an explicit and engaging context that can help those seeking therapy to understand their own experiential landscapes more intimately and more expeditiously proceed towards achieving the most favorable outcomes.[8]

My central interest in this connection between literature and therapy rests in the testimonial intersections that link the lived experiences of African American women with the fictional first-person "tellings" of various characters that inhabit the works of Toni Morrison. As I have begun to explore the work of other theorists in the field with similar foci, I have been particularly intrigued by emerging the work of Kyeong Hwangbo. Through her focus on trauma as a paramount motivation for therapy, her work braids the too-often therapeutically siloed threads of trauma; gender, race, and ethnicity; and literature.

According to Hwangbo, racism has the power to instigate "intergenerationally transmitted trauma, in its relation with other social factors such as gender, class, and age, produces synergistic effects of multiple marginalization."[9] It must be noted that a reader's experience of trauma in the fictional world of a narrative is more mediated and constrained than the reader's direct experience of trauma in his or her own life. Hwangbo borrows Morrison's term *unspeakable things unspoken* to describe the "known but unacknowledged presence of devalued, denigrated others."[10] Through this form of testimony, Morrison's work gives a voice to the unvoiced, thereby creating potentially therapeutic narrative with particular saliency for those who are marginalized.

In many ways, reading a work of Toni Morrison mirrors aspects of what Hwangbo champions as a new and ideal approach to the therapy process and relationship. Literary critic Phillip Page asserts that Morrison forces her readers "to delve beyond the what into the more problematic how and why, with her nonlinear, polyvocal, multi-stranded narratives."[11] A therapeutic relationship that can pattern itself after Morrison's ambitions and formal actualizations would be both efficacious and democratizing. For African Americans, development of therapeutic applications grounded in emulating the relationship generated between Toni Morrison's works and her most engaged and participatory readers is particularly promising and necessary because we continue to be underserved with respect to dynamic, non-hierarchical models for mental health delivery that are not rooted in the racist and patriarchal paradigms of the dominant culture. Evidence of this need is readily apparent in differences between African-Americans and other groups in the areas of access, evaluation, and treatment within the mental health system and also by the pervasive problem of the overrepresentation of youth from culturally and linguistically diverse backgrounds in the special educational system.[12]

Again, Hwangbo proves instructive in investigating the possibilities for constructing a Morrison-inspired therapeutic modality. She asserts that Morrison's *The Bluest Eye* does more than just give a voice to the unheard; the novel *talks back* to the victimizing and repressive forces that push against African American communities. This testifying call-and-response helps to create spaces for therapeutic progression and for self-healing by clients. The novel's testimonial regarding the necessity of narratives of respect and dignity foregrounds the imperative of relationships grounded in mutual esteem as equivalent to survival for mistreated sufferers like Morrison's protagonist, Pecola.

II. Feminist Counseling and Therapy (FCT) and Multicultural Counseling and Therapy (MCT)

Traditional theories of counseling and therapy (psychoanalytic, cognitive-behavioral, and existential humanistic) do little to explore how societal power affects an individual's development and psychological well-being. Both theoretical movements developed in the United States during the cultural revolutions of the 1960s and 1970s — approximately the timeframe that Morrison emerged on the literary scene — and are based on principles of social justice.[13]

Within FCT, there are three principal concepts that are particularly relevant in the context of generating bibliotherapeutic possibilities when thinking of the intersections between these theories and Morrison's artistic missions. First, FCT considers the role of the manifestations of power in society as central. Second, sexism has harmful effects on the psychological development of women and men. Third, the *self-in-relation* concept holds a central place in FCT.[14] I would like to advocate for a new approach to bibliotherapy that emphasizes these constructs of the FCT and MCT movements. Although my thinking about these possibilities is in its nascent stages, it seems to me that there are myriad potentialities suggested specifically by Morrison's self-description of herself as a reader in her essay "The Reader as Artist."

> My own reading skills were enhanced in schools, but my pleasure in, my passion
> for the art of reading came long before. . . . The result was a heavy reliance on
> my own imagination to provide detail; the specific color of things, the feel of the
> weather, the space characters occupied, their physical features, their motives,
> why they behaved as they did, and especially the sound of their speech, where

so much meaning lay. Listening required me to surrender to the narrator's world while remaining alert inside it. That Alice-in-Wonderland combination of willing acceptance coupled with intense inquiry is still the way I read literature: slowly, digging for the hidden, questioning or relishing the choices the author made, eager to envision what is there, noticing what is not. In listening and in reading, it is when I surrender to the language, enter it, that I see clearly. Yet only if I remain attentive to its choices can I understand deeply. Sometimes the experience is profound, harrowing, beautiful; other times enraging, contemptible, unrewarding. Whatever the consequence, the practice itself is riveting. I don't need to "like" the work; I want instead to "think" it.[15]

Morrison's definition of the reader as an individual with agency and as possessing a subjectivity that is contextual, astute, and perceptive presents a promising model for the merger of her vision of the reader as artist with the fundamental assumptions of FCT and MCT.

III. Conclusion: Trauma, Testimony, and Therapeutic Change

Trauma refers not only to a single event, but also series of events or life conditions. Maria Root, a feminist psychotherapist cited in the work of Hwangbo, describes insidious trauma as trauma related to oppression and "the communal experiences of women, children, and minority groups who have been neglected in the development of theory."[16] Hwangbo paraphrases Jerome Bruner by stating, "to tell a story in which testimony collapses is still to testify. By telling a story where memory fails, the self disintegrates, and witnessing collapses."[17] Modeling Root and Bruner, Hwangbo explores the relationship between trauma and the social injustices that result from racism.

> Unless translated into a meaningful narrative and placed in a proper context, strengthened by communal support and the willingness of both survivors and bystanders to engage attentively in the arduous process of undoing the injury, traumatic events and the memories of the events will remain either disparate, fragmented bits of information and empty noises, or the toxic remains of the past people want to avoid and turn their backs on.[18]

Here, Hwangbo highlights the importance of the relationship between narrative and memories (collective and individual), and implies that memories of trauma should not be avoided, but should instead be processed in order to understand their impact. This process can be facilitated through the both the model and the direct employ of Morrison's work.

Acting out as a consequence of trauma is considered to be a pathological way of remembering.[19] But narrative, specifically Morrison's canon, can be utilized in a therapeutic manner to encourage conscious (re)membering of trauma and the exploration of trauma's impact on development and psychological well-being through literature. The healing power of remembering has been documented and there is some critical consensus that the crux of the narrative of *Beloved* rests on the conflict between remembering and forgetting.[20] Extrapolating this reading of the novel's central conflict to the therapeutic relationship redefines its tension as rooted in the question of an individual's cognitive ability to acknowledge the traumas of the past without obsession. The key to confronting this dilemma lies in developing the skills to transform collective and individual memories of trauma into knowledge about oneself— to paraphrase *Beloved's* Sixo "to gather the pieces."[21]

One of the undergirding principles of any bibliotherapeutic modality modeled on the principles Morrison exemplifies through her works is to use the narratives and their complex engagements with trauma to catalyze optimal outcomes for clients — manifested as tangible life changes and psychological health. Synthesis of various understandings of bibliotherapy with analyses of the works of Morrison is the beginning of this journey for me. Examination of Morrison's work in light of generating and developing new methodologies and approaches will positively impact and transformative the practices of counseling and therapy, and I look forward to continuing to explore this topic and developing applied uses for the work of Morrison within counseling and therapy — and to testifying, whenever possible, about the possibilities and uncharted paths that lay in that direction.

NOTES

1. Louis Martinie and Sallie Ann Glassman, *The New Orleans Voodoo Tarot* (Rochester, VT: Destiny Books, 1992), 148.
2. Kyeong Hwangbo, "Trauma, Narrative, and the Marginal Self in Selected Contemporary American Novels," (PhD diss., University of Florida, 2004), 68.
3. Donald Cosentino, "Who is that fellow in the many-colored cap? Transformations of Eshu in Old and New World Mythologies," *Journal of American Folklore* 100 (1987). 261-75.
4. Audre Lorde, *Sister Outsider: Essays & Speeches by Audre Lorde* (Berkeley: Crossing Press, 2007, orig.published 1984) 40.
5. Amie Sullivan and Harold R. Strang, "Bibliotherapy in the Classroom: Using Literature to Promote the Development of Emotional Intelligence," *Childhood Education* 79, no. 2 (2002): 74-80.
6. Joseph M. Furner, "Using bibliotherapy to Overcome Math Anxiety," *Academic Exchange Quarterly* 8, no. 2 (2004): 209-13; Fran Lehr, "Bibliotherapy," *Journal of Reading*, 25, no. 1 (1981): 76-79.
7. Melissa A. Heath, Dawn Sheen, Deon Leavy, Ellie Young, and Kristy Money, "Bibliotherapy: A Resource to Facilitate Emotional Healing and Growth," *School Psychology International* 26, no. 5 (2005): 170-94; 563–80; Mary Anne Prater, Marissa L. Johnstun, Tina Taylor Dyches, and Marion R. Johnstun. "Using Children's Books as Bibliotherapy for At-Risk Students: A Guide for Teachers," *Preventing School Failure*, 50, no. 4 (2006): 5-13.

8. C. J. Cook, "Told in Memory of God's People: *Beloved*," *Pastoral Psychology* 59, no. 6 (2010): 725-35.

9. Hwangbo, "Trauma, Narrative," 25.

10. Ibid., 8.

11. Phillip Page, "Furrowing all the brows: Interpretation and the Transcendent in Toni Morrison's *Paradise*," *African American Review*, 35, no. 4 (2001): 637.

12. H. E. Briggs, A. C. Briggs, and J. D. Leary. "Promoting Culturally Competent Systems of Care Through Statewide Family Advocacy Networks," *Best Practices in Mental Health* 1, no. 2 (2005): 77–99; Charles R. Ridley, *Overcoming Unintentional Racism in Counseling and Therapy: A Practitioner's Guide to Intentional Intervention*, 2nd ed. (Thousand Oaks, CA: Sage Publications, 2005); William Turner, Elizabeth Wieling, and William D. Allen. "Developing Culturally Effective Family-Based Research Programs: Implications for Family Therapists," *Journal of Marital and Family Therapy* 30 (2004): 257–70; Darren Woodruff, "Reducing Minority Student Disproportionality in Special Education: Schools and Families Working Together," *Focal Point: A National Bulletin on Family Support and Children's Mental Health* 16, no. 2 (Fall 2002): 26–28.

13. Allen Ivey, Michael D'Andrea, Mary Bradford Ivey, and Lynn Simek-Morgan, *Theories of Counseling and Psychotherapy: A Multicultural Perspective*, 6th ed. (Boston: Pearson Education, Inc., 2007).

14. Ibid.

15. Toni Morrison, "The Reader as Artist," *Oprah Magazine*, Harpo Productions (July 2006), http://www.oprah.com/omagazine/Toni-Morrison-on-Reading.

16. Hwangbo, "Trauma, Narrative," 21.

17. Ibid., 69.

18. Ibid., 4.

19. Ibid.

20. Cook, "Told in Memory of God's People: *Beloved*."

21. Toni Morrison, *Beloved* (New York: Random House-Knopf, 1987), 321.

Koritha Mitchell

Koritha Mitchell is Assistant Professor of English at the Ohio State University, where she teaches and writes on African American literature of the late nineteenth and early twentieth centuries, racial violence throughout American literature and culture, and black drama and performance. Her first book is *Living with Lynching: African American Drama, Performance, and Citizenship, 1830-1930* (2011); she has also published articles in scholarly journals, and edited volumes. Her research has been supported by the David Driskell Center for the Study of the African Diaspora, the Ford Foundation, and the American Association of University Women. Her essay for this volume traces her own upbringing and professional development alongside the narratives of race and gender in Toni Morrison's novels. In reading Morrison, who sketches and develops the tensions of gender alongside those of race, Mitchell recognizes the complexities of having to negotiate two separate and yet profoundly-intertwined identities. These questions inform and infuse her own scholarship as fiercely and as hauntingly as they do Morrison's novels.

Belief and Performance, Morrison and Me

KORITHA MITCHELL

The black won't rub off! It really isn't dirt!
—CHILDHOOD PLAYMATE

Accused of rape? That's what he gets for messin' with them white girls.
—COLLEGE FRIEND

*That's right, class: Toni Morrison won this year's Nobel prize. You
know, it's a good time to be black and a woman.*
—GUEST LECTURER

Girl, you better act like you know.
—MY MAMA, LAVERNE MITCHELL

Reading Toni Morrison's *The Bluest Eye* at age eighteen ultimately led me to pursue a Ph.D. in Literature, so Morrison's work literally shaped the life I now lead as a college professor. The insights I gleaned from that novel have proven valuable throughout my journey as a black woman living in the United States. When I encountered Morrison's first novel during my freshman year of college, I had reached that point in my life admitting, quite reluctantly, that race would shape my experiences. Try as I might, I could not make racial difference go away. And this surprised me as much as not being able to rub my color off had surprised my friend on that unforgettable afternoon.

By the time that I entered college, I was still resisting the idea that color could shape my life, but I could not deny the significance of events that told me otherwise. Still, nothing had prepared me to consider the relevance of gender, not just race. Morrison's *The Bluest Eye* did precisely that, and once it did, I began to recognize the many moments when people would try to make me choose whether I would prioritize race or gender when things got tough. And it seemed that issues of sexuality made times get tough more quickly than anything else! We were college students — away from our parents — dealing with sexual freedom, but that was not the only reason for the tension around gender and race. Anxiety attended these issues even in class, when seemingly staid matters were up for discussion, such as merit or intellectual rigor.

Now, as I look back, I recognize the wisdom of something that I had heard growing up but whose enduring value I would have to learn over time, and over and over again. As a black woman in the United States, I had better *act like I know*. Sometimes the most important thing to know is that this is a racist, sexist, heterosexist, classist society. Operating as if I don't know that is foolish, I believe; but I also think that recognizing these truths about my environment keeps me from believing some of the nation's lies.

My first encounter with Morrison showed me that American culture is structured to ensure that my race and gender will matter in all situations. Then, the experiences that I had after reading *The Bluest Eye* showed me that I would be expected to perform in accordance with accepted notions of gender and race. Recognizing those pressures made me realize that belief and performance are always intertwined. They sometimes work in concert, sometimes not, but they are never distinct from each other.

I. Discovering Gender

Growing up on the outskirts of Houston, Texas, I was familiar with racist behavior, but I was fairly committed to interpreting it as anything but racism. I was determined to live in a world in which only the triumphs I associated with

Martin Luther King, Jr. really mattered. I insisted that race would not shape my life. But there were a few incidents that I could not explain away. My best friend's attempt to wipe my "dirt" off was one of them, but it mostly made me angry with myself. Why had that incident hurt my feelings? I knew that her grandfather was a mean old man, and that's the only reason she would say something like that. She was a true friend; in fact, she liked me more than she liked her grandpa. Because I could always reassure myself with these reminders, I was most upset by the fact that I seemed unable to forget that day.

Years later, a similarly unforgettable incident occurred during my senior year of high school. It was the first time I remember actually being called a *nigger*. Class was being held in the library so that we could conduct research. Two classmates were talking while locating books for the assignment. The library shelves towered high above our heads, so as we searched for our books on opposite sides of the same shelf, I could hear them but not see them. One of the boys complained that I had taken the topic that he would have chosen if it had been available by the time the teacher called on him. John responded: "What a shame. She's a nigger; you would've done a better job with it." The complainer was silent, apparently stunned. I heard John pipe up again, chuckling: "What? It's just the truth."

By the time I arrived at a small liberal arts college in Ohio, I was beginning to accept that race would in fact shape many of my experiences; however, I was not prepared for the notion that gender would help determine the experiences I would have. In my freshman year, I enrolled in a Women's Literature class. Early on, I was taken with the feminist arguments made in *How to Suppress Women's Writing*. This study lists the various ways in which women's literary contributions have been denigrated: "*She didn't write it*. But if it's clear she did the deed . . . *She wrote it, but she shouldn't have*. (It's political, sexual, masculine, feminist.) *She wrote it, but look what she wrote about*. (The bedroom, the kitchen, her family. Other women!) *She wrote it, but she wrote only one of it*. ("Jane Eyre. Poor dear, that's all she ever. . . .") *She wrote it, but she isn't really an artist, and it isn't really art*. (It's a thriller, a romance, a children's book. . . .) *She wrote it, but she had help*. (Robert Browning. Branwell Brontë. Her own "masculine side.") *She wrote it, but she's an anomaly*. (Woolf. With Leonard's help. . . .) *She wrote it, BUT. . . .*" I found the entire book engrossing, and I kept scribbling in the margins, "Why can't you see that this applies to black-authored works?"[1]

I began to wonder if the silence around this obvious parallel was deliberate, but I was far from prepared to ask the question. I may have been wrong, but I assumed that I would be considered a troublemaker for offering the observation. I liked the class and the professor, and I didn't want to bring negative attention to myself. I never said anything about the silence that accompanied our discussions of *How To Suppress Women's Writing*, which served as our touchstone throughout the course, but it suddenly did not matter. We read *The Bluest Eye* toward the end of the semester, and I was no longer interested in naming what I believed to be the hypocrisy of our discussions of "women's literature." Because my professor introduced me to that novel, I gained an understanding of my surroundings that I doubt could have come from her or my classmates.

The novel felt like it had been written for me! I am dark-skinned and was called "fat, black, and ugly" nearly every day of my teenage years. Claudia MacTeer, who narrates much of the action, is also dark, but I was struck by her ability to question assessments of beauty and worth. For example, when her peers have "a loving conversation about how cu-ute Shirley Temple was," Claudia could not join them "because I hated Shirley."[2] Likewise, other children love blue-eyed baby dolls, but she revels in dismembering them. To my mind, these were unthinkable displays of strength. And it became clear that this was a strength particularly valuable for black *girls*. It was not simply being black or being dark-skinned that mattered; it was being those things while also being female. When I was called "fat, black, and ugly" at the bus stop every morning, I was not the only black child, nor was I the only dark-skinned child in the group. We were all black, but I was the only girl . . . and I was dark. As a girl, though I did not realize it at the time, it was my duty to look a certain way so that I would be pleasing or at least acceptable. Not doing so came with a price.[3]

Besides questioning beauty standards, Claudia gives voice to feelings with which I was quite familiar. At one point, Claudia and her sister Frieda have an argument with Maureen Peal, a middle-class girl with a fair complexion. The disagreement ends with Maureen's declaration: "I *am* cute! And you ugly! Black and ugly black e mos. I *am* cute!"[4] Claudia explains her and her sister's response in these terms:

> We were sinking under the wisdom, accuracy, and relevance of Maureen's last words. If she was cute—and if anything could be believed, she *was*—then we were not. And what did that mean? We were lesser. Nicer, brighter, but still lesser. Dolls we could destroy, but we could not destroy the honey voices of parents and aunts, the obedience in the eyes of our peers, the slippery light in the eyes of our teachers when they encountered the Maureen Peals of the world. What was the secret? What did we lack? Why was it important?[5]

These were questions that I had never asked, but I was familiar with the feelings that I suddenly believed should have inspired them.

Surely, if I had had the confidence Claudia possessed, I would have asked these questions, but before I could become preoccupied with criticizing my younger self, the novel gave me reason to show mercy. Morrison has Claudia continue, "And so what? Guileless and without vanity, we were still in love with ourselves then. We felt comfortable in our skins, enjoyed the news that our senses released to us, admired our dirt, cultivated our scars, and could not comprehend this unworthiness."[6]

Gender also came into stark relief when I encountered Cholly Breedlove's back-story. A teenaged Cholly goes into the woods with a girl named Darlene during a church picnic. They are having sex when two white men happen upon them and force them to continue at gunpoint. Morrison's handling of that scene made clear for me that both characters endured a racist assault, but Darlene experienced the violence and its implications in ways that differed from Cholly's experience of it. Neither was more or less traumatic, but there was a difference. Therefore, there was reason to believe that being a man or a woman factors into all experiences. I was not sure that I wanted to understand all that this could mean, but I was intrigued. Certainly, I was not interested in ignoring the truth that I had gleaned.

During my sophomore year, scandal overtook our small liberal arts college: a white woman had accused her black boyfriend of rape. As small liberal arts schools are wont to do, the university scheduled an arbitration hearing, which would determine disciplinary action without involving the police.[7] At the time, what most shaped my experience of the controversy was the fact that student leaders encouraged "all members of the black community" to support "our brother" by gathering outside of the arbitration room. The intended result: the complainant, defendant, and school officials would have to walk through a silent crowd of African and African American students. The black defendant would feel supported, and the others would know that he was supported. A friend and I decided that we would not be a part of such a display because we did not know enough about what had happened to take sides. We were disappointed that so many of our peers had planned to do exactly that without any more information than we had.

My not having stood in (black) "solidarity" led to some debates, but more than I recall explaining my decision, I remember a comment made when only black women were present. We gathered at the beginning of the controversy, when all we knew was that our classmate had been accused and would have to defend himself. Someone said, "Well, that's what he gets for messin' with them white girls." Several women agreed, some of us said nothing, but no one disagreed. I didn't disagree either. I sensed a kind of truth in this declaration but would not have been able to explain why it felt accurate. The remark haunted me. Why would the accused have avoided problems by dating a black woman? Because we don't believe rape happens between lovers? Or, because we won't air the race's dirty laundry even if it does? The implications were many, and all of them were frightening, yet none seemed to be out of step with what I had come to believe. For that reason, the comment would remain with me as I continued on a journey now shaped by the knowledge *The Bluest Eye* had given me.

Determined to raise awareness, including my own, I became interested in living in the Women's House where residents sponsored campus programming on women's issues, including sexual harassment, rape survival and prevention, and negotiating society's beauty standards. Soon, it was all settled; at the beginning of my junior year, I would move out of the dorm and into the Women's House. At the same time, the House of Black Culture was slated to become co-ed for the first time in its history. I was active in black student organizations, so some asked me why I would opt for the Women's House rather than the House of Black Culture. And, of course, some were bold enough to declare that I should have chosen the latter. Their criticism was frustrating, but over time, I had reason to be frustrated with my peers in the Women's House, too. My white housemates would sometimes suggest that healthy body image or domestic violence, for example, were clearly "women's issues" that had nothing to do with race. In other words, like so many other black women before and since, I was pressured to prioritize either race or gender.

Having read *The Bluest Eye* made me see that gender, not just race, factored into the experiences that I would have. That fact came into even starker relief with the interracial rape case. I could not avoid the way that sexuality, power, vulnerability, and allegiance were staring me down, demanding attention and urging me to at least attempt to find answers. How would I negotiate these forces?

That question was already a constant companion when my favorite magazine, *Essence*, published an article about the tensions between white and black women. The piece vividly captured the frustrations that I had regarding both black men and white women; clearly, what I felt was nothing new. I therefore became intensely interested in whether black and white women had ever successfully worked together for political change. I had some inkling that, in making their case for voting rights, white women had insisted that it was wrong for former slaves to enjoy suffrage while white men's own wives and mothers did not have the privilege. Yet, I also knew that black men had made their case for suffrage partly based on the fact that they were men who were no longer slaves; they deserved the "manhood rights" of citizenship. It seemed that both black men and white women made arguments that did not necessarily include black women. So, in addition to being curious about when black and white women worked together, I was also interested in what black women were saying during the decades when no one else seemed eager to claim allegiance to them. In short, I became fascinated with what black women had written between 1870, when black men won the vote, and 1920, when women did.

Graduate school seemed to be a way to pursue these interests, but I was not ready to give up on my life-long dream of becoming editor-in-chief of *Essence* magazine. I enrolled in a study abroad program that arranged an unpaid internship at a magazine in New York. However, I wanted to move to the city in the summer, rather than wait for the fall, and I landed a paid internship with *Travel Holiday*. Based on my work there throughout the summer, the editor allowed me to keep the job through the fall, so I did not have to take the unpaid internship. I lived and worked in New York for six glorious months. Because the entire experience was so positive and educational, when I ultimately decided to pursue graduate school, I did so without regret. I chose an academic path out of desire, not because a magazine career was unattractive.

When I returned for the Spring semester of my senior year, I was fairly certain that I would apply to Master's programs, but I enrolled in a class that changed my life as much as *The Bluest Eye* did. Ohio Wesleyan had hired the only woman-of-color professor that I had seen during my college education. Dr. Anu Aneja offered a seminar on Women of Color authors. Morrison entered our discussions not as a novelist, but as a critic ("Unspeakable Things Unspoken: The Afro-American Presence in American Literature"). Still, I was mesmerized; my other classes had simply not prepared me to believe that women of color had created such rich literary traditions. Our readings included *I, Tituba, Black Witch of Salem, Like Water for Chocolate, The Mother of Dreams,* and *Meatless Days.* In Dr. Aneja's class, it was clear that the literature was significant, not because it was important to represent "minority" voices or even because I related to its characters, but because it was part of a literary tradition worthy of serious study. I had read African American authors before, but because the curriculum seldom incorporated them, my doing so seemed more like a hobby than intellectual endeavor. Dr. Aneja changed that, thereby sparking my desire to teach at the graduate and undergraduate levels. The implicit but powerful message that I received was that you don't have to love Shakespeare to study serious literature.

It was settled, then: I would pursue the Ph.D., and the questions that Morrison had raised for me would be my guiding light. I was determined to face issues that continued to disturb me regarding the rape case.[8] I was also eager to better understand the claims that most annoyed me: "X is clearly about race," and "Y is clearly about gender." Why had Dr. Aneja been the first woman-of-color professor I had encountered?[9] That seemed like a question worth pursuing, and I suspected that the answer was related to the other issues that claimed my attention. After all, the silence around that question reminded me of the silence that accompanied discussions of *How To Suppress Women's Writing.*

II. Tripping and Trippin' on Hierarchies

The same year I encountered *The Bluest Eye* in a Women's Literature course, a guest speaker visited my other English class, which was taught by a professor who had quickly become my favorite. Our visitor was a creative writer, introduced as a real talent to be respected. Because he was invited by my favorite professor, it never occurred to me to think of this guest as anything less than awe-inspiring. He dazzled us with readings from his own work and a discussion of his understanding of literary traditions more generally. Toward the end of the class period, he asked whether we could name the latest winner of the Nobel prize for literature. Someone offered, "Toni Morrison." The guest confirmed the answer and asked if we could list past winners. A string of men's names followed. I had heard of most of them, but not all. Soon, familiarity with these authors' work proved to be irrelevant because the purpose of the exercise became crystal clear. The guest declared, "Toni Morrison won this year's Nobel Prize. You know, it's a good time to be black and a woman."

Suddenly, I felt several sets of eyes on me. Students' eyes. The guest speaker was too caught up in himself to look in my direction. I was uncomfortable and avoiding the glances that came my way, but I remember looking at my favorite professor; he was watching his guest with pride. He sat atop a student desk to the side of the lectern from which the guest spoke. As he let his leg hang off the desk, he was the picture of relaxed reassurance; the speaker's presentation delighted him.

Somehow, I was vaguely aware that I was in the middle of an age-old scenario. This educational experience was shaped by the easy confidence of the white men at the front of the classroom, the racial affirmation that my white classmates had not requested but nevertheless received, and the amorphous cloud of unearned shame that affected the posture and facial expression of the one black student in the room. And I could see that a strong belief was operating, though I was far from having the language to name it. The speaker believed that race and sex did not factor into the success of any of the Nobel Prize winners . . . except Morrison. Being white and male somehow had nothing to do with the prize being bestowed upon most winners. However, being black and a woman had everything to do with the committee recognizing Morrison and her work. I was silently being encouraged to believe this too, and I wasn't sure that I didn't because I had no tools to resist the assumptions. Still, I suspected that if I accepted those beliefs, I would be paralyzed and doomed to a life of mediocrity.

This incident stayed with me for the rest of my college career, and though it did not keep me from applying to graduate school, it certainly haunted me while I did so. I spent several months developing a writing sample for my application;

it examined *The Bluest Eye* with more sophistication than was possible when I wrote about the novel in my freshman year. As proud as I was to have discovered many more critical essays on Morrison's work than I would have dreamed existed, I wondered whether I was making the right life choice. If Morrison's achievement could be so easily diminished, what would happen to me?

III. Acting and Knowing

Because I knew how easily Morrison's work could be dismissed, fear and anxiety were constant companions as I pursued my Ph.D., but the lessons that I learned from *The Bluest Eye* sustained me and helped to shape my work now that I am a professor and scholar. I have come to understand the insights that the novel inspired in terms of belief and performance, and that understanding has fueled my interest in Performance Studies. Belief and performance are always intertwined. In fact, "every performance enacts a theory, and every theory performs in the public sphere."[10] For example, believing that whites naturally belong in places of honor (and blacks don't), the guest speaker publicly questioned the Nobel Prize committee's decision to recognize Morrison. Viewing that fateful day in terms of belief and performance also sheds light on why it seemed like an age-old scenario; its power arose from the fact that it was routine. Because this scene has been repeated so often in American schools, my encounter with it was "at once a reenactment and re-experiencing of a set of meanings already socially established."[11] Looking back, I now recognize a powerful element that I had not been able to identify at the time: when that guest speaker cast himself as an arbiter of merit, his whiteness lent credibility to his performance.[12]

Because it revealed how much being black and a woman factors into my experiences, *The Bluest Eye* eventually helped me to see a simple truth: to recognize the role of whiteness in others' lives is to attend to the semiotics of everyday existence. In this country, "white" skin is not neutral; it carries meaning in all interactions. Those meanings translate into the person with white skin being granted basic respect and the benefit of the doubt, because he is assumed to have intelligence and integrity. Whiteness is privileged and advantaged, and part of the privilege is being able to pretend that skin color has nothing to do with one's achievements. Whites are encouraged to believe that the respect granted to them is based on actual "qualifications" or "merit." However, white professors (for example) are not "just" professors or "just" scholars. They are professors whose racial markers lead most of their students to assume that they are smart and lead most of their colleagues to assume that they deserve their position—unless they routinely prove unproductive. (Several examples of ineptitude won't be enough to undo the assumption of competence. Lackluster performance must be continual and impossible to ignore in order for there to be even a hint of a question about whether they are qualified.) Therefore, it is not an accident that American English departments, for example, are full of certain kinds of people and represent certain kinds of knowledge. These conditions are not the result of a benign tradition; they are evidence of how refusing to admit how whiteness matters *only further advantages those who are already heavily represented.* To put it plainly, United States universities do not look like they do because whites are so brilliant, but because these institutions are set up to ensure that whites are viewed that way.

It is one thing to know that racism and white privilege exist; it is another to understand this fact in theatrical terms that account for semiotics. Recognizing how whiteness is interpreted allows me to gain perspective in countless situations, which in turn helps me to identify what is driving belief. For instance, when I realize that a colleague's being white and male shapes interpretations of his every move, then I understand that even if I duplicated his demeanor in the classroom, students would read me differently. Because a white person's behavior is interpreted generously, they are affirmed nearly everywhere they turn; that makes a difference for them, and it is important to note, rather than ignore, that fact. It puts whites at an advantage so that their experience is not the norm of what American universities feel like or of how these institutions treat faculty members. Theirs is an advantaged, privileged experience. Because I remember this, I am less likely to absorb the beliefs that are promoted, including the myth that *my* success is a direct result of the social and political climate: you know, the United States has gotten to be so liberal (and charitable) that it's a good time to be black and a woman.[13]

The emphasis that Performance Studies places on semiotics has made it a particularly inviting field for me. It enriches my work as a literary critic because it encourages critical readings of the written word as well as spoken words, props, gestures, movement. I have also found that scholars committed to Performance Studies refuse to pretend that they can float above the implications of how their bodies are read.[14] This kind of awareness would do our nation's classrooms a lot of good. However, it is too often only scholars of color who are attentive to how their bodies are read in the classroom, and white professors' refusal to do the same only exacerbates the problems scholars of color face. Research shows how routinely professors who are not white, male, and heterosexual receive student evaluations whose content and tone reflect reactions to much more than instruction.[15] While my teaching experiences have often corroborated these findings, I will not recount them here. I will simply say that an awareness of semiotics has helped me to deal with some of the disturbing ways in which

I have been interpreted by students and colleagues. However, the emphasis on semiotics is just one of the reasons that I find the field empowering; it has also kept me cognizant of the dynamic interplay of belief and performance.

The Bluest Eye helped lead me to Performance Studies because it equipped me to see that assumptions around race and gender animate interaction in everyday life. Beliefs about race and gender create an environment in which people are expected to perform in certain ways. Approaching my research with this awareness has been invaluable, but it has also helped me to navigate the treacherous terrain of American life and culture. After all, one must interpret much more than words to recognize the dynamic ways in which gender and race, power and vulnerability, alienation and allegiance write the scripts that are enacted in everyday life.

I conclude this essay by sharing a recent experience that reiterated the enduring value of the insights I first gleaned from *The Bluest Eye*, especially because I now see them through a performance lens. As I share what follows, I understand that while it is a personal experience, widespread, institutionalized conditions made it possible, so it is also quite common. In this way, it is not specific to me, the senior colleague involved, or even to the institution that employed us. As a scenario in which white privilege is in play, it is "an act that has been going on before one arrived on the scene."[16] In order to survive the "white bourgeois elite intellectual traditions codified as 'the academy,'"[17] scholars of color must negotiate incidents like this all the time, so this story is not unique (though it is not often told in public).

As a tenure-track professor, I needed several classroom observation reports from senior members of the faculty. I asked a senior colleague to observe one of my upper-level undergraduate classes. The colleague is a white woman whose research and overall demeanor I greatly admire. While in attendance, she noticed that students were in the habit of saying "N" whenever they came across "nigger" while reading passages aloud. When she and I debriefed afterward, she acknowledged that the students seemed comfortable with the practice, but she wondered why I had actually made it a policy in the syllabus.[18] We discussed it a bit, and I shared some of my personal reasons. She shared that the issue arises only when she teaches Mark Twain, but she does not shy away from the word. In fact, she used it during this meeting with me. She was not at all self-conscious about it, despite the fact that this was a conversation about my attempts to avoid hearing that word in the workplace. Wanting to enlighten me by sharing her teaching methods, she explained that she makes clear to her students that when the word is used in class discussions, it is "in quotation marks."

So, here I am: a young, untenured professor talking to a senior colleague whom I not only respect but also admire, and she is using the N-word, knowing that I don't appreciate hearing it. My beliefs have been articulated, but her beliefs are also being articulated and performed. Immediately, I must launch into a performance of my own. I strive to control the tone and volume of my voice, my body language, and my facial expressions. I work to convey appreciation and understanding while concealing the many thoughts and feelings that it would not have been "professional" to express. As we have learned from political theorist James Scott, "a convincing performance may require both the suppression or control of feelings that would spoil the performance and the simulation of emotions that are necessary to the performance."[19]

The situation demonstrated how thoroughly conceptions of professionalism privilege whiteness. How many white professors would find themselves in this position, so how much easier might it be for them to be interpreted as professional? Indeed, her cool demeanor was, as always, the epitome of "professionalism." She was being rational and intellectual, wasn't she? Furthermore, she was being generous, not only sharing her wisdom with a junior colleague, but also preparing to take the time to write an observation report.

As I suppressed feelings in order to perform "appropriately," I simultaneously grappled with conceptions of professionalism and collegiality. As others have observed, given the power of white privilege, "the term 'collegiality' becomes a particularly loaded one, offering very little potential for dissent."[20] As I labored to be read as professional and collegial, my task was made more difficult because anger was not the only feeling I had supressed. As cultural theorist Anne Cheng observes, anyone who has been in a racially painful situation knows the "vexing web of feelings that ensues: shock mixed with expectation, anger with shame, and yet again shame for feeling shame."[21] I performed well enough to leave the meeting on a pleasant note. After all, ". . . the prudent subordinate will ordinarily conform by speech and gesture to what he knows is expected of him — even if that conformity masks a quite different off-stage opinion."[22] It was not wise to say everything that I was thinking and feeling. I could not forget that this colleague would soon write a report that would go into my permanent file, to be revisited when I am reviewed for tenure. By that time, my file already contained reports noting "red flags" in my teaching evaluations, including student testimony that I walk into the classroom "like Darth Vader."[23] I was careful about what I said and did, despite how fiercely I disagreed with what was taking place in this conversation. To use the vernacular, my mama didn't raise no fool.

Nevertheless, I could not remain silent for long. I could not sleep that night — partly out of the shame of having performed well enough that I was the only one who left upset. So, I wrote her a letter, focusing on the notion that her students understand that, in her class, "nigger" is always "in quotation marks." Among other things, I said that her rationale fails to "account for the fact that the word refers to me and mine, not my white counterparts."

Speaking from the perspective of a black student in her class, I explained that her practice does not even acknowledge that "I'm the one who feels the sting of that word." Instead, the student receives a powerful message: "If you get the nuances and complexity and subversiveness, then you wouldn't be offended and you wouldn't feel a sting." I continued:

In our racist society, a black student is constantly faced with the knowledge that everyone assumes she's intellectually inferior. So, when she comes into a class and this *quotation mark* scenario is set up, she must find a way to deal, because she sees herself as capable and she wants to prove that she can do as well as anyone else. So, she might say to herself, "If I'm really smart enough, I'll get the distinction, the nuance, the subtlety."

One of the many results: When a class is set up this way, a black student has invisible labor. The word applies to/stings her in ways that it doesn't sting the teacher and other students using/reading it. So, she has to find a way to *work around* what she feels about that word being spoken (in this room in which she is the only or one of few that this word has historically applied to). She has to *work around* the mountain of feeling that it creates for her in order to engage the material and/or engage in discussion and/or enjoy and learn from you. She has to do something with her feelings about what you're doing in order to continue to see you as a teacher who cares about her learning. And the thing about it is this—she'll likely do that work. I certainly did. There will be other evidences that you're a good teacher and that you care about the learning atmosphere you're creating, etc. so the student will do lots of work to ignore that pain and accept that it's just her own sensitivity. (And society is constantly telling her that her feelings are not justified and don't matter anyway.) So, she'll do that work and not feel exactly right about it but never have the words to articulate to herself or to you why it caused unnecessary injury.

Let's also note that this scenario puts white students at a distinct advantage. They aren't just in the majority; they are at an advantage. They don't have to do that extra emotional work in order to engage the class and shine as a student. The course has been structured in ways that don't assault them with racial epithets. This is to say nothing about the fact that they're in an educational system that constantly affirms them by showing that almost all that is worthy of study is white — and the vast majority of people worthy of teaching them are white. Yes, white students are at a distinct advantage.

After writing that letter, I could sleep. If it accomplished nothing more, that was a victory. But it was also a way of reassuring myself that my beliefs were intact, despite my necessary performance.

My mother was right when she said, "Girl, you better act like you know." This advice is powerful in at least two senses. On the one hand, I need to *act* according to what I know is expected of me in situations where power — the power of whiteness — is unmistakable. I did that by acting like a grateful junior colleague who had never considered the brilliant utility of quotation marks. On the other hand, "acting like I know" means operating in this society aware of its history and tendencies. One way I do that is to recognize that white privilege is real, so little in the academy or the nation gives this colleague reason to hear me or to care about what I tried to share about my experiences or the potential experience of her students. Knowing that, I also know that her confidence in disregarding what I said does not mean that her beliefs are more valid; they are just endorsed by a society that routinely accommodates and affirms whites. I say that she disregarded my input because, even after the private meeting in which I shared some personal reasons for the policy and even after the email from which I quote here, she joined the other senior colleagues in my annual review meeting as they criticized my N-word policy. As I had learned from *The Bluest Eye*, gender matters, not just race, but just as surely, race matters. The fact that we are both women did not magically create common ground.

So, "acting like I know" involves recognizing that whites often have the leeway to disregard others. I must be prepared to have them behave in ways designed to convince me that I am crazy or overly sensitive or somehow dreaming up professional disadvantage, lack of support, etc. But being prepared for this also keeps me from believing that race has nothing to do with their success. They may take on the unearned arrogance of believing that their whiteness does not help them, but I don't have to believe the hype.

In a hostile society, survival sometimes requires performing out of sync with one's beliefs. In fact, doing so can often be the best way to preserve those beliefs. I must sometimes behave as if I accept American myths. By doing so, I can claim the psychic space needed to maintain and nurture my own views in the midst of a society that wants to convince me that my perspective is skewed.

When we first met, I did not have the strength that Claudia MacTeer exhibited in resisting assessments of her beauty and worth, but she and Toni Morrison remain with me as I continue to gather the tools to do precisely that.

NOTES

1. Looking back at the book now, I see the opening pages evince some awareness on the author's part of black authors, but I remain confident that I had been right at age 18 to observe that this awareness was not woven throughout the logic of the study.
2. Toni Morrison, *The Bluest Eye* (New York: Random House-Knopf, 1970 and 1994; repr. New York: Holt, Rinehart and Winston, 1993), 19.

3. A similar distinction is made throughout Wallace Thurman's novel *The Blacker the Berry* (New York: Macaulay Company, 1929). The protagonist has gotten a clear message that a dark-skinned man will find success and happiness, but his female counterpart will encounter many more roadblocks.

4. Morrison, *The Bluest Eye*, 73.

5. Ibid., 74.

6. Ibid.

7. It is possible that the victim did not want the police involved, but the fact that this criminal matter was not treated as such is symptomatic of our society's tendency to diminish the crime and injury of rape.

8. Once I began graduate study, I soon realized that the black rapist myth emerged after black men gained voting rights, so it was a powerful political tool. White men labeled black men rapists and insisted that lynching was the best way to avenge the rape of white women and prevent future attacks. Rape can certainly occur between lovers, and the only thing that I know for sure about the campus case is that I don't know what happened between my peers. However, because these issues stayed with me, and I looked for historical alliances between white and black women, I began studying lynching — initially believing that the movement to end it had been truly interracial. Instead, I found that the black rapist myth had been invented for political reasons, and I found black women activists calling on white women to join them in the fight against the mob *for decades* before white women responded in force in 1930.

9. Attending an HBCU was not within my reach. Having that experience has always seemed like a privilege to me, because I needed financial assistance that I was not able to secure from majority-black institutions.

10. Diana Taylor, *The Archive and the Repertoire: Performing Cultural Memory in the Americas* (Durham, NC: Duke University Press, 2003), 27.

11. Judith Butler, "Performative Acts and Gender Constitution: An Essay in Phenomenology and Feminist Theory," in *The Performance Studies Reader*, 2nd ed., ed. Henry Bial (New York: Routledge, 2004), 193.

12. Scholars (more brilliant and experienced than I am) have explained why "white" and "whiteness" are accurate and appropriate terms for dealing with the discourses and practices that I am addressing. George Lipsitz offers a seminal discussion of (among other things) how maintaining the whiteness of institutions often hinges on an investment in pretending that whiteness has nothing to do with how the institution works. See Lipsitz's *The Possessive Investment in Whiteness: How White People Profit from Identity Politics* (Philadelphia: Temple University Press, 1998).

13. To the extent that conditions are better in this country, the debt I owe is to African and African American forerunners who struggled to make a path for me. For more on this, see my article "Generative Challenges: Notes on Artist/Critic Interaction," *Callaloo* 32, no. 2 (2009): 605-15.

14. Of course, I would never claim that Performance Studies approaches prevent obliviousness around race, gender, class, and sexuality. That is perhaps one reason that Black Performance Studies has begun emerging as a vibrant field.

15. The research is extensive. A few citations include, (1) Michael A. Messner, "White Guy Habitus in the Classroom: Challenging the Reproduction of Privilege," *Men and Masculinities* 2, no. 4 (2000): 457-69; (2) Susan A. Basow, "Student Evaluations: The Role of Gender Bias and Teaching Styles," in *Career strategies for Women in Academe: Arming Athena*, eds. L. H. Collins, J. C. Chrisler, and K. Quina (Thousand Oaks, CA: Sage, 1998), 135-56; (3) Nicole Buchanan, "The Nexus of Race and Gender Domination: The Racialized Sexual Harassment of African American Women," in *In the Company of Men: Re-discovering the Links between Sexual Harassment and Male Domination*, eds. by James Gruber and Phoebe Morgan (Boston: Northeastern University Press, 2005), 294-320; (4) Eros DeSouza, and A. Gigi Fansler, "Contrapower Sexual Harassment: A Survey of Students and Faculty Members," *Sex Roles* 48 (2003): 519-42.

16. Butler, "Performative Acts," 193.

17. E. Patrick Johnson, "Black Performance Studies: Genealogies, Politics, Futures," in *The Sage Handbook of Performance Studies*, eds. D. Soyini Madison and Judith Hamera (Thousand Oaks, CA: Sage, 2006), 461.

18. I express my views on this issue as part of a classroom covenant which is placed at the end of my syllabus and course policies. The statement that has inspired comment from people reviewing my teaching is the second to the last of 5 statements. It reads: The "N" word won't be used in this class by a person of any race, even though it consistently appears in our texts.
19. James Scott, *Domination and the Arts of Resistance: Hidden Transcripts* (New Haven, CT: Yale University Press, 1990), 28-29.
20. Anu Aneja, "Of Masks and Masquerades: Performing the Collegial Dance," *symploké* 13, no. 1-2 (2005): 145.
21. Anne Anlin Cheng, *The Melancholy of Race: Psychoanalysis, Assimilation, and Hidden Grief* (New York: Oxford University Press, 2001), x.
22. James Scott, *Domination and the Arts of Resistance*, 36.
23. Students' ability to see me as Darth Vader is particularly telling given that I am only 5'2", wear size 2-4, and dress in a very feminine and conservative manner when teaching.

Mendi + Keith Obadike

Mendi + Keith Obadike make music, art, and literature. Keith is Assistant Professor in the College of Arts and Communication at William Paterson University, and Mendi is Assistant Professor in the Department of Humanities and Media Studies. They have collaborated on several acclaimed works, including *The Sour Thunder: An Internet Opera, Crosstalk, American Speech Music*, Big House/Disclosure (a 200-hour public sound installation at Northwestern University), and *Four Electric Ghosts* (an opera-masquerade commissioned by the Kitchen). They have exhibited at the New Museum, the New York African Film Festival and Electronic Arts Intermix, Whitechapel Art Gallery, the Gene Siskel Film Center, the Studio Museum in Harlem, and the Whitney Museum. Their piece for this collection, "The Good Hand (Praise Song for Toni Morrison)," beautifully collects and composes Morrison's characteristic imagery of loss, mourning, hope and loving attentiveness. "Praise the good hand / That loves what its fingers hold," Mendi + Keith remind us through stirring lyrics and subtle, haunting sound.

Praise Song for Toni Morrison

MENDI + KEITH OBADIKE

One of Toni Morrison's contributions to artistic interdisciplinary innovation was her creation, in 1994, of the Princeton Atelier arts program. The program was designed to support and nurture interdisciplinary collaborations between artists and students from different disciplines. The program attracts artists who are considered to be among the best in their fields because the artists are intrigued by the possibilities inherent in such fertile collaborations.

Historically, the program has offered four course sections with different artists and themes in the spring semester. Each section of the Atelier enrolls ten students, and the size of the class allows for close and intimate interactions between faculty, artists, and students. The guest artists live in residency on the Princeton campus and therefore are more available for engaged participation. Morrison has said that she was inspired to begin the program because of the richness of her own interdisciplinary collaborations.

While working as guest artists in Morrison's Atelier in 2005, Mendi and Keith collaborated with Princeton students in order to craft a multimedia production entitled *Four Electric Ghosts*. The Obadikes' creation was inspired by Amos Tutuola's 1954 novel *My Life in the Bush of Ghosts* and Pac-Man (the videogame created by Toru Iwatani in 1980). According to the Obadikes, "*Four Electric Ghosts* considers the question, 'What does it mean to be invaded by an innocent?'"

We first met Toni Morrison when we were invited to serve as visiting artists in Morrison's Atelier. Like millions of others, we had long been fans and avid students of her craft. So we were thrilled, surprised, and a bit nervous to hear that we would have an opportunity to meet with Ms. Morrison before the program began. In that first discussion, we talked about African literature, the summer weather, and a decorating discovery made when she had paired a new flat screen television with an antique Chinese bench. We soon began to realize that Ms. Morrison had moved from having a casual conversation to making a commentary on our plan to combine new and old forms in our current project. This brief conversation encouraged us to reflect on the power of storytelling in our day-to-day conversations and on the sometimes-thin line between life and art. Over the next few months, not only did we continue to be inspired by our discussions with Morrison about art, we also witnessed her work as a visionary, teacher, and administrator. Having already learned so much from her writing, to benefit as well from these other labors was a truly humbling experience. In honor of her many achievements, we have written a praise song based on her Nobel lecture.

The recording of "The Good Hand," Mendi and Keith's praise song for Toni Morrison, can be found by following the QR code or visiting www.bucknell.edu/Praisesong.

The Good Hand
(Praise Song for Toni Morrison)

At the village brim,
At home, a blind sage waits
For wonder's lost children,
Seeking her weathered face.

As twilight comes,
Suspicious youth arrive.
They hold a hidden dove
They ask if it's dead or alive.

(CHORUS):
Sometimes what's held is not just a bird.
It could be the charged and necessary word.
Unbound quills inscribe the sky,
Calling us to fly.
And the sage says:

Once in the hand,
All dreams of flight depend
On the holder's plan,
Not on the blowing wind.

So praise her good hand
Cherish her brilliant soul.
Praise the good hand
That loves what its fingers hold.

(CHORUS):
Sometimes what's held is not just a bird.
It could be the charged and necessary word.
Unbound quills inscribe the sky,
Calling us to fly.

(BRIDGE):
Circling around a
Nest of the sublime,
Though word cannot land,
It arcs toward our plight

(CHORUS):
Sometimes what's held is not just a bird.
It could be the charged and necessary word.
Unbound quills inscribe the sky,
Calling us to fly.

So praise her good hand.
Cherish her brilliant soul.
Praise the good hand
That loves what its fingers hold.

Barack Obama

Barack Obama is the 44th President of the United States.

Morrison and Obama

I. A Literary Question for Barack Obama

In the series Presidential Questions, *CBS News anchor Katie Couric asks questions that move the candidates well beyond the usual sound bites. Some questions concern policy. Others are more personal. All will give you a better sense of who these men are — and what has shaped them. What follows is Couric's question — and the candidates' full answers.*[1]

KATIE COURIC: What is your favorite book of all time?

BARACK OBAMA: Well, the Bible is the book that shaped me and moved me the most. But, in addition to that, Toni Morrison's *Song of Solomon* might be one of my favorite books. It's just a beautiful, beautiful book. And I've gotten a chance to know Toni Morrison during the course of this campaign, and she's just as elegant and wise and thoughtful as you would want her to be. You know, it's always nice to meet somebody and they turn out to be just like you want them to be. She's just a spectacular writer and a spectacular woman.

II. President Barack Obama about Toni Morrison
Upon Award of the Presidential Medal of Freedom, June 2012

"As a single mother working in a publishing company by day, she would carve out a little time in the evening to write, often with her two sons pulling on her hair and tugging at her earrings. Once a baby spit up on her tablet, so she wrote around it. Circumstances may not have been ideal, but the words that came out were magical.

Toni Morrison's prose brings us that kind of moral and emotional intensity that few writers ever attempt. From *Song of Solomon* to *Beloved*, Toni reaches us deeply using a tone that is lyrical, precise, distinct and inclusive. She believes that language 'arcs toward the place where meaning might lie.' The rest of us are happy to be following along for the ride."[2]

III. Toni Morrison on Obama

"When Obama was elected, Morrison says, it was the first time she felt truly American. 'I felt very powerfully patriotic when I went to the inauguration of Barack Obama. I felt like a kid. The marines and the flag, which I never look at — all of a sudden it looked... nice. Worthy. It only lasted a couple of hours. But I was amazed, that music that I really don't like — God Bless America is a dumb song; I mean it's not beautiful. But I really felt that, for that little moment.'"[3]

NOTES

1. Katie Couric, "Candidates Name Their Favorite Books," CBS Nightly News, transcript, October 2008, http://www.cbsnews.com/2100-18563_162-4557194.html, n.p.
2. Cynthia Gordy, "Toni Morrison Receives Medal of Freedom," *The Root*, May 29, 2012, http://www.theroot.com/blogs/medal-freedom/toni-morrison-receives-medal-freedom, n.p.
3. Emma Brockes, "Toni Morrison: 'I Want to Feel What I Feel. Even If It's Not Happiness,'" *The Guardian*, April 13, 2012, http://guardian.co.uk, n.p.

Linden Peach

Linden Peach is Dean of the Faculty of Arts and Humanities at the University of Wales. Formerly a Professor at Edge Hill University, Peach taught previously at the University of London, Bretton Hall University of Leeds, Loughborough University — where he was awarded a Personal Chair in Modern Literature — and the University of Gloucestershire. He has published widely on Morrison's work, including an edited collection of contemporary critical essays on the author, and a monograph — *Toni Morrison: Historical Perspectives and Literary Contexts*. He has written extensively on women authors, including Virginia Woolf and Angela Carter. He is also a specialist in Irish and Welsh literature. Peach's contribution to this volume contemplates the various abled and disabled bodies that populate Morrison's fiction, arguing for an analogy between the body difference experienced by Morrison's characters and their experience as black women in a masculinist, white-dominated society. The performative and mutable nature of such bodies, Peach maintains, allows Morrison to simultaneously evade and confront the powers that try to pin "Other-ed" bodies down.

Body Difference
in Toni Morrison's Fiction

LINDEN PEACH

The principal signifiers of body difference in Toni Morrison's fiction are race and skin color, although her fiction complicates them through her invocation of miscegenation, in novels such as *Jazz*, and her exploration of difference within black communities, in novels such as *Tar Baby* and *Paradise*. However, there are other body signifiers apart from these in her work that have not received the same attention as race and skin color, important as they are to her fiction. With the exception of the physical war injuries inflicted on Shadrach and the psychological wounds suffered by Plum in *Sula*, it is women in Morrison's fiction who have significant body difference or deformity, such as Eva Peace, who has one leg, (*Sula*); Pilate, (*Song of Solomon*); who does not have a navel; Sethe,(*Beloved*) whose back has been ripped open by a whipping; Junior, (*Love*) whose feet have been crushed. The subject of this essay is Morrison's exploration of the stigmatization of body difference other than skin color and of how this process of shaming is countered by a performative view of body identity.

The breadth of Morrison's concern with body difference reflects the extent to which her fiction explores the experience of being "different" in one's body *per se.* In this regard, her fiction contributes not only to black studies, but to our wider understanding of body image — how bodies are assigned cultural meanings — and disability. In fact, it is Pilate who does not have a navel, who cautions another character (and through him the reader) that there are many different kinds of black.

Pilate's realization that she is unlike other women is a startling moment of body awareness for her, having previously believed that women were different from men in not having a navel. Prior to when another woman disabuses her of this misconception, she hadlived in an Edenic, pre-Fall state in which difference as a negative concept had little part. But coming to a different knowledge of her body, as did the Biblical Adam and Eve, Pilate is made to feel ashamed and stigmatized because she is different from others. It is through such elisions of difference and shame that Morrison's fiction broadens its concern with the way in which non-white skin color became a stigma as a result of the dominance of white ideologies.

The exploration of body difference and stigma brings together the two dimensions of Morrison's fiction, the socio-analytical and the experiential, often in some of her most powerful writing. Erving Goffman, writing at a time when publishing convention was for the masculine third person singular, distinguishes three categories of stigma:

First there are the abominations of the body — the various physical deformities. Next there are the blemishes of individual chararcter perceived as weak will, domineering or unnatural passions, treacherous and rigid beliefs . . . . Finally there are the tribal stigma of race, nation and religion, these being stigma that can be transmitted through lineage . . . In all of these various instances of stigma, however . . . . the same sociological features are found: an individual who might have been received easily in ordinary social intercourses possesses a trait that can obtrude itself upon attention and turn those of whom he meets away from him, breaking the claim that his other attributes have on us.[1]

I. Experiencing Stigmatization

Morrison's exploration of how traits in each of the categories that Goffman identifies "obtrude itself upon attention" is part of a larger examination in her work of how body "otherness," as Susan Wendell argues in a discussion of disability, "is maintained by culture but also limits culture profoundly."[2] In other words, stigmatising those who are physically different does not simply maintain particular cultural ideals of what a body should be but prevents that culture from engaging with difference in ways that would ultimately enable it to develop and survive. Morrison makes a similar point in relation to skin color in an episode in her first novel, *The Bluest Eye,* in which a Jewish American shopkeeper refuses to place coins in the palm of Pecola, a black child. His action causes her to see herself and her difference from white people negatively. Looking into the shopkeeper's eyes, she sees "[t]he total absence of human recognition — the glazed separateness."[3] This proves to be a defining moment in her life, afterwhich her childhood innocence is displaced by awareness of the ingrained divisiveness of human society. Because "she has seen interest, disgust, even anger, in grown male eyes,"[4] she has crossed a boundary which makes a return to innocence, as in Pilate's case, impossible. But the lack of recognition, as manifested in the shopkeeper's behavior, also freezes it, suggesting that it cannot move forward, and the diviseness in human society which the child now sees says as much for white Western culture generally.

In this episode, as in the moment when Pilate realizes the extent of her body diffference and is made to feel stigamatized as a result (which will be discussed in more detail), the focus is on how body difference is not so much a physical fact as a social and cultural construction. Morrison's contribution to our understanding of this sociocultural phenomenon is that, as a novelist, she presents us not simply with perceptive sociolocultural analysis from an African American perspective, but with a narrative of stigmatization from the point of view of those who are ostracized. Her configuration of the experience of stigmatization based on race and skin color highlights its emotional, mental, and social dimensions in ways that are relevant to those who encounter what Pecola experiences because of other corporeal features.

In Pecola's encounter with the shopkeeper and Pilate's recognition that her lack of a navel sets her apart from other humans, the initial defining moment of shaming freezes the prior experience of difference and what had previously been accepted without a sense of inferiority. In each case, the individual who is different is stigmatized, and thereby defined by, what she sees in the eyes of those who do not have the same body characteristic(s). Having seen the hatred in the shopkeeper's eyes, the black child experiences a new way of looking at herself and her world as a whole: "All things in her are flux and anticipation. But her blackness is static and dread."[5] It is worth considering for a moment how Morrison writes the deepfelt experience of stigma. The word "dread" cryptically suggests also "dead," which then influences the affect that "static" has upon the reader. And Morrison's writing is particularly effective here because of the contrast between the moment of post stigmatization, when not only Pecola's "blackness" but her inner self "is static and dread," and her previous condition as a child. The innocence and excitement of being a child, irrespective of skin color or other distinctive body feature, is rooted in an experience of the world as perpetually new. However, this is a moment not only of psychological change but of emotional transference, based on the internalization of the shopkeeper's horror and disgust which leads to another kind of spiritual deadness.

The episode in which Pilate is made to realize that she has no navel depicts the subject's experience of stigmatization in a way similar to that in which Pecola comes to see her skin color negatively, especially in the freezing of her sense of self — in this case, her fluidity, spontaneity, and inner pschology as a woman begins not just with the strangeness of Pilate's navel-less abdomen, but with the way in which a black woman's navel (and the way in which the umbilical cord), a reminder of the perceived destiny of so many black women as mothers, is rendered "strange" and "Other" in Pilate's eyes: "Pilate saw the little corkscrew thing right in the middle, the little piece of skin that looked like it was made for water to drain into, like the little whirlpools along the edges of a creek."[6] The language here, invoking amniotic fluids, de-familairizes a hitherto familiar body feature and relinks the human body with nature and the female body, in particular, with flowing and circling water. But Pilate's view of herself is determined by the way in which the black woman who makes her aware of how different she is looks at her: "And from the horror on the older woman's face she knew there was something wrong with not having it."[7] While she had always accepted her body, unworried by the difference between men and women, she now internalizes the horror in the woman's eyes (as Pecola was frozen by what she saw in the shopkeeper's face) and is stunned by the way in which she is now defined negatively by what differentiates her from others. Recognizing that male and female were different was acceptable because it seemed to reflect and confirm what she perceived as a wider natural order: "It was just like the thing her brother had on his stomach. He had one. She did not. He peed standing up. She squatting down. He had a penis like a horse did. She had a vagina like the mare. He had a flat chest with two nipples. She had teats like the cow."[8] Ironically, this whole episode is haunted by the familiar Freudian concept by which women, lacking a penis, are defined by a sense of lack. However, Morrison does not simply transfer a Freudian concept of lack to a woman who does not have a navel but suggests that a negative view of body difference, including deformity, is sustained by similar paradigms as support Freud's thesis, in which the female is inevitably defined against the male rather than in relation to herself. In other words, body difference is inevitably defined negatively against a body norm.

II. Countering Stigma and Shame

The episodes discussed so far — one based on the stigmatization of skin color and the other on the stigmatization of another form of body difference — are disturbing because they are anchored not only in harrowing moments of shaming, but because they also encapsulate the prejudice that will thereafter characterize their lives, probably on a daily basis. This is the case for all who are ostracized because of their body difference. In discussing *The Bluest Eye*, Jill Matus underscores how "[s]hame displaces anger more thoroughly in Pecola's negotiations with the world."[9] But what is especially important in this seesaw of emotions, between shame and anger, from the perspective of someone shunned by body difference, is the distinction between these two emotions, to which Matus draws attention: "Anger feels better than shame because it empowers her; shame is a crippling emotion that leaves her merely humiliated, disempowered."[10]

Morrison makes a similar point in *Sula* with her depiction of Eva Peace, whose lost leg is the subject of diverse stories about her, including one that suggests she placed her leg on a railway line in order to secure insurance money. But, unlike in Pecola's case, shame does not displace anger in Eva's response to her disability. She has an assertive, almost aggressive, enthusiasm for life, refusing to allow others to define her body difference as a disability. Indeed, she engages in self-mythologization when "in some mood of fancy, she began some fearful story about [the fact that she has only one leg] — generally to entertain children."[11] The incident in the novel that occurs on one body night in 1921 contrasts Eva as disabled, "hoisting herself up on her crutches,"[12] and Eva as bodily different but not disabled when, taking control of her crutches, she "swooped on through the front room, to the dining room, to the kitchen, swinging and swooping like a giant heron. . . ."[13] Eva's actions and the bird imagery in the word "swooped" conjure up the myth of the flying African, based on a folktale about a slave who flew to freedom, which is the principal motif in *Song of Solomon*. But here, the myth is given a female center, and what was a story about overcoming the culturally constructed disablement of race and skin color is invoked in a narrative of eschewing physical difference. Not allowing her loss of a leg to become a disability or to ostracize her, Eva's physcial difference actually enables her to become more a part of the community: "The Peace women loved maleness, for its own sake. Eva old as she was, and with one leg, had a regular flock of gentleman callers, and although she did not participate in the act of love, there was a good deal of teasing and pecking and laughter."[14] The loss of a limb is a signifier not only of body difference, but of the sense of loss African American women experience as black in a white-dominated culture and as women in a black, male-oriented community. A similar point is made in the novel when Sula cuts off the tip of her finger to frighten boys who are poised to attack her and her friend Nel. But Eva's principal role in the novel is as a signifier of how physical difference can change one's personal, social, and communal center of self in relation to marginalization and disempowerment.

Given the recurring concern in Morrison's fiction with the types of stigma that Goffman identifies (based on race, character differences, or physical deformities), it is not surprising that the experience and the origins of shame are dominant motifs in all of her novels. Indeed, in *Song of Solomon*, it is not only Pilate who suffers shame; Milkman is so named because his mother breast fed him for much longer than was usually the case in the community in which they lived. The origins of the name lie in the sense of shame that the community thereafter inflicts upon him. But, throughout Morrison's work, as in Milkman's case, the experience of shame is interwoven with an exploration of the process of projection itself. The representation of negative perceptions of body difference in her writings, including skin color but embracing the other stigmas to which Goffman draws our attention, enables Morrison to explore stigmatization, which is of course central to prejudice and stereotyping, as a social, cultural, and personal-oriented phenomenon, based as much on fear; (the permeabilty of boundaries between acceptable and unacceptable behaviors), as on personal security as an ideology. Wendell, again discussing disability but drawing on Simone de Beauvoir's work, points out that those we define as "Other" are seen as "symbolic of something else — usually, but not always, something we reject and fear and project onto them."[15] However, in Morrison's concern with stigma based on body difference, the key focus is on how shaming and the maintenance of power are inextricably linked in nations, units of a nation (such as communities), and, indeed, in units of a community (such as families).

In her examination of disability as difference, Wendell also argues that "Othering" is "something we can all do to each other, but the process is often not symmetrical, because one group of people has more power than another to call itself the paradigm of humanity and to make the world suit its own needs and validate its own experiences...."[16] Similar ideas are expolored in Morrison's work in relation not only to white and black racialism, but to differences within the black community, a perspective that acquires increasing importance in her work. For example, one of her later novels, *Paradise*, set in Oklahoma in the 1970s, recalls the foundation of all-black townships in the mid-West in the 1870s and the 1920s, where the men running one of those townships project their fears onto the women in a Convent seventeen miles away and also on mixed-race people from whom the townships were established to separate themselves. But, in focusing on categories of stigma other than race and nation in her fiction, Morrison further explores the relation between indivdual self-worth and alignment with cultural body ideals that in *Paradise* leads, as in Nazi Germany (which idealized a pure Aryan race), to a kind of corporeal fascism. Eva's loss of one of her legs, Pilate's lack of a navel, and Junior's deformed foot are vehicles through which Morrison explores how body difference distinguishes them from other black women and locates them in an experience of self in which they, in turn, define themselves in specifc ways and in which each is potentially stigmatized and mythologized, or self-mythologized. But Eva's need to invent stories about the loss of her leg, Pilate's positioning of herself on the margins of society, and Junior's need to hide her feet from the gaze of others are strategies to resist a totalizing cultural view of the body that is unsympathetic, if not actively hostile, to body difference.

Wendell maintains, "When people cannot ground their self-worth in their conformity to cultural body-ideals or social expectations of performance, the exact nature of those ideals and expectations and their pervasive, unquestioning acceptance become much clearer."[17] The "pervasive, unquestioning acceptance" of cultural body ideals, of which Wendell speaks, is the constant presence that Eva, Pilate, and Junior threaten to destabilize in the societies in which they live and that ultimately marginalizes them or always threatens to do so. It is explored with regard to a wider variety of contexts in Morrison's work through the status of mixed race peoples (for example, in *Jazz*), black women's pursuit of white beauty (for example, in *The Bluest Eye* and *Tar Baby*), and other body differences in the three characters on whom we have been focussing. But what these three protaogonists also demonstrate is how Morrison's examination of body difference is usually positioned at the boundary between the stigmatization and mythologization of the body.

III. Mythologizing Body Difference

One of the principal subjects that Morrison explores in respect to the boundary between stereotyping and mythologizing is how far body difference affects self-perspective and the experiences of people who are different from those who conform to the principal body ideal in a particualr culture, society, or community. This is evident in the case of Pecola, as well as Pilate, who lives a life in an all-female household, associated with alternative therapies, music, song and an affiliation with nature. Although, as Matus points out, "Pilate's line neither thrives nor survives,"[18] she occupies a significant and contrary place in a novel that is concerned with fathers and, on a number of levels, male possession of the power of flight (for example, in the myth of the flying African and Milkman's journey into the South). As Matus observes, "[T]here is something free and exciting about her household of women, its nutritional and other eccentricities, wonderful singing, and hand-to-mouth existence."[19]

Drew Leder has suggested that "the body tends to be absent to consciousness except in times of suffering, disruption, rapid change (as in puberty or pregnancy)."[20] To this list, Morrison's fiction adds "body difference." It goes without saying that the experience of body difference in Morrison's fiction is often negative, involving extreme physical and psychological trauma at the hands of whites, in the case of the black slaves in *Beloved*, or at the hands of other African Americans — and even family — in *Paradise* and *Love*. But, as a novelist, Morrison is particulalry interested in aspects of what happens when the body, to employ Leder's terminology, comes "to consciousness...in times of suffering, disruption, [and] rapid change." One of the most horrific examples in Morrison's fiction of a body coming "to consciousness" through an episode of suffering is the way in which Sethe transforms the mess of scars on her back into the shape of a beautiful tree. Sethe does something similar at another traumatic moment in her life when she sees her mother's body (from which she, like other slave children on plantations, was separated from birth) hanging from a sycamore tree that in her mind is transformed into a sublime image. Sethe's response to trauma involves her choosing, as Wendell says in relation to disability and transcendence of the body, "to exercise some habits of mind that distance oneself from chronic, often meaningless physical suffering, increases freedom, because it expands the possibilities of experience beyond the miseries and limitations of the body."[21] This can also be said of Junior, whose feet are left deformed by having a truck driven over them. But Morrison is not simply interested in body transcendence. She is concerned with how the motif of body difference, interwoven with the wider human need to interpret and re-interpret body experience, can be a vehicle for exploring cultural body identity from a variety of historical, social, cultural, religious, and mythological perspectives.

Severe and minor body differences in Morrison's fiction, especially in regard to women, often invite sociocultural and mythological interpretations. Before Sula Peace is ostracized for her promiscuity, she is singled out because of her birthmark, which can be seen either as the mark of the beast or the rose of Christ, depending on the perspective which one chooses to adopt. The possession of such a provocatively ambiguous birthmark challenges the ideal of the pure unmarked body upon which white concepts of cultural beauty and purity were based at that time. But it also disrupts the male-oriented view of the female body (prevalent in both white and African American culture and society, and hence of women in general) as passive and compliant. Indeed, the ambiguity of Sula's birthmark reflects how complexity and dissidence in the mother figure were seen as undermining the way in which the moral upbringing of the family — and ultimately the social staus quo — was entrusted to the mother. But Sula's birthmark also challenges the way in which Christian ideas about Christ and the devil (and about good and evil) are traditionally based on a binarism in white culture that is displaced in African, and hence African American, culture by the conviction that they exist on a continuum. In other words, good and evil exist in a relative and shifting relationship to each other in which the boundaries between them are much less distinct. Moreover, the community's sense of itself is also challenged by Sula's birthmark, for it actually encapsulates an ambiguity which is to be found in their behavior as well as hers.

The extent to which body difference in Morrison's fiction invites diverse mythological interpretations is especially evident in the case of Pilate. Her lack of a navel underscores the novel's concern, and the concern of all of Morrison's fiction, with improbable beginnings. In this regard, Pilate (her name suggests "pilot" as well the Biblical Pilate) reflects *Song of Solomon* as a whole, in which Milkman, under Pilate's guidance, rediscovers and connects himself with his black ancestry. She also reflects Morrison's fiction more generally, in that individual novels begin in a present but undertake a journey into the past, and the way in which her oeuvre can be seen as returning (for example in the exploration of the origins of slavery in *Beloved* and *A Mercy*) to deconstruct a past of which the traditional view is rendered unreliable.

Pilate's missing navel takes us back to the improbable notion, from a scientific point of view, that the human race began with Adam and Eve as the Bible suggests. However, the absence of a navel aligns her with African American mythologies, which include the folktale of the flying African slave on which *Song of Solomon* as a whole is based, and locates her in the mythic dimension of Morrison's fiction and of black culture more generally, as do Pilate's occupations as a natural healer, wine maker, singer, conjure woman, and soothsayer. The fact that she does not have a navel acquaints Pilate with Eve, who presumably would not have had a navel because she was created from one of Adam's ribs. If we follow the story of Adam and Eve to its logical conclusion, it would only have been the children of Adam and Eve, born in incest and in sin, who would have had a navel. Thus, the navel itself becomes, like Sula's birthmark, an ambiguous signifier suggesting the individual's links with her/his mother but also, from the story of Adam and Eve, with incest and sin. Moreover, it is also a symbol of the cutting of the umbilical cord, which leaves each child with an irrecoverable sense of loss, and of Eve's act of transgression, in which eating of the Tree of Knowledge broke Adam and Eve's covenant with God. Thus, Pilate's navel-less abdomen, perceived negatively by others because it is physically different, can be seen as a more positive signifier than bodies that are not physically different from the norm. Without a navel, Pilate's body is neither a persistent reminder of the loss of the mother through the severed umbilical cord, nor of the lasting desire to restore this link with her. There is also a Catholic dimension to Pilate in that she acts as a midwife, to Ruth for example, and supports other women in general; this is redolent of the Virgin Mary, who, according to Catholic teaching, enters and supports the lives of suffering women, with whom she is able to identify despite her own virgin birth and through witnessing her own son's torture and death. The way in which Pilate's involvement in the lives of other women is redolent of the Catholic veneration of the Virgin Mary raises some interesting theological questions. Does Pilate's abdomen, physically different from that of other women, suggest that Mary, who was born outside of sin, was also without a navel, a symbol of the incest and sin into which Adam and Eve's children were inevitably born?

IV. Body Difference and Performance

While the absence of Pilate's navel idenifies her with Eve, Junior's deformed foot links her to the devil and the infamous Salem witch trials, in which the male inquisitors sought signs of the devil in women's bodies. Junior, of course, is a very different character from Pilate. In her independence and sexual assertiveness, she is redolent of Sula. Long before the reader learns of her injury, it is Junior's body and the way in which she carries herself that separates her from the other women in the community and, as in Sula's case, attracts the attention of men. In this regard, she is also comparable to Pilate, who also finds a kind of personal freedom in her body difference.

The way in which Junior constructs and uses her body image to play into and against male fantasies of women, as well as more conservative representations of women, is a theme that Morrison pursues throughout her fiction in works as diverse as *Sula*, *Tar Baby*, and *Paradise*, where independently minded and body-assertive women resist traditional totalizing images of womanhood. Junior's merged toes are a permanent signifier of how the men in her family tried to control and restrict her. But like Sula's birthmark, they suggest that she might have something of the devil in her. Moreover, while Pilate's body difference leads to her mythologization, Junior's deformity, which is constantly hidden by the black boots that she wears even when she is having sex, leads to her fetishization. In making love with Romen, naked apart from her boots, both are aware of the difference that she creates from the way in which other women in the somewhat conservative African American community might be presumed to have sex.

A key element of this body difference, which displaces Junior's concealed disfigurement, is her performance of sexual fetish, of which there is a legacy in African American culture that can be traced back to Josephine Baker and mid-twentieth-century black dancers whose performances were dependent upon a combination of nakedness and fetish. In the bedroom, Romen actually contributes to the fetish by giving Junior his grandfather's military cap, underlining the difference between Junior as an idealized, fetishistic image and Junior as a disfigured female. The dialectic between these two images is similar to that between Eva swooping on her crutches and Eva as disabled because each involves concealing the disablement through recognizing the performative elements in their own bodies. Important to a full understanding of Morrison's approach to body difference here is Judith Butler's argument that identity is based on a dialectic between cultural and personal configurations.[22] In the course of the novel, Junior moves from reliance upon her boots to hide her injuries to a greater dependency upon performance as a way of thinking of herself as a vibrantly sexual women rather than a woman with deformed feet.

Unlike Pilate, who is born with her physically different body, Junior and Eva acquire their body difference through injury that is either inflicted by others (as in Junior's case) or is (allegedly) self-inflicted (as far as Eva's is concerned). Each novel raises questions about body identity and a sense of self. First, there is the question about the relationship between the pre- and post-injury self and, second, the interconnection between self and body when the body that changes over time (through injury, illness, disease, or the process of aging) becomes literally different. This is especially evident in Eva's case, where the narrative stresses her aging, as well as her disablement. Thus, in engaging with diverse body differences, Morrison counters stigmatization through suggesting that body difference is not a static, fixed phenomenon but one that is itself fluid, through recognition of the potential performative nature of the body.

NOTES

1. Erving Goffman, *Stigma: Notes on the Management of Spoiled Identity* (New York: Simon & Schuster, 1963), 4-5.
2. Susan Wendell, *The Rejected Body: Feminist Philosophical Reflections on Disability* (London and New York: Routledge, 1996), 65.
3. Toni Morrison, *The Bluest Eye* (New York: Random House-Knopf, 1970 and 1994; repr. New York: Holt, Rinehart and Winston, 1993), 36.
4. Ibid.
5. Ibid., 37.
6. Morrison, *Song of Solomon* (New York: Random House-Knopf, 1977), 143.
7. Ibid.
8. Ibid.
9. Jill Matus, *Toni Morrison* (Manchester: Manchester University Press, 1998), 45.
10. Ibid., 46.
11. Morrison, *Sula* (New York: Random House-Knopf, 1973), 30.
12. Ibid., 45
13. Ibid., 46.
14. Ibid., 41.
15. Wendall, *The Rejected Body*, 60.
16. Ibid., 61.
17. Ibid., 69
18. Matus, *Toni Morrison*, 84.
19. Ibid.
20. Drew Leder, *The Absent Body* (Chicago: University of Chicago Press, 1990), 92.
21. Wendall, *The Rejected Body*, 178.
22. Judith Butler, *Gender Trouble: Feminism and the Subversion of Identity* (London and New York: Routledge, 1987), 128.

Nancy J. Peterson

Nancy J. Peterson is Professor of English and American Studies at Purdue University, where she studies and teaches contemporary American literature and culture, specifically, ethnic American literatures. She is the author of numerous books on American literature and on Morrison specifically, including *Beloved: Character Studies*, her edited collection *Toni Morrison: Critical and Theoretical Approaches*, and her book *Against Amnesia: Contemporary Women Writers and the Crises of Historical Memory*. Peterson's essay for this volume recounts Morrison's 2006 lecture and special exhibition at the Musée de Louvre in Paris, "The Foreigner's Home" ("Étranger chez soi"). With a deft and insightful analysis of the exhibition's centerpiece — Théodore Géricault's 1819 painting *The Raft of the Medusa* — Peterson aligns the "incendiary art" of Morrison's literary aesthetic with that of Géricault's own provocative, visually-stunning narrative. In chronicling Morrison's intention to make this particular painting the powerful and, indeed, problematic center of her exhibition, Peterson portrays Morrison not only as a prescient artist herself, but also as a revolutionary and perceptive reader of art.

Toni Morrison, Théodore Géricault, and Incendiary Art

NANCY J. PETERSON

On November 6, 2006, Toni Morrison delivered a lecture titled "The Foreigner's Home" (or as it is translated into French, "Étranger chez soi") at the Musée de Louvre in Paris, introducing this theme as the connective thread for the exhibitions and events she organized as a guest-curator for the museum. In her keynote address, Morrison points out that the apostrophe in the phrase "the foreigner's home" can be used to mark possession — meaning the home belonging to the foreigner — or to indicate a contraction — meaning the foreigner is at home (or has come home). In this striking phrase, Morrison's lecture evokes a series of potential contradictions and connections between foreignness and indigeneity, between self and other, between rootedness and mobility, between being at home, having a home, and being homeless.

As a guest-curator, Morrison designed a remarkably diverse series of exhibitions, performances, and events to explore "the foreigner's home." "Corps étranger: danse, dessin, film," a collaborative work between Morrison, the American choreographer William Forsythe, and the German artist Peter Welz, explored the body in motion and one's own body as a space sometimes seeming quite foreign, through video and film, dance, painting and drawings brought into dialogue with one another. "Étrangers dans les societies anciennes Mésopotamie, Égypte, Gréce" included works from the Louvre's vast holdings in ancient Egyptian, Greek, and Assyrian art, selected for their representations of foreignness and difference, and often displaying hostility, fear, conquest, and the forced exile of the other. Morrison's commitment to taking an expansive approach to questions of foreignness, as embodied in ethnicity and race, gender and sexuality, nationality, and other identity markers, made innovative use of the Louvre's collections. Morrison also turned the museum into a place where "foreigners" could find a "home" when she included a slam poetry performance among the events related to her theme. On November 10, 2006, in one of the main galleries of French classical paintings, slammers from the banlieue spoke rhythmically and eloquently about identity, exile, and belonging, and the crowd that came out for the performance included immigrants and young people from the suburbs who may never have visited the Louvre previously. Morrison's guest curatorship at the Louvre was especially timely: widespread protests took place in November 2005 in the suburbs of Paris occupied largely by immigrants, particularly those of Middle Eastern or African background, and one of the reasons Morrison was invited to serve as a guest curator by the Louvre was to open up public discussion of such loaded issues.

Morrison has described one of her goals as a writer as trying "to convert a racist house into a race-specific yet nonracist home,"[1] and the complex sense of race and foreignness she evoked during her guest-curatorship at the Louvre reveal Morrison as a public artist-intellectual, calling into question received ideas of home and exile, displacement and belonging, and using the critical potential of art to create conditions for cross-cultural understanding and social change. This theme emerged quite strikingly in her keynote lecture at the Louvre, when she singled out one work in particular from the museum's vast holdings to evoke the theme "the foreigner's home": a monumental painting (4.91 x 7.16 meters) by Théodore Géricault from 1819 titled *The Raft of the Medusa* (or *Le radeau de la Méduse*, in French).

Morrison's remarks about the painting during her lecture included a description of the visual aspects that particularly intrigued her, as well as some of the gripping, horrific details of the story that inspired Géricault's painting.[2] The first part of this essay brings Géricault and Morrison into conversation as artists to suggest the way that art can function as an urgent aesthetic and critical discourse, and the second part extends this framework to Morrison's 2008 novel, *A Mercy*.

Théodore Géricault, *The Raft of the Medusa*, 1819

I. Morrison and Géricault as Artists

As Morrison mentions in her keynote lecture, Géricault's painting was created in response to the outrage provoked by the sinking of the ship *Medusa* off the coast of West Africa in July 1816. While Morrison has time to mention only some of the more glaring aspects of these events, it is worth taking some time to understand the full dimensions of the story behind Gericault's painting to appreciate Morrison's interest in re-telling the narrative in her lecture.[3] The *Medusa* was one of a convoy of ships transporting soldiers and settlers from France to what was then known as the colony of Senegal. The captain of the *Medusa*, a royalist, was commanding a ship for the first time in twenty-some years because of the Bourbon return to power that followed Napoleon's defeat at Waterloo. Under his command, the *Medusa* outran the other ships in the group. Trying to maneuver through shoals along the coast of Mauritania, the captain went his own course, ignored the advice of his more experienced crew, and ran the ship aground. After two days of being unable to free the frigate, the captain decided to abandon ship. During the evacuation, it became apparent that there would not be enough lifeboats for all those on board. Defying maritime tradition, the captain and his senior officers placed themselves among the 250 people who made it into the lifeboats; the remaining 150 on board were relegated to an immense raft, constructed out of lumber from the ship tied together with ropes. The original idea was for the larger lifeboats to tow the raft to shore, but the swell of the sea made for an unwieldy situation, and within hours, those in the lifeboats cut the towropes.

The focus of Géricault's painting is on the raft — the raft, in fact, as it appeared after various disasters overtook it after being set adrift. The historical accounts of the events make clear that the raft was overloaded, and only those who could make it to the center section were safe from being swept overboard by the waves. On the second day afloat, there was a mutiny: despairing soldiers who had taken to drink attempted to kill their officers and to slash through the ropes holding the raft together. They were eventually subdued by violent conflict or by being thrown into the sea. By day three, it became clear to all that there was a very short supply of provisions on board the raft. In a desperate attempt to survive, some turned to eating the flesh of those who had died; within a few more days, all were eating flesh to prolong their own lives. As days passed without the sight of any ship on the horizon, a series of terrible calculations were forced upon those aboard the raft: some survivors were seriously ill, and the relatively healthy members on the raft held a meeting to decide how to ration their dwindling supply of wine. They decided to throw into the sea anyone who was close to dying. When it was set afloat, the raft held approximately 150 people; by day six, only 28 survivors remained; on day 13, when the ship the *Argus* finally spotted the raft, only 15 survivors were aboard, and 5 of those 15 perished soon after being brought to shore.

A bestselling book written by two of the survivors, Alexandre Corréard and Jean Baptiste Henri Sevigny, inspired Géricault to begin work on his monumental painting. The artist met with the authors and talked with them at length about their ordeal; he also commissioned the *Medusa*'s carpenter to build a scale model of the raft for him. Géricault's quest for authenticity in his painting even led him to the morgues and hospitals of Paris to observe dead bodies and putrefying flesh, and to bring body parts back to his studio to study and sketch in detail. Still, Géricault faced the difficult choice of selecting exactly which scene from the dramatic story of the *Medusa* to use as the basis for his painting. In *Géricault's Raft of the Medusa*, art historian Lorenz Eitner explains that Géricault considered at least five possibilities.[4] Sketches and studies preceding Géricault's work on the painting show that he considered depicting the moment when the sailors on the raft mutinied against the officers, and he considered depicting the desperate turn to cannibalism on the raft. Both of these painterly prospects dwelled upon dreadful aspects of the episode. Géricault also worked on two possibilities that highlighted the redemptive aspects of the story: the sight of the longboat as it approaches the raft, and the rescue itself as the survivors leave the raft and board the boat. In the end, however, Géricault decided to use the moment when the survivors on the raft sight the distant rescue ship as the basis for his painting, and in this brilliant move, Géricault found a way to depict both the horrific conditions on the raft, as well as the possibility of hope.

The story behind Géricault's painting is disturbing and memorable, and it is not surprising that whole books have been written about Géricault and the painting. But significantly, Géricault did not confine himself to documenting the event itself in his painting; rather, he reinterprets the scene symbolically, mixing aesthetics, politics, and critique. A few tantalizing aspects are worth observing. While Géricault's preparations for the painting were extensive and many commentators — including Morrison herself — note his quest for authenticity as part of the power of the work, the survivors in the painting are in fact not depicted realistically. After 13 days on the raft, the actual survivors were emaciated, weak, and severely sunburnt; Géricault's survivors, on the contrary, with their sculpturesque bodies, seem inspired by Michelangelo, whose works Géricault studied and copied extensively during a trip to Italy in 1817. It is also worth noting that unlike other historical paintings of his time, which focused on royalty, nobility, and those with power, Géricault's painting focuses on common men but uses the same monumental scale and technique to sympathize with their struggle.

Géricault's decision to place a black man at the highest position in the painting, waving a piece of cloth to catch the attention of the distant ship, is one of the most striking aspects of the painting. As Jonathan Miles asserts in his recent book, this decision by Géricault was "daringly, dangerously avant-garde" given the racial hierarchies of his time.[5] Corréard and Sevigny, whom Géricault interviewed during his work on the painting, protested the slave trade and were abolitionists, and art historian Albert Alhadeff has argued that Géricault's painting deserves "a fresh analysis, one focusing on the slave trade, its horrors, and the protests that attended it."[6] For Alhadeff, the elevation of the black man represents both "the surge of hope" that takes hold of the survivors as they see rescue on the horizon, as well as the hope that French society might fully embrace the national ideals of liberté, égalité, and fraternité embodied in the composition of Géricault's painting.[7]

While Alhadeff adamantly sees the painting as embodying hope, it is important to notice that in the actual painting the survivors seem to be waving to an empty ocean. Even for someone standing in front of the vast painting (which reaches approximately 16 feet high by 24 feet long) in its magnificent salon at the Louvre, it is almost impossible to see the *Argus* on the horizon. An analysis of the sketches and smaller paintings that Géricault completed while working on a final composition for the full scene shows that the size of the rescuing ship became smaller and smaller in subsequent studies until, in the final version, we can barely spot the ship at all and the raft takes center stage.[8] Through its composition and design, Géricault's painting insists that viewers place themselves on board, alongside the survivors, facing the tumultuous sea, quite uncertain that there will be any rescue. How do human beings react in the face of such crisis? Some with utter despair, others with what might be called deluded hope, and some with resilience: Géricault's painting depicts a full range of response.

In her keynote address at the Louvre, Morrison commends the painting because of Géricault's insistence on history and authenticity. In fact, these are significant elements in Morrison's own fiction, as we recall the newspaper account about Margaret Garner that inspired *Beloved*, or the James Van Der Zee funereal photograph that led to *Jazz*, or the advertisements soliciting Black Exodusters that sparked *Paradise*. Morrison also remarks on Géricault's ability to balance oppositional tensions, to attend equally to the realistic and the symbolic resonances of the scene, to depict "breath and death." Indeed, the father mourning his dead son in the foreground of Géricault's painting receives equal attention as the men signaling the far-off ship. In Géricault's canvas, we are plunged into the midst of distress, death, and despair, along with a desire to gesture upwards, toward hope.

Both Morrison and Géricault as artists understand how to make history come alive by narrowing it and deepening it. Like *Beloved*, which takes the story of Margaret Garner, along with the history of slavery and Reconstruction, and distills them into a family drama focusing on Sethe, Denver, Beloved, and Paul D, Géricault's painting of the raft of the *Medusa* provides an intimate look at a monumental event. And like *Beloved*, which celebrates collective will and community even as it details the manifold violence of slavery, Géricault's work recognizes a collective, egalitarian effort that is forged amid devastation. And like Morrison's *Beloved*, where Baby Suggs tells her followers in the Clearing that "the only grace they could have was the grace they could imagine,"[9] reminding them of the power of their own self-definition and attitude, Géricault's survivors can barely see the ship on the horizon and thus are left to do the best they can with what little they have: a sign of crisis *and* the opportunity to take the measure of one's humanity and inner strength.

As powerfully imaginative artists, both Morrison and Géricault have been subject to criticism and controversy at times. Think, for a moment, of the infamous review of *Beloved* that Stanley Crouch published in 1987 in the *New Republic*, or the fact that *Beloved* was passed over for the National Book Award, leading a group of African American intellectuals and writers to write a letter of protest and support for Morrison that was published in the *New York Times* in January 1988. Géricault's *The Raft of the Medusa*, in order to be exhibited at the officially sanctioned Salon of 1819, was retitled simply as "*scene de naufrage*," or shipwreck scene, erasing all specific reference to the actual incident on which it was based. It won no honors at the Salon, the Louvre did not express any interest in purchasing the painting at the time, and Géricault was plunged into despair. As Lorenz Eitner astutely observes, the painting "seemed to have no point" to spectators and critics of the time; it "violated the norms of national history painting" that Géricault's contemporaries followed; it lacked "hero or message" and presented "martyrdom . . . without glory."[10] The painting did not have clear politics, and its aesthetics were suspect as well, in terms of mingling beauty and horror. It is precisely these unsettling qualities that Morrison admired when she refers to Géricault's painting in her lecture at the Louvre as a great example of art that exceeds its frame: "un exemple parfait de l'art excédant son cadre."[11]

"Art is incendiary and properly so," Morrison proclaims in the talk she gave at the MLA convention in 2004. She adds, "It sharpens us, makes us vulnerable, makes us fierce, coherent, and it can even frighten us. All of which is to say that the practice of great art is the practice of knowledge unseduced by its own beauty."[12] Certainly, Géricault's painting is, in Morrison's sense, an *incendiary* work of art: the painting, after all, depicts not only a devastating shipwreck; it also depicts the failure of Empire, the collapse of a belief that those of rank or those in power are figures of enlightened civilization. But the world itself does not collapse: on the raft of the *Medusa*, amid horrible conditions, some of the survivors are able to create a fragile sense of community, surpassing class and racial stratifications as they come together to lift an African man to a position of prominence. Géricault's painting offers us a powerful look at what comes after empire, and one aspect includes the possibility of reimagining community in unanticipated ways — a project that Morrison explores further in her 2008 novel, *A Mercy*.

II. A Mercy *and Incendiary Art*

On Friday, November 17, 2006, as part of her Louvre exhibition, Morrison read excerpts from her forthcoming novel, which she then planned to call simply "Mercy." One of the scenes she read aloud is the encounter that the slave girl Florens has with a group of people charged with determining whether someone is a witch, a scene that unhinges Florens at the core as they express horror at the color of her skin and wonder whether she is Satan's minion. Like *The Raft of the Medusa*, where Géricault reverses social hierarchies by showing the specter of the fall of empire and by elevating an African man to a heroic position, this scene from Morrison's novel powerfully renders the arrogance and inhumanity of white religious and juridical authority of the time and critiques the way that these representatives of civilization in effect incite wild and devastating turmoil for Florens. *A Mercy* echoes the longing for home, community, freedom, and belonging symbolized in Géricault's great painting and utilizes a richly symbolic setting to explore these issues.

A *Mercy* is set in the 1690s in the colonies of North America — long before the idea of revolution and a "united states" would even be contemplated. Choosing this setting allows Morrison to unmoor received and familiar notions of history and to insist that readers imagine desires, interests, and conflicts from a new angle of vision. Reading *A Mercy*, we step into a land where religion and wealth — perhaps more so than race — set up rigid boundaries between people, and Morrison has commented in interviews that she was interested in exploring a "period before a race hierarchy was established legally . . . when people were more preoccupied with religious differences,"[13] and a time when whether people "were black or white was less important than what they owned and what their power was."[14]

Like Géricault's monumental scene, Morrison's novel depicts harrowing circumstances: almost every character has some kind of personal trauma that he or she struggles to escape. Florens, a young black woman, is the main narrator of the novel and a central character. She has been traded to Jacob Vaark in partial payment for an outstanding debt. She never forgets the moment her mother held on to her brother while offering her daughter to the trader, and that primal betrayal shapes all of the other relationships she enters into in the novel. Sorrow, a "mongrelized" girl whom Vaark also brings to his homestead out of pity, has experienced a devastating shipwreck and creates an alter ego and a series of protective behaviors to survive. Lina, a young Native woman, has lost her tribe and family to the ravages of a plague, probably smallpox; Vaark's purchasing her to work his land becomes a means of escape from the beatings and rape she encountered in her previous domestic situation. Rebekka is the wife for whom Vaark arranges, sight unseen; she is willing to sail across the ocean in horrible steerage conditions and marry a man she knows nothing about in order to escape the indifference and hostility of her own family and to escape the brutalities of London, where public executions, drawings and quarterings, and various forms of inhuman mutilation are a source of common entertainment. Then there are Willard and Scully, two poor white men who have fallen into indentured servitude, who have little hope for much of the novel of accumulating enough money to repay their debts, let alone the "freedom fee" that will be added to the original sum. There are all kinds of slavery, Morrison's novel points out, even as it suggests the dehumanizing awfulness of the slave trade through the understated, yet critical characterization of Senhor, originally from Portugal, who has made his money by transporting Africans from Angola (which was then a Portuguese colony) to the plantations of Brazil, to Barbados, and to "Mary's Land" on this continent.

Even in the midst of devastation and brutality, A Mercy depicts unexpected moments of bonding and compassion. Jacob Vaark sees the child Florens as a human being, not as a piece of property, and so her mother sends the girl to him to try to protect her. He also brings home Sorrow out of his sympathy for orphans. Lina and Rebekka transcend lines of class and race to experience moments of deep friendship and affection. Lina also finds her mothering and protective capacities evoked by Florens's arrival at the Vaark homestead. In her depiction of this household, which becomes a family of sorts, Morrison presents a multi-racial community that parallels the motley crew of survivors that Géricault places on the raft of the Medusa. This family, too, is formed out of fragile bonds, as the novel demonstrates by the end, but nonetheless something human and hopeful has arisen — if just for a while — amid a swirl of competing and sometimes brutal self-interests.

Perhaps the most unexpected moment of community building occurs on the ship that brings Rebekka from England to the New World. She finds herself thrown together to endure the voyage with several "exiled, thrown-away women" in the ship's hold next to pens that house animals, in a cramped, dark, and smelly space.[15] The other women have much more worldly experience than she does; they have eked out an existence as pick-pockets, prostitutes, and thieves. What could Rebekka, who is revealed to be a virgin, possibly have in common with these other women? Yet, what she finds is good company and companionship, and Morrison's novel tells us that "Together they lightened the journey; made it less hideous than it surely would have been."[16] Like Géricault's survivors on the raft, the women form a community in the midst of harrowing circumstances as they make their journey of escape, towards land and the possibility of rescue. Once on shore, the women part ways unsentimentally, without making any false promises to see one another again, and so Morrison's novel underscores the fleeting quality of such coalitions. And yet, the memory of the good company of women stays with Rebekka for the rest of her life, until she hardens into the Mistress who puts Florens up for sale, who distances herself from Lina, and who withdraws from human connections into the Anabaptist Church and its dogmatic teachings.

Several reviewers have noted the Edenic imagery that arises in Morrison's novel from time to time, and John Updike has argued that the novel depicts the "new world turning old, and poisoned from the start."[17] Indeed, the novel ends tragically in many ways, as Rebekka settles into her brittle and harsh widowhood; as Florens carves her story of loss and longing into the wood floors and walls of the ostentatious new house that will never be lived in, knowing her former lover will never be able to read her words; as Florens's mother finally tells her side of the story, not of betraying her daughter but of protecting her, granting her "a mercy," but without being able to reach Florens, so that she will hear the tale. It is up to the reader at the end of Morrison's novel to pull the full story together and to contemplate with terror and pity the missed connections and failed opportunities so dramatically wrought throughout *A Mercy*. The novel, as a work of incendiary art, strikingly reveals the tremendous costs of isolationism on individuals without communities.

As an incendiary work of art, *A Mercy* also offers a strong re-vision of the early settlement of America. One of the most powerful "memories" the book creates for readers is of a continent that is not yet a nation, that is not yet a "United States" founded on white male privilege and the power of wealthy property owners. Some of the characters in Morrison's book, of course, carry that baggage with them to the New World, but the difficult conditions of making a living and sheer survival create openings—openings, though, that will quickly disappear once the familiar, normative way of doing business in America takes hold. What Morrison's novel offers readers is not a romanticized view of the "fresh green breast of the New World" summoned up at the end of F. Scott Fitzgerald's *The Great Gatsby*; rather, it returns to a teeming and pre-national 1690s to remember opportunities for cross-cultural and mixed racial encounters, at a time before legalized racism would take effect. Surely, Morrison's novel returns readers to this particular historical era, a time when there seemed to be enough land to offer a "home" to all, as a critical and urgent reflection on the kinds of debates about mobility and immigration, foreignness and belonging that continue to preoccupy the United States today.

Morrison closed her keynote lecture at the Louvre in 2006 by reminding the audience, "We live on earth, after all, which is every foreigner's home,"[18] an insight that resonates in A Mercy and The Raft of the Medusa. Like Géricault's painting, which combines an extraordinary design and aesthetics with powerful social critique to evoke the ideals of liberté, égalité, and fraternité, Morrison's novel brings together eloquent prose narration and an incisive look into American history to appeal to democratic and humanistic principles. Incendiary art presents a full, unsparing picture of devastation and hope in order to spark what Morrison calls "the moral imagination": "certain kinds of trauma visited on peoples are so deep, so stupifyingly cruel," Morrison plaintively notes in her MLA presentation, that "art alone"—not money, vengeance, good will, or justice —"can translate such trauma and turn sorrow into meaning."[19] The point of incendiary art is not to aestheticize or beautify cruelty or trauma through art; such an approach would pacify the audience and work against the possibility of recognizing trauma as a kind of woundedness that never completely heals. Incendiary art yokes beauty and devastation together in a tense, uneasy relationship to provoke the audience and to produce deep, penetrating knowledge of inhuman cruelty *and* human possibility. As works of incendiary art, Géricault's The Raft of the Medusa and Morrison's A Mercy reimagine the possibility of a radically democratic world where we are all foreigners, and all equally at home.

1. Toni Morrison, "Home," in The House That Race Built, ed. Wahneema Lubiano (New York: Pantheon, 1997), 5.

2. In fact, when the Louvre published the French translation of her lecture, they included a reproduction of Géricault's painting to underscore its importance. See Toni Morrison, "Étranger chez soir." [French translation of "The Foreigner's Home" lecture.] Toni Morrison, invite au Louvre, trans. Anne Wicke, ed. Christian Bourgois, (Paris: Louvre Museum, 2006), 20-21.

3. The series of events that led up to the shipwreck has proven to be riveting not only to Morrison, but also to many historians, contemporary artists, and other writers. To cite just a couple of these works from diverse genres: Julian Samuel has produced a video documentary inspired by Géricault's painting, titled The Raft of the Medusa, Five voices on Colonies, Nations and Histories; a company known as the Plagiarists performed a stage version called The Wreck of the Medusa in Chicago in April 2010; and Kara Walker's cover for the August 27, 2007, issue of the New Yorker juxtaposes images from New Orleans in the aftermath of Hurricane Katrina onto the composition of Géricault's raft.

4. Lorenz Eitner, *Géricault's Raft of the Medusa* (London: Phaidon, 1972), 23.
5. Jonathan Miles, *The Wreck of the Medusa: The Most Famous Sea Disaster of the Nineteenth Century* (New York: Grove, 2007), 179.
6. Albert Alhadeff, *The Raft of the Medusa: Géricault, Art, and Race* (Munich: Prestel, 2002), 137.
7. Ibid, 151.
8. The Louvre has in its holdings two important small-scale paintings that Géricault worked on prior to beginning his work on the full-scale canvas: in salle 61 is the first study (R.F. 2229), and even on a small canvas (38 by 46 cm.), the Argus, with its masts and full sails, is clearly visible on the right side. The second study (65 by 83 cm.) is located in salle 69 (R.F. 1667), and while the sky is considerably darker and cloudier, the ship remains easily spotted on the right side of the canvas. Both of these studies may be viewed online at the Louvre's website: http://www.louvre.fr/.
9. Toni Morrison, *Beloved* (New York: Random House-Knopf, 1987), 103.
10. Eitner, *Géricault's Raft of the Medusa*, 195.
11. Morrison, "Étranger chez soir," 22.
12. Toni Morrision, Presentation for "Roundtable on the Future of the Humanities in a Fragmented World," *PMLA* 120, no. 3 (2005): 717. Morrison's comments about "incendiary art" clearly echo an often-quoted phrase from her 1984 essay, "Rootedness: The Ancestor as Foundation," in *Black Women Writers (1950-1980)*, ed. Marie Evans (New York: Random House-Doubleday, 1984), where she describes the best art as being "unquestionably political and irrevocably beautiful at the same time." See Morrison, "Rootedness," 345. While the 1984 formulation eloquently insists that aesthetic and political concerns need not be oppositional, and in fact work together in great works of art, her more recent idea of "incendiary art" goes a step further in insisting upon a productive friction between beauty and horror, aesthetics and politics, in order to forge works of art that can seize hold of the viewer/reader to illuminate a disturbing situation.
13. Jamin Brophy-Warren, "A Writer's Vote: Toni Morrison on Her New Novel, Reading Her Critics and What Barack Obama's Win Means to Her," *Wall Street Journal*, November 7, 2008, W5.
14. Boris Kachka, "Toni Morrison's History Lesson," *New York Magazine*, September 1-8, 2008, 90.
15. Toni Morrison, *A Mercy* (New York: Random House-Knopf, 2008), 82.
16. Ibid, 96.
17. John Updike, "Dreamy Wilderness," review of *A Mercy*, by Toni Morrison, *New Yorker* (November 3, 2008): 113.
18. The French translation reads: "Nous vivons sur cette terre, après tout. Et la terre est bien le «chez soi» de tous les étrangers." See Morrison, "Étranger chez soir, 26.
19. Morrison, Presentation, 717.

Christine Jessica Margaret Reilly

Christine Jessica Margaret Reilly is a poet and has been published in the *Anemone Sidecar, Asinine Poetry, Breadcrumb Scabs, Blood Lotus, Canopic Jar, Bijou Poetry Review*, CaKe and *Blinking Cursor*, as well as in the Bucknell University publications *Fire and Ice* and *Mirth Grinder*. The two selections featured here highlight the alternating combinations of arresting and comforting imagery that characterize Toni Morrison's own writing. In her preface to the poems, Reilly acknowledges the tensions between "oppressive" and "generative" language that constitute the primary thematic tensions her poetry, particularly these works that were catalyzed by Morrison's own vision and aesthetic.

Morrison as Muse: The Poetic Process

CHRISTINE JESSICA MARGARET REILLY

Throughout her novels, Toni Morrison displays and critiques uses of tyrannical language and, in so doing, illuminates the destruction such violations may cause. She demonstrates her belief in the power of non-tyrannical language by utilizing non-destructive language. In that vein, many of her characters employ language as a generative force. Morrison believes that language can be used as a preventive measure in the spread of oppression. It is Morrison's linguistic practice that has been the greatest inspiration for the development of my own poetic language.

My poem "Blackberry Lips," inspired by Morrison's *Song of Solomon*, explores feelings for a sister who does not actually exist in my life but who is based on Morrison's character Pilate. The lines, "My sister, / didn't know what was possible or impossible / to digest, tried to swallow the universe, / but had to settle for kissing clouds, / open-mouthed, instead" illustrate my view of Pilate's mythical "earth mother" persona. Pilate's role as "big sister" is one that demands protection, careful observation, and a close relationship with the speaker of my poem. The speaker has a plethora of complex feelings toward her sister, mostly pity for her. In spite of her older sister's defiant nature, the speaker realizes that she ultimately fails in whatever she intends to prove or do in her life.

I use my poem "Out of Sethe's Back," inspired by Morrison's *Beloved*, as a means of expressing another thoroughly abstract and universal topic: not death, but birth. In this poem, I do not write frantically with a mission, but rather attempt to paint a picture of a messy, organic, and thoroughly natural life process. In this scenario, I do not search for a prescribed understanding of birth, but seek to capture its pure aesthetic beauty. I compare birth to a symphony of cicadas and describe the female body delicately as I pray for the mother's and child's health and life.

I have always been drawn to the philosophy that reading and writing poetry can be therapeutic or a coping mechanism for both the writer and reader. I hope that my poems reflect the richness I've gained from Morrison's language. In the end, my hope is that the psychological value of my work is based on the spirit of Morrison's ability to utilize specific literary techniques and engage universal spaces and themes.

Out of Sethe's Back

I. The Tree

Her back furrowed and scarred into a constellation resembling
a tree. She gave life while her skin died. She lay
entangled in bedsheets, a white orchard.

II. The Root

When she was dead tired from her whipping she took off her clothes.
I barely knew her; we were by the side
of the road and in this moment
I saw her root-like scars protruding like wings. Her body swathed
in white bedsheets, five petals
from the earth. Her skin like transparent cicada wings.
I salted her back with my tears and prayed
for one more ring of life.

III. The Branch

The branch protects all those
who dwell under it, reach out
to nourish the apples that lie between the bedsheets.
The weeping willow weeps for two.

IV. The Fruit

Fermented grapes in her mouth, blood between the white sheets.
When the baby finally arrived, against
the sun-cracked window, light fluttered in.
Her bones and breasts were full, the baby cried like
a cicada. The baby began to root.

Blackberry Lips

My sister with the Lady Godiva hair, long and lean
like a milkweed seed, played her jazz records
whenever there was rain because she couldn't
tell the difference between the two. My sister,
mouth breather with oven-warm hands,
liked to sing songs in a key that hadn't been invented yet.
My sister, the smoker with big hips and blackberry lips,
made a promise to our mother at the age of five
she could stop chewing her split ends,
the first of many broken promises in her life.
My sister with the oven-warm hands, who whistles
through her teeth, was christened a *smartass*
by boys down the street because she let words
slip from her lips like ribbons of water. The other parents said
put a muzzle on that one. My sister,
who said the word *fuck* like *sunshine.* My sister
with oiled tongue, who gave head to bread, chocolates
and sweet cashews, vomited them up as a sacrifice.
My sister, who was breastfed for too long,
thought every stranger and boy down the street
was the milkman and trusted too much. My sister,
who didn't know what was possible or impossible
to digest, who tried to swallow the universe
but had to settle for kissing clouds,
open-mouthed, instead.

Sonia Sanchez

Sonia Sanchez is one of the most important African American poets and thinkers of the last forty years. She is the author of more than sixteen books including *Homecoming, We A BadddDDDDD People, Does your house have lions?, Like the Singing Coming Off of the Drums: Love Poems,* and her most recent work, *Shake Loose My Skin.* She is the recipient of numerous awards and accolades, notably the Community Service Award from the National Black Caucus of State Legislators, the Lucretia Mott Award, the Peace and Freedom Award from Women International League for Peace and Freedom, the Pennsylvania Governor's Award for Excellence in the Humanities, a National Endowment for the Arts Award, and a Pew Fellowship in the Arts. She has lectured at more than five hundred universities and colleges in the United States and has traveled extensively, reading her poetry around the world. She was the first Presidential Fellow at Temple University and held the Laura Carnell Chair in English there until her retirement. Her selections for this volume — a series of fifteen haiku dedicated to Morrison — capture the enormous possibilities of imaginative writing as it struggles to free itself from its own beautifully restrictive form.

15 Haiku
~ *for Toni Morrison* ~

SONIA SANCHEZ

1

We know so little
about migrations of souls crossing
oceans seas of longing;

2

we have not always been
prepared for landings that help
us suspended about our bones;

3

in the beginning
There was we and they and others
Too mournful to be named;

4

or brought before elders
even held in contempt. they were
so young in their slaughtering;

5

in the beginning
when memory was sound. there was
bonesmell, bloodtear, whispercream;

6

and we arrived
carrying flesh and disguise
expecting nothing;

7

always searching
for gusts of life
and sermons;

8

in the absence
of authentic Gods
new memory;

9

in our escape from plunder
in our nesting on agitated land
new memory,

10

in our fatigue at living
we saw mountains tracking
skulls, purple stars, colorless nights;

11

tree praising our innocence
new territories dressing our
limbs in starched bones;

12

in our traveling to weselves
in the building, in the journeying
to discover our own deaths;

13

in the beginning
there was a conspiracy of blue eyes
in iron eyes;

14

new memory falling into death
O will we ever know
what is no more with us;

15

O will weselves ever
convalesce as we ascend into wave after
wave of bloodmilk?

A. J. Verdelle

A. J. Verdelle currently teaches in the MFA Program at Lesley University in Cambridge, MA. She is a prize-winning fiction writer and essayist. Her debut novel, *The Good Negress*, won five national prizes — including awards from the American Academy of Arts and Letters, the Bunting Institute at Harvard University, and the American Library Association. She has published essays on wide-ranging subjects. She has interviewed Morrison for *Essence Magazine*, *Doubletake Magazine*, and for the *Literary Conversations Series*. She was also on the faculty with Toni Morrison at Princeton University. Her latest novel about black cowboys is scheduled for publication in 2012. In her contribution to this volume, Verdelle composes a series of letters to Morrison. These letters are imaginative non-fiction that presents a novelist, an aspiring writer, and a child growing up encountering the successive publications that mark Morrison's career. In so doing, Verdelle demonstrates how considerably different — and yet unexpectedly continuous, indeed comfortably stable — that relationship has been. Her impressions of Morrison across twenty years — as either "preserving" or "unnerving," or perhaps both — ring as true as her initial impression of Morrison as an enigma, like her home state of Ohio, which "sounds like it could be the same frontwards and backwards, except when you see the spelling, you know it's not."

The Making of a Novelist (Epistolary)

A. J. VERDELLE

Very Near Now
[A Mercy]

Dear Mistress of the Middle View:

The short view of slavery is the traditionally novelistic. Exploring the tawdry, bestial, inhumane intimacy from Big House to slave shack, from private room to public exposure, from ship to sand, from drawn corset to seasonal shoelessness, from Spencer to sacking, from wainscoting to whip. You cover this intimate inhumanity, as do the rest of us, but with better, ascendant words. You lance this part of slavery — whoa, no, not just habitual; friezing how undue and truly pathologic, how morbid, how septic, deranged. You whipsnap through these slavery routines — synoptic, piercing, lickety split. Why linger over the known grotesque? Your way of smacking the intimate truth awake: slaves lined up summarily during their interrupted rest, the spirit of the murdered daughter refusing to die, the slave man made to dance in the woods, TK MERCY. Clean insight. In every key. In every slave century. All across your books. Drawing out the panorama: centuries of evil done, hundreds of years of psychological abuse, laid frayed end of rope to frayed end of rope. So carefully, I wonder if your back hurts. So lyric, so clean, I could call you: ask if you play piano.

The long view of slavery is germane, routine, in history, which is not, exactly, our field. The ports glutted, the seas traveled, the ships consigned, employed or built. Even run aground. The kings involved, the countries engaged, the profits made estimated insured. The cruelty and shock, the dehumanizing, the crude and caustic profiteering. History and psychology entwined. Still astounding, how, in our long history of jurisprudence, we squawk and craw about cruel and unusual punishment, and yet this gangrene, multiple centuries of deep stagnant wounds, so deeply and intentionally knifed and twisted that old blood still congeals, crimson — still hurts, and screams. Nations spend days and months and decades and centuries — tomes and pages of text — trying, brokeback, to deny or ignore, reduce or retract. Protective psychology and survivalist capitalism entwined. History dousing itself — cosmetic sweet.

Between whipsnap and Longview — middle distance. Impatient to be rescued from never-been-done. Of course, nothing about the Past is new or undiscovered, but you rip the skirt off the unmentionable, writing through the colonies, calling them for what they were: wigged, Dutch, shipped, Spaniard, giddy, Portuguese, claimed by Brits, by king. The Europes. When you have the little girl stand up on order, and her coat and shoes are taken to keep someone whiter warm, you still hold on the middle distance — she is not raped, not then, and she is not stolen, not then. She is in a middle hell, where she lives but does not own her name, where she travels but cannot name her destination, where she breathes, but must suffer and shiver and nearly freeze if some snarky watchful white thief decides.

As I sit to write this letter, and compile the others, I can't help but be astonished at how thoroughly I have read your novels. About no other writer can this be said. My Morrison reading is as Complete as Sorrow's chosen name. And this has happened without duty, without fanfare, or trumpet. Your production has been the horizon of my literary coming of age.

I could call you. Tell you I did not hear enough about *A Mercy*. But then, my own distraction, no? Maybe, maybe not. I have been in a dugout, building a series of sodhouses, with Harriett and her cowboy brood. My characters. Your work has taught me about us as characters: rocking crazy or hurrying, harried or walking grit-teeth through this chaos we call our country. I have been preoccupied with my Harriett's whole family: children born, and dead, and trying to survive. Skirting assaults in real centuries, or dying as a result, even as their trials and names and birthdays are completely made up.

I could call you but what can I say to you that you haven't heard or thought of? Still, I could call because I should say I see you write about slavery from a middle distance. Like the middle passage? Yes, no? Not painful like, but true. You made this choice. Silly to question or think otherwise. Do I dare comment on something you surely already recognize? Reading you makes all us think you must have thought or heard of everything.

I know I shouldn't say reading you because you refuse to be read. Reading your work, or your book, is the better expression. Name the book I know.

How *A Mercy* redefines "read"! Just amazing: you are able to take the simple the routine and implode. You did with rememory, again with read. Europe/ Europes too. I started and started *A Mercy* afresh, getting only as far as "but can you read?" until, of course, I managed to routine read the whole. Some insights require that we put a book down — and your œuvre contains a hefty share of these — and go about our day recalling, revisiting, shaking our heads at your perception. This "but can you read?" rocked me. Inside insight. Middle distance. Not about one heart, but not about crowds either. Internal, interior, intimate intelligence. Common to clans — not hordes, but more than one. Conjure-truth rise up. Plenty of us who can read have lost the ability or willingness to read-as-you-remind-us. Life (and the universe) is full of arrangements and symbols and dregs, which would teach if we would (or could) read. Constellations are these. Just as much as tea leaves or smoke. Maybe the time for reliance on these arrangement messages has passed. Maybe these conjure-skills, or spirit-wakings forever gone the way of blood drawings, or cave art, or quills.

Sometimes, it's hard to know whether you are preserving or unnerving.

Very Sincerely,
Verdelle

Nota bene:

I can't help but continue to wonder or to marvel at how (long) you (must) work your amazing phrases. Today, I am thinking of those phrases that are shock full of insight and warning, even as they cross centuries — those you write about, those you write in — like, " . . . the shattering a free black man would cause." We are still, today, forty years after *The Bluest Eye* and a mere two after *A Mercy*, watching this shattering. We do our mediocre cultural best to bear the slicing . . .

I know I should be ashamed, remarking on your phrasing in a Note. But then, it would take a lifetime to write all the notes on you. Would take ten thousand letters, and who would read? Wherever I can say what I can line up the words to say gives me one wrap, which amounts to an articulation. N.B., P.S., even Also, or Finally — individually or together, now or yesterday. Beats a blank. As forty years of your writing has proven, to write and to keep writing is to think and to keep thinking, to live and to keep living. Nota bene, postscript, all of the above, or all of the below.

Circa '03
[*Love*]

Dear Morrison,

Who knew you'd go as far as Heed the Night? And, who would question you? Which one of us could do anything but throw our heads back, remark? Even thinking — three words, one of them heed, one of them the sleep time — reminds us, if nothing else, of all the many names you are known for. Legions of them. You name with the strength of scripture. Names none of us could have thought of, even if we had all the authors the Bible boasts. The topography of naming literary negroes is yours, practically yours alone. Over and over, in twenty years of reading you, I get stunned by the names you lay down. Time and again I've had to put down the book, and call somebody. Did you read? Did you see? Can you believe? You get credit for some doozies, sacks of humdingers: Heed, Denver girl, Beloved, Milkman, Soane, Lone, Save-Marie. Deacon. Steward. Joe Trace, Doctor Street, Rose Dear, Cosey, Vida, Billy Boy, Niggerhead Rock. Cholly, the Peaces, Consolata, Mary Magna, Ming, Pallas, Soaphead Church. First and Second Corinthians. Sorrow, Complete. Violet, Plum, Blue.

We all have a few assertions we always make. One of mine: people grow into their names. I think I got this from characters growing into their names. Or maybe from my grandmothers? I say to my students, you have to know what your characters' names mean. Yes, I know, you choose them. But, choosing does not excuse you from knowing the meaning they carry, beyond the sound or the rememory that lured you to your chosen word. Did I surmise this from you? Or who? Did I decide this on my own for real? The beginning — of a thought or of a book or of a writer or of a woman — is never as crystalline as sunlight suggests. I can say that I don't even know whether names would wave in the wind, little flags, surrenders — if your work had not made me consider them, hold them up to heat, decipher where they come from and what they carry. Parse them for parts. Throwback? Invention? Scripture? Song?

Maybe one day. I'll make a list of the Morrisons. How many names might there be? A directory. Maybe: Inhabitants of Morrison.

Full names, aliases, former names (if given).

Formal names, if known.

Specific place of residence.

[No capers.]

Address: Perhaps their pages, in first editions. (To be consistent.)

If there are addresses in the texts, those too can be displayed. [Absent affect.]

For example: Beloved, 124.

Signed,

A. J. Verdelle

Circa '96
[*Paradise*]

Dear Mother of the Antique Black Twins; Creator of the Oven, Coven, Convent:

You are writing back in history. From now to before now; telescoping from how we are to the way we were. Used to be — twins ran in families. (We had this conversation, you and I.) Used to be people accepted the moniker of mother as always a compliment. (We've half-had this conversation, maybe you rememory.) I realize neither of these used-to-be's are much true anymore. But, you are the mother of the twins in Paradise: the girls dead in the car; and the men: Deacon and Steward, and Zechariah and his brother, say as much about black men as a corps of them, individuals lumped together as a result of a lazy, suspicious and non-empathic world. Mirrors, duos, a quartet; church men, mayor men; renegades, gun-toters; pillars of their time. Their onslaught on us women is inside out, perplexing. Violence not unusual in the main, but stalking, with bullets, a shock and a shame.

Miss Consolata. With her sunglasses and her light sensitivity, she is the blazing star. With her raising by the nun(s) and then her raising up in midlife. Her hot peppers and her demonstration of your particular rendering of love-sickness. (Consolata and Florens battle for that win.) Her walking the road she had not for years or decades traveled. Her mounting the truck and wildly reaching before she smelled the other him. Deacon walks the town in his sock feet or bare feet, one. Shoeless as a slave. Penitent for crimes he cannot (do enough to) assuage. Ruby holds a mirror to our sins against each other: insistence, impertinence, resistance, removal, refusal, denial, telling girls they have no history, before the tea-brown sea.

How you write about love and sex! Next to crosses and habits of religion. Ghosts in the garden. Men in overalls. The wrong men in driver's seats. The biting, fear, blood. Pages show our same drive and hungers. We are not as unique as we think. The nightgown over Mavis's face. Her never seeing her kitchen again.

Paradise keeps slapping *Bluest Eye* and *Beloved*, getting in front of the line. My new favorite book. Your new best book. Deacon and Steward and Lone and Soane stand certain and rooted and determined, while Pecola and Denver and ghosts and rememories half-whine, What about me? I tell the ghosts and children to stop their figment-jostling, ask the Ruby founders to halt their beat-down. I appreciate your agreeing to the interview. And I haven't stopped remembering yet.

Memory is the first test. Of everything, if emotional geography is not compromised, not flooded, not backhoed or otherwise destroyed. I realize these interruptions apply to great territories, but for many, for me, memory works, serves. If I don't remember, then what? What? If I do remember, then yes, there is meaning. Reading, reading, reading, reading, all these words, all these years, I have carried the Consolata you made. Her drive, her tenderness, her sensitivity, her hot green thumbs. She has come with me as a woman of three worlds, or four, or more. Religion and relic, mid-life waking, kindness & devotion, wildness & nurture. Many words and scenes between, before, and after, and she stays, hovers, does not flinch, does not cry. What this means I may still learn. For now, she remains — a memory, a mystery, a living part of *Paradise.*

Mystified, fortified,
A. J. Verdelle

Circa '95
[*Jazz*]

Dear (Noble) Laureate,

I got late with my reading, but I have a good excuse. I wrote a book. It was Hard. My book has been in to the publisher, and they gave it back to me. And then there was some arguing, and then I responded to more queries than is seemly, and now I have had proof pages and galleys and the first editions will be coming soon. I like to think you would be proud of me. How presumptuous. How far away.

Anyhow, it's amazing (I just finished), *Jazz*. The whole time I was reading I was thinking about my own book. Or, the whole time I was writing I was thinking about swing. Jazz relies on swing. Jazz that don't swing ain't jazz.

Jazz has been out for three years already. I had my head so deep in my own novel-one, I couldn't crack the covers. I dutifully bought a hardcover, and *Jazz* has waited, with its jaunty purple teal-trimmed spine.

Now I have read it, and now I know that sometime soon I will read *Jazz* again. There are some amazing lines, as is true of any composition, especially with rounds of solos. You are, of course, doing choruses, solos, riffs. Your singing story swinging round the corners of the City, showing out, snapping time; violent, violet, sometimes sweet. I hollered when you wrote: "The dark hat she wore made her darker. And, when I see them now they are not sepia, losing their edges to the light of a future afternoon."

Jazz plays with time. Syncopates. And rockets. Grooves. Might at night, in cities. Sounds off from stages, beyond which people dance. Smokes. In cave-like rooms, where people whisper-nice or argue. Jazz avoids wide starlight, open fields — where music gets sucked up, suffocated, and where human undulations go silent against miles of dirt and grass. Jazz studies us, our history, our place here, our inventiveness. Jazz places us, and gives us a name.

Truth be told, I love the swing and sultry, the light shifting; the struggle, the outcome, the phrase and the bridge. The chords, the shade and rise. Truth be told, I love this groove, this very phrase: "Midway between was and must be." Is that the middle distance? Verbs upturned; made places, states. I stand there now, Laureate, Morrison. My own work turned to is. I am out here: writing reading reaching.

Astounding to be living in your time.
A. J. Verdelle

Circa '87
[*Beloved*]

Dear Professor Morrison:

Mercifully, I can now afford to buy hardcover books. This seems almost trivial. By now, I have been working — statistics, research, reading, trying to figure out if I, too, can write. I am at the place now where the publication of one of your works does not get by me. My paying attention to publishing — what books come out, when they come out, who's writing new books — is all new, or news, to me. So, I bought the pristine hardcover of *Beloved*, and because I have to finish some work before I can focus my attention and read it, I leant it to a woman who used to be my good friend. We went to another huge church, this time in Boston, where I've accepted a job, to see you. I asked her to bring my book so I could get it signed. She brought it. Without its dust jacket. The white cover was smudged with (her) lipstick. I spoke mean words and thought meaner thoughts. She explained that she thought the dust jacket needed to be preserved — not torn, not mishandled. She thought it would be better to sully the cover of the book. I decided that I was too hot, and the book was too damaged, to warrant asking for your signature. I am uncertain about all this book signing drama, but I do love to hear you read. I'm glad to not have to wait in line for that. I arrive early. You come. You read. It's satisfying.

I've heard you were involved in theater at Howard. You read as if this is true. Very impressive that you knew what you wanted and did what you wanted so early.

Sully might be a good name for a character.

You don't need me to tell you what hot is — *Beloved* is. Who gives a house an attitude but you? Who could imagine the exchange with the stonecutter? Who makes a child so rightly speechless? Who makes a real righteous ghost?

Of course there are ghosts of our murders, our seizures, our struggles to contain our rage. Of course there are ghosts of our mothers, their efforts, their trials and their bleeding feet. Of course there are ghosts of porridge mornings, and hiding, and of incomprehensible struggles to get free. Of course there are ghosts. Of course, mad spirits. Around us and in. You. Me.

Very, very impressed,
A. J. Verdelle

Circa 1984
[*Tar Baby*]

Dear Ms. Toni Morrison:

Getting through college was not easy. University of Chicago was no joke. What I did not realize before I went was that the quarter system meant you had one more term than most college students. When you go to college, you don't compare yourself as much to people in your school, because your friends have all gone to many schools. So, you compare schools. I had to finish a quarter early so that I could finish my incompletes so I could graduate on time. I graduated on time.

In my last term, I went to see you at the Trinity Church on the South Side. Felt like reward. I love the South Side. Hyde Park is on the South Side, but just like people don't admit that Egypt is in Africa, they also don't admit that Hyde Park is on the South Side. Once again, only black people know the truth, and once again, black people live on the south side of truth. My mother has insisted that white people are, in the main, duplicitous, and the more I learn, the more this proves to be true. To call Egypt the Middle East is duplicitous. To call Hyde Park anything other than the South Side is the same. I suspect the University of Chicago, planting and nurturing this Hyde-Park-is-not-exactly-the-South-Side. This seems like a houseplant they would water, set in sun.

There were gobs of people there to see you. At Trinity Church. I thought I had you more to myself. I thought you were closer to my private author. I thought that since I had not yet met many people who were reading, or re-reading, your books, that there would not be many people at the Church. It was a Church, after all. It was a big church. This was a big awakening, to see so many readers throng to see you, to listen to you read, to hear what you have to say about your writing. I still live in Hyde Park, even though I have graduated. I've started a Master's degree, and I plan to move to the north side this summer. Rent will be cheaper. I was not able to keep up with my reading while I was getting my B.A. Especially since I did not major in English, but instead majored in Political Science and Statistics. My parents both say I have to have a career to fall back on. I have decided not to become a lawyer. So many lawyers plan to eventually be writers. I don't want to buy into eventually.

I did not bring my books to be signed. This turned out to be a good idea because the line for you to sign books was longer than any line I have ever seen. I was at the March on Washington in '63, and there were more people there. But, that was not a line, it was a throng. It was a movement. It was a national change in tide. As for an orderly line, I have not seen more people standing, waiting, than I saw that night for signatures in *Tar Baby*, and their carried copies of *Song of Solomon* and *Sula* and *Bluest Eye*. People collect hardcover books. I did not realize that. I'm getting rid of every one of my old textbooks. I will never have a need for *American Demography*, and I know this. Your books, I need.

I've gotten behind in my reading. I'm going to read *Tar Baby* next. And then *The Street*. And then *Scarlet Sister Mary*. And I'm going to read *Eva's Man* again too. Was that book a trip, or what?! Last summer, I did read *The Big Sea*, and *I Wonder as I Wander*. I was a little bit pissed that I hadn't read those books already. Who doesn't love Langston? We all cut our teeth on Langston. Did you? Did you meet him? Why didn't I know about his books beyond poetry? I hate feeling late on the scene.

I'm writing a thesis on women's occupational choices. Testing the hypothesis that women's occupations are less self-selected than men's. I'm calling it "I Want to Be an Engineer." Seems insignificant, even in advance. This dry study mostly douses what rises out of me. After I finish this Master's, I'm going to backpack through West Africa. A lot of my university friends backpack through Europe, but why should I? I've studied French all this time — since fourth grade, since meeting Pecola, who could go nowhere. There are French speaking countries in West Africa. I'm going. I want to cast my eyes on our yanked-from places, even as my lens is now.

But first, I'm going to catch up on my reading. I did want to talk to you at Trinity Church, but eleven or twelve o'clock would have come before I could catch the train home. Too late. Not safe. We all have to make decisions. When to go. Where to stay.

Sincerely,
A. J.
Graduate student,
University of Chicago

Circa 1978
[*Song of Solomon*]

Dear Ms. Morrison:

I talked my mother into letting me take a few days off school to finish my college application essays. I am applying to Harvard and Princeton and the University of Chicago. Michigan State is my safe school. I have visited all these places. They have paid for me to come and have a weekend and meet the other students. If I get in, I think I might go to the University of Chicago because I like cities. I like to be able to go see plays and dance — Alvin Ailey Dance Theater of Harlem Raisin in the Sun Your Arms Are Too Short to Box with God. I like to be around black people, and go to black church if I want to. I like to be able to hear black people talk like black people, and not like white people. If you talk like white people, then you sound ashamed, to me. My grandmother preferred that I talk like white people. I switch back and forth.

The whole time I was reading *Song of Solomon*, I was thinking that I should be writing my college essays. But I read the whole book, before I started trying to get my essays organized. Sometimes when I get caught up in a book, I can't think until I know how the book has ended, until I know what has happened, until I know what the writer is taking all those twists and turns to do. I was the same way with *Manchild in the Promised Land*. I've read that book three or four times in the last five or six years. I hope Claude Brown is OK. And his friends. But mostly him. Readers really learn to root for writers.

Milkman nursing from his mother after he was big enough to walk and talk and run even is just as strange as boys frying shrimp, in the shells, in Vaseline. One of these is a group activity and the other is sort of a secret. Shrimp and baby milk are both food, really. Boys as mama's babies and boys as criminals — both are roles. Neither one is the right kind of man. It's not a straight road for boys turning into the kind of Negro men we expect. Or we need. Or we want. Or their mamas wish they would become.

We have been studying symbolism and theme in English. Seems like for years. In honors English, we were allowed to choose our own books to write our reports, but my English teacher doesn't want me to write about either one of your books. I started with *Bluest Eye*. I've read that book every summer because I root for Pecola, and since I have known that I was going to be able to go to college, I have felt more sorry for her and for Claudia and both their confused mothers. Of course, I still love the way you ~~wrote~~ spelled Cholly, even though Cholly Rich, down the block from Ma Jones — well, he's dead now. They say Negro men do end up dead. Early. Dead — or in jail, which is same as dead sometimes. People they know who are not related to them don't get chance to see them no more. That's what being dead is — not being seen anymore.

After my English teacher said no *Bluest Eye*, then I skipped over asking about Sula because I heard that you had a new book, *Song of Solomon*. As soon as I heard, I asked my sister, who is in college in New York, to send me *Song of Solomon* and she did. I remember the day it came in the mail. I love a new paperback book. The pages are flat at the edges; no yellow; no curls; no marks. Nobody has had the book but me. *Song of Solomon* is a thick book! For adults, I imagined.

As soon as I started reading, I was surprised about Milkman drinking milk, and could see how his nickname would be an embarrassment and would reveal how late he drank from his mother. His history and his nickname were both a burden. The long story of Milkman and his community tell a tale of burdens, of embarrassments, and of doing the same things for too long. I asked to write a report on *Song of Solomon* before I had even finished the book. My teacher said no. I asked why, and my teacher said not to get belligerent. I said I am not getting belligerent and my teacher said fine, choose another book. I said I would like to write about *Sula*. I knew better, but I was mad, which is on the way to belligerent. My teacher said that neither she nor any of the other students in Honors English knew either of these books, or knew of this author. My teacher asked if my mother gave me permission to read the books. I told her that at the moment I was asking for her permission to write about the books, and that whether I had read the books was already history. She said I could bring a note from my mother saying that I had her permission to read any book by "this author" or I could choose a book from the list she gave me. And she wrote out a list. I think it had five books on it. I remember Jane "Air" was one. I can't stand the way white writers refuse to spell things like they say them. They like to pretend that readers don't have ears. I don't remember which book I chose. Maybe a Brontë. Maybe an Alcott. I wrote so many themes my senior year, I could hardly keep them stacked on my desk. Papers sliding. I got very good grades. ("Belligerence" and all.) My English teacher couldn't really argue with me, not about what I read, or how I wrote about what I read. I was determined to be as uniform as a meat grinder, about reading. Steak in, hamburger out: ground meat neat and uniform as worms. But, Mrs. Henderson could close the gate on my choices, since we had to have the books we chose approved. My mother hates writing teacher notes. My mother hates me being confrontational. I did not ask my mother to approve *Song of Solomon*, or any of your other books. My mother no longer has time to read.

Do you listen to Nina Simone? You must. You know her song "I Wish I Knew How It Would Feel to Be Free"? You must. I cannot count the number of times I have listened to that song. Maybe a thousand. Maybe two (thousand). No, actually, maybe 2536 if you count once a day, minus weekends, since I was nine. (Some days I listen to I Wish I Knew How 3 or 4 times, but then there are days not at all. Once a day is an average. And a vitamin.) I remember when I discovered that song. Silk & Soul. Red cover, do you know it? I remember when my mother discovered her record was scratched. She bought another 33 — thank the Lord. I stopped playing the album on the weekends after that, because my mother told me in no uncertain terms not to scratch her second record, not to mess with her music. Nina Simone, especially that song, is my music too. Anyway there's a line in the lyric that talks about flying — like a bird in the sky. (You too are lyric.) About how sweet it would be to find you (I) could fly. About soaring to the sun, and looking down at the sea. That's how you know how it feels to be free. Did Nina Simone help you give birth to Milkman? Does music help you that way? Is it OK for me to ask?

Wondering,
A. J.
Age: 17.

P.S. — I know Song of Solomon uses the Bible as a touchstone. There is so much to read, the Bible included. I am going to read Corregidora next. I discovered Gay Jones this year because my uncle gave me a hardcover (!) of her stories. I have never had a book of my own that had a hard cover and a dust jacket before. I read the stories, and now I'm going to read *Corregidora* and *Eva's Man*. After I read Gayl Jones's novels, I will try to read the Bible.

Circa 1974
[*Sula*]

Dear Ms. Morrison,

I am elated that you have another book. I think I have read *The Bluest Eye* five times since I found it. I remember looking in the library among the PS's and PZ's, since I learned *The Bluest Eye* was listed there. Since discovering that there is a literary section of the library with all the novels and fiction books, I have done a lot of reading and browsing. Thank you for leading me to the literary section of the library. Before I found *The Bluest Eye* on my mother's shelf, I only read books they gave us in school, or that I found at my grandmother's house, or that my mother said. Before I found *The Bluest Eye, Meet Abe Lincoln* and the biography series like that were my favorite books. My sister has all the Bobbsey twins, and I think I read all of those before *The Bluest Eye*. At school we have Nancy Drew, but those go so fast, it's almost not like real reading. I don't care about solving the mysteries; I like seeing what new words there are. Some people read for the story, but I read for the words. I am always looking for new words. Sometimes I read the dictionary, but words are more exciting to discover in context. My grandmother (whose name is Jimmie — you might be interested) bought us a set of books that is like an encyclopedia. It's called the Negro Heritage Library, and was very expensive. I like to read these books on Saturdays after music, or on Sundays after church. There are wax paper pages overtop of the illustrations. I love leaning close to examine the pictures. My grandmother has a magnifying glass that sometimes I hold over the pictures, so that I can see all the details: like what the street signs say, or the bills of slave sale say, or what the white men are holding in their hands. Usually guns or quills or dollar bills. I try not to damage the wax sheets. I always wash my hands before I start my afternoons with the Negro Heritage books. I bet you have these books too. Or, at least that's what I imagine as I study my Negro history. My grandmother was a teacher before she started working for the government. Although she works for the government now, she still behaves as a teacher, if you know what I mean. She wants us to speak the King's English and will not listen to what we say if we speak incorrectly. She wants us to have good penmanship and sees no reason why we wouldn't. She wants us to practice piano every day and to play classical music. She wants us to read read read!

I read constantly. In the library I have found more books to read than I knew there were. I hope that when I grow older, I am able to afford books like at the library. I don't want all the books at the library. You might already know this: There are so many sections, with all different books coordinated in their sections. Although I like science and start my science projects as soon as the school year starts, I don't need the science books at the library. There are many sciences like geology, which is the science of the hard earth and its rocks and its metals at many temperatures, and chemistry which is part naming and part math, and zoology which is the study of animals, and which makes me sneeze just thinking about it. Jerry Lewis is a zoologist in the movie The Nutty Professor. (Jerry Lewis is a chameleon. He's funny on film, and manly in real life, and has a great singing voice, which is a big surprise. My mother says most actors have to be able to act and dance and sing. Jerry Lewis can do all of these although his acting seems to be what he really does and his dancing and singing seems like him when he's real.)

I like writing. I like your writing. You can see through writing. When you read an author's writing, you can see what they think, and what they invent — like engineering. You can see what a writer chooses to write about. You can see what a writer chooses. Writing is like looking through a window. No, reading is like looking through a window. Reading is like looking through a window that the writer creates. The writer would be like an engineer. On the other side of the window, the other side from the reader, the writer has made a world. The world is really words, but the words work to show the reader something like a movie. But this only works if you can read. My grandmother said not everybody can read, even as well as I can. I test in the 12th grade reading level now. After 12th grade is college. I am going to college. But not until I finish twelfth grade. That will be in four years.

Writers do not use every word they could. Writers have to choose which words to use. You have taught me this. And the writers you have led me to in the PS's and the PZ's have taught me this. James Fenimore Cooper uses very different words than James Baldwin. This is part because of the time when they lived and wrote. But James Fenimore Cooper chooses different words than Henry James, because JF Cooper writes about hunting, and animals, and Indians, and white heroes, and H James writes about manners and ideas (and white heroes?). You choose different words than Irving Stone, and you write whole big stories with a lot less words than Irving Stone's big books. Sula is more like Irving Stone than The Bluest Eye would have made me think. If I had to guess what kind of book you would write next, I would have guessed that you would have let Pecola go to college and find a nice boyfriend. Sula is more like girls having a catfight. And a family of women not understanding each other. My family is mostly women. They do get mad at each other and even stop speaking sometimes. I will never stop speaking to anybody in my family. Life is too short, and too many questions to ask.

I have not told anyone I read Sula. I have been waiting and waiting for Sula to come. Well, waiting for your next book to come. But now, I do not think it is appropriate for me to report that I read *Sula*. I cannot even say what *Sula* is about, but I do remember the two of them on the floor all the time. When I am not at all expecting to think of them on the floor, there they are. Poor Nel. Wild Sula. When I am washing dishes, or when I wake up, or when I open a new book to read, or when I am not paying attention at school because we already went over what is up on the board — there they are. If I knew you, I would ask you why you put them on the floor like that. I don't understand why, but I know you made a choice. And I would ask you why you made that choice. It is hard to get that choice out of your mind.

Anyway, I am glad you wrote another book. Even if I can't tell anybody what I read. I think you are really not writing for readers my age. Fortunately, I am growing older, and once I am in college, I can tell anyone I want that I read *Sula*. I am sure I will read *Sula* again. At some time, when I discuss *Sula*, maybe I will understand why you put them on the floor for the reader to look at through the writing window. I don't understand right now.

Reading on and wondering,
A. J.
Summer after 8th grade

Circa, June, 1972
[*Bluest Eye*]

Dear Author:

I chose your book to read, and I chose you as the author I will write to. Pecola Breedlove is my same age. Your character has an unusual first name and last name. I like the characters in your novel. This is the first novel that I have read that is not a book slanted just for children. I got your book off my mother's bookshelf and my mother doesn't really allow me to read her books unless I ask first. I got engrossed in *The Bluest Eye* and I forgot to put it back on the shelf and left the book open on the couch. My mother saw that I was reading *The Bluest Eye* and did not get mad. I was surprised. That this is a book not written for children is what my mother told me when I said, The main character is my age. But she did not make me stop reading.

Our assignment tells us to say why we chose a book. I chose *The Bluest Eye* because of the title. I wondered about the bluest eye, because it is singular and superlative. We live in Washington, D.C. We are native Washingtonians, third generation. My father is always reminding us of this. He says this is very important because most people who live in Washington, D.C. come here. My grandmother takes over the Washingtonian story at this point. She says Washington was a freedman's community as much as it was a national capital. My grandmother always says that free Negroes built themselves up from their bootstraps more than anybody or as much as anybody. My grandmother says that bootstraps are more than we had starting out because slaves often did not have shoes. Especially if they ran off to get free. I know it seems like I am getting off the subject, but I am not. Freedom and blue eyes are related or maybe the same. If you have blue eyes, then mostly you would automatically be free. But if you do not have blue eyes, and you are running off like my great-great-grandparents did, then blue eyes would be in the faces of the people you have to worry over, who might yank you back to the slavery you had scratched and clawed to get away from, to get to Washington DC to be in a freedmen's community and escape. I think if you had the bluest eye of all, then you might be a monster and a yank-person. I thought your book would be a little scary for the girl who is the main character. I thought she might be running off. Or that she might be having a nightmare. Or that she might be chased by a yank-monster who had the bluest eye.

Your title fooled me. Your book is not about blue-eyed monsters. Pecola Breedlove is not running off and she lives much closer to now than to slavery. In order to run off she would have to live in the time of Abraham Lincoln or his mother Sarah Todd Lincoln, and she does not live back then. Your book does not say exactly when Pecola lives, and so that means we are to interpret that she lives close to now, when the book is published, which is 1970. I was ten then. Now I am twelve, like Pecola. Your main character's title is about her doll. I like books more than dolls, as maybe you can tell from my letter. I am very experienced with books. My older sister and my younger sister both like dolls much more than me. My older sister, Brenda, saves her dolls and sits them up like a big collection of little people watching over her while she does her homework and cleans her room on Saturdays. My little sister, Noonie, plays with her dolls as much as I read. My little sister is still mad at me that I took the wire out of her Kathy Quick Curl but she made me so mad always fixing that doll's hair and thinking the hair was magic! Now I am getting off the subject of the book, but it was science, that there was wire in Kathy Quick Curl's hair. I wanted to show my sister the science, and stop her from silly pretending about a silly doll. Now her Kathy Quick Curl's hair does not curl anymore, and my sister is mad. Of course Kathy Quick Curl has the bluest eyes a factory could come up with. Superlative is kind of relative, as long as you are specific. My little sister has lots of other dolls to play with; she should read some anyway. She does not like books enough. She likes doll combs and brushes and dolls way too much to be any fun. Pecola Breedlove does not seem to have doll combs and brushes although she does envy the doll with the bluest eyes, just like my little sister.

What else I like about your book is that evil as he is you spell Cholly like it is said. I know a man named Cholly. Cholly Rich. He is the neighbor one house away at my grandmother's house on Eighth Street. This is my grandmother Ma Jones, not my grandmother Ma Howell. Ma Howell lives on Irving Street and her neighbors that we know are Mr & Mrs Cook, and Mrs Newton. Mrs Newton has five children and they are Jehovah's Witnesses. They are the only Jehovah's Witnesses we know except the Jackson Five. Well, we don't know the Jackson Five but we went to the Baltimore Civic Center to see them, and they are the only other Jehovah's Witnesses we have heard of except for the Newton's, our neighbor's at our grandmother's house on Irving Street, who are the Jehovah's Witnesses we know. But Cholly Rich, well his real name is Charlie. I told Ma Jones that we don't say Char-lee, we say Cholly. Ma Jones said Cholly is another way of saying Charlie, but my mother laughed. I wrote down Cholly, just like you did, and my mother laughed more. My grandmother didn't even look at the correct spelling of how we say Charlie, but my mother laughed until she had tears. I like to make my mother laugh, but Cholly is real. Cholly Rich, down the street. He is never in our house close-up, even though his sister comes. Cholly Rich seems nice enough, or his sister does. Now that I have read your book I understand that negroes probably say Cholly instead of Charlie, even in other parts of the country. It is good to know when you are not the only one. I was glad to see that somebody else than me understood how to spell Cholly the way we say. Even though Pecola's Cholly is not somebody to be calling their name.

There are two really sad parts about your book, even though the book is sad overall. That Pecola's mother has the short leg and is so strained about herself and her not-good husband and her girls. Just as well that Cholly ran off. I wrote not good, but folks around here mostly say no good. And the other sad thing is that after all that, the flowers don't grow and Pecola doesn't get herself or the baby. Pecola goes berserk. All bad things heaped one on top of the other. My mother does not let us do anything by ourselves. We're in the habit now. Even though we take turns washing dishes, we usually are two or three in the kitchen. My mother (and father) say one daughter, two daughters, three daughters — we all do everything at once. Alone is not safe because men are dogs. As you might imagine, my mother says this part more than my father. She does not mean my father or grandfathers. We don't have any brothers. But we do have boy cousins — three of them who are almost our same age. They are a little bit round the way boys. My mother means men we don't know who want to do nasty things to girls. I am surprised to be writing this in a letter to an Author! But you wrote this in your book, so you wrote this first. Although this very bad thing happens to Pecola because of her uncaring father Cholly, and this makes me feel scared and sad, I like that you say it is a bad thing, and don't make it seem half bad and half good.

Thank you for writing *The Bluest Eye*, even if you did write the book for grownups. I have good reading skills, and I score tenth and eleventh grade level in reading all the time. Grownup reading is beyond these grades, but I understood what you wrote, and I liked meeting Pecola Breedlove and her sister, and especially seeing how Cholly spelled his name even though he was a terrible man. We go to Catholic school in the suburbs and so I know you will probably never see us. But, if you ever come to Washington, D.C., I hope that my mother will bring us to see you. I would like to hear you say Cholly out loud, to see if it sounds the same as how we say Cholly. I know that people from different places say vowels different ways, and I know you are from Ohio, not here. I like the word Ohio; it sounds like it could be the same frontwards and backwards, except when you see the spelling, you know that it's not.

Well, I have answered all the questions, and more. I hope that Teacher will choose my letter to be sent off. I have already found the address of your publisher in New York, just in case my letter gets picked.

Sincerely yours,
A. J.
6th grader, St. Margaret's Catholic grade school

L. Martina Young

L. Martina Young is a dancer and choreographer who formerly directed the Dance program at the University of Nevada, Reno and is now a Somatic Pilates Educator at her studio loft, The Lighthouse / Studio 5 0 2 in downtown Reno. She is a co-founding member of the Institute for the Pilates Method in Santa Fe, New Mexico. She is currently writing a book on Joseph and Clara Pilates, and she has earned a Ph.D. in Mythological Studies, with an emphasis in Depth Psychology. In her contribution to this collection, Young weaves an account of *Beloved* that reads the movement and circulation of bodies and their energies as a means of conflating past with present, of bridging love and despair. Young's work, which considers the gap between unconscious and conscious, mind and body, in Toni Morrison's writing, brings the collection full circle in its reading of the Clearing as a liminal space, a territory that is both named and unnamed, and the source of raw psychic energy in Morrison's work.

Beloved Bodies:
Gestures toward Wholeness

L. MARTINA YOUNG

Beloved is an ordeal — a story about memory and forgetfulness, denial and retrieval. Like a conjure woman, Toni Morrison invokes the hidden and forgotten experiences from the recesses of Sethe's flesh and coaxes memory from the shadows of oblivion. She brings a past into a present, ripples onto the surface of consciousness, toward the region where memory's movement can be felt — *must be felt* — so that Sethe can put herself back together in "all the right order."[1] Between a wrecked soul and its wounded limbs, Morrison palpates the gap between conscious and unconscious being. She identifies precisely where healing must take place, where possibility itself abides, and where grace can be imagined: at the most immediate and phenomenal locale — the human body.

"So Sethe and the girl Denver did what they could, and what the house permitted . . . . Perhaps a conversation . . . . So they held hands and said, 'Come on. Come on. You may as well just come [in].'"[2] Thus Morrison begins her ritual, a call, an invitation to the soul "raising hell from the other side" to make an appearance.[3] Morrison is in proprioception to the body's intellectus, and through a performed ritual, she propels her intention to re-implace, reclaim, and restore personal ownership of that body. She does this against the legal and institutionalized framework of American slavery — the historical practice that issued denial of ownership of a 'self' — and a system that reduced black bodies to the status of property and chattel.

As ritual text, *Beloved* performs its healing by the back and forth rhythmic movement of separating and bringing together — actions that are performed by the characters themselves and that underscore the creative contents of the story. Physical acts such as walking, cooking, dancing, folding laundry, and the inching of fabric between fingers — subtle in their perfunctory ordinariness — become the looming occasions for the transformative impulse at the hearts of the author's intention.

Morrison has her finger on the pulse of the ritual archetype. She knows that it is through repetitive rhythmic acts that change occurs. Indeed, ritual *is* rhythm, and it is its active repetition that the transformative arcs around and over linear trajectories. The purposive rhythm in *Beloved* activates a process that, according to writer Wole Soyinka, is a "symbolic disintegration and retrieval of the protagonist ego [and thereby] reflects the destiny of being."[4] The ordeal is a clearing. Furthermore, Morrison's reader is part of this clearing and retrieval process. She asserts: "The Black novel should try deliberately to make you stand up and . . . feel something profoundly in the same way a Black preacher requires his congregation to speak, to join him in the sermon . . . , to stand up and to weep and to cry . . . to change and to modify."[5]

Insisting on the participatory nature of her work, Morrison beckons us to participate, as those gathered around a storyteller, to listen with our whole bodies, to position ourselves forward, poised on the tongues of words, the intakes of breath, and on the wager of the pause. In doing so, we become complicit in addressing what author Dennis Patrick Slattery sees as "a national and communal wound [that] runs so deep that its scar tissue will [never] disappear."[6] Scars do not disappear; on the contrary, they mark and remind — they are carriers of private and public memory like silent soliloquies of human being-ness. *Beloved* is both place and enactment for attending to this communal wound and Morrison invites us — body and soul — to expand our sense of self and wend our way toward a renewed stature of dignity through a clearing ritual.[7]

As archetypal practice, ritual clears the way for resuscitating of a *body of memory* to give birth to a remembered body. In a larger sense, it is the recovery of a people's history, palpating possibility for moving forward and refiguring experiences of grace. Central to its structural workings, *Beloved's* ritual functions by way of Morrison's use of enfleshed language, body-words that are especially grounded in the ritual ethic: as image, actions are linked to memory, carrying continuities through discontinuous bodily movement; as language, ritual refigures notions of freedom and gives grace a new face; as ethos, ritual situates and establishes *Beloved's* logic and worldview. Finally, ritual discloses a metalanguage that adds torque and spin to Morrison's unraveling project.

In her Nobel Lecture, Morrison states: "[Language] is generative; it makes meaning that secures our difference, our human difference — the way in which we are like no other life. We die. That may be the meaning of life. But we *do* language. That may be the measure of our lives."[8] That "measure" connotes a way of being, and language is an echo given form from the depths of that being. Mingling imagination with history, language conveys a way of knowing; it weaves together multiple levels of perception, actualizing a self who belongs to a larger cosmos. In Morrison's *oeuvre*, language not only implies a level of human functioning that marks certain belonging, it also presents itself in a myriad shapes and forms.

As "fixing ceremonies,"[9] the ritual archetype pulses through *Beloved* as music, dance, and poetry — *gestured languages*, ways of knowing and being — that perform Morrison's sweeping poeisis toward healing and making whole what has been torn asunder. Morrison trusts the generativity of all of these languages. She relies on the imaginative capacities of the body to speak in ways that are not only curative but also nourishing to the soul that inhabits it.

"Any analysis of *Beloved*," asserts Marc C. Conner, demands "a sensitivity to what Nellie McKay terms *ways of knowing*."[10] In Morrison's work, these are "*bodily ways of knowing* [informed through] myth and language, African-American musical traditions of the spirituals, blues, and jazz, alternative approaches to history, religion, and ancestry, and the culture specific concepts and philosophical ideas of time and cosmology . . . ."[11] These "ways of knowing" are in relationship to the rhythm and flow of life's circularities and the enfoldings of time: "Oh but when they sang. And oh but when they danced and sometimes they danced the antelope. The men as well as the ma'ams . . . . They shifted shapes and became something other."[12]

The "something other" is precisely what Morrison conjures, and it is the poethical imperative underpinning ritual. The dance of the antelope retrieves a mythic portrait of one's self. Initiating a spatial-temporal shift, one *becomes* the antelope, recalling qualities of being that have been forgotten, lost, or otherwise unattended. In this light, dancing retrieves one's *ante-loping* self — the animal *anterior* or *interior to* the worldly human. Danced ritual becomes the psychological opening by which parts of one's self are gathered and re-implaced in new order, when a body recognizes a soul portrait that is transpersonal, transcending spatial-temporality, even long-held belief systems.

In *Beloved*, rituals are polylogic conversations that revitalize contact with parts of one's self in the physical world as well as in the spirit world. "[A] little communication between the two worlds" reflects Morrison's mythopoetic intent.[13] Along with Sethe, we enter a chthonic world, an undertaking. The story is a cauldron, heat and poultice for drawing out excesses of ruin. By its end, a cooling agent comes on the forgiving breeze of a pause for letting go and letting be.

I. Beloved Rhythms

Beloved's bodies move with a sense of time that is synchronized to a cosmological rhythm. Memory moves in a similar way. Not only does memory rudely disrupt chronological and linear time, but it also asserts and inscribes itself on life's fleeting affairs, invoking the forward and backward motion that repasts the present: Sethe's "brain was devious. . . . Nothing else would be in her mind . . . . Just the breeze cooling her face as she rushed toward water . . . . Then something. . . . and suddenly there was Sweet Home rolling rolling rolling out before her eyes . . . and she could not forgive her memory for that."[14] Morrison weds what might be called mythic or cosmic time with that of linear or chronological time: "Sethe had had twenty-eight days — the travel of one whole moon of unslaved life," and in that cycle of time, she had known "[d]ays of healing, ease, and real-talk."[15] Though Sethe "couldn't read clock time . . . she knew when the hands were closed in prayer at the top of the face [she] was through for the day."[16]

Likewise, Sixo, who "went among the trees at night"[17] moved to the rhythm and gleam of a distant satellite: "Time never worked the way Sixo thought . . . . Once he plotted down to the minute a thirty-mile trip to see a woman. He left on a Saturday when the moon was in the place he wanted it to be, arrived at her cabin before church on Sunday."[18] Morrison's time reflects an awareness not of mere chronological time; rather, she is in relation to the *how* of experiencing time — in its poetic dimensions.

Constructing images that, in effect, slow time down, Morrison slows the rhythm of the reader's relationship to the narrative. Suddenly, the reader's own spatial-temporal locale has shifted; she, too, gazes at the positioning of the moon and, hesitant to move too soon, pauses there and breathes quietly, until the moon has risen one hand's length above the horizon. Synchronizing one's subjective viscera with the celestial bodies, Morrison evokes an empathetic reading weighted with ethical overtones.

Rhythm thus is at the heart of Morrison's project, constituting its transformative process. Throughout, rhythmic images are *embodied* images: the pace with which Baby Suggs, holy — Sethe's mother-in-law — unearths Sethe's hidden earrings "still knotted up" in the (soiled) petticoat;[19] the tactile timing in Sethe's hands as she "took a little spit[tle] from the tip of her tongue with her forefinger. Quickly, lightly touched the stove. Then she trailed her fingers through the flour, parting, separating small hills and ridges . . . then sprinkling water, she formed dough."[20] As Sethe performs *lysis* and *physis* in the making of bread — first separating, then . . . bringing the ingredients into a unified whole — a transformative poeisis takes place. Sethe's body incarnates the actions of *Beloved*'s plot: separating (differentiating), sifting (clarifying), and reintegrating in a new order.

As a bodily act, cooking does not merely suggest a particular kind of rhythm, but is its manifestation: kneading and preparing the dough, baking, and the time it takes to heat and transform the substance — all this is participation with rhythm's nourishing quality. Redressing the body in its poethical consciousness, that is, in its move toward balance, elevates Morrison's narrative. In this light, no image in *Beloved* can be considered arbitrary without risk of collapsing the aesthetics and ethical momentum of the work. Morrison is always in proprioception to this ethos. By not losing touch with the caduceus-like rhythm of an ethical aesthetic, she expands the consciousness of both her reader and her novel's characters, raising both to a higher level of being.

Morrison's bodies are engaged in what Gaston Bachelard considers "pure acts";[21] they wholly inhabit every act in such a way that each gesture speaks with a sentience that both buoys and betrays meaning and purpose. In *Beloved*, moving bodies unfold memory's presence:

> Sethe . . . lifted a sheet and stretched it as wide as her arms would go. Then she folded, refolded and double-folded it. . . . She had to do something with her hands because she was remembering something she had forgotten she knew. [What] was getting clear and clearer as she folded and refolded was the woman called Nan . . . who used different words . . . Sethe could not recall nor repeat now.[22]

The repetition of bodily acts, like the repetition of words in a poem or the measured beats in a song, mnemonically calls to deep memory. With every fold is an unfolding. Sethe's material fold traces memory back. Tracing memory's movement, Morrison summons the way one glides in and out of the present moment, like daydreaming, returning to the present with some snatch of memory, some kind of find that one belongs to or has need of — a retrieval — and, as if having journeyed on the tides and waves of timelessness, is then able to put back one's parts in all the right order.

Employing what Peter Hewlett identifies as "messianic time," Morrison's dual sense of time may be understood as having a biaxial structure: "a horizontal axis of linear time, action and the power to forget intersecting a vertical axis of synchronistic time, stasis and memory."[23] *Beloved* is a matrix of linear time and eternal time — *kronos* and *kairos*. This biaxial notion of time recalls the polyrhythmic schema central to African and African American dance and music forms, and *Beloved* conjures relation to this construct of motion. The body itself becomes the middle ground, indeed the crossroads, where these two temporalities meet and are experienced.

II. The Rhythm of Knots

Morrison's unraveling project is performed the way knots are untied: by fingering and following the trajectories in retrograde — backwards — then pulling the twine forward a bit, feeding it back a bit, then gently pulling it forward again until the knot is undone. The "knot" is a trope; it is an image of rhythm. It is also an image of stasis; its rhythm is tied to the pause. In *Beloved*, the knot connotes several ambiguous functions: healing and protection, and preludes to grace.

Throughout the text, Morrison wields a magic that activates the rhythm of the knot. She traces the knot back and loosens it so that a way forward can be imagined. Tracing memory's lead becomes a creative act that occasions memory's presence. In the backward trace, Morrison "bit by bit" discloses the healing properties that memory holds for constructing a future.[24]

After Sethe arrives safely at 124 Bluestone Road, Baby Suggs, holy suggests tossing Sethe's tattered clothes away because "nothing worth saving in here."[25] Sethe replies: "Wait. Look and see if there's something still knotted up in the petticoat." Then, "Baby Suggs inched the spoiled fabric through her fingers and came upon what felt like pebbles."[26] Hidden in the knotted fabric are "the stones," glittering crystal earrings that Mrs. Garner — the mistress of the plantation Sweet Home — gave to Sethe as a wedding gift, a ceremony that — with "dancing maybe . . . a little sweet william in [Sethe's] hair" — never takes place.[27] With bittersweet humor, Baby Suggs encourages Sethe to put the earrings on, that perhaps they will guide her son Halle, Sethe's husband, home: "Maybe they'll light his way."[28] Rather, the stones light Sethe's way; they are lights born on the back of memory reflecting possibilities yet to be.

The "inching" of the fabric slows to the rhythmic cadence of release. In this instance, the knot is undone, and gemstones are revealed. Sethe's gemstones are apertures of light; they receive light only to project it out in streams of illumination. Morrison is engaged in the dynamics of materiality; thus, the reader too is made sensitive to its workings. The image brings into dialectic tension the rotted and spoiled fabric as an emblem of Sethe's escape from Sweet Home with the image of un-knotting gifts that hide a beauteous light. "[The] knotted earrings in her underskirt" ignite the memory, "when she was soft, trusting."[29] These were gifts "that made her believe she could discriminate among" trustworthy and untrustworthy white people. Morrison limns the trope of the knot and undoes just enough of the story so that some light can shine through. The image of the knot becomes a dynamic healing image that inch Sethe and the reader toward new consciousness — the way full exhales initiate new breath patterns.

Morrison's poetic yields to the dynamics of these images and particularizes the smallest of human gestures, foregrounding them with equal stead to larger, looming images. In this way, the reader is given glimpses of the implicit movement in *Beloved*. The "inching of fabric" between fingers lends the *feel* of how Morrison poeticizes the body and at the same time "[undoes] a bit the cloth" so that "light appears."[30]

The knot functions in another way in *Beloved*. Stamp Paid, "born Joshua" and who "ferried contraband humans across the river,"[31] shows Paul D — one of the Sweet Home men — a picture of Sethe from a newspaper clipping after she had killed her child: "From the solemn air with which Stamp had unfolded the paper, the tenderness in the old man's fingers as he stroked its creases and flattened it out, first on his knees, then on the split top of piling, Paul D knew that it ought to mess him up."[32] Stamp Paid unfolds the newspaper on his knees with a ritual solemnity that carries knowledge of the fragility shame and horror can wield on a human being; this quality alerts Paul D to the gravity of the news. In antiquity, the knees, according to Richard B. Onians, were not only considered to be the seat of vitality and strength, but also perceived as having sanctity; it was a joint of "empty space" that if pierced, "the spirit flows away."[33]

Unable to read the newsprint, Paul D reads Stamp Paid's body instead: the placement and cadence of Stamp Paid's hands; the belabored act of unfolding the paper.[34] Together with the picture of Sethe who *is not* Sethe — "Uh, uh. No way. A little semblance round the forehead maybe, but this ain't her mouth"[35] — Paul D is altered.

Paul D descends to the cellar of the community church, "Holy Redeemer," to sleep and where it is "cold as charity."[36] He "[holds] his wrists between his knees,"[37] Morrison writes, "not to keep his hands still but because he had nothing else to hold on to."[38] Knotted and folded in the void, Paul D holds has only the sanctity of his being to hold on to. Morrison creates a double or two-way tension: on the one hand, she presents a grave image — the cellar of the spiritual house — an image *down under*, weighted by the tragic contents of Paul D's life; on the other, the image of Paul D *knotted up* gives the reader an image by which to experience empathy for a human body. Paul D *is* the knot. His body is wrested and whipped; it weeps. The knot performs its double by positioning and situating, preparing and bracing Paul D's immanent unfolding.

Noting the aesthetic imperative of an image of tragedy in terms of music and dance as portrayed in traditional Yoruba drama, Soyinka writes: "Tragic music is an echo from [the] void; the celebrant [initiate] speaks, sings, and dances in archetypal images from within the abyss. All understand and respond, for it is the language of the world."[39] Morrison attends to this language. She invokes empathic response through the knot because it is an *experience* in the world. Locked against what he cannot imagine, Paul D is arrested by the truth of Sethe's act. He folds into the pause, into the void.

Rendered still between truth and understanding, the knot — the pause — is the only place from which he gains insight into himself and, into Sethe. "Truth," writes Hannah Arendt, "can reveal itself in complete human stillness."[40] The knot as pause serves as bridge toward understanding, a translation of a deeper truth. In literary criticism, the "pause" according to Aristotle, is "the elaboration of poetic diction."[41] Thus poet Rainer Maria Rilke writes: "Sometimes during a brief pause, a tender look edges forward to bridge the chasm."[42] Morrison invokes our most tender look.

Within African cosmology, and within Yoruba culture in particular, Soyinka further explains that the *off beat* or silent beat is embraced as a perception "within the whole of the life's rhythm."[43] In ritual, it connotes "the resting place for the departed, and a staging-place for the unborn."[44] Thus, the pause is a place of transition; it is the moment for rites of passage. *Beloved's* ethic abides in this understanding of the "integrated acceptance of this temporal sense of the life-rhythm."

The knot is an image of the poetic pause; it is snare and bridge that act on behalf of *Beloved's* structural and rhythmic sense. As a catalyst, it asserts Morrison's intention to invoke the harmonious existence within the individual self, as well as between the community and the cosmos. "Human life is holy, all of it."[45] Affirming "the principle of continuity" inherent in the ritual archetype,[46] she carves out a place and time for regaining physical and psychic balance, gathering up all the parts and refashioning them in the most appropriate order, for the individual and for the world.

Connoting a contemplative and chthonic realm, the pause functions like an underground seed that contains all potential and possibility; it signals the still point from which Paul D gathers all the parts of himself. Being the knot is prelude to his ability to walk toward Sethe. The knot performs the test and resolve of Paul D's greatest agency: grace — an integrative knowing of what is, what has been, and what could possibly be.

There are moments in "other times, [when] Beloved curled up on the floor, her wrists between her knees . . . ."[47] The knot re-appears and alerts Denver to the gravity of the situation. Seeing Beloved's contorted body is the catalyst that gives birth to Denver's dignity, a glimpse of her burgeoning self and her sense of being *other*. Beloved as the *knot* pronounces Denver's peripeteia, her turnaround. In this regard, the knot performs as protective agent, signaling not only caution but also the recognition of "having a self" to be cautious for. When Stamp Paid delivers Sethe and the baby Denver to the other side of the river, he "leaves the old sty open when there's a crossing. Knots a white rag on the post if there's a child too."[48] In this context, the knot "preserves the newly born."[49]

There is a delicate yet muscular rigor to Morrison's project of knotting and unknotting that constitutes *Beloved*'s dynamic and ethical fiber. Just below the brow of consciousness, the music of the spheres can be heard; it takes the form of an eternal rhythm pulsing through all things, a rhythm that is the movement of consciousness itself. In all its guises, rhythm is a constant presence, and its rituals articulate *Beloved*'s anatomies toward freedom and grace. To further illuminate Morrison's poetics, the Greek term *stoicheiosis* is applied, where the meaning of the word reflects the rich complexity and craft of *Beloved*.

III. Stoicheiosis: Activating the Image

In its classical context, the root form *stoicheo* means, "to be in a line," and "to march in rank and file." According to Proclus, Greek philosopher and mathematician, the term refers to the movement of "the elementary principles of the world": that is circularity.[50] Thus, the line is a round, and the elements of the world move in an orderly circle; they are in relational proprioception to one another. Further, the term recalls Plato's imagination of heavenly bodies: the sun, moon, and stars as the "moving gods" of the cosmos.

The noun form, *stoicheion*, suggests, "that which belongs to a series." In terms of music, *stoicheiosis* refers to the overtones produced by the notes, also referred to as the "shadow-lines." In *Beloved*, "[they] were not holding hands, but their shadows were. Sethe looked to the left and all three of them were gliding over the dust holding hands . . . . Nobody noticed but Sethe."[51] The passage exemplifies the term *stoicheion* in the sense that the position of the sun activates the image through a cast of shadows. The shadows are the overtones produced between heavenly and earthly bodies. Morrison brings our attention to this relationship: "[On] the way home, although leading them now, the shadows of the three people still held hands."[52] The position of the sun has shifted, and so has the image. The interlaced shadows lead the trio home; it is a generative image that projects possibilities for Sethe: "It was a good sign. A life. Could be."[53] The movement of the sun and the forward and reverse movement of the characters recall the circular round of Greek poet Pindar's *strophe, antistrophe,* and *epode;* it is the movement that mirrors the round dance of the stars.[54]

In its variant forms, *stoicheiosis* connotes relational motion, connoting meanings having to do with the rhythmic nature of things. In aesthetics, this is also the case, as it implies the activation of images "by specially magical processes."[55] Magic often implies the work and actions of supernatural powers — the invisible made visible. Activating the image implies that the image comes with a life force, possessing a certain power that causes the image to "act" with its own agency. Morrison's poetics palpate this life force in a concrete way, viscerally, through movement and rhythm. Using the organizing principle of rhythm's nature, Morrison leans on what Owen Barfield calls the "progressive incarnation of life in consciousness."[56]

The dramatic oscillation of the text mirrors the way one reads it. As the eye shuttles back and forth across the page between the past and the present, a momentary experience of dislocation occurs, followed by integration. In the oscillation, continuity is created. Insights are awakened and meanings revealed, as the reader, in time, discovers the novel's unity amidst its disparate and fragmented parts. Morrison's writing performs *stoicheiosis*.

In the same way that the inter-textual reading of the Bible is key to understanding its continuity and wholeness, Morrison uses *stoicheiosis* to bring her characters face-to-face with their past so that a looming grace may point toward a future. The movement is akin to cross-stitching, a folding and unfolding over and under, renewing relationship to self and community in the present, while moving back and forward in time's history.

The meaning of the text is found in the resonances between the past and the present — the echo between them. The overtones are felt when the past and present meet. In this light, "meaning" is a continuous project that unravels itself over time, in the flow and flux of movement — in the reading of events, backward and forward. Meaning thus blossoms from the wrestle between what Arendt terms "*vita activa*" and "*vita contemplativa*" — "[the] only truly free way of life."[57] Morrison's characters are engaged in the wrestle of not only making their lives, but also making meaning from the lives they live. They are involved in what Martin Buber calls "life's rhythm of pure relationship."[58]

Stoicheiosis serves to underscore a poethical dynamic that establishes integration through physical and psychic proprioception. The healing pattern in this relationship is one in which the body is continuously engaged; a body always moves toward balance while maintaining awareness by which it fully participates in the process of *parousia*.[59]

Circularity oscillates throughout *Beloved*. I call it *the round*. This round is anticipated in the address: 124 Bluestone Road. Morrison invokes the tone of the "Blues," by which she voices and re-stories the lives within a community. A traditional African American musical form, the blues follow a round structure based on a three-line stanza, the last verse or melodic line is repeated or recapitulated at the end of each cycle. As a poetic form, it embodies a narrative through-line that is propelled forward and backward; it mingles memory with emotional experiences of love and loss in an improvised soliloquy, to the gods and to one's community. Repetition, memory, and the numinous cajole and constellate one another, singing into presence a new image of universal order. The blues aesthetic embodies ethical imperatives.

Numbers play a significant role in *Beloved*. In particular, the number "3" often emerges; it is the number left out in the address — *124 Bluestone*. The presence of its absence underscores Morrison's reference to the unaccounted for, the disremembered, and the figure of Beloved herself.[60] *Three* "symbolizes spiritual synthesis; [it] forms a half-circle comprising birth, zenith and descent; [it] is the harmonic product of the action of unity upon duality; and expresses . . . the growth of unity within itself."[61]

Another significant aspect to the appearance of numbers in *Beloved* is their symbolic reference to the ineffable as well as the unquantifiable. In this sense, their images are embodied symbols of what is not spoken. They point to a presence of the invisible. They are silent outcries as much as they are the silent speech of grace.

Throughout the novel's narrative, new order is in progress; the body's intelligences and its relations to time implicitly propel its telling round. Escaping from Sweet Home, Paul D and Sixo, whose "wrists [are] bleeding" are tied and surrounded.[62] Sixo sings. His song and laughter split the night with a triumphant and final chord:

> Tied at the waist to a tree, he sings "by the light of the hominy fire," and then he laughs. A rippling sound . . . . His feet are cooking; the cloth of his trousers smokes. He laughs. Something is funny. Paul D guesses what it is when Sixo interrupts his laughter to call out, "Seven-O! Seven-O!" [They] shoot him to shut him up.[63]

Sixo's Thirty-Mile[64] woman is pregnant with child. "She is lit [with] some glowing, some shining that comes from inside her."[65] The "shining" is the seventh generation in Sixo's lineage; he laughs knowing that a new order is in the making. The number seven is "symbolic of perfect order, a complete period or cycle"[66]; it is also the number that "forms the basic series of musical notes, of colours and of the planetary spheres."[67] Finally, it is "the symbol of pain." When added together, the numbers in 124 Bluestone Road equal the number seven.

Within Judeo-Christian thought, *seven* is cast with particular significance. The creation of the world was formed in seven days. In the Book of Joshua, the number seven denotes the *herem* (ritual) ceremony initiating the fall of Jericho.[68] For Paul D, seven also signals a new order: "[Then] came the miracle. [He] earned a coin for helping "unload two trunks from a coach cab," bought "a bunch of turnips."[69] "That was when he decided that to eat, walk, and sleep anywhere was life as good as it got. And he did it for seven years . . . ."[70]

One of the most visceral images in *Beloved* is the gathering of the community of thirty women, en masse, on behalf of Sethe. They signal the return of the community to bring one of their own back into the fold and to tie a new knot of unity and belonging. According to Heraclitus, the number "[thirty] names the moon of generation."[71]

The women are moved to perform an exorcism; they enact the counterbalance to what has been out of balance for too long. In an improvisatory ritual to rid the house and Sethe of Beloved's gripping hold, Ella, who had "junked [Sethe] for making no gesture to anyone,"[72] was, however, moved by Denver's courage to ask for help: "The daughter [appeared] to have some sense after all." "So thirty women made up that company and walked slowly, slowly toward 124. It was three o'clock in the afternoon on a Friday" "Ella begins the sound. They [took] a step back to the beginning. In the beginning there were no words. In the beginning was the sound, and they all knew what the sound sounded like." Eventually, "[the] sound broke the back of words"; it was "a wave of sound wide enough to sound deep water and knock the pods off chestnut trees. It broke over Sethe and she trembled."[73]

Like the resounding ring of ancient crystal bowls, the primal keening of the thirty women body forth an apotropaic sound from memory that ushers from far beyond their personal histories; it is a mythic sound — transpersonal and generative. "As soon as the body sings," observes writer Assia Djebar, "memory that had been hibernating for many long years revives."[74] The hibernating voice echoes from the body's cellular memory, and its call is familiar to every other body because it is "the language of the world."[75]

Stepping "back to the beginning" is a step into primal time, that is, the time before *time,* before words, when everything was vibration, the primal hum of possibility — an eternal "source of light."[76] The thirty women coalesce, forming an image of grace[77] — the "mothers of the Waters."[78] They've come to wipe clean what had been dirtied and to *rememory* an eternal covenant, the "universal principle of the survival of the species."[79] These "mothers of the Waters" are the embodiment of "peace, evolution, and re-birth,"[80] and they utter a cape of sound to be "wrapped around in, like arms to hold,"[81] a protective shield and armor of "predictive grace" ("àshe") that steadies and guides one along the course of life.[82]

The thirty women keening perform the novel's peripeteia, the poetic turnaround — the generative moment. Their sound-image is the point of human and spiritual insertion, *expression*; their voicing enfolds and unfolds the eons when no words existed. These thirty women thereby bring forth the continuity to which they all belong. Their sounding is the overtone that breaks the backs of words and speaks with knowledge of belonging to a unitary consciousness; it is the creative sound of a profound love.

A telling in the round, *Beloved*'s storyline is a spiral that folds and turns back on itself; not in the sense of a regression, but rather, as refiguration. It is the return to self and community, to *be loved*. "All evolution involves a return," asserts theologian Jean-Yves Leloup, "to the place that is our origin and our destiny. [We] return to the Source, not to our beginning."[83] A "conscious return" is what awaits Sethe. By novel's end, she is poised on the threshold of possibility: a renewed image of a self with a future.

IV. From Earth's Body: The Silent Language of Flowers

"Denver's secrets were sweet [and] accompanied every time by wild veronica."[84] Miss Bodwin, on the other hand, "[talked] of a war full of dead people . . . and although her voice was heavy as a man's, she smelled of flowers."[85] In these passages, Morrison scents her text with the subtle yet potent images of flowers, trees, and plants. She creates a lyric and vegetative landscape that evokes an *Artemisian* presence, harkening the Greek goddess *Artemis* — the personification of the wild and uncanny aspects of nature. This mythic presence weaves its earthy aroma throughout *Beloved*, creating a counterpoint to the persistent denigrations of racism and economic poverty.

Though apparently silent, flowers speak in rhythm, color, and scent. Of the Artemisian imagination, Walter Otto writes: "Here is a teeming concourse of elements, flora and fauna, life unnumbered which sprouts, blooms, spreads its scent . . . and sings; an infinity of sympathy and discord, pairing and struggle, rest and feverish movement, yet all is related, interwoven . . . ."[86] Blooming and fading, their fragrances attend the cycles of life, death, and re-birth, offering a kaleidoscope of stains and odors. In *Beloved*, they echo possibility. Keeping nothing to themselves, they gesture reveries of generosity.

Informed by the traditional folkways of the African American community, Morrison utilizes the silent language of flowers and trees as protective wisdom and as agents of healing: Baby Suggs, holy, tends Sethe's swollen feet by soaking them in "salt water and juniper."[87] Juniper is one of the smallest of coniferae flowers and grows in "inhospitable areas," reminds botanist Marcel Lavabre: "[I]ts presence is like a consolation."[88] One of its medicinal benefits, furthermore, is that as a tonic for the nervous system, it "fortifies the memory."[89]

In his escape north from the chain gang — the "Free North. Magical North" — Paul D was advised by the Cherokee to "follow the trees, [only] the tree flowers. As they go, you go."[90] So Paul D:

> raced from dogwood to blossoming peach. [He] headed for the cherry blossoms, then magnolia, chinaberry, pecan, walnut and prickly pear. . . [He] reached a field of apple trees whose flowers were just becoming little knots of fruit. . . . [When]

he lost them, . . . paused, climbed a tree on a hillock and scanned the horizon for a flash of pink or white in the leaf world that surrounded him.[91]

The world of plants, flowers, and trees is a secret world; it is also a healing world where the articulation of language is silence. Morrison's Artemesian consciousness invokes *Harpocrates,* the mythic god of silence.[92] The paradoxical function of this silence, however, lifts the story from under the veil, *sub rosa,* from "under the rose." The phrase is associated with confidentiality, and the sense-meaning of the "rose" is traced to the myth of Cupid (*Eros*) who, as a bribe, gave a rose to Harpocrates to not betray the confidence of Venus (*Aphrodite*). Hence, "council rooms, and meeting places in the sixteenth and seventeenth centuries were painted with roses" to remind guests that what was spoken *sub-vino* — under the influence of wine — was spoken in secrecy, in silence — *sub rosa.*[93]

In *Beloved,* roses signal silence *and* betrayal, life's truths and its secrets, and they make their appearance in the form of dying roses: "The closer the roses got to death, the louder their scent, and everybody who attended carnival associated it with the stench of rotten roses."[94] Their potent scent announces the arrival of the carnival, and carnival is life's appearances turned upside-down and on its ear, topsy-turvy; it is a deliberate display of life's imbalances aesthetically employed to return a sense of balance.

Philosopher Mikhail Bahktin explains that carnival is a reversal of prescribed social norms; it is a shattering of conventions, staging the world and its bodies in the form of the grotesque. The grotesque is identified by images of "excessiveness, superabundance, [and] the tendency to transgress all limits."[95] Morrison typifies this condition through the 'entertaining bodies' at the carnival. Lifting the veil momentarily, carnival reveals the grotesque in *Beloved.* It "gave four hundred black people" the "breathless excitement" of "seeing the spectacle of whitefolks making a spectacle of themselves."[96]

Evoking memory, Baby Suggs scents the arrival of Beloved: she smells "a dark and coming thing."[97] The vegetable world is a presence, double-edged and thorny: Sethe "remembered when 124 was busy as a way station [and] the very hour when everybody stopped dropping by. [Now], the shoulder weeds of Bluestone Road were all that came toward the house."[98] As the shoulder weeds edge close, they draw the boundary line between Sethe and the community. Shoulder weeds carry the weight of a greening separation.

Silence thus blooms and echoes the tenor of life through its images of flowers; they are the voice of origins that tell of nascent values. It is a greening voice, and the color green, asserts psychologist Peter Bishop, is a "bridge or intermediary" between the elemental worlds.[99] For Morrison, it is a "blessed greenness," for there was "not one touch of death in the definite green of the leaves."[100] Sweet Home's Sixo, "privately, alone, [went] among the trees at night [for] dancing, to keep his bloodlines open."[101] Denver remembers how her grandmother, Baby Suggs, holy, "smelled like bark in the day and leaves at night."[102]

The brilliant array and paradoxical qualities that flowers possess — gentleness and vulnerability as well as resilience, color, and scent — challenge and foil the gray, black, and white world harboring the meagerness of human hatred and the tragedies life. Like "insistent rue" and the force with which the bitter herb pushes its yellow flowers through too "tight soil,"[103] Morrison moistens the greening of her opus with a tender touch, weighted against a seeming hopeless and unfertile climate. In this way, she offers remembrance of the inter-relatedness between earth's body and the human body, between silence and language, and between consciousness and evolution.

Denver's birthplace, that is, her original home, is amidst flowing river water, then on land, among the "silver-blue lines [lying] right at the river's edge."[104] The image of bluefern claims, marks, and shapes the person Denver becomes. Spores that grow "in the hollows" are an image of Denver's *daimon*, her "guiding genius."[105] Quietly floating between land's edge and the river's flow lay Denver's potential, her blooming genius. In the story, Morrison tells us that bluefern spores "are often mistook for insects — but they are seeds in which the whole generation sleeps confident of a future."[106] This confidence, however, is fraught with uncertainty, as Denver struggles against "a loneliness [that] wore her out. *Wore her out*"; but "Denver's secrets were sweet," and she sought refuge "in the woods, between the field and the stream."[107]

Remembering happier days with her sons Bulgar and Howard, Sethe recalls that "something sweet [lived] in the air."[108] "[The] peas still had flowers [and] the grass was [full] of white buds and those tall red blossoms people call Diane."[109] "[Perfumes]," Bachelard claims, "nourish the world."[110]

Language, in Morrison's hands, bursts and blossoms. She pollinates the page with the healing powers of plants such that a peripheral sweetness impugns a world bent on disorder. The pleasing odors of flora renew the sweetness in life and capture the contagious beauty of the world. Perfumes not only appease the gods and soften the hearts of humans, but they signal a divine presence: "When the Lord smelled the pleasing odor, the Lord said in his heart, 'I will never again curse the ground because of humankind ... nor will I ever again destroy every living creature ....'"[111] The pleasing odor ensures that the earth's nourishing cycles will be preserved.

Like the seasonal blooms that clothe earth's body, *Beloved* redresses the human body in its regenerative capacities, in the way flowers, trees, and plants are "a blessing [to] lean on."[112] Flowers invite participation with beauty at its most intimate level, "[a] beauty to be held in the palm of one's hand."[113] Thus, Sethe is able to take some of "the ugly out," and replace it with "a gesture of tenderness"[114] — creating the feeling of having a home of her own. Sethe's intimate thought suggests the tilling of one's own soil. Her body *is* her garden and home — the possible landscape of her own design.

At the heart of Morrison's poetic is the possibility for the experience of an epiphany, of self-ness, of becoming the radiant *parousia* through a poetic consciousness of being a body. When Morrison utters, "this is not a story to pass on,"[115] she includes those stories that have been construed by a culture that has "systematically looted" language, substituting "its nuanced, complex, mid-wifery properties for menace and subjugation."[116] *Beloved* may indeed be a story not to pass on, but its telling, much like the slippery project of language, betrays its ambiguous nature. *Beloved* thus is mid-wife to an agency that presupposes a future, for "[discovering] what it may become."[117]

V. Beloved Bodies Grace and Wisdom

"Here, in this here place, we flesh; flesh that weeps, laughs; flesh that dances on bare feet in grass."[118] This is how Baby Suggs, holy, began her "unchurched" preaching, her "fixing ceremony,"[119] on every Sabbath in the Clearing. Baby Suggs, holy stands at the heart of *Beloved* as a quintessential image of a body of wisdom and grace, who — though she "walked like a three-legged dog" because of her injured hip — "danced in the sunlight" what her "big old heart" had to say.[120] The "holy" was "a small caress after her [name],"[121] an honor given by the community for making 124 Bluestone — like Solomon — a temple in the desert.[122] "Holy" means "whole" and "hallowed,"[123] and Baby Suggs is holy because she is blessed.

In the Clearing — "the green blessed place . . . misty with plant steam" and known only "to deer"[124] — Baby Suggs, holy, ritually delivers her sermons. "Situating herself on a huge flat-sided rock" circled by a ring of trees, Baby Suggs appears like the tree of wisdom herself, "in the center of things,"[125] resolute yet swaying, bowing her head and praying in silence. She invokes a "divining," a "practice," according to Giambattista Vico, performed by the "theological poets" with what he called "the science of the language of the gods."[126] Baby Suggs, who "had a listening way about her" and "devoted her freed life to harmony,"[127] does not tell the people to "clean up their lives or to go and sin no more,"[128] for Suggs' wisdom resides in knowing just what to say and when to say it: "Everything depends on knowing how much," she says, and "Good is knowing when to stop."[129] Rather, what she tells them is that "the only grace they could have was the grace they could imagine," and that "if they could not see it, they would not have it." With these words, Baby Suggs summons that which mirrors the "possible." She pronounces bodily being as the locus of grace as she directs each member of the community to acknowledge, with love, the very flesh of their being.

In the Clearing, Baby Suggs, holy, establishes a "praise house," a place of worship designated to sing oneself in grace and glory through the "praise song." The progenitor of traditional spirituals, praise songs are "chanted sermons," asserts Bernard Bell, "inspired by the Bible, informed by the group experience, and characterized by [rhyme], improvised graphic phrases, and . . . call and response."[130] According to MacLachlan, "praise songs, carrying a quality of *alatheia* — disclosure of truth or unveiling — have a creative power."[131] In Greek myth, the praise song was acknowledged as the domain of the *Charites*, the Greek Graces.

The Clearing is thus a place of ritual. It is here that Baby Suggs invokes the transcendent experience. She is a conjure woman, voicing the imperative of love through a celebration of the grace of the body. Baby Suggs, holy attends to her community the way a gardener tends a garden, being both source and nourishment. The grace-filled experience, like its ancient religious roots, revitalizes the people toward new life. Baby Suggs' chanted sermons are the enchanted enactments of grace. The body in this light becomes the "cultural signifier"; potentiality and creative possibilities rests in the renewal of its text and tissue, its soul and spirit. Through Baby Suggs' invocations, Morrison ritualizes the anatomy of freedom and maps its course by way of the body's physiognomy.

In Baby Suggs's eyes, grace is palpated by the laying of one's own hands on the body of one's own person. Here lies the healing gesture: "love that dissolves the flesh," writes Hesiod.[132] Grace *is* the body; it is the gift of one's hands, feet, shoulders, back, skin, eyes, and heart. Grace is the "dark, dark liver" which, in antiquity, was considered to be "the inmost spring of the deeper emotions."[133] Morrison redresses the body not only as the way to grace, but more pointedly, as *being* grace. In the Clearing, grace is a body that "[you've] got to love . . . stroke . . . and hold . . . up."[134]

Amy Denver, a white indentured slave who meets Sethe on the back roads of the woods, serves as a "bridge" between "black and white, racism and understanding, destruction and renewal."[135] Etymologically, "Amy" means "beloved," and thus offers another image of a body of grace and wisdom. Like Baby Suggs, holy, Amy tends to Sethe's body, the gateway to her psychic wounds. She has a knowing way about her and is "good at sick things."[136] With "fugitive eyes and [a] tenderhearted mouth," Amy "rearranged the leaves (on the ground) for comfort" and "knelt down to massage [Sethe's] swollen feet.[137]

In Yoruba culture, "kneeling" is a posture of honor and generosity. Amy makes shoes for Sethe by "[tearing] two pieces from Sethe's shawl, [filling] them with leaves and [tying] them over her feet."[138] Amy, the "white girl [with] hair enough for five heads,"[139] uses the fabrics of nature as healing agents. With "thin little arms,"[140] she hunts "spiderwebs [and returns] with two palmfuls . . . ." Draping "Sethe's back [like] stringing a tree for Christmas,"[141] she stitches Sethe together with the web of life, and with her own hands midwives the birth of Denver. Amy acts as an overarching bridge of grace between Sethe — who "limped" between life and death — and the "whimpering, trembling" Denver. The three of them are haloed by bluefern. Sending out "sticky spiderwebs" with which Morrison's characters "touch one another,"[142] Sethe, Amy, and baby Denver form a knot that good loving creates; it is a knot they tie together, and they do it "appropriately and well."[143]

Paul D, whose body is an "an arc of kindness,"[144] has "ever-ready love" in his eyes — "easy and upfront, the way colts, evangelists and children look at you: with love you don't have to deserve."[145] Morrison frames Paul D as a body of grace: "There was something blessed in his manner. Women saw him and wanted to weep — to tell him that their chest hurt and their knees did too."[146] Paul D is described as having "no mockery coming from his gaze. [It] felt soft in a waiting kind of way. [Judging] but not comparing . . . : interested."[147] Likewise, Hesiod writes in his description of the Greek Graces: "beautiful is their glance from under their brows."[148]

Paul D walks back to Sethe at 124 Bluestone where he finds her in Baby Suggs, holy's "keeping room," and "[his] coming was the reverse route of his going."[149] Sethe "knows the danger of looking at him,"[150] for looking is also seeing. By seeing, Sethe must confront a new way of being. The aesthetic round must be fulfilled: Sethe must accept herself as *whole* through the gift of being seen. Grace is relational. Seeing Sethe, Paul D "leans over and takes her hand. With the other he touches her face."[151] Sethe "opens her eyes," and "looks at" Paul D.[152]

Offering Sethe his "holding hands," he thinks, "there are too many things to feel about this woman," and when Sethe bemoans that Beloved — "her best thing" — has gone, Paul D tenderly asserts, "You your best thing, Sethe. You are."[153]

In a whisper, Sethe breathes out her final words: "Me? Me?" This first person singular statement, though meek, nevertheless resounds acknowledgement of a self. While author Naomi Mandel suggests that Sethe's "stutter" signals "disbelief" and concludes that Sethe is incapable of "[laying] claim to the ontological verb 'to be,'"[154] Mandel's reading does not permit the two imperatives central to Morrison's poetics: firstly, that Sethe's "fractured body" *is* her agency, allowing that the body as agent "is a process [that] strives for stability and balance"[155]; and that secondly, in order to have grace, one must be able to "imagine grace" — that is — *see* grace.

The moment Sethe speaks and responds to her own call, she affirms the subjective noun "me." Framed as a question, she echoes an answer. Sethe is not only being seen — she is being heard. She breaks the silence that, according to Mandel, threatens to "possess" her. Her "recognition" of a self, "is a change from ignorance to knowledge"[156]; she is poised on the threshold where the imagination has an opportunity to blossom into possibilities. Rather than being couched in disbelief, Sethe is suspended in wonderment. Caught by surprise between the gaze and possibility, Sethe wonders aloud, a voice that hears its own agency striving toward imagining grace.

Paul D's gaze provides the reflexive aperture by which Sethe sees herself. Paul D embraces Sethe's personhood in its entirety, just as she had embraced him: "The pieces I am, she gather them and give them back to me in all the right order."[157] Paul D was given the gift of Sethe's gracious gaze, seeing all his parts and gave them back in the right order. The glance back creates the bridge of possibility. "The gaze of the beloved," suggests Barbara Shapiro, "recognizes and affirms the wholeness and intrinsic value of one's being."[158] Thus Morrison writes: "And she had nothing to fall back on: not maleness, not whiteness, not ladyhood, not anything. And out of the profound desolation of her reality, she may very well . . . invent herself."[159]

There is a responsibility Morrison demands of the reader: to allow the imagination to conjure generative responsiveness. The task is to bridge the gap with the reader's own body by bringing the texture (text) of his/her own body's consciousness into proprioceptive relationship with Morrison's narrative. Together, they flesh out the overtones of the novel. In this way, Morrison establishes the "joint space" or opening by which the inter-textuality between the reader and the story is made. The reader not only participates ethically by virtue of his/her own response-*ability*, but more specifically, by abiding in the silence between the words where the text harbors creative possibilities.

Beloved forges a clearing place for the reader to enter and participate. Through the bodily act of reading, one enters the ritual space for a healing and transformative experience. As an artist, Toni Morrison's *charis*, her grace, has been guiding, protecting, and celebrating the efforts of the reader; for "the power of *charis*," MacLachlan notes, "resides in its unerring ability to provoke a response."[160]

Sethe takes pause in her body; she is suspended between what was and what could be. In the mystery, wonder tilts its head toward a future. As Sethe murmurs, "Me . . . Me . . . " her mouth broadens slightly at the edges as the gesture lifts toward a peripheral light.

NOTES

1. Toni Morrison, *Beloved* (New York: Random House-Knopf, 1987), 273.
2. Ibid., 4.
3. Ibid., 5.
4. Wole Soyinka, *Myth, Literature and the African World* (New York: Cambridge University Press, 1990), 36.
5. Morrison qtd. in Michael Awkward, *Inspiriting Influences: Tradition, Revision, and Afro-American Women's Novels* (New York: Columbia University Press, 1991), 146.
6. Dennis Patrick Slattery, *The Wounded Body: Remembering the Markings of Flesh*, SUNY Series in Psychoanalysis and Culture. (Albany: State University of New York Press, 1999), 207.
7. The meaning of the term "dignity" is understood within the context that Friedrich Schiller implies, who, while acknowledging the near impossibility of defining the word, nevertheless suggests that it is a "complex consisting of free will, inclination, duty, moral strength, and natural impulse." See Friedrich Schiller, "On Grace and Dignity," in *Schiller's "On Grace and Dignity" in Its Cultural Context: Essays and a New Translation*, trans. Jane V. Curran, eds. Jane V. Curran and Christophe Fricker (New York: Camden, 2005), 2.
8. Toni Morrison, *Lecture and Speech of Acceptance, Upon the Award of the Novel Prize for Literature, Delivered in Stockholm on the Seventh of December, Nineteen Hundred and Ninety-Three* (New York: Random House-Knopf, 1994), 50.
9. Morrison, *Beloved*, 86.
10. Marc C. Conner, ed., "Introduction," in *The Aesthetics of Toni Morrison* (Jackson: University Press of Mississippi, 2000), xiii.
11. Ibid., xiv.
12. Morrison, *Beloved*, 31.
13. Ibid., 257.
14. Ibid., 7.
15. Ibid., 95.
16. Ibid., 189.
17. Ibid., 25.
18. Ibid. 21.
19. Ibid., 94.
20. Ibid., 16.
21. Gaston Bachelard, *Air and Dreams: An Essay on the Imagination of Movement*, trans. Edith R. Farrell and C. Frederick Farrell (Dallas, TX: Dallas Institute, 1988), 133.
22. Morrison, *Beloved*, 62.
23. Peter Hewlett, "Messianic Time in Toni Morrison's *Beloved*," *Agora: Online Graduate Humanities Journal* 1, no. 1 (2001): 2, http://www.humanities.ualberta.ca/agora/Articles.cfm@ArticleNo=121.html.
24. Morrison, *Beloved*, 95.
25. Ibid., 94.
26. Ibid.
27. Ibid., 58.
28. Ibid., 94.
29. Ibid., 188.
30. Anne Carson, Introduction, "On the Text," in *If Not, Winter: Fragments of Sappho*, trans. Anne Carson. (New York: Vintage, 2002), x.
31. Morrison, *Beloved*, 169.
32. Ibid., 154
33. Richard Broxton Onians, *The Origins of European Thought: About the Body, the Mind, the Soul, the World, Time, and Fate* (Cambridge: Cambridge University Press, 1951), 181.
34. See Denver's soliloquy: "So quiet. Made me have to read faces and learn how to figure out what people were thinking, so I didn't need to hear what they said . . . ." Morrison, *Beloved*, 206.
35. Morrison, *Beloved*, 157.
36. Ibid., 186. Many visual depictions of the Greek Graces often show the center Grace with her back toward the viewer, that is, without her face showing. This posture is perhaps a personification of time's own waiting nature, time's grace, what cannot be seen, and thereby suggests the "coldness"

of charity. It is an image that connotes the "between" time of being and becoming. On the other hand, Weil writes: "Supernatural love . . . does not protect the soul against the coldness of force, the coldness of steel." See Simone Weil, *Gravity & Grace*, trans. Arthur Wills (Lincoln: University of Nebraska Press, 1952), 23.

37. Morrison, *Beloved*, 188.
38. Ibid., 218.
39. Soyinka, *Myth, Literature and the African World*, 145.
40. Hannah Arendt, *The Human Condition: A Study of the Central Dilemmas Facing Modern Man* (Garden City, NY: Doubleday Anchor, 1959), 16.
41. Aristotle, *Poetics*, trans. S. H. Butcher (Toronto: Dover, 1997), 52 pt., 24.
42. Rainer Maria Rilke, *Duino Elegies*, trans. Edward Snow (New York: North Point, 2000), 31.
43. Soyinka, *Myth, Literature and the African World*, 2.
44. Ibid.
45. Morrison, *Beloved*, 260.
46. Soyinka, *Myth, Literature and the African World*, 11.
47. Morrison, *Beloved*, 251.
48. Ibid, 91.
49. Mircea Eliade, *Images and Symbols: Studies in Religious Symbolism*, trans. Philip Mairet (Kansas City, KS: Sheed Andrews and McMeel, 1961), 112.
50. Proclus's theories of "epicycles" and "eccentric cycles" state: "Earth is in the centre of a circle [. . .] with smaller circles rotating round its circumference," while the latter theory suggests that "the planets move round in circles whose centres do not coincide with the Earth" ("Proclus Diadochus," online). See the Introduction in my dissertation, Young, "Where Grace May Pass: A Poetics of the Body" (PhD. diss. Pacifica Graduate Intitute, 2007), n2.
51. Morrison, *Beloved*, 47.
52. Ibid., 49.
53. Ibid., 47.
54. See chap. 2, n3, Young, "Where Grace May Pass," for a discussion of strophe, antistrophe, and epode.
55. David Freedberg, "Arousal by Image," in *Uncontrollable Beauty: Toward a New Aesthetic*, eds. Bill Beckley with David Shapiro (New York: Allworth, 1998), 126.
56. Owen Barfield, *Poetic Diction: A Study in Meaning* (Middletown, CT: Wesleyan University Press, 1973), 181.
57. Arendt, *The Human Condition*, 15.
58. Martin Buber, *I and Thou*, trans. Walter Kaufmann (New York: Simon & Schuster, 1970), 162.
59. Parousia is a Greek word that means, "coming, arrival, personal presence," and is used 24 times in the New Testament. In the Greek world of the New Testament it meant among other things, "a State visit" or "the presence or appearance of a deity during worship e.g. by divine fire." It was a range of meanings comparable to that of the archaic English word visitation. Also parousia, meaning, "a being near," i.e. "advent. " In its physical aspect, it means "coming" and "presence."
60. Dividing her novel into three books, Morrison chronicles the past and present events of a community torn asunder by the ravages of slavery. As a novel that addresses the presence of absence and unaccounted for, *Beloved* resonates with the book of I Chronicles from the Hebrew Bible. Modern scholars suggest that Chronicles, "the book of the events of the days," ("seper dibre hayyamim") as well as the Chronicles in the Septuagint, the Greek Paralipomena, is a record of "the things left out" — left out of "earlier biblical history" and is a summary of "divine history." See *The New Oxford Annotated Bible*, 3rd ed. (Oxford: Oxford University Press, 2001), 576. Beloved herself is the divine "third," the voice left out, and it is a history made present that inscribes itself onto the texts of those who remember it.
61. J. E. Cirlot, *A Dictionary of Symbols*, 2nd ed., trans. Jack Sage (New York: Philosophical Library, 1971), 232.
62. Morrison, *Beloved*, 225.
63. Ibid., 226.
64. The number three and the words thirteen, and thirty, are found throughout the novel, as are other references to the number three: e. g., "In all [Paul D's] escapes, not one had permanent success . . . the longest had been . . . three years." See Morrison, *Beloved*, 268. What Paul D thought would be "the walk of his life" was his walk from Selma to Mobile when he saw twelve dead blacks in the first

eighteen miles (269). Twelve and eighteen add up to thirty. Sethe is thirteen when she arrives at Sweet Home; her sons, Bulgar and Howard, are thirteen when they leave 124 Bluestone (39).

65. Morrison, *Beloved*, 225.
66. Heraclitus, *Fragments*, trans. Brooks Haxton (New York: Penguin, 2001), 88.
67. J. E. Cirlot, *A Dictionary of Symbols*, 2nd ed., trans. Jack Sage (New York: Philosophical Library, 1971), 233.
68. Joshua 6:2-5.
69. Morrison, *Beloved*, 269.
70. Ibid., 270.
71. Heraclitus, *Fragments*, trans. Brooks Haxton (New York: Penguin, 2001), 55.
72. Morrison, *Beloved*, 256.
73. Ibid, 256, 257, 259, 261.
74. Djebar qtd. in Nada Elia, *Trances, Dances, and Vociferations: Agency and Resistance in Africana Women's Narratives* (London: Garland, 2001), 11.
75. Soyinka, *Myth, Literature and the African World*, 145. See reference to Nietzsche in my dissertation, Young, "A Glance Back: The Graces," chap. 2, n1.
76. Morrison, *Beloved*, 4.
77. Teresa N. Washington, *Our Mothers, Our Powers, Our Texts: Manifestations of Àjé in Africana Literature* (Bloomington: Indiana University Press, 2005), 236.
78. Ibid.
79. Ibid.
80. Ibid., 326.
81. Ibid., 152.
82. Robert Farris Thompson, *Flash of the Spirit: African & Afro-American Art and Philosophy* (New York: Random House-Vintage, 1984), 9. See Morrison, *Beloved*, 152: After Sethe kills her child and is taken to jail, the community "stopped murmuring" and "made no gesture" toward her. "Was her back too straight . . . head too high? Probably. Otherwise the singing would have begun at once . . . . Some cape of sound would have quickly wrapped around her, like arms to hold and steady her on the way." There were "no words. Humming. No words at all." This signals the disowning of Sethe by the community, and it is exemplified by the lack of the group body's timeless and mythic "sound."
83. Jean-Yves Leloup, *The Gospel of Mary Magdalene*, trans. Joseph Rowe. (Rochester, VT: Inner Traditions, 2002), 46.
84. Morrison, *Beloved*, 28.
85. Ibid.
86. Walter F. Otto, *The Homeric Gods*, trans. Moses Hadas (London: Thames, 1955), 81.
87. Morrison, *Beloved*, 93.
88. Marcel Lavabre, *Aromatherapy Workbook* (Rochester, VT: Healing Arts, 1990), 78.
89. Ibid.
90. Morrison, *Beloved*, 112.
91. Ibid., 113.
92. Note the reference to Harpocrates in the name "Harpo Marx," the non-verbal Marx Brother who nonetheless speaks through gesture and silence, and in Oprah Winfrey's production company, Harpo Productions, the company that produced Beloved for film, and works "in the background" to assist persons in need throughout the world through "The Angel Network."
93. Marina Heilmeyer, *The Language of Flowers: Symbols and Myths* (Munich: Prestel, 2006), 74.
94. Morrison, *Beloved*, 47.
95. Mikhail Bahktin, *Rabelais and His World*, trans. Hélène Iswolsky. (Bloomington: Indiana University Press, 1984), 306.
96. Morrison, *Beloved*, 48.
97. Ibid., 139.
98. Ibid., 163.
99. Peter Bishop, *The Greening of Psychology: The Vegetable World in Myth, Dream, and Healing* (Dallas, TX: Spring Publications, 1990), 16.
100. Morrison, *Beloved*, 17, 138.
101. Ibid., 25.
102. Ibid., 19.
103. Ibid., 138.

104. Ibid., 84.
105. See my discussion of the daimon in chap. 2, Young, "A Glance Back," in "Where Graces May Pass."
106. Morrison, *Beloved*, 84.
107. Ibid., 28-9.
108. Ibid., 192.
109. The flower called Diane evokes an Artemisian presence. The Latin name is Artemisia vulgaris, and is considered to be "a magical plant," according to Marcel Lavabre, "known to increase psychic power." See Lavabre, *Aromatherapy Workbook*, 75.
110. Gaston Bachelard, *Air and Dreams: An Essay on the Imagination of Movement*, trans. Edith R. Farrell and C. Frederick Farrell (Dallas, TX: Dallas Institute, 1988), 44.
111. Genesis 8:21.
112. Morrison, *Beloved*, 23.
113. Bachelard, *Earth and Reveries of Will*, 225.
114. Morrison, *Beloved*, 26.
115. Ibid., 275.
116. Morrison, *Lecture and Speech of Acceptance*, 49.
117. William R. Hadley, "The House a Ghost Built: Allegory, Nommo, and the Ethics of Reading in Toni Morrison's *Beloved*" *Contemporary Literature* 36, no. 4 (1995): 701.
118. Morrison, *Beloved*, 88.
119. Ibid., 86.
120. Ibid., 139, 86.
121. Ibid., 87.
122. See the introduction to Psalms, where it is explained that Solomon, son of David, constructs the Jerusalem Temple. Baby Suggs' son, Halle, "constructs" his mother's freedom by buying her time at Sweet Home. Halle is the architect of her freedom; yet Baby Suggs is the architect of the temple of 124 Bluestone. King David and Solomon conflate in the image of Baby Suggs. Furthermore, Psalms is the second book of the Poetical and Wisdom Books. It is a collection of sung poetic prayers; song and movement are rituals of "tehillim" (praises). The Clearing is "the blessed place" where these "praises" are sung. Also, cf. Revelations 21:22-26.
123. Eric Partridge, *Origins: A Short Etymological Dictionary of Modern English* (New York: Macmillan, 1958), 292.
124. Morrison, *Beloved*, 89.
125. Ibid., 137.
126. Vico qtd. in Marguerite Fernández Olmos, and Lizabeth Paravisini-Gebert, eds., *Sacred Possessions: Vodou, Santería, Obeah, and The Caribbean* (New Brunswick, NJ: Rutgers University Press, 2000), 152.
127. Morrison, *Beloved*, 156, 171.
128. Ibid., 88.
129. Ibid., 87. See Exodus 36:2-6 for the sense of "too-muchness."
130. Bernard W. Bell, *The Contemporary Afro-American Novel: Its Folk Traditions and Modern Literary Branches* (Amherst: University of Massachusetts Press, 2004), 26.
131. Bonnie MacLachlan, *The Age of Grace* (Princeton, NJ: Princeton University Press, 1993), 102.
132. Hesiod, *Theogony and Works and Days*, trans. with intro. M. L. West (New York: Oxford University Press, 1988), 909.
133. Onians, *The Origins of European Thought*, 84.
134. Morrison, *Beloved*, 89.
135. Nicole M. Coonradt, "To Be Loved: Amy Denver and Human Need-Bridges to Understanding in Toni Morrison's *Beloved*," *College Literature* 32, no. 4 (2005): 168-87, *Project Muse*, http://muse.jhu.edu/, 2.
136. Morrison, *Beloved*, 82.
137. Ibid., 79, 83.
138. Ibid., 83. Amy, in this act, is a poetic mimesis of Baby Suggs, holy in the sense that Baby Suggs is herself a shoemaker.
139. Ibid., 77.
140. Ibid., 76.
141. Ibid., 80.
142. Ibid., 65.

143. Ibid., 85.
144. Ibid., 17.
145. Ibid., 161.
146. Ibid., 17.
147. Ibid., 25.
148. Hesiod, *Theogony*, 909-10.
149. Morrison, *Beloved*, 263.
150. Ibid., 272.
151. Ibid., 273.
152. Ibid., 272.
153. Ibid., 273.
154. Naomi Mandel, "I Made The Ink: Identity, Complicity, 60 Million, and More" *Modern Fiction Studies*. 48, no. 3 (2002): 599.
155. Thomas Hanna, *The Body of Life*. (New York: Random House-Knopf, 1979), 6.
156. Aristotle, *Poetics*, pt. 11, 20.
157. Morrison, *Beloved*, 273.
158. Barbara Shapiro, "The Bonds of Love and the Boundaries of Self in Toni Morrison's *Beloved*" *Contemporary Literature* 32, no. 2 (1991): 200.
159. Morrison qtd. in Washington, *Our Mothers, Our Powers, Our Texts*, 111.
160. MacLachlan, *The Age of Grace*, 37.

Bibliography

Works by Toni Morrison
(Editions cited in this volume listed in the order cited in this volume)

Morrison, Toni. *The Bluest Eye*. New York: Random House-Knopf, 1970 and 1994. Reprint, New York: Holt, Rinehart and Winston, 1993.

——. "What the Black Woman Thinks About Women's Lib." *New York Times Magazine*. August 22, 1971, 14, 63.

——. *Sula*. New York: Random House-Knopf, 1973.

——. *Song of Solomon*. New York: Random House-Knopf, 1977.

——. *Tar Baby*. New York: Random House-Knopf, 1981.

——. "Rootedness: The Ancestor as Foundation." In *Black Women Writers (1950-1980)*, edited by Marie Evans. New York: Random House-Doubleday, 1984.

——. *Beloved*. New York: Random House-Knopf, 1987.

——. "James Baldwin: His Voice Remembered; Life in His Language." *New York Times Book Review*. December 20, 1987, 27.

——. "Unspeakable Things Unspoken: The Afro-American Presence in American Literature." *Michigan Quarterly Review* 28, no. 1 (1989): 1-34.

——. *Jazz*. New York: Random House-Knopf, 1992.

——. *Playing in the Dark: Whiteness and the Literary Imagination*. New York: Random House-Vintage, 1992.

——. *Lecture and Speech of Acceptance, Upon the Award of the Novel Prize for Literature, Delivered in Stockholm on the Seventh of December, Nineteen Hundred and Ninety-Three*. New York: Random House-Knopf, 1994.

——. "Home." In *The House That Race Built*, edited by Wahneema Lubiano, 3-12. New York: Pantheon, 1997.

——. *Paradise*. New York: Random House-Knopf, 1998. Reprint, New York: Penguin-Plume, 1999.

——. *The Dancing Mind*. New York: Random House-Knopf, 2003.

——. *Love*. New York: Random House-Knopf, 2003.

——. Presentation for "Roundtable on the Future of the Humanities in a Fragmented World." *PMLA* 120, no. 3 (2005): 715-17.

——. "Étranger chez soir." [French translation of "The Foreigner's Home" lecture.] *Toni Morrison, invite au Louvre*. Translated by Anne Wicke. Edited by Christian Bourgois, 13-26. Paris: Louvre Museum, 2006.

——. "The Foreigner's Home." Opening Lecture for the special exhibition. Louvre Museum, Paris, 6 November 2006.

——. *What Moves at the Margin: Selected Nonfiction*, edited by Carolyn C. Denard. Jackson: University Press of Mississippi, 2008.

——. "How Can Values Be Taught in the University?" In *What Moves at the Margin: Selected Nonfiction*, edited by Carolyn C. Denard, 191-7. Jackson: University Press of Mississippi, 2008.

——. "Speaking of Reynolds Price." In *What Moves at the Margin: Selected Nonfiction*, edited by Carolyn C. Denard, 95-99. Jackson: University Press of Mississippi, 2008.

——. *A Mercy*. New York: Random House-Knopf, 2008.

____. *A Mercy*. New York: Vintage International, 2009.

——. "A Bench by the Road: *Beloved*." In *Toni Morrison: Conversations*, edited by Carolyn C. Denard, 44-50. Literary Conversations Series. Jackson: University Press of Mississippi, 2008.

——. "The Reader as Artist." *Oprah Magazine*. Harpo Productions (July 2006). http://www.oprah.com/omagazine/Toni-Morrison-on-Reading (accessed March 2011).

——. *Home*. New York: Knopf, 2012.

Naylor, Gloria, and Toni Morrison. "A Conversation." *Southern Review* 21, no. 3 (1985): 567-93.

Other Sources (cited in this volume)

Aguiar, Sarah Appleton. "'Passing On' Death: Stealing Life in Toni Morrison's *Paradise*." *African American Review* 38, no. 2 (2004): 513–19.

Alhadeff, Albert. *The Raft of the Medusa: Géricault, Art, and Race*. Munich: Prestel, 2002.

Aneja, Anu. "Of Masks and Masquerades: Performing the Collegial Dance." *symploké* 13, no. 1-2 (2005): 144-51.

Angelou, Maya. *I Know Why the Caged Bird Sings*. New York: Random House, 1970.

Arendt, Hannah. *The Human Condition: A Study of the Central Dilemmas Facing Modern Man*. Garden City, NY: Doubleday Anchor, 1959.

Aristotle. *Poetics*. Translated by S. H. Butcher. Toronto: Dover, 1997.

Awkward, Michael. *Inspiriting Influences: Tradition, Revision, and Afro-American Women's Novels*. New York: Columbia University Press, 1991.

Bachelard, Gaston. *Air and Dreams: An Essay on the Imagination of Movement*. Translated by Edith R. Farrell and C. Frederick Farrell. Dallas, TX: Dallas Institute, 1988.

———. *Earth and Reveries of Will*. Translated by Kenneth Haltman. Dallas, TX: Dallas Institute, 2002.

Bahktin, Mikhail. *Rabelais and His World*. Translated by Hélène Iswolsky. Bloomington: Indiana University Press, 1984.

Baker, Houston A., Jr., and June Jordan, et al. "Black Writers in Praise of Toni Morrison." *New York Times Book Review*. January 24, 1988, 36.

Barfield, Owen. *Poetic Diction: A Study in Meaning*. Middletown, CT: Wesleyan University Press, 1973.

Barthes, Roland. *S/Z*. Translated by Richard Miller. New York: Hill and Wang, 1974.

Basow, Susan A. "Student Evaluations: The Role of Gender Bias and Teaching Styles," In *Career strategies for Women in Academe: Arming Athena*, edited by L. H. Collins, J. C. Chrisler, and K. Quina, 135-56. Thousand Oaks, CA: Sage, 1998.

Bell, Bernard W. *The Contemporary Afro-American Novel: Its Folk Traditions and Modern Literary Branches*. Amherst: University of Massachusetts Press, 2004.

Bercovitch, Sacvan. "The A-Politics of Ambiguity on *The Scarlet Letter*." *New Literary History* 19, no. 3 (1988): 629-54.

———. "Hawthorne's A-Morality of Compromise." Special Issue: American Reconstructed 1840-1940. *Representations* 24 (Autumn1988): 1-27.

Bishop, Peter. *The Greening of Psychology: The Vegetable World in Myth, Dream, and Healing*. Dallas, TX: Spring Publications, 1990.

Blackburn, Sara. "Review of *Sula*. 'You Still Can't Go Home Again.'" *New York Times Book Review*. December 30, 1973, 3.

Braxton, Joanne, and Andree Nicola McLaughlin, eds. *Wild Women in the Whirlwind: Afra-American Culture and the Contemporary Literary Renaissance*. New Brunswick, NJ: Rutgers University Press, 1990.

Briggs, H. E., A. C. Briggs, and J. D. Leary. "Promoting Culturally Competent Systems of Care Through Statewide Family Advocacy Networks." *Best Practices in Mental Health* 1, no. 2 (2005): 77–99.

Brockes, Emma. "Toni Morrison: 'I Want to Feel What I Feel. Even If It's Not Happiness.'" *theguardian*. April 13, 2012. http://guardian.co.uk (accesed May 2012).

Brophy-Warren, Jamin. "A Writer's Vote: Toni Morrison on Her New Novel, Reading Her Critics and What Barack Obama's Win Means to Her." *Wall Street Journal*. November 7, 2008, W5.

Brown, Caroline. "Golden Gray and the Talking Book: Identity as a Site of Artful Construction in Toni Morrison's *Jazz*." *African American Review* 36, no. 4 (2002): 629-42.

Buber, Martin. *I and Thou*. Translated by Walter Kaufmann. New York: Simon & Schuster, 1970.

Buchanan, Nicole. "The Nexus of Race and Gender Domination: The Racialized Sexual Harassment of African American Women." In *In the Company of Men: Re-discovering the Links between Sexual Harassment and Male Domination*, edited by James Gruber and Phoebe Morgan, 294-320. Boston: Northeastern University Press, 2005.

Burton, William E. "Review of Poe's The Narrative of Arthur Gordon Pym." *Burton's Gentleman's Magazine* 3 (1838): 210-11. *Edgar Allan Poe Society of Baltimore*. http://www.eapoe.org/papers/misc1827/18380900.htm (accessed August 30, 2011).

Butler, Judith. *Gender Trouble: Feminism and the Subversion of Identity*. London and New York: Routledge, 1987.

——. "Performative Acts and Gender Constitution: An Essay in Phenomenology and Feminist Theory." In *The Performance Studies Reader*. 2nd ed, edited by Henry Bial, 187-206. New York: Routledge, 2004.

Byrd, Rudolph P., and Alice Walker, eds. *The World Has Changed: Conversations with Alice Walker*. New York: The New Press, 2010.

Cade-Bambara, Toni. *The Black Woman: An Anthology*. New York: Penguin Books, 1970.

Candelaria, Cordelia Chávez, "The 'Wild Zone' Thesis as a Gloss in Chicana Literary Study." In *Feminisms: an Anthology of Literary Theory and Criticism*. 2nd ed, edited by Robyn R. Warhol and Diane Price Herndl. New Brunswick, NJ: Rutgers University Press, 1997.

Carmen, Karen. *Toni Morrison's World of Fiction*. Troy, NY: Whitson, 1993.

Carter, Susan, et al., eds. *Historical Statistics of the United States, Millennial Edition*. New York: Cambridge University Press, 2001. http://www.hks.harvard.edu/fs/phall/HSUS.pdf.

Carroll, Noël. "The Wheel of Virtue: Art, Literature, and Moral Knowledge." *Journal of Aesthetics and Art Criticism* 60, no. 1 (2002): 3-26.

Carson, Anne. "On the Text." In *If Not, Winter: Fragments of Sappho*. Translated by Anne Carson. New York: Vintage, 2002.

Cheng, Anne Anlin. *The Melancholy of Race: Psychoanalysis, Assimilation, and Hidden Grief*. New York: Oxford University Press, 2001.

Cirlot, J. E. *A Dictionary of Symbols*. 2nd ed. Translated by Jack Sage. New York: Philosophical Library, 1971.

Clausen, Christopher. *The Moral Imagination: Essays in Literature and Ethics*. Iowa City: University of Iowa Press, 1986.

Conner, Marc C., ed. "Aesthetics and the African-American Novel." In *The Aesthetics of Toni Morrison*. Jackson: University Press of Mississippi, 2000.

——. "Modernity and the Homeless: Ethics, Aesthetics, and Religion in the African-American Novel." forthcoming.

Cook, C. J. "Told in Memory of God's People: *Beloved*." *Pastoral Psychology* 59, no. 6 (2010): 725-35.

Coonradt, Nicole M. "To Be Loved: Amy Denver and Human Need-Bridges to Understanding in Toni Morrison's *Beloved*." *College Literature* 32, no. 4 (2005): 168-87. *Project Muse*. http://muse.jhu.edu/ (accessed September 28, 2006).

Cooper, James Fennimore. "To the Abbate Giromachi, &C. &C., Florence." In *Norton Anthology of American Literature*. Vol. 1, 3rd ed, edited by Nina Baym. New York: Norton, 1989.

Corréard, Alexandre, and Jean Baptiste Henri Sevigny. *Naufrage de la frégate la Méduse, faisant partie de l'expédition du Sénégal en 1816*. Paris, 1818.

Cosentino, Donald. "Who is that fellow in the many-colored cap? Transformations of Eshu in Old and New World Mythologies." *Journal of American Folklore* 100 (1987). 261-75.

Counihan, Carole, and Penny Van Esterik, eds. *Food and Culture: A Reader*. 2nd ed. New York: Routledge, 2008.

Couric, Katie. "Candidates Name Their Favorite Books." CBS Nightly News. Transcript. October 2008. http://www.cbsnews.com/2100-18563_162-4557194.html (accessed May 2009).

Crouch, Stanley. "*Aunt Medea*." *Review of* Beloved *by Toni Morrison*. New Republic. October 19, 1987, 38-43.

Davis, Angela. *Angela Davis: An Autobiography*. New York: Bantam Books, 1975.

Davis, Christina. "Interview With Toni Morrison." In *Toni Morrison: Critical Perspectives Past and Present*, edited by Henry Louis Gates Jr. and K. A. Appiah, 412-20. New York: Amistad, 1993.

Davis, Thadious. *Faulkner's Negro: Art and the Southern Context*. Baton Rouge: Louisiana State University Press, 1983.

Denard, Carolyn C., ed. *Toni Morrison—Conversations*. Literary Conversations Series. Jackson: University Press of Mississippi, 2008.

Derrida, Jacques. *Writing and Difference*. Translated by Alan Bass. Chicago: University of Chicago Press, 1978.

DeSouza, Eros, and A. Gigi Fansler. "Contrapower Sexual Harassment: A Survey of Students and Faculty Members." *Sex Roles* 48 (2003): 519-42.

Eagleton, Terry. *Literary Theory: An Introduction*. Minneapolis: University of Minnesota Press, 1983.

Eitner, Lorenz. *Géricault's Raft of the Medusa*. London: Phaidon, 1972.

——. *Géricault: His Life and Work*. Ithaca, NY: Cornell University Press, 1983.

Elia, Nada. *Trances, Dances, and Vociferations: Agency and Resistance in Africana Women's Narratives*. London: Garland, 2001.

Eliade, Mircea. *Images and Symbols: Studies in Religious Symbolism*. Translated by Philip Mairet. Kansas City, KS: Sheed Andrews and McMeel, 1961.

Eliot, T. S. "The Love Song of J. Alfred Prufrock." In *T. S. Eliot: The Complete Poems and Plays (1909-1950)*, 3-7. New York: Harcourt, Brace, 1971.

Emerson, Ralph Waldo. "The Burial of Nathaniel Hawthorne." In *The Journals of Ralph Waldo Emerson.* Vol. 10. Cambridge: The Belknap Press, 1969.

——. "The American Scholar." In *Emerson's Prose and Poetry*, edited by Saundra Morris, 56-69. New York: Norton, 2001.

——. "The Poet." In *Emerson's Prose and Poetry*, edited by Saundra Morris and Joel Porte, 138-97. New York: Norton, 2001.

——. "Self-Reliance." In *Emerson's Prose and Poetry*, edited by Saundra Morris, 120-37. New York: Norton, 2001.

Espinosa, Aurelia. "Notes on the Origin and History of the Tar-Baby Story." *Journal of American Folklore* 43, no. 168 (1930): 129-209.

Evans, Mari. *I Am a Black Woman.* New York: Quill, 1970.

Faulkner, William. "The Art of Fiction No. 12." Interview by Jean Stein. *The Paris Review* 12 (Spring 1956).n.p. http://www.theparisreview.org/interviews/4954/the-art-of-fiction-no-12-william-faulkner (accessed August 30, 2011).

Fishman, Charles. "Naming Names: Three Recent Novels by Women Writers." *Names: Journal of the American Name Society* 32 (March 1984): 33-44.

Freedberg, David. "Arousal by Image." In *Uncontrollable Beauty: Toward a New Aesthetic*, edited by Bill Beckley with David Shapiro, 115-45. New York: Allworth, 1998.

Foucault, Michel. *Madness and Civilization: A History of Insanity in the Age of Reason.* Translated by Richard Howard. London: Travistock Publications, 1967.

——. *The Order of Things: An Archaeology of the Human Sciences.* New York: Random House, 1970.

——. *The Archaeology of Knowledge.* Translated by A. M. Sheridan Smith. New York: Pantheon Books, 1972.

 ——. *Discipline and Punish: The Birth of the Prison.* Translated by Alan Sheridan. New York: Random House, 1977.

——. *The History of Sexuality: Vol. I, An Introduction.* Translated by Robert Hurley. New YorK; Pantheon Books, 1979.

——. *Power/Knowledge: Selected Interviews and Other Writings, 1972–1977*, edited by Colin Gordon. New York: Pantheon Books, 1980.

Fullilove, Mindy. *Root Shock: How Tearing Up City Neighborhoods Hurts America, and What We Can Do About It.* New York: Random House-Ballantine, 2004.

Fultz, Lucille P. *Toni Morrison: Playing with Difference.* Chicago: University of Illinois Press, 2003.

Furner, Joseph. M. "Using bibliotherapy to Overcome Math Anxiety." *Academic Exchange Quarterly* 8, no. 2 (2004): 209-13.

Gerstenberg, Alice. *Overtones*. New York: D. McKay, 1914.

Gillespie, Carmen. *Critical Companion to Toni Morrison*. New York: Facts On File, Inc., 2008.

Gilroy, Paul. *Postcolonial Melancholia*. New York: Columbia University Press, 2006.

Gioia, Ted. *The Imperfect Art: Reflections on Jazz and Modern Culture*. New York: Oxford University Press, 1988.

Giovanni, Nikki. *Black Feeling, Black Talk, Black Judgement*. New York: William Morrow. 1970.

Goffman, Erving. *Stigma: Notes on the Management of Spoiled Identity*. New York: Simon & Schuster, 1963.

Gordy, Cynthia. "Toni Morrison Receives Medal of Freedom." *The Root*. May 29, 2012. http://www.theroot.com/blogs/medal-freedom/toni-morrison-receives-medal-freedom (accessed May 31, 2012).

Greenfield-Sanders, Timothy. *The Black List Documentary*. Directed by Timothy Greenfield-Sanders and Elvis Mitchell. HBO Documentary Films, 2008.

——. "Artist Statement" *The Black List*. National Portrait Gallery Exhibition. October 28, 2011-April 22, 2012. http://www.npg.si.edu.

Grewall, Gurleen. *Circles Of Sorrow, Lines Of Struggle: The Novels of Toni Morrison*. Baton Rouge: Louisiana State University Press, 1998.

Guardini, Romano. "The Meaning of Melancholy." In *The Focus of Freedom*. Translated by Gregory Roettger Helicon, 55-92. Baltimore: Helicon, 1966.

Hadley, William R. "The House a Ghost Built: Allegory, Nommo, and the Ethics of Reading in Toni Morrison's *Beloved*." *Contemporary Literature* 36, no. 4 (1995): 676-701.

Hanna, Thomas. *The Body of Life*. New York: Random House-Knopf, 1979.

Hansberry, Lorraine. *To Be Young, Gifted and Black: An Informal Autobiography*. New York. Signet Paperback. 1970.

Harris, Trudier. *Fiction and Folklore: The Novels of Toni Morrison*. Knoxville: University of Tennessee Press, 1993.

Hayes, Elizabeth T., ed. "'Like Seeing You Buried': Persephone in *The Bluest Eye*, *Their Eyes Were Watching God*, and *The Color Purple*." In *Images of Persephone: Feminist Readings in Western Literature*, 170-94. Gainesville: Florida University Press, 1994.

Heath, Melissa A., Dawn Sheen, Deon Leavy, Ellie Young, and Kristy Money. "Bibliotherapy: A Resource to Facilitate Emotional Healing and Growth." *School Psychology International* 26, no. 5 (2005): 170-94; 563–80.

Heffernan, Carol Falvo. *The Melancholy Muse*. Pittsburgh: Duquesne University Press, 1995.

Heilmeyer, Marina. *The Language of Flowers: Symbols and Myths*. Munich: Prestel, 2006.

Heraclitus. *Fragments*. Translated by Brooks Haxton. New York: Penguin, 2001.

Hesiod. *Theogony and Works and Days*. Translated with an introduction by M. L. West. New York: Oxford University Press, 1988.

Hewlett, Peter. "Messianic Time in Toni Morrison's *Beloved*." *Agora: Online Graduate Humanities Journal* 1, no. 1 (2001): n.p. http://www.humanities.ualberta.ca/agora/Articles. cfm@ArticleNo=121.html (accessed October 24, 2006).

Homans, Margaret. "'Her Very Own Howl': the Ambiguities of Representation in Recent Women's Fiction." *Signs* 9, no. 2 (1983): 186-205.

Holloway, Karla F. C., and Stephanie Demetrakopoulos. *New Dimensions of Spirituality: A Biracial and Bicultural Reading of the Novels of Toni Morrison*. New York: Greenwood Press, 1987.

Hwangbo, Kyeong. "Trauma, Narrative, and the Marginal Self in Selected Contemporary American Novels." PhD diss., University of Florida, 2004.

Ivey, Allen, Michael D'Andrea, Mary Bradford Ivey, and Lynn Simek-Morgan. *Theories of Counseling and Psychotherapy: A Multicultural Perspective*, 6th ed. Boston: Pearson Education, Inc., 2007.

Jarmon, Laura. *Wishbone: Reference and Interpretation in Black Folk Narrative*. Knoxville: University of Tennessee Press, 2003.

Jefferson, Thomas. "Query 14 'Laws' The administration of justice and description of the laws." *Notes on the State of Virginia*. London: John Stockdale, 1787.

Johnson, E. Patrick. "Black Performance Studies: Genealogies, Politics, Futures." In *The Sage Handbook of Performance Studies*, edited by D. Soyini Madison and Judith Hamera, 446-63. Thousand Oaks, CA: Sage, 2006.

Johnson, Mark L. *Moral Imagination: Implications of Cognitive Science for Ethics*. Chicago: University of Chicago Press, 1993.

Kachka, Boris. "Toni Morrison's History Lesson." *New York Magazine*. September 1-8, 2008, 90-91.

——. "Who is the Author of Toni Morrison?" *New York Magazine*. April 29, 2012. http://nymag.com/news/features/toni-morrison-2012-5/ (accessed May 15, 2012).

Kanthak, John F. "Feminisms in Motion: Pushing the 'Wild Zone' Into the Fourth Dimension." *Literature Interpretation Theory* 14 (2003): 149-63.

Klein, Donald, and Hisham M. Amin. "Racial Legacies." *African American Review* 28, no. 4 (1994): 659-63.

Kopley, Richard. "Readers Write: Nineteenth-Century Annotations in Copies of the First American Edition of Poe's The Narrative of Arthur Gorgon Pym." *Nineteenth-Century Literature* 55, no. 3 (2000): 399-408.

Kristeva, Julia. *Black Sun*. New York: Columbia University Press, 1989.

Krumholz, Linda J. "Reading and Insight in Toni Morrison's *Paradise*." *African American Review* 36, no. 1 (2002): 21-34.

Lavabre, Marcel. *Aromatherapy Workbook*. Rochester, VT: Healing Arts, 1990.

LeClair, Thomas. "'The Language Must Not Sweat': A Conversation with Toni Morrison." In *Conversations with Toni Morrison*, edited by Danille Taylor-Guthrie, 119-28. Literary

Conversations Series. Jackson: University Press of Mississippi, 1994.

Leder, Drew. *The Absent Body*. Chicago: University of Chicago Press, 1990.

Lee, Maurice S. "Absolute Poe: His System of Transcendental Racism." *American Literature* 75, no. 4 (2003): 751-81.

Lehr, Fran. "Bibliotherapy." *Journal of Reading,* 25, no. 1 (1981): 76-79.

Leloup, Jean-Yves. *The Gospel of Mary Magdalene*. Translated by Joseph Rowe. Rochester, VT: Inner Traditions, 2002.

Lepenies, Wolf. *Melancholy and Society*. Translated by Jeremy Gaines and Doris Jones. Cambridge, MA: Harvard University Press, 1992.

Leonard, John. "Three First Novels on Race." *New York Times*. November 13, 1970, 35.

Lepow, Lauren. "Paradise Lost and Found: Dualism and Edenic Myth in Toni Morrison's *Tar Baby*." *Contemporary Literature* 28, no. 3 (1987): 363-77.

Lorde, Audre. *Sister Outsider: Essays & Speeches by Audre Lorde*. Berkeley: Crossing Press, 2007. Originally published 1984.

Li, Stephanie. *Toni Morrison: A Biography*. Santa Barbara: Greenwood Biographies, 2010.

Lipsitz, George. *The Possessive Investment in Whiteness: How White People Profit from Identity Politics*. Philadelphia: Temple University Press, 1998.

MacLachlan, Bonnie. *The Age of Grace*. Princeton, NJ: Princeton University Press, 1993.

Mandel, Naomi. "I Made The Ink: Identity, Complicity, 60 Million, and More." *Modern Fiction Studies*. 48, no. 3 (2002): 581-612.

Marshall, Paule. *Brown Girl, Brownstones*. New York: Holt, Rinehart and Winston, 1970. Originally published 1959.

Martinie, Louis, and Sallie Ann Glassman. *The New Orleans Voodoo Tarot*. Rochester, VT: Destiny Books, 1992.

Matus, Jill. *Toni Morrison*. Manchester: Manchester University Press, 1998.

Mayberry, Susan Neal. *Can't I Love What I Criticize? The Masculine and Morrison*. Athens: University of Georgia Press, 2007.

McIntosh, Peggy. "White Privilege and Male Privilege: A Personal Account of Coming to See Correspondences through Work in Women's Studies." In *Working Paper No. 189*. Wellesley, MA: Center for Research on Women, Wellesley College, 1988.

McKay, Nellie. "An Interview with Toni Morrison." In *Toni Morrison: Critical Perspectives Past and Present*, edited by Henry Louis Gates Jr. and K. A. Appiah, 396-411. New York: Amistad, 1993.

McWilliams, John P. "Introduction." In *The Last of the Mohicans*, by James Fenimore Cooper, ix-xvi. New York: Oxford University Press, 1990.

Messner, Michael A. "White Guy Habitus in the Classroom: Challenging the Reproduction of Privilege." *Men and Masculinities* 2, no. 4 (2000): 457-69.

Miles, Jonathan. *The Wreck of the Medusa: The Most Famous Sea Disaster of the Nineteenth Century.* New York: Grove, 2007.

Mitchell, Koritha. "Generative Challenges: Notes on Artist/Critic Interaction." *Callaloo* 32, no. 2 (2009): 605-15.

Mullin, Amy. "Moral Defects, Aesthetic Defects, and the Imagination." *Journal of Aesthetics and Art Criticism* 62, no. 3 (2004): 249-61.

The New Oxford Annotated Bible. 3rd ed. Oxford: Oxford University Press, 2001.

Nussbaum, Martha. *Love's Knowledge.* New York: Oxford University Press, 1990.

Obama, Barack. "A Just and Lasting Peace." Nobel Prize Acceptance Lecture. *Los Angeles Times*, December 10, 2009. http://latimesblogs.latimes.com/washington/2009/12/barack-obama-nobel-peace-prize-speech-text.html.

Olmos, Marguerite Fernández, and Lizabeth Paravisini-Gebert, eds. *Sacred Possessions: Vodou, Santería, Obeah, and The Caribbean.* New Brunswick, NJ: Rutgers University Press, 2000.

Onians, Richard Broxton. *The Origins of European Thought: About the Body, the Mind, the Soul, the World, Time, and Fate.* Cambridge: Cambridge University Press, 1951.

Otto, Walter F. *The Homeric Gods.* Translated by Moses Hadas. London: Thames, 1955.

Page, Phillip. "Furrowing all the brows: Interpretation and the Transcendent in Toni Morrison's *Paradise*." *African American Review,* 35, no. 4 (2001): 637-49.

Partridge, Eric. *Origins: A Short Etymological Dictionary of Modern English.* New York: Macmillan, 1958.

Peterson, Nancy J. "Introduction: 'The Canonization of Toni Morrison.'" *Toni Morrison. Modern Fiction Studies.* Special Double Issue. 39, no. 3-4 (1993-94): 481-833.

Poe, Edgar Allan. *The Letters of Edgar Allan Poe.* Edited by John Ward Ostrom. New York: Gordian Press, 1966.

——. *The Narrative of Author Gordon Pym.* Boston: David R. Godine, 1973.

——. "Philosophy of Composition." In *Essays and Reviews*, edited by G. R. Thompson, 13-25. New York: Literary Classics of United States, 1984.

——. "Nathaniel Hawthorne: *Twice-Told Tales*." In *Essays and Reviews*, edited by G. R. Thompson, 569-77. New York: Literary Classics of United States, 1984.

Pollan, Michael. *The Botany of Desire.* New York: Random House, 2001.

——. *The Omnivore's Dilemma: A Natural History of Four Meals.* New York: Penguin, 2006.

Pollock, Channing. *The Fool.* New York: Brentano's, 1922.

——. *The Enemy.* New York: Brentano's, 1926.

——. *Mr. Moneypenny.* New York: Brentano's, 1928.

——. *The House Beautiful.* New York: S. French, 1931.

Prater, Mary Anne, Marissa L. Johnstun, Tina Taylor Dyches, and Marion R. Johnstun. "Using Children's Books as Bibliotherapy for At-Risk Students: A Guide for Teachers." *Preventing School Failure,* 50, no. 4 (2006): 5-13.

Randolph, Laura B. "The Magic of Toni Morrison." *Ebony* 43, no. 9 (1988): 100-106.

Reed, Ishmael. "Op-Ed: Fade to White." *New York Times.* February 5, 2010, A25. http://www.nytimes.com/2010/02/05/opinion/05reed.html (accessed August 17, 2011).

Ridley, Charles. R. *Overcoming Unintentional Racism in Counseling and Therapy: A Practitioner's Guide to Intentional Intervention.* 2nd ed. Thousand Oaks, CA: Sage Publications, 2005.

Rilke, Rainer Maria. *Duino Elegies.* Translated by Edward Snow. New York: North Point, 2000.

Robinson, Edwin Arlington. "Richard Cory." In *Selected Poems of Edwin Arlington Robinson,* edited by Morton Dauwen Zabel, 9-10. New York: Macmillan, 1966.

Rowe, John Carlos. "Antebellum Slavery and Modern Criticism." *At Emerson's Tomb: The Politics of Classic American Literature.* New York: Columbia University Press, 1997.

Russell, Danielle. *Between the Angel and the Curve: Mapping Gender, Race, Space, and Identity in Will Cather and Toni Morrison.* New York: Routledge, 2006.

Samuels, Wilfred D., and Clenora Hudson-Weems. *Toni Morrison.* Twayne's United States Authors Series, 559. Boston: Twayne, 1990.

Sanchez, Sonia. *We A BaddDDD People.* Detroit: Broadside Press, 1970.

Sapphire. "Letter—Why Stories Like 'Precious' Need to Be Told." *New York Times.* February 12, 2010, A20. http://www.nytimes.com/2010/02/12/opinion/l12sapphire.html (accessed August, 17 2011).

Sardello, Robert. "The Landscape of Virginity." In *Images of the Untouched: Virginity in Psyche, Myth and Community,* edited by Joanne Trout and Gail Thomas, 39-48. Dallas, TX: Spring Publications, 1982.

Scarpa, Giulia. "Narrative Possibilities at Play in Toni Morrison's *Beloved.*" *MELUSI,* 17, no. 4 (1991): 91-103.

Schiller, Friedrich. "On Grace and Dignity." In *Schiller's "On Grace and Dignity" in Its Cultural Context: Essays and a New Translation.* Translated by Jane V. Curran. Edited by Jane V. Curran and Christophe Fricker, 123-70. New York: Camden, 2005.

Scott, Bonnie Kime, ed. *Gender in Modernism: New Geographies, Complex Intersections.* Urbana: University of Illinois Press, 2007.

Scott, Bonnie Kime, and Mary Lynn Broe, eds. *The Gender of Modernism: A Critical Anthology.* Bloomington: Indiana University Press, 1990.

Scott, James. *Domination and the Arts of Resistance: Hidden Transcripts.* New Haven, CT: Yale University Press, 1990.

Shange, Ntozake. *For Colored Girls Who Have Considered Suicide When the Rainbow is Enough.* New York: Charles Scribner, 1977.

Shapiro, Barbara. "The Bonds of Love and the Boundaries of Self in Toni Morrison's *Beloved.*" *Contemporary Literature* 32, no. 2 (1991): 194-210.

Showalter, Elaine. "Feminist Criticism in the Wilderness: Pluralism and the Feminist Critique." *Writing and Sexual Difference. Critical Inquiry* 8, no. 2 (1981): 179-205.

Slattery, Dennis Patrick. *The Wounded Body: Remembering the Markings of Flesh.* SUNY Series in Psychoanalysis and Culture. Albany: State University of New York Press, 1999.

Smith, Barbara. "Toward a Black Feminist Criticism." In *But Some of Us Are Brave,* edited by Gloria T. Hull, Patricia Bell Scott and Barbara Smith, 157-75. Old Westbury, NY: Feminist Press, 1982.

Smith, Victoria. "Generative Melancholy: Women's Loss and Literary Representation." *Mosaic* 41, no. 4 (2008): 95-109.

Soyinka, Wole. *Myth, Literature and the African World.* New York: Cambridge University Press, 1990.

Stave, Shirley Ann. "*Jazz* and *Paradise.*" In *The Cambridge Companion to Toni Morrison,* edited by Justine Tally, 59-74. Cambridge: Cambridge University Press, 2007.

Sullivan, Amie, and Harold R. Strang. "Bibliotherapy in the Classroom: Using Literature to Promote the Development of Emotional Intelligence." *Childhood Education* 79, no. 2 (2002): 74-80.

Tally, Justine. "The Morrison Trilogy." In *The Cambridge Companion to Toni Morrison,* edited by Justine Tally, 75-91. Cambridge: Cambridge University Press, 2007.

Taylor, Diana. *The Archive and the Repertoire: Performing Cultural Memory in the Americas.* Durham, NC: Duke University Press, 2003.

Taylor-Guthrie, Danille, ed. *Conversations with Toni Morrison.* Literary Conversations Series. Jackson: University Press of Mississippi, 1994.

Thompson, Robert Farris. *Flash of the Spirit: African & Afro-American Art and Philosophy.* New York: Random House-Vintage, 1984.

Thurman, Wallace. *The Blacker the Berry.* New York: Macaulay Company, 1929.

Toomer, Jean. *Cane.* New York, Harper & Row, 1923 and 1969. Reprint, New York: Norton, 2011.

Turner, William, Elizabeth Wieling, and William D. Allen. "Developing Culturally Effective Family-Based Research Programs: Implications for Family Therapists." *Journal of Marital and Family Therapy* 30 (2004): 257–70.

Walker, Alice. *The Third Life of Grange Copeland.* New York: Harcourt Brace Jovanovich, 1970.

——. "Sula." Letter to the Editor. *New York Times.* January 20, 1974, 328.

——. *Meridian.* New York: Harcourt, 1976.

——. *The Color Purple: A Novel.* New York: Harcourt, 1982.

——. *In Search of Our Mothers' Gardens: Womanist Prose.* San Diego: Harcourt, 1983.

Washington, Teresa N. *Our Mothers, Our Powers, Our Texts: Manifestations of Àjé in Africana Literature.* Bloomington: Indiana University Press, 2005.

Weil, Simone. *Gravity & Grace*. Translated by Arthur Wills. Lincoln: University of Nebraska Press, 1952.

Wendell, Susan. *The Rejected Body: Feminist Philosophical Reflections on Disability*. London and New York: Routledge, 1996.

Werhane, Patricia H. *Moral Imagination and Management Decision Making*. New York: Oxford University Press, 1999.

Whalen, Terrance. "Average Racism: Poe, Slavery, and the ways of Literary Nationalism." In *Romancing the Shadow: Poe and Race*, edited by Gerald Kennedy and Liliane Weissberg, 3-40. New York: Oxford University Press, 2001.

Wilber, Richard, ed. "Introduction." In *The Narrative of Arthur Gordon Pym*, by Edgar Allan Poe. Boston: David R. Godine, 1973.

Williams-Forson, Psyche. *Building Houses out of Chicken Legs: Black Women, Food, and Power*. Chapel Hill: University of North Carolina Press, 2006.

Witt, Doris. *Black Hunger: Food and the Politics of U.S. Identity*. New York: Oxford University Press, 1999.

——. *Black Hunger: Soul Food and America*. Minneapolis: University of Minnesota Press, 2004.

Woodruff, Darren. "Reducing Minority Student Disproportionality in Special Education: Schools and Families Working Together." *Focal Point: A National Bulletin on Family Support and Children's Mental Health*, 16, no. 2 (Fall 2002): 26–28.

Updike, John. "Dreamy Wilderness." Review of *A Mercy*, by Toni Morrison. *New Yorker* (November 3, 2008): 112-13.

Young, Linda Martina. "Where Grace May Pass: A Poetics of the Body." PhD. diss,. Pacifica Graduate Intitute, 2007.

Yu, S. "Race, Psychoanalysis and Female Subjectivity in Toni Morrison's *The Bluest Eye*." Presentation at the Hawaii International Conference on Arts and Humanities. Honolulu, HI, January, 2003.

Secondary Sources

A comprehensive bibliography of secondary sources on Morrison's work was compiled for readers of *The Clearing*. The bibliography can be accessed by going to the url or QR code listed below.

http://www.bucknell.edu/ClearingBibliography